THEORIES OF CONSCIOUSNESS

"This is a fine book, a fascinating set of discussions of an extremely interesting area."
John Leslie, University of Guelph

"This is an excellent survey of recent theories of consciousness."
Barry Loewer, Rutgers University

The most remarkable fact about the universe is that certain parts of it are conscious. Somehow nature has managed to pull the rabbit of experience out of a hat made of mere matter. *Theories of Consciousness* explores a number of ways to understand consciousness and its place in the physical world. Spectacularly diverse, the spectrum of theories ranges from those that identify consciousness with particular brain processes to those that seemingly *deny* that consciousness even exists.

The attempt to understand consciousness is only as old as the scientific revolution. As William Seager shows, Descartes can be seen as the pioneer of this project and some aspects of his position still set the stage and the agenda for modern work. His views vividly illustrate the problem of explaining the physical 'generation' of consciousness and point to the fundamental importance of – or perhaps reveal the basic error in – an appeal to the notion of *mental representation*. After addressing Descartes, Seager considers theories that identify certain particular elements of conscious experience (the so-called *qualia*) with 'vector codes' within abstract spaces defined by neural networks. From there, Seager proceeds to HOT theory, which regards consciousness as the product of higher order thoughts *about* mental states. The influential and provocative views of Daniel Dennett are closely examined. *Theories of Consciousness* devotes a lot of attention to the new representational theory of consciousness and the special problems created by the phenomena of conscious thought, which lead to the conclusions that representation is indeed essential to consciousness but that an *internalist* account of representation is required. In his final chapter, Seager explores more speculative terrain: the idea that consciousness might somehow be a *fundamental* feature of the universe, perhaps ubiquitous and maybe linked to bizarre features of quantum physics.

Theories of Consciousness serves both to introduce a wide array of approaches to consciousness as well as advance debate via a detailed critique of them. Philosophy students, researchers with a particular interest in cognitive science and anyone who has wondered how consciousness fits into a scientific view of the world will find this book an illuminating and fascinating read.

William Seager is Professor of Philosophy at the University of Toronto at Scarborough. He is the author of *Metaphysics of Consciousness* (Routledge, 1991).

PHILOSOPHICAL ISSUES IN SCIENCE
Edited by W. H. Newton-Smith
Balliol College, Oxford

REAL HISTORY
Martin Bunzl

BRUTE SCIENCE
Hugh LaFollette and Niall Shanks

LIVING IN A TECHNOLOGICAL CULTURE
Mary Tiles and Hans Oberdick

THE RATIONAL AND THE SOCIAL
James Robert Brown

THE NATURE OF THE DISEASE
Lawrie Reznek

THE PHILOSOPHICAL DEFENCE OF PSYCHIATRY
Lawrie Reznek

INFERENCE TO THE BEST EXPLANATION
Peter Lipton

TIME, SPACE AND PHILOSOPHY
Christopher Ray

MATHEMATICS AND THE IMAGE OF REASON
Mary Tiles

EVIL OR ILL?
Lawrie Reznek

THE ETHICS OF SCIENCE
An Introduction
David B. Resnik

PHILOSOPHY OF MATHEMATICS
An Introduction to a World of Proofs and Pictures
James Robert Brown

THEORIES OF CONSCIOUSNESS
An introduction and assessment
William Seager

THEORIES
OF
CONSCIOUSNESS

An introduction and assessment

William Seager

London and New York

First published 1999
by Routledge
11 New Fetter Lane, London EC4P 4EE

Simultaneously published in the USA and Canada
by Routledge
29 West 35th Street, New York, NY 10001

© 1999 William Seager
Typeset in Times by the author

Printed and bound in Great Britain by
Redwood Books, Trowbridge, Wiltshire

British Library Cataloging in Publication Data
A catalogue record for this book is available from the British Library

Library of Congress Cataloging in Publication Data
Seager, William, 1952–
Theories of Consciousness: an introduction and assessment/William Seager.
p.   cm. – (Philosophical issues in science)
Includes bibliographical references and index.
1. Consciousness   2. Mind and body.   I. Title. II. Series
B808.9.S4 1999
128–dc21   98–34492
                                                 CIP
ISBN 0–415–18393–6 (hbk)
ISBN 0–415–18394–4 (pbk)

TO MY PARENTS

CONTENTS

ACKNOWLEDGEMENTS

Most of this book was written while on a sabbatical leave from the University of Toronto and my thanks go to my university for continuing to support the notion of a research leave.

Some of the book has appeared before. A small part of chapter 3 was published in *Analysis* as 'Dretske on Hot Theories of Consciousness' (Seager 1994). The bulk of chapter 4 originally appeared in *Philosophy and Phenomenological Research* as 'The Elimination of Experience' (Seager 1993a); a version of the minimalist explication of Dennett's four-fold characterization of qualia also appeared in my previous book, *Metaphysics of Consciousness* (Seager 1991a). I give it here again for the convenience of the reader. A earlier version of a good part of chapter 5 can be found in *Inquiry* as 'Verificationism, Scepticism and Consciousness' (Seager 1993b). Parts of chapters 6 and 7 were published in a critical notice of Fred Dretske's *Naturalizing the Mind* in the *Canadian Journal of Philosophy* (Seager 1997). An early version of chapter 9 was published in the *Journal of Consciousness Studies* (Seager 1995) and some of my 'A Note on the Quantum Eraser' (Seager 1996) from *Philosophy of Science* has been interpolated into chapter 9 as well.

I would like to thank the many people who have discussed this material with me. My students at the University of Toronto have been an invaluable help. The philosophers at Dalhousie University have suffered over the years through almost the whole manuscript, always providing an enthusiastically critical outlook on the work. Early versions of chapter 8 were presented at a conference, *Conscience et Intentionalité*, held at the Université du Québec à Montréal in 1995, organized by Denis Fissette, to a conference on *Consciousness in Humans and Animals*, held at the Centre for Process Studies in Claremont in 1994 and organized by David Griffin, and to the meetings of the *Canadian Philosophical Association* in Calgary also in 1994. A preliminary version of chapter 5 was presented to the *Toronto Cognitive Science Society* in 1993. My thanks to the organizers and participants of all these events.

Finally, I would like most of all to thank Christine, Emma, Tessa and Ned for being there.

PREFACE

Recently there has been a tremendous surge of interest in the problem of consciousness. Though it has always lurked in the vicinity, for years there was little or no mention of consciousness as such in either the philosophical or scientific literature. Now books and articles are flowing in an ever widening stream. This is strange. Hasn't the mind–body problem always been about consciousness? There is no mind–body problem without the dream of a complete physical science, a dream first clearly entertained by Descartes who then had no choice but to invent the modern mind–body problem. And for Descartes, the mind–body problem *is* the problem of consciousness for there is, according to his understanding of the mind, nothing else for the mind to be. It is consciousness that sits square across the advancing path of the scientific world view. I doubt that Descartes, were he to admit the possibility of unconscious mentality, would think that it posed any serious challenge to a materialist view of the world.

I think it was the growth of psychology as a potential and then actual science that forced upon us the idea that there could be a *generalized* mind–body problem, of which the problem of consciousness would be but one aspect. Scientific psychology both posited and seemed to require unconscious processes that were in their essential features very like the more familiar conscious mental processes of perception, inference and cognition. And far from retreating, the contemporary science of psychology, along with the upstart sciences of artificial intelligence and cognitive science, has shown ever more reliance upon the hypothesis of non-conscious mental processes. Thus, just as psychology carved out a problem-domain independent of consciousness so the philosophy of mind saw its task redirected on to a mind–body problem whose focus was on the mental processes appropriate to the new problem space (especially the problems of mental representation and the nature of cognition). Is it an unworthy suspicion that the absence of consciousness was not unwelcome?

Then it came to seem that perhaps consciousness could be relegated and confined to one esoteric and increasingly baroque scholastic corner of the mind–body problem which has come to be known as the 'problem of qualia'. What are *qualia*? They are the particular experienced features of consciousness: the redness of the perceived or imagined poppy, the sound of an orchestra playing in your dreams, the smell of burnt toast (perhaps as evoked by direct neural stimulation as in the famous experiments of Wilder Penfield). They are what makes up the way it feels to be alive and they are, I am sure, the ultimate source and ground of all value. The problem of qualia is of that peculiar sort that arises in philosophy where a good many students of the subject doubt the very existence of the 'objects' supposedly creating the problem. This doubt sent us down an enticing path. If the problem of consciousness could be reduced to the problem of qualia, and if there were no qualia after all, then, as surely as night follows day, there just would be no problem of consciousness. The solution to the unconscious mind–body problem would be the solution to the whole problem.

This is too easy; there are no shortcuts. The facts of consciousness cannot be hidden under a rug woven from certain philosophical interpretations of these facts, at least not without leaving tell-tale lumps. To solve the problem of consciousness involves telling a story that encompasses the problem of qualia in some way – even if that means denying their existence – but that goes beyond it to grapple with consciousness itself. There are some remarkable philosophical theories that attempt this feat. I don't blush to confess that they are not *scientific* theories (though in fact all of them more or less explicitly aim to be compatible with future science), for in fact there are no scientific theories yet conceived that address the *nature* of consciousness as opposed to its neural substrate. What I want to do in this book is take a critical look at philosophical attempts to tell us what consciousness *really is* while remaining, if possible, within the bounds of the modern descendant of Descartes's scientific picture of the world.

What the theories I examine share is the central significance of the notion of representation, although they deploy this notion in spectacularly different ways. The underlying common problem which they face is to account for the nature and genesis of consciousness within the natural world, as described in our burgeoning scientific picture. Though the philosophical theories could all be described as anti-Cartesian, the application of the notion of representation to the problem of the mind and the fundamental problem of the genesis of consciousness both stem from Descartes. A closer look at some infrequently appreciated aspects of Descartes's philosophy of mind will set the stage for all of the modern theories to come and highlight the problems they will face. So I begin with the great-great-grandfather of the mind–body problem.

William Seager
Bathaven, 1998

1

THEMES FROM DESCARTES

Box 1.1 • Preview

The 'modern' problem of consciousness begins with Descartes, who back in the 17th century could already see and was helping to forge the scientific world view. Especially he saw that the physical seat of consciousness, the brain, is separated *from* the world by the very things that connect it *to* the world. Pursuing the scientific vision into the brain itself, the separation of consciousness from physical activity appears to continue. We are left with the difficult problem, which I call the *generation problem*, of explaining precisely how the physical workings of the brain generate or underlie conscious experience. Famously, Descartes 'solved' the problem by announcing the absolute separation of consciousness from the brain: mind and brain are utterly different kinds of thing. But this is not what is most important in Descartes's philosophy of mind. Rather, we should pay attention to Descartes's suggestive remarks linking consciousness to the notion of *representation* and his brain-theory of the generation of consciousness. Since Descartes maintains that every state of consciousness involves an *idea* and ideas are basically representational, Descartes is suggesting that consciousness is in some fundamental way itself representational. Furthermore, Descartes postulated that the brain is teeming with purely physical 'representations', and he has surprisingly modern sounding views on the function and creation of these representations. This is the birth of cognitive science. Descartes also had an interesting theory of how consciousness was generated. This theory is a molecular-compositional theory which posits, at the simplest level, a brute causal power of the brain to produce elementary 'units' of conscious experience. Thus Descartes sets the themes of this book: the nature of consciousness and its generation, and begins the exploration into them.

Technology only very slowly begins to match philosophical imagination. When Descartes worried that his experience might be systematically deceptive, generated by a malicious being capable of presenting to consciousness ersatz experiences indistinguishable from those presented by the real world, he sowed the seed of the nascent technology we call Virtual Reality (VR for short). Others before Descartes had of course worried about the problem of illusion, but his philosophical position was based on two key ideas which underwrite the technical realization of VR: first, the separation of consciousness from the world which stems from – the second idea – a reasonably sound notion of how the physical world interacts with the body and brain in the generation of conscious experience. By now we know so much more about the second of Descartes's ideas that we must repudiate his most fundamental belief about it: that the final stage in the generation of conscious experience transcends the

1

physical world. But this repudiation is ironically accompanied by a continued acceptance of what is really significant about the separation of consciousness and the world. So much so that we find the opposite view difficult even to understand: *of course* if we duplicate the subject's sensory inputs then the experiences will also be duplicated (all else about the subject being equal). Our VR engineers deny Descartes's dualism as part of an effort which actually depends upon, and reinforces the significance of, Descartes's separation of mind and world, for the question of the ontological status of the mind turns out not to be the most important feature of Descartes's dualism. We might say that the important feature is a certain understanding of the rather elementary physiological discovery that there are *nerves* standing between the world and the mind.

A core idea behind Cartesian dualism is that there is a radical independence between mind and matter, an independence which can be summarized in the possibility of variance of mind without variance in the world, where this variance is allowed by the laws which govern the world as a whole (that is, including both mind and matter). Thus the Evil Genius's VR machine is not ruled out by any law of nature or law of mind but by the sudden and astonishing interposition of a moral rule which is, curiously and if we are lucky, also the only reason human brains will not be unwillingly immersed into future VR engines. Modern physicalists can't abide this uncompromisingly extreme degree of variance, but something like it seems undeniable: the world can be decoupled from the mind because the mind is only contingently connected to the world via a host of information channels. Naturally, such decoupling is rare and technically difficult to achieve insofar as the mind is an ultra-complex evolved feature of organisms long mated to an extremely information rich environment by sensory systems that can deal with and positively expect huge floods of information and which come already dependent upon their input information meeting a host of structural constraints. Thus the dual flow of inferences to and from the world and the structure of the mind (and brain) remains no less in order than our everyday acceptance of the world as we see it.[1]

These days there is much talk about *embodiment* in a variety of philosophical and 'cognitive science'-type works for a variety of reasons (see for example Damasio 1994, Johnson 1987, Lakoff 1987, Varela, Thompson and Rosch 1991). It is surely true that the body is so deeply infused into the mind, both literally and metaphorically, that all of our experience and even the conceptual resources with which we face the world are pretty thoroughly dependent upon the facts of our particular embodiment. If the emphasis on embodiment is aimed at reminding us that our mental attributes stem from a concrete biological base whose nature depends upon a convoluted, contingent and particular evolutionary history, then no one could quarrel with it. But sometimes this emphasis is placed in direct opposition to Descartes's presumed denial of the body (as the very title of Damasio's book was meant to suggest). I think this is somewhat unfair to Descartes. While Descartes allowed for disembodied minds he never denied the significance of the body for the action of *our* minds (recall how Descartes *denied* that we are like pilots in ships). In fact, in Cartesian terms, it is rather hard to imagine what the experience of a disembodied mind would be like except for the special case of a mind being 'fed' sensory experiences as if from an embodied existence (this is the VR situation). One reason for this is Descartes's admission that emotions are fundamentally dependent upon the body and stem from the evaluation of bodily states as being either good or bad for the body. Even the 'purest' and most highly developed emotions, such as those involved in wholly intellectual pursuits, inherit this base in the body (see Descartes 1649/1985, p. 365).[2] So it is unclear how a disembodied mind would fare when faced with the task of handling a body merely on the basis of intellectual information about that body's situation in physical/biological/social space (that is, when we make this mind no more than a pilot in the ship of the body). Without guidance from the body in the form of what Descartes called passions there would seem to be little to provide the disembodied mind with any motivation to act at all, as opposed to just continuing to think.[3]

This is not the place to defend Descartes's theory of the emotions (which is doubtless inadequate), nor his dualism (which is doubtless false). The point is that the errors of Descartes are not so profound as his insights. At least, it remains true that modern research on the mind is in essence Cartesian, and that Cartesian themes will still provide an appropriate guide to the problems of consciousness.

Descartes used his VR thought experiment to reconsider old questions about knowledge in the new light of the scientific revolution and his scientific nerve-theory of experience. Scepticism is not my target, but the sceptical possibilities of the VR thought experiment depended upon another distinctive Cartesian position which is vital to modern thinking about cognition, one which also stemmed from Descartes's view of the nerve-link between world and mind. This is the representational theory of the mind. According to Descartes, what the action of the nerves eventually excites in the mind are *ideas*, which are one and all representations, sometimes of the body, sometimes of the world beyond, sometimes of pure abstract objects (of which mathematics provides the most obvious and best examples).[4] Descartes's philosophy is distinguished by the claim that *all* that enters consciousness is ideas, and all ideas, says Descartes, are essentially two-faced. On the one side they are just what they are: modifications of the special mind-stuff or relaxation states of neural networks or whatever. Descartes, following scholastic nomenclature, labelled the intrinsic nature of our mental states their 'formal reality'. But on their other side ideas all possess representational content, which Descartes called 'objective reality'. The notion that consciousness is essentially representational is a remarkable doctrine, for it has always been, and pretty much remains, the common wisdom that consciousness involves at least two distinctive and basic elements, namely, thoughts and sensations. Sensations are supposed to be utterly non-conceptual, to possess no representational content, to be 'bare feelings'; they are the qualia that so vex our understanding of consciousness.

3

Thoughts, on the other hand, are essentially conceptual, possess representational content as their very function, are not 'felt' and, in themselves, present no purely qualitative features to consciousness. Although thoughts can be conscious, it is supposed that they are usually – perhaps even necessarily – accompanied by qualitative consciousness, as for example in the visual images that often are deployed in thought. In fact, the consciousness of thoughts in the absence of some attendant qualitative consciousness is rather mysterious on the common view; it may be that the view supposes, though this is seldom explicitly admitted, that certain features of qualitative consciousness provide the vehicles of our thought contents (in something like the way that ink provides a vehicle for word contents). Descartes is again distinguished by his claim that there are no such vehicles (this issue will return when we examine the pure representational theory of consciousness, especially in chapter 7 below).

Notoriously, Descartes denied to animals all aspects of mind, but he sometimes allowed that animals have sensations. Does this mean that Descartes's reduction of consciousness to thought was merely a verbal ploy? No, for it is clear from his writings that the term 'sensation' as applied to animals refers only to certain bodily conditions, especially of the brain, caused by the interaction of the world with sense organs of various sorts (what Descartes calls 'organic sensation' 1641b/1985, p. 287). These organic sensations are not in any sense conscious experiences. Of course, we share organic sensation with the animals, but our conscious sensations are a species of thought, albeit, as Descartes usually puts it, *confused* thoughts. Sensations in animals are only the brain activity that, if they possessed *enminded* brains, would lead to the kinds of thoughts we call (conscious) sensations. Here, once again, dualism becomes unnecessarily embroiled in the central issue: is conscious experience a species of thinking, does *every* state of consciousness have representational content (or what philosophers call *intentionality*)?

To this, Descartes answers 'yes' and if we follow him we arrive at a very interesting understanding of consciousness, though one subject, as we shall see, to a variety of interpretations. Notice something else: Descartes's vision of the mind is the foundation of modern cognitive science. The linchpin idea of this upstart science is that the mind is in essence a field of representations – encompassing perception and action and everything in between – some conscious, most unconscious, upon which a great variety of cognitive processes operate. Descartes's view is apparently extreme. According to him, all these representations are present to consciousness and the operations are presumed to be inferences, though by no means are all of these logically impeccable. So, despite its transparency, Descartes does allow that we make mistakes about the operation of the mind: for example, the untutored do not realize that *seeing* is actually *judging*. In Meditation Two Descartes gives this famous example:

4

> ... if I look out of the window and see men crossing the square, as
> I just happen to have done, I normally say that I see the men them-
> selves. ... Yet do I see any more than hats and coats which could
> conceal automatons? I judge that they are men. And so something
> which I thought I was seeing with my eyes is in fact grasped solely by
> the faculty of judgement which is in my mind.
>
> (1641a/1985, p. 21)

Not only is the equation of perception with judgement strikingly modern and in line, once again, with orthodox cognitive science, the ground of Descartes's assimilation is similarly modern. Since the mind is a field of representations, the *contents* before the mind are such as can be either correct or incorrect. Even when I 'bracket' the referential nature of my representations they remain 'in the space of' truth, they present a way the (or a) world could *be* – this is a source of the VR problem once again. The notions of correctness and incorrectness lie within the realm of judgement and belief, rather than in some putative zone of pure sensation. Descartes's writing is so beautifully compressed that it might be missed that Descartes is *not* denying that we see the men; he is reforming the notion of *seeing*: seeing = judging. To be properly circumspect here, the kind of judgements that perception delivers to consciousness are defeasible in at least two ways: they can be overturned by further perception (as when the bear one sees in the bush thankfully transforms itself into some swaying branches upon further inspection), and their authenticity can be rejected by reason. Reasoned rejection of validity does not, typically, lead to transformed perceptions but this does not show that perception is not in the realm of judgement, for we are still presented with 'a way the world could be' rather than suddenly a mere patchwork quilt of sensory qualities even after our reasoned rejection that the world is *that way*.

The fact that we make the 'mistake' of supposing we just plain *see* the men in the street is also extremely significant to the problem of consciousness. For what we are normally conscious of is *people in the street*, whereas we are not conscious solely of *hats and cloaks* (it is common to be able to recall that one saw some people without being able to remember whether or not they were wearing hats, cloaks etc.) nor, as the determined empiricist would have it, various *pure sensory qualities*. Even if such qualities play a role in seeing, they are certainly not the normal objects of conscious-ness; it is, rather, that we see right through them to the world of people, hats and cloaks. Our consciousness of people *as* people, complex systems *as* complex or threatening situations *as* threatening means that in some way the concepts by which we organise and categorize the world infiltrate our states of consciousness – all the way down to perceptual states. Descartes implicitly suggests that insofar as our consciousness is composed of ideas, conceptual structure constitutes our conscious-ness. This is an interesting view even if one that many would find highly implausible. It is, however, quite in line with the intuition, which I share, that all consciousness is consciousness *of* something, and of that something *as* something or other. In Cartesian terms, the view can be summed up as denying that the formal reality of our states of consciousness is available to consciousness; what is available is only the objective reality of these states. Of course, the formal reality can be indirectly accessed if there is some state whose objective reality represents the true nature of states of consciousness.

For a materialist, this is actually an attractive picture, for while we do not experience our brain states *as* brain states, there are obviously states which do represent brain states as such. One might even imagine that with sufficient 'training', of the sort envisioned by Paul Churchland for example (see his 1979, 1985), someone might come to experience certain brain states *as* brain states. This is not the place to develop the following thought in any depth but it is worth noting here. No matter how much training, or conceptual re-education, we will *not* be able to experience 'seeing red' *as* a brain state for the simple reason that we already can experience *as red* and this is not an experience *as of a brain state*. In itself, the experience tells us nothing about the brain. If I could experience some sensorially induced state *as* a brain state this would be a state entirely distinct from any of the conscious states I now can enjoy. So there is no hope of apprehending, no matter how much 'training' I might be subjected to, my current states of consciousness *as* brain states. Even if they are brain states, this fact is irredeemably invisible to our current consciousness of them. I think this point is of some importance if one imagines that the problem of consciousness will just disappear with the gradual acquisition of a new set of conceptual tools which we may be able to apply 'directly' to ourselves. It will never be 'just obvious' (a matter of observation) that states of consciousness are brain states, unless, perhaps, we also imagine a serious impoverishment in the range of states of consciousness which humans can enjoy.[5]

Some mitigation of Descartes's extreme claims of transparency and representationality can be found in his picture of the brain. Within the Cartesian brain we find a shadowy legion of representations realized as particular nerve pathways through which the quicksilver-like 'animal spirits' flow. Descartes calls these representations 'images' but goes out of his way to stress that they need not resemble, in any strong sense, the object of which they are the image (see 1637b/1985, p. 164) and he hints that they could represent in the arbitrary way that either spoken or written words do. Descartes's notion of how these images function in memory is startlingly (or perhaps dismayingly) modern, and is worth quoting at length:

> To this end, suppose that after the spirits leaving gland H [this is the magic region of dualistic interaction, but let that pass] have received the impression of some idea, they pass through tubes 2, 4, 6, and the like, into the pores or gaps lying between the tiny fibres which make up part B of the brain. And suppose that the spirits are strong enough

to enlarge these gaps somewhat, and to bend and arrange in various ways any fibres they encounter, according to the various ways in which the spirits are moving and the different openings of the tubes into which they pass. Thus they also trace figures in these gaps, which correspond to those of the objects. At first they do this less easily and perfectly than they do on gland H, but gradually they do it better and better, as their action becomes stronger and lasts longer, or is re-peated more often. That is why these figures are no longer so easily erased, and why they are preserved in such a way that the ideas which were previously on the gland can be formed again long afterwards without requiring the presence of the objects to which they corre-spond. And this is what memory consists in . . .

(1664/1985, p. 107)

It is tempting to find in Descartes the first intimations of Hebbian learning and distributed representation.[6]

Be that as it may, it cannot be denied that the core idea of the representational mind is to be found in Descartes, and that it is this vision that provides the foundation of what is really the only viable scientific picture of how cognition works. An important distinction should be introduced here to forestall a premature objection. It must be admitted that there are legitimate approaches that dispute the particularities of the *computationalist* view of cognition. Both connectionism and the more general 'dynamical systems' approach (see van Gelder 1995 on the latter and its distinctness from connectionism) will dispute the computationalist definition of cognition as syntactically defined operations on formal symbol systems. But doubts about computationalism are not necessarily doubts about representationalism. Only very special pleading would make a theory of brain function that had no place for represen-tations and operations upon those representations into a theory of cognition. It is evident in recent connectionist work that the notion of representation remains central to an understanding of cognition. And I think that van Gelder's (1995) provocative assertion that the steam engine governor is a better model of cognition than the Turing machine should be taken only to mean that cognitive operations will be seen to work more like the governor than like the Turing machine. But the fact that the governor does not work with representations only shows that it is not a system engaged in cognition; only an eliminativist cognitive theory would elevate *this* feature of the governor to a central place in cognitive psychology. In Descartes's frequent appeal to inference and logic as the machinery of cognition we can no doubt see the seeds of computationalism.[7] There is, however, a curious and interesting twist in Descartes's picture. As we shall shortly see, only the conscious mind performs true feats of reasoning, deliberation and inference, yet the field of cognition remains for Descartes much more extensive than the bounds of consciousness.

7

So, Descartes says that between the mind and the world stands the nervous system, which serves (among other functions) to lay down representations of the world in the brain. These representations do not represent in virtue of resembling their objects. Descartes does not have a theory of representation which pins down the relation between a brain representation and its object but we glean from passages like the above that it is some kind of causal/historical covariance theory, with admixtures of some kind of a 'topological-homomorphism' resemblance theory thrown in now and then for good measure. Their informational value stems from at least four sources: the first is the link to motor pathways which facilitate the appropriate response to the object which they represent. Arnauld complained to Descartes that his denial of thought to animals was just too implausible:

> But I fear that this view will not succeed in finding acceptance in people's minds unless it is supported by very solid arguments. For at first sight it seems incredible that it can come about, without the assistance of any soul, that the light reflected from the body of a wolf on to the eyes of a sheep should move the minute fibres of the optic nerves, and that on reaching the brain this motion should spread the animal spirits throughout the nerves in the manner necessary to precipitate the sheep's flight.
>
> (1641/1985, p. 144)

Nonetheless, this is exactly what Descartes maintained. But he did *not* deny that the sheep has a representation of the wolf at work in its cognitive economy. The sheep has a 'corporeal image' of the wolf and, either because of an instinctual linkage or through learning, this image is such as to direct the animal spirits in just the manner Arnauld indicates.[8] And there is no reason to deny that the operations working on the corporeal images of the wolf should be cognitive operations, best described in informational terms (in fact, at the level of brain organization where it makes sense to talk of 'images' there seems little chance of a purely 'mechanical' description of the brain's activity).

The second informational role also involves memory, but more broadly conceived. The mind can reactivate these representations to retrieve sensory information (by directing the animal spirits back through the appropriate pathways). Descartes does seem to have believed that sensory memory is stored intact as a copy of earlier experience, but since our awareness of memory is a mental function there will have to be judgements implicated in the production of conscious memory experience, and in these judgements we will surely find room for a more plausible reconstructive view of memory.[9]

These brain representations also serve, third, as the source of imagination, which according to Descartes requires a 'corporeal figure' for the mind to contemplate.

Imagination is straightforwardly constructive, for the mind can direct the brain to combine and reconfigure these corporeal representations.

A fourth information function is the production of conscious experience itself and here Descartes's view is richly suggestive. For, we might ask, if the brain can store a variety of representations sufficient to encode past experience and actually direct, all by itself, behaviour appropriate to these representations' content, is there not a danger that the mind may be usurped by the brain? Descartes's well known reply is that the brain cannot accomplish the more intellectually demanding tasks characteristic of human cognition (he gives as examples the use of language and the cognitive abilities which depend upon language use; see Descartes 1637a/1985). This suggests a two (or more) layer view of representation: the bottom layer being representations of combinations of sensory qualities, the higher layer being the representations of cognitively rich content, the prime examples of which are simply the ideas constituting the states of consciousness involved in our normal intercourse with the world. The brain can achieve the bottom layer of representation, and so can the mind of course, but the mind evidently cannot preserve these representations except by the continual consciousness of them and hence requires them to be stored up in some more durable medium. But while the brain can, as it were, store ideas, *only* the mind can support the high level cognitive processes characteristic of human thought.

Now, this is deeply puzzling. For if Descartes is saying that memory is entirely a function of the brain, then how could any entirely disembodied mind enjoy any coherent chains of thought? The puzzle is only deepened when we consider that Descartes's treatment of deductive reasoning gives memory an essential role (see for example Descartes 1684/1985) in as much as we must remember each intuitively obvious step in any deduction of even very moderate length. But haven't we always been told that Descartes allowed that a mind, whether embodied or not, could perform feats of logical calculation? On the other hand, if memory is a proper function of the soul itself then there must be mental structure that is not present to consciousness. This is the whole point of memory: to 'hold' information which is not currently before the mind. The problem is made worse if we think about the difference between so-called 'semantic' and 'episodic' memory. The latter is what Descartes, and the rest of us, usually talk about; it is the felt memories of events in which we participated in the past; it is the re-experiencing of the past. The former is simply the immense field of information which at one time we learned, and which we now retain and use throughout our daily lives, such as our 'memory' of the meanings of words, or what a cow looks like, etc. It seems obvious that, say, the appearance of a cow must in some sense be stored within us (this is not intended as an endorsement of some kind of template matching theory of perceptual recognition) even though we are never conscious of it as such even when we are recognizing or imagining a cow.

It is no answer to this difficulty to say, as did Locke, that memory is just a dispositional property of the mind to have certain experiences upon certain occasions.

Locke perceives the problem of memory very clearly but merely avoids addressing it when he says:

> This is memory, which is as it were the store-house of our ideas. . . .
> But our ideas being nothing but actual perceptions in the mind, which
> cease to be any thing, when there is no perception of them, this laying
> up of our ideas in the repository of the memory, signifies no more but
> this, that the mind has a power in many cases to revive perceptions,
> which it has once had, with this additional perception annexed to
> them, that it has had them before. And in this sense it is, that our ideas
> are said to be in our memories, when indeed they are actually no-
> where . . .
>
> (1690/1975, bk. 2, ch. 10, p. 149)

Of course, Locke has no right to speak of 'reviving' perceptions 'once had', but there is a more serious problem. It is a sound principle that there are no free-floating dispositions: every disposition or capacity must be realized in some structure which provides a causal ground of the disposition or capacity. If the mind has structure sufficient to ground these memory dispositions then there are elements of mind that are not open to consciousness.[10]

The tension is evident in Descartes's reply to Arnauld, who complained about the 'transparent mind' thesis (that is, the thesis that the mind is conscious of whatever is in it) with the rather ill chosen objection that an infant in the mother's womb 'has the power of thought but is not aware of it'. To this, Descartes says:

> As to the fact that there can be nothing in the mind, in so far as it is
> a thinking thing, of which it is not aware, this seems to me to be self-
> evident. For there is nothing that we can understand to be in the mind,
> regarded in this way, that is not a thought or dependent on a thought.
> If it were not a thought or dependent on a thought it would not
> belong to the mind *qua* thinking thing; and we cannot have any
> thought of which we are not aware at the very moment when it is in
> us. In view of this I do not doubt that the mind begins to think as soon
> as it is implanted in the body of an infant, and that it is immediately
> aware of its thoughts, even though it does not remember this after-
> wards because the impressions of these thoughts do not remain in the
> memory.
>
> (1641b/1985, p. 171)

Descartes generally reserves the use of the word 'impression' for the action of the senses or the mind upon the brain (there are, admittedly, some passages that may allow for 'impression' to be interpreted as a feature of the mind, but they are few and, I believe, ambiguous, as the above). So interpreted, the quoted passage makes sense and coheres with the view expressed in the passage quoted above from the *Treatise on Man* (1664/1985): the infant's mind thinks from implantation, is necessarily aware of these thoughts while they occur, but, because of the relatively undifferentiated nature of the newly associated brain's 'memory zones', no impressions of any strength can be as yet laid down in the brain as a record of these thoughts or the ideas which make them up. (Descartes also says, elsewhere, that the infant's thoughts are almost exclusively sensory thoughts about the state of the body.[11])

However, this interpretation has the apparently distressing conclusion that a pure, disembodied mind could not remember what it had thought, and thus could not engage in any deductive process of thought. I believe that this is Descartes's view, although Descartes is characteristically cagey about stating it outright; he does say, in reply to Hobbes's objections to the Meditations, that 'so long as the mind is joined to the body, then in order for it to remember thoughts which it had in the past, it is necessary for some traces of them to be imprinted on the brain; it is by turning to these, or applying itself to them, that the mind remembers' (1641b/1985, p. 246). Why the mind would be free of this need when disembodied Descartes declines to inform us. This 'corporeal memory' interpretation explains why Descartes demanded that the proofs in the early part of the Meditations be graspable without any memory of the deductive steps involved: the arguments must end up with the thinker in a state of intuitive apprehension of the truth of their conclusions. Of course, it is ridiculous to think that the arguments for the existence of God in Meditation 3 or 5 can actually reduce to a flash of insight – and this would be so even if they were sound. Yet that is what Descartes claims, and must claim, to have achieved. In Meditation 3, after presenting the arguments for God's existence he says: 'The whole force of the argument lies in this: I recognize that it would be impossible for me to exist with the kind of nature I have – that is, having within me the idea of God – were it not the case that God really existed' (1641a/1985, p. 35). In Meditation 5 we find this statement: 'Although it needed close attention for me to perceive this [i.e. God's existence], I am now just as certain of it as I am of everything else which appears most certain' (1641a/1985, p. 48). The object of the proofs is to get your mind into this state of intuitive certainty of God's existence: a certainty which supposedly carries a self authenticating validity in exactly the manner of Descartes's famous 'I think, therefore I am', a certainty that can be produced and grasped by a single thought.

It does not follow that Descartes can employ a kind of transcendental argument which moves from the fact that I remember things to the existence of the body (as in 'I reason, therefore my body exists'). Descartes does consider such an argument at the beginning of Meditation 6 and sensibly concludes that it could at most justify a certain probability that corporeal substance exists. There are two sceptical difficulties with such an argument. The radical sceptical problem – implicitly recognized by

Descartes – is that Descartes has no right to suppose that his purported memory experiences are really the product of memory or, indeed, that there is any past to remember at all. The less radical worry is that the structures required for memory are themselves unknown (at least in the stage of enquiry represented by the Meditations). The radical worry trumps the lesser one, but even if we ignore extreme sceptical possibilities, the most we could hope to prove is that the 'body' exists – some kind of stuff able to support the cognitive architecture required for coherent conscious experience. (It was Kant who thoroughly worked out this line of thought, accepting the above limitation.)

I have gone into this at such length only to arrive at this last point. Although Descartes is famous for the 'transparent mind' thesis, and although there is no doubt that he accepted the thesis, he did not deny and in fact his views positively require that the mind be supported by a massive structure that operates in the shadows, outside of or below consciousness. Unlike Locke, for example, Descartes explicitly recognized the need for such a structure and with typical elegance both proved the existence of the body and explained much of our thinking and behaviour, as well as all of animal behaviour by appeal to it. What is more, this structure is what we would call a cognitive structure. It is a system of representations, subject to a variety of transformative operations initiated both by the mind and – in the vast majority of the cases – by the brain alone. This structure is so extensive, so capable (by itself, it can orchestrate *all* animal behaviour and almost all human behaviour) and the mind would appear to be so helpless without it that I am sometimes tempted to doubt that Descartes was really a Cartesian dualist. Perhaps the fiction of the separate soul was merely a politically useful anodyne, easing the pain of the devout and potentially helpful in avoiding the fate of Galileo (a tactic comparable, then, to the far less subtle rhetorical manoeuvring that permitted Descartes to 'deny' that the Earth was in motion, 1644/1985, pp. 252 ff.). Well, that would be to go too far, but my imaginary Descartes fits in so nicely with the modern outlook that he is quite an attractive figure.[12]

No matter which Descartes we take to heart, an error for which the true Descartes has been much taken to task recently would remain. This is the error of the Cartesian Theatre (or, more generally, of Cartesian Materialism – of which our fictive Descartes would presumably be a strong proponent – indeed, if not the originator of the doctrine, at least the paradigm case). According to Daniel Dennett (1991b) this is the error of supposing that there is some one place in the brain where the elements of experience (or what will create experience) must be united. This is said to be a very natural and common error, even today and even among those whose job is to study the brain, so it would be no surprise if the man who pioneered research on the brain-experience connection should fall into it. In Descartes's case, though, is it not less an error than just the simplest hypothesis from which to begin? Still, did not Descartes flagrantly and ridiculously commit the error with a vengeance in supposing that the mind received from and transmitted to the brain at one particular spot: the pineal gland (selected on the factually incorrect and in any case rather arbitrary ground that it is the brain organ that is distinguished by not coming in pairs)? Yet even here we could plead Descartes's case a little.

What Descartes says about the pineal gland is indeed that it is the seat of the soul. But Descartes exploits the fact that the gland is *not* a mere point in the brain but is an extended body. It is the *motions* of the gland that give rise to conscious experience or, to ignore the mind for the moment, it is the motions which are produced by the combined actions of the animal spirits on the whole surface of the gland which are the 'final' representations which guide behaviour. So although the pineal gland is the place where 'it all comes together', the coming together is nonetheless spread out over the pineal gland. We might say that the representations at the gland are superpositions of the various shoves and pushes which the gland receives from all the 'pores' leading to it. Descartes slips up a little in his discussion of how perceptual consciousness is created at the gland, but we can read him in a more or less generous way. What he says is this:

> . . . if we see some animal approaching us, the light reflected from its body forms two images, one in each of our eyes; and these images form two others, by means of the optic nerves, on the internal surface of the brain facing its cavities. Then, by means of the spirits that fill these cavities, the images radiate towards the little gland which the spirits surround: the movement forming each point of one of the images tends towards the same point on the gland as the movement forming the corresponding point of the other image, which represents the same part of the animal. In this way, the two images in the brain form only one image on the gland, which acts directly upon the soul and makes it see the shape of the animal.
>
> (1649/1985, p. 341)

Here is the most flagrant case of Cartesian Theatre-itis one could imagine (straight from the horse's mouth too). Clearly, however, Descartes did not need to suppose that the two images (which, note, are *spread out* over a part of the pineal gland) actually coincide. It is *motions* of the gland that communicate with the soul, and the two images could, presumably, produce a motion just as easily if they hit the gland in distinct regions (unless, I suppose, they arrived so precisely aligned as to exactly cancel each other's effect[13]). So, the generous reading of Descartes has him saying only that all the elements of our current conscious experience must be somehow combined or linked together. His attempted explanation of this linkage is to suppose that our unified experience at any moment stems from a superposition of motions of the pineal gland. Descartes first identifies the sources of primitive or basic conscious experience – *every* motion of the gland is associated with some conscious experience, *no* motion is unexperienced – and then proposes that the unity of diverse possible states of consciousness into one is a matter of vector addition of motions. It would appear that any conscious experience that anyone has ever actually had is already the result of a very complex set of superposed motions (since, for one thing, visual images are spread out on the pineal gland and so any image of any spatial extent must produce a complex motion in the gland). Nonetheless, the model is clear: each point on the pineal gland is at any time subject to some force from the animal spirits; the motion of the gland is then determined by the vector sum of all these forces. We must always remember, though, that the vast majority of cognitive operations occur in the brain without any inclination to produce motions in the pineal gland and what is more, many of these cognitive operations can nonetheless *influence* those processes which will or can lead to pineal motions. Less happily, we must also remember that, according to strict Cartesian doctrine, not all conscious experience is the result of some motion of the pineal gland, for the mind has powers of its own at least sufficient for pure intellectual apprehension of a certain class of ideas.[14]

We recognize this motion-theory as an attempted solution to a high-level example of what are now called 'binding problems' (the solution to one version is the topic of Francis Crick's recent book, *The Astonishing Hypothesis* 1994). This version of the problem is how the appropriate diverse features of a possible experience are linked together in consciousness. For example, a good ventriloquist makes one experience his voice as coming from, or belonging to, his dummy – an entertaining effect which can be startlingly robust. It is psychologically interesting too, for we really do consciously experience the dummy as the one doing the talking (well, we are smarter than that, but at least the sounds do seem to come from the dummy even if we know otherwise). There must be some process which associates in our experience the sight of the dummy and the sound of the ventriloquist's voice. More generally, out of all the things that we *might* be conscious of at any moment, some subset is selected, 'bound together' and presented in a single state of consciousness. *Any* theory of consciousness must address this problem, though it is possible to deny that there is some special or particular brain process that accomplishes binding[15] – a view which then makes the binding problem (at least at the level of concern here) a kind of artifact of our own *understanding* of consciousness.

Within the problem of consciousness, the binding problem appears as an almost purely neuroscientific problem; the usual run of solutions appeal to neurological processes. There must also be a cognitive dimension, for what is bound together in consciousness is sensitive to cognitive factors. The ventriloquist example cries out for an explanation in terms of covert expectations and inferences, and this carries over to an immense range of conscious perceptual states. Sympathetically taking into account his necessarily limited knowledge of the brain, Descartes's view is a nice combination of the neurological and cognitive, for the 'neural' story of how the animal spirits, in concert, sway the pineal gland will be enhanced by knowing that the movements are all brought about by neural processes that are also representations whose route to the final pineal destination has been modified by a host of processes sensitive to their representational qualities.

Reading Descartes very generously and abstractly, we find him advancing a view something like this: in general, a state of consciousness is a state in which a variety of potential states of consciousness are unified. This unification is accomplished by the superposition of the factors which would, each by each, produce a state of consciousness the content of which would be one of the elements to be unified; the result is a state distinct from all of its components though in a sense containing them all. Descartes's particular model has it that the relevant factors are motions of the pineal gland as a whole and thus that the relevant superposition principle is a vector summation of the forces acting on the pineal gland, which are simply impact forces caused by the animal spirits striking upon the gland. The motion producing processes themselves are modified by more or less hidden cognitive processes which are not all such as to produce any consciousness of them. The basic model is very general and, I think, remains attractive. It observes a great scientific maxim: explain the complex by the concerted action of a multitude of simpler entities. At the same time, it preserves our phenomenologically reinforced notion that in any state of consciousness a multitude of distinct features are combined into a unified state. It is an atomic-molecular theory of the generation of states of consciousness. This basic model is so general that one might object to it on the ground of unfalsifiability. It must be admitted that alternatives to the 'atomic-molecular' picture of the generation of any phenomenon are hard to come by. Descartes's general picture should be thought of as a kind of metaphysical underpinning of the scientific enterprise as practised for the last three hundred years – a practice for which Descartes of course bears a great deal of responsibility – and so in truth it is not falsifiable in the same sense as any particular scientific hypothesis (for more on this issue, see my discussion of what I call 'physical resolution' in Seager 1991a, chapter 1).

But did Descartes stop with a mere enunciation of a general picture of how science should advance in the study of complex phenomena? No, he produced a particular instantiation of the general view which was in line with the scanty brain knowledge of the day (as well, naturally, as according with Descartes's 'higher' metaphysical principle of the dualism of mind and matter) and which was empirically testable, albeit not testable in his own time but obviously actually testable since in the general advance of neuroscience it has been found to be false.

Cartesian Materialism of the pineal gland variety is certainly false. The more circumspect Cartesian Materialism that still asserts that there is one place in the brain where all the elements of consciousness must literally come together in space and time is very probably false. The idea that all the elements of a state of consciousness must be 'bound together' by some process is not obviously false, and remains accepted by many, probably most, researchers who study the brain mechanisms of consciousness. If they are right, it would not be surprising if the binding process was superpositional in nature. There will be some bundle of forces or factors or whatever which stitch together the diverse components of our conscious experience.[16] Certainly we expect something like an atomic-molecular theory of the unity of consciousness – it is hard to think of an alternative that would count as scientific.

Descartes is said to have led us into error in many ways, most fundamentally in both the nature of knowledge and of mind. The two primary errors about the mind are the transparent mind thesis and the separation of conscious experience from its sources in the world. Descartes is characteristically radical in the versions of these views that he defends: everything in the mind is available to consciousness and mind is ontologically distinct from matter. But even a brief examination of Descartes's views from the point of view of the problem of consciousness finds more than radical error in these two central theses. The transparent mind thesis is mitigated by Descartes's belief in a vast cognitive-representational system that lurks below or outside of consciousness which appears to be – though Descartes is cagey about this – crucial to the operation of the 'true mind'. Even the dualism of Descartes seems to embody a valuable insight: conscious experience is separable from the world because of the details of its generation by a nerve-net standing between the world and experience. Many a modern functionalist goes so far as to say that conscious experience is at bottom a purely organizational property, utterly indifferent to the nature of its realizing material. In a certain sense, this is a dualism no less radical than Descartes.[17]

I have been trying to reclaim certain elements of Descartes's philosophy that I want to enlist in the battle to understand consciousness. I am not so foolhardy as to defend his dualism. I am not – I don't think anyone is – in a position to defend a modern version of his superpositional theory, nor do I think that such a theory would solve the problem of consciousness even though it would obviously be a tremendous advance in our knowledge. I do want to set out a range of questions which drive current theories of consciousness. These questions stem from the Cartesian outlook and they infuse the work of even the most rabid anti-Cartesians. They set an agenda which any theory of consciousness must, for now at least, follow. After consolidating these Cartesian themes as clearly as possible in modern terms it will be time to look at particular theories of consciousness.

In broadest terms, there are but two themes of central interest: the nature of consciousness and the production of consciousness. A now commonplace worry about the former theme is that the term 'consciousness' covers such a broad range of phenomena (even, perhaps, some pseudo-phenomena) that there is no hope and should be no expectation of discovering *the nature* of consciousness (for example, see Wilkes 1988 and, for a decidedly different view of the issue, Flanagan 1992, pp. 66–7; Lycan 1996, chapter 1, notes eight distinct senses of 'consciousness' and finds no fewer than twelve possible problems associated with sense 7 alone). No doubt there is something to this worry, but I want to borrow from Descartes one crucial choice-point in our most general views of consciousness: is consciousness essentially representational or is there a significant non-representational component to it? Another way to put this choice is this: are all states of consciousness states with a representational content or can there be some states of consciousness devoid of such content? In philosophers' jargon, the question is whether or not all states of consciousness possess intentionality. Descartes, as I read him, embraces the first element of all these dilemmas: whatever else consciousness might be it is essentially representational in nature. Although this is now a minority view amongst philosophers I will argue, in chapters 6, 7 and 8, that it is correct and that, at the very least, its acceptance makes for an interesting view of consciousness. In any case, putting the problem of the nature of consciousness in this Cartesian form is very fruitful. It makes the problem somewhat tractable and nicely encompasses the extant philosophical theories of consciousness. It provides an elegant entry into one of the key issues now dividing philosophers: the nature of qualia or the problem of subjective experience. The Cartesian dilemma also demands an examination of something else which is often neglected in discussions of consciousness: what is *representational content* (or, in philosophers' terms, what is intentionality)? Even if one disagreed with Descartes's strong position that *all* states of consciousness possess representational content, how could one deny that at least *many* states of consciousness represent the world as being in such and such a state? A lot can be said about representation without mention of consciousness but in the end I don't think that one can hive off the problem of consciousness from the problem of intentionality (or *vice versa*). At the same time, the encounter between 'representational consciousness' and current theories of representational content is not entirely friendly. This makes the problem of consciousness harder but also potentially more illuminating.

Box 1.2 • Two Main Questions

What is the nature of consciousness, and how is it generated or 'implemented' by the brain, are the two primary questions that any theory of consciousness must address. A way to get a handle on the first question is to ask whether consciousness is thoroughly representational, whether all states of consciousness are representational states, or whether there are some non-representational elements of consciousness. Each of the theories to be examined grapples with this issue in a distinctive way. The second question is about explanation and many attitudes to it are possible. A crude division of opinion divides those who think we can from those who think we cannot attain any explanation of how matter generates consciousness. The latter are sometimes labelled 'mysterians'; the former come under many labels. One can hold that it is no more than a 'brute fact' that certain configurations of matter are capable of implementing conscious experience. Leaving aside his infamous dualism, Descartes is an example of such a 'brute mysterian'. Another sort of mysterian holds that while, in some abstract

---

Box 1.2 • Two Main Questions (cont.)

sense, there is an explanation of the matter–consciousness link, we humans lack the intellectual ability either to discover or understand it. Non-mysterians face what at least the intellectual ability either to discover or understand it. Non-mysterians face what at least appears to be a very serious problem. What we could know about the brain is limited to how it is structured and how it physically functions. We might thereby come to know how the brain links perception to action and we might even be able to correlate distinct brain-states with states of consciousness. But we want to know *how* the correlated brain states do the job of generating or implementing states of consciousness. How could one explain, in terms of the brain, the generation of experience as opposed to the generation of behaviour?

Now, even if we could get straight the relation between intentionality and consciousness, including a satisfactory account of qualia (even if perhaps an eliminativist one), a serious problem would appear to remain, which I will call the 'generation problem'.[18] The generation problem can be vividly expressed as the simple question: what is it about matter that accounts for its ability to become conscious? We know, pretty well, how matter works, and there is no sign of consciousness in its fundamental operations (but see chapter 9 below for some speculative doubts about this), nor in the laws by which matter combines into ever more complex chemical, bio-chemical, biological and ultimately human configurations. We know enough about complexity not to be surprised that the behaviour of complex configurations of matter will surprise us, but consciousness is not a matter of surprising *behaviour*. We have a glimmering of how the brain can orchestrate behaviour, smoothly and appropriately matching it to the world in response to the physical information brought to the brain through many sensory pathways. In fact, it seems almost evident that that is *all* that the brain is doing, and that is what evolution selected the brain for, and that by the very nature of matter, there is nothing more that the brain could be doing. Conscious-ness can appear to be a miraculous, seemingly unnecessary, upwelling – a cool spring bubbling up in the midst of a vast, arid desert.

Some physical systems in the world are conscious and others are not. Let us suppose that somehow we could with perfect accuracy divide up the world into the conscious and the non-conscious systems.[19] Let us further suppose, an even more unlikely assumption, that we find that all the conscious systems have some physical property, P, which all the non-conscious systems lack and which we take to underlie consciousness. The generation problem is to explain precisely how the possession of property P generates or produces (or underlies, subvenes, constitutes, realizes, whatever) consciousness in those systems that possess it (for an argument that the problem is absolutely insoluble, see McGinn 1989). The problem is beautifully expressed in a passage from Aldous Huxley's *Point Counter Point*:

... the scraping of the anonymous fiddlers had shaken the air in the great hall, had set the glass of the windows ... vibrating; and this in turn had shaken the air in Lord Edward's apartment. ... The shaking air rattled Lord Edward's *membrana tympani*; the interlocked *malleus, incus* and stirrup bones were set in motion so as to agitate the membrane of the oval window and raise an infinitesimal storm in the fluid of the labyrinth. The hairy endings of the auditory nerve shuddered like weeds in a rough sea; a vast number of obscure miracles were performed in the brain, and Lord Edward ecstatically whispered 'Bach'! He smiled with pleasure. ...[20]

(1963, p. 44)

Maybe this problem becomes clearer if we compare it to a simpler but perhaps analogous problem: how do gases, when heated at constant volume, generate increasing pressure. Here we know the answer, expressed in terms of the mechanical theory of gases; we can use the theory, along with technical know-how, literally to generate desirable fluctuations in pressure and we understand why our heat engines work the way they do. Given our hypothetical property P, we would also, in principle, be able to generate consciousness, but would we know *why* our consciousness-engines work? It can very easily seem that we would not and that, unlike the case of the pressure of a gas, the generation of consciousness is a brute feature of property P (as in the functionalist quote in note 17 above). Brute features are, by definition, inexplicable and so if the ability to generate consciousness is a brute feature of P then the generation of consciousness is inexplicable. This is one way to be a 'mysterian' about the relationship between consciousness and its physical ground. Another is to suppose that there is an explanation of how P generates consciousness but that this explanation so transcends our intellectual abilities that we will never be able to grasp it (see McGinn 1989, 1991 for this brand of mysterianism).

Descartes is actually a rather good example of a brute mysterian, casting aside, once again, his dualism which is really irrelevant here. For Descartes, the property P is just the possible motions of the pineal gland – a perfectly good physical property – for these are the generators of conscious experience. How does the gland do this? Descartes says, in many places, that the connection between the gland's movements and consciousness is just 'ordained by nature'. For example: '... nature seems to have joined every movement of the gland to certain of our thoughts from the beginning of our life, yet we may join them to others through habit. Experience shows this in the case of language. Words produce in the gland movements which are ordained by nature to represent to the soul only the sounds of their syllables when they are spoken or the shape of their letters when they are written ...' (1649/1985, p. 348; compare again Boyd's remarks in note 17 above). That is, it is a brute fact.

Of course, it does seem very likely that there are brute facts, at the very least in our theories of the world but also, if these theories are sufficiently complete and accurate, in the world as well: the values of various constants of nature, the mass ratios between certain sorts of particles, the generation of fundamental forces are all brute facts. These facts are themselves inexplicable and must be simply accepted as true and used in the explanations of other phenomena.[21]

On the other hand, the brute facts with which we are familiar and comfortable are all what might be called 'elementary' facts about the world; they reside at or near the bottom of the world's unfathomable complexity and from their brute simplicity generate all that complexity. In fact, it is *because* brute facts are elementary that the physical sciences are able to go so far in mastering the complexity of the world. Consciousness however does not seem to be an elementary fact of this kind. It seems to exist only as the product of the combined operation of vast numbers of what are themselves intrinsically complex physical systems. We may well wonder how any phenomenon depending upon the concerted action of a vast myriad of such sub-components could be brute. Once again, I think Descartes's picture helps bring this problem into better view. In one sense, Descartes responds to the brute fact problem in the proper scientific spirit, that is, by reducing the bruteness to the most elementary level possible. An 'elementary unit of consciousness' corresponds to the simplest motions of the pineal gland; we might read Descartes as holding that these motions are the ones normally produced by the force of the animal spirits from a *single* nerve source. It is no complaint that we actually never experience these elementary units of consciousness, since whenever we are conscious a vast number of nerve sources are active, for their role is postulational – they mitigate the bruteness of the production of consciousness. The discomfort we should feel in supposing that the matter/consciousness link is a brute fact is also evident in Descartes's treatment: really, it is entirely absurd that a particular chunk of matter should be such that its motions magically generate consciousness. After all, the pineal gland is itself made of a myriad of particles and we should wonder at *their* role in the production of consciousness. For what it is worth, Descartes will play his trump card here in the appeal to God as the source of this particular layer of brute facts; but this is of little interest to us.

Box 1.3 • Two Strategies

Perhaps the intractability of the generation problem is a sign that it is the *problem* itself which is defective rather than our attempts to answer it. Two ways to undercut the generation problem are the *identity strategy* and the *dissolution strategy*. Suppose that X is identical to Y (as for example lightning is identical to electrical discharge). It then makes no sense to ask *how* X manages to generate Y. The identity strategy is promising but may simply yield a new version of the generation problem. At bottom, this is because systems that lack the physical state targeted as *identical* to consciousness can behave indistinguishably from systems that possess it. Unless we embrace a kind of

---

Box 1.3 • Two Strategies (cont.)

behaviourism we face the question of why only some of the 'behaviourally sufficient' states are *really* identical to states of consciousness. The dissolution strategy tries to show that the generation problem is merely a pseudo-problem, conceptual confusion masked as intellectual difficulty. But the most straightforward attempt at dissolution requires substantial and implausible assumptions about the nature of thought and concepts, and alarmingly appears to 'dissolve' the whole enterprise of cognitive science. More subtle efforts at dissolution ask us to rethink our idea of consciousness in various ways, some of them quite radical. Many of the theories examined below attempt this sort of moderate dissolution.

So the idea that the matter/consciousness link is a brute fact does not seem very satisfactory, which drives us back to the original and intractable form of the generation problem.[22] Seeing that it is so hard even to imagine what a solution to the generation problem could look like we might begin to suspect that there is something wrong with the problem itself rather than with our intellectual abilities. There are two rather obvious ways to sidestep the generation problem (that is, obvious to state, not so obvious to work out or assess). Let's call the first manoeuvre the 'identity strategy'. In general, if X = Y there shouldn't be an intelligible question about how Y *generates* X. The questions that take the place of the generation problem are the questions whose answers support the identification of X and Y in the first place. In an explanatory context, the identification of X with Y will tell us what X is, and the identification will be supported by showing how the properties of Y can explain the usual causes and effects of X. If the identification is accepted the only generation problem left will be how Y is generated. In the case of consciousness this sounds hopeful: we will identify consciousness with certain brain processes (say) and then the generation problem reduces to the problem of how these brain processes are generated and while this is doubtless an exceedingly complex problem it is entirely within the realm of the physical world, with none of the *metaphysical* worries that attended the original generation problem. It is a problem for which one could devise a reasonably clear research strategy. Obviously, this approach trades on our familiarity with and love of various reductive successes in the physical sciences.

However, I fear that there is only the appearance of progress here. For a problem which is entirely analogous to the generation problem (really, I think it is the very same problem) will now surely arise. Identifications are made on the basis of a discovery of the sources of some phenomenon's causes and effects. But while conscious experience has its set of causes and effects it is also a phenomenon in its own right and it is far from clear that just anything that occupies the appropriate effective and affective position in the world is a case of consciousness. We might call this the 'simulation' version of the generation problem (John Searle has exploited our intuitions about this problem in a number of places, originally and most notably in his 1980 but carrying through to his 1992): is it possible to simulate consciousness without producing consciousness? Either it is or it isn't. Suppose that it is: then we have (at least) two candidates for identification with consciousness, call them U and V, both of which mesh with the world appropriately but only one of which can truly be identified with consciousness. The problem, which is a form of the generation problem, is to give the correct answer to 'which of U or V is identical to consciousness?' and to *explain* why this is the correct answer. On the other hand, try to suppose that you can't simulate consciousness without producing consciousness so that consciousness is, so to speak, extremely multiply realizable. This leads to the various absurd implementations or *realizations* of mind which philosophers are so very good at dreaming up (see e.g. Block 1978, Maudlin 1989, Peacocke 1983, pp. 203 ff.; see chapter 9 below as well). One of the first thought experiments of this kind can be found in Leibniz, who envisaged the pre-programmed robot counterexample to extreme multiple realizability:

> There is no doubt whatever that a man could make a machine capable of walking about for some time through a city and of turning exactly at the corners of certain streets. A spirit incomparably more perfect, though still finite, could also foresee and avoid an incomparably greater number of obstacles. This is so true that if this world were nothing but a composite of a finite number of atoms which move in accordance with the laws of mechanics, as the hypothesis of some thinkers holds, it is certain that a finite spirit could be so enlightened as to understand and to foresee demonstratively everything which would occur in a determinate time, so that this spirit not only could construct a ship capable of sailing by itself to a designated port, by giving it the needed route, direction, and force at the start, but could also form a body capable of counterfeiting a man. For this involves merely a matter of more or less. . . .
>
> (1702/1976, p. 575)

One might complain that Leibniz's example is simplistic: the counterfeit man would cease to behave like a man if put into counterfactual situations (not all the absurd realizations – none of the modern ones – have this fault).[23] But why, exactly, should the existence of consciousness in the here and now depend upon appropriate behaviour in counterfactual situations? I am not saying that it doesn't; the point is that the question is a version of the generation problem. My brain won't support appropriate behaviour in counterfactual situations of the right sort (e.g. under conditions of stimulation of my brain that lead to paralysis or seizure) but that gives no reason at all to think that I am unconscious *now*. Thus, we can demand that a distinction be drawn

22

between those counterfactual situations that should eliminate consciousness from those that should not. This is just the generation problem rearing its head once again.

I would like to press this issue a little further. Is it true, in general, that the failure to behave appropriately in counterfactual situations shows that an actual system, as it is in the actual world, does not possess a mind or is not conscious? It seems rather obviously not so. Let us permit the wings of our imagination full flight. Consider a person, P, someone who uncontroversially can be allowed to have a mind and to enjoy states of consciousness. Now, take one feature of Leibniz's example: the possibility that a finite mind could predict (to a sufficient degree of accuracy) all the events that P will interact with or be a part of for the course of his or her natural life. Let this finite mind rig a device, entangled deep within and spread throughout P's brain, constructed so that were P to encounter any event other than those predicted by our finite but nonetheless super-mind, P will become completely paralysed (we can even imagine that this paralysis is relatively peripheral so that the central components of P's brain continue to function more or less normally), or perhaps P will start to produce completely random behaviours, or perhaps P's brain will simply explode. Of course, the device will never have a chance to function for the conditions of its functioning are counterfactual conditions, which the super-mind knows will never come to be. So, in fact, our subject will pass a life seeming to be entirely normal. And, of course, this fiction is not really physically possible (too much information needs to be collected, too much calculation time is required, etc.) but its point is clear. P will never act appropriately, rationally, *as if* possessed of a mind, or *as if* feeling anything or being aware of anything in *any* counterfactual situation. But I can't see that this gives us any reason to doubt that P is any less conscious than you or I. I don't think that appeal to counterfactual normalcy goes any way at all towards *explaining* what it is that makes a normal brain conscious. Our subject has been *de-counterfactualized* but still thinks and feels for all of that (for more on the peculiar problem of de-counterfactualization, see chapter 9 below).

A really solid identity hypothesis will provide the ground of the distinction between the conscious and the non-conscious systems of course, but at the cost of returning to the first of our disjuncts. If, say, we identify consciousness with brain state X then consciousness persists just so long as, and through any counterfactual situation in which, brain state X persists. It seems very likely though that the causal role of any particular complex physical system, such as X, can be duplicated by some physical system which is non-X.[24] The creature operated by non-X will appear to be conscious, will make sounds that sound like utterances in which it claims to *be* conscious, etc. But if the creature lacks X then it won't be conscious. There is then an obvious question as to just what about X makes *it* the thing to identify with consciousness. This is the generation problem as it arises in an identity theory. It is no more tractable in this form than in the earlier version.

Perhaps it's worth explicitly emphasizing that functionalist theories face the identity theory version of the generation problem no less than more 'classical' identity theories. In fact, the situation is worse in at least two ways.

Functionalist theories are, in effect, restricted identity theories (see Seager 1991a, chapter 2) and face the generation problem in the form: why does just *this* functionally definable architecture produce consciousness. Any complex system will have multiple 'functional levels' at which it could be described. For example, within the brain, there appear to be 'modules' with more or less specific functions (such as speech comprehension systems, speech production systems, a large variety of sensory detection systems, form and motion detection systems, emotion generation systems etc.) in terms of which cognition can be defined (at least, such definition seems to come into the realm of the possible if we assume that some day we will isolate all the relevant modules). Such a functionalism is at a very high level (and more or less corresponds to the so-called computational theory of the mind). The very same system can be – still functionally – described at the very low level of the functional systems within the individual neurons (e.g. signal summing systems, energy transport systems, 'ion channels', microtubules, etc.). There are myriads of functional descriptions of the brain intermediate between these extremes (such as, notably, the system described in terms of the functional interconnection amongst the neurons, abstracting from the – still functional – description of the implementation of each neuron, which system more or less corresponds to 'connectionist' theories of the mind). The generation problem then arises as the difficulty of explaining why a *certain* level of functional description, or the functioning of a system described at *this* level, is appropriately *identified* with consciousness (see chapter 9 below for more on this difficulty). If we define the relevant functional level in terms of ultimate ability to produce behaviour then we will have the bizarre realization problem breathing down our necks; if we step back from behaviour we will need to explain why only some behaviourally equivalent systems are really conscious. And the identification of consciousness with (implementations of) certain functionally defined states, or functional states at a certain level of functional description, as a *brute* feature of the world is, to my mind, exceptionally bizarre and implausible. Metaphorically speaking, the world has no idea of what functions it might or might not be implementing as the atoms combine in this or that configuration.

The second way in which the situation is worse for the functionalist is that unless physicalism is taken to be necessarily true, the candidate functional property could be implemented by non-physical realizers. Thus, functional properties are not physical properties at all, for they are instantiated in radically non-physical possible worlds. I am not altogether sure what to make of this difficulty, but see below for some additional remarks. I suspect there are deep tensions between the commitment to physicalism and pretty strong intuitions in favour of multiple realizability (some of these tensions have been explored by Jaegwon Kim 1989, 1993).

Whether one agrees with John Searle's view of consciousness or not, his views provide a particularly clear example of the generation problem in the context of an identity theory (for these views see Searle 1992). Searle says that consciousness is 'caused by and realized in' our neural machinery, rather in the way that the liquidity of water is caused by and realized in the molecular structure of water between 0 and 100 degrees C.[25] What is crucial is that the neural machinery has the causal powers appropriate to supporting (i.e. causing and realizing) consciousness. Searle's clear opinion is that these powers are not just the power to produce behaviour which gives every indication of consciousness but, we might say, the power *to be* consciousness. Searle is also clear that discovering what features of the world have these particular causal powers is not easy. Thus it might be that a computer which can at least simulate consciousness-indicating behaviour could well be actually conscious, so long as its circuit elements had the requisite causal powers. On the reverse of this coin, we find the more disturbing prospect of certain physical states possessing the causal power to cause and realize consciousness, as Searle puts it, while lacking the power to produce appropriate behaviour (a possibility accepted and graphically described in chapter 3 of Searle 1992). The analogue of the generation problem is clear here: why do only certain physical states have the causal power to be consciousness, whether or not they suffice to support the appropriate sort of behaviour? It also seems that Searle's position is an instance of the brute fact approach we examined above. There doesn't seem to be any way on his view to explain, in general, why certain physical states have while others do not have the power to cause and realize consciousness; it is, in the words of Descartes, just 'ordained by nature'.

If the brute fact approach is unsatisfactory and the generation problem is no less a problem for identity theories of consciousness than for more traditional productive accounts, philosophers still have one card to play, which I will call the 'dissolution manoeuvre'. It is said that some philosophical problems are not to be solved but rather *dissolved*; dissolution proceeds by showing that a correct outlook on a seemingly refractory problem reveals that there is no problem whatsoever and that the appearance of difficulty stemmed from a mistaken understanding of the problem space. I can't think of any real philosophical problem that has been satisfactorily dissolved; attempted dissolutions seem to rely upon their own set of controversial philosophical theses (for example, verificationism, behaviourism, implicit theories of meaning, e.g. meaning as *use*, etc.)[26] that proceed to manufacture their own set of more or less intractable and genuine philosophical problems – this is called progress. One can make up toy examples however. If some idiot was, somehow, seriously worried about how the average family could have 2.4 children, given the obvious fact that children come in integer units, his problem would be dissolved by setting him straight about the concept of the 'average family'. Dissolutions don't provide a solution to the problem as it is posed (as if we could find a family that sawed up its children and kept 0.4 of one of them) but rather reform the problem so that its problematic nature disappears. There seem to be two kinds of philosophical dissolution however that deserve to be distinguished. The first, and more radical, strategy is to declare that the whole problem space is misconceived because of a fundamental confusion about the nature of the concepts in which the relevant (pseudo) problems are posed. My toy example would fall victim to this kind of dissolution if we try to imagine that the relevant error lies in supposing that the notion of 'the average family' is entirely analogous to that of 'the Jones family'.

The second kind of dissolution is more familiar when it is described as 'eliminative reduction'; such dissolutions proceed by showing that the worrisome problem stems from an incoherent, or at best extremely implausible, background understanding of the problem space. The purification of the background will, almost just as a by-product, eliminate the bothersome elements which are creating the problems. The purification process can take several forms. One is to let science perform the rites (see note 26); since our views of many problematic aspects of the world have been recast by science as it advances we can hope that our particular problem space will be similarly reformed (this hope is reinforced in the case of the problem of consciousness insofar as we believe that science is only just getting around to this difficulty).[27] Another is to rethink the problem in terms of other concepts already to hand which, it is believed or hoped, will not simply lead to yet more difficulties once they are applied to the problem at issue. The two sorts of dissolution shade into each other here for often the presumed misunderstanding of the concepts generating the problems will be explicated in terms of other concepts of which, it is supposed, we have a firmer grasp. The primary difference between the two modes of dissolution is that the second mode does not necessarily charge anyone with a 'misunderstanding' of a concept (or the 'role' of a concept) but, more typically, charges them with deploying in their thinking a covertly *incoherent* concept or, at least, a concept actually useless for the tasks in which it is employed.[28]

In the philosophy of mind, Ryle's *Concept of Mind* (1949) and various of Wittgenstein's writings (primarily 1953/1968) surely provide examples of the attempt to dissolve rather than solve the mind–body problem in the radical, first sense of 'dissolution'. Ryle says that the Cartesian errors stem from a variety of more or less subtle *category mistakes*, which are misunderstandings of concepts (or the role of concepts). Wittgenstein says that 'everything in philosophy which is not gas, is grammar' (Wittgenstein 1980, as quoted in Hacker 1993) and, I take it, philosophical grammar consists in setting forth a proper understanding of the nature and role (or use) of concepts. Of course, the proper understanding of Ryle and Wittgenstein is not the labour of a couple of paragraphs. Still, it is tempting to give their views short shrift on the basis of the following argument. In general, the propriety of the notions of *category mistake* and *philosophical grammar* presupposes an acceptable and clear distinction between analytic truths (those truths true in virtue of the meanings of words or the 'form' of concepts) and synthetic truths (those truths true in virtue of the empirical state of the world). But there is no acceptable or clear analytic–synthetic distinction (see, of course, Quine 1953). So the fundamental philosophical machinery required for this sort of radical dissolution of the problem of consciousness is simply not available. The dissolution cannot get off the ground.

For example, using Hacker (1993) as a convenient and comprehensive guide to the views of Wittgenstein (and if Hacker is not reliable on such basic features of Wittgenstein's views then I can't see how we will ever know what Wittgenstein thought about these issues) we find that computers cannot think, infer or reason because 'thought, inference and reason are capacities of the animate' (1993, p. 80). Now, what is the *philosophical grammar* of 'animate'? We find that 'if in the distant future it were feasible to create in an electronic laboratory a being that acted and behaved much as we do, exhibiting perception, desire, emotion, pleasure and suffering, as well as thought, it would arguably be reasonable to conceive of it as an animate, though not biological, creature. But to that extent it would not be a machine . . . ' (1993, p. 81). This seems to suggest either that the possession of mental qualities can be, as a matter of 'grammar', equated with *behaving* in certain ways or the tautologous claim that we will not be able to build a computer that thinks and etc. unless and until we can build a computer that thinks and etc. (and then we won't *call* this computer a machine). The first disjunct is simply logical behaviourism, which, we are repeatedly assured, was *not* Wittgenstein's (or, for that matter, Ryle's) view.[29] The second is empty: the questions are *how* do we build or what is involved in building, if we can build, a device that is conscious, and exactly how did our construction process generate consciousness (as opposed to, or in addition to, various behavioural capacities)? It is not much of an answer to be instructed to proceed by building a device that is conscious. (Whereas, note, the logical behaviourist at least gives us relatively clear cut instructions on how to proceed since behavioural capacities are all we need to produce.)

Given that the study of the mind–brain remains in its early phases, part of our problem lies in devising the proper models or the proper language for describing and explaining how cognition works. The radical dissolution manoeuvre threatens to undercut these early efforts, if in its attempt we are led to impose draconian strictures on the language of science, even if only on the language of something as evidently ridiculous and error-ridden as 'so-called "cognitive science"' (Hacker 1993, p. 2). And such strictures do seem to be drawn wholesale from the detached brow of philosophical grammar where we find that 'it is "nonsense on stilts" to suppose that a brain classifies and compares, . . . constructs hypotheses and makes decisions' (1993, p. 71). The whole thrust of cognitive science is that there are sub-personal contents and sub-personal operations that are truly cognitive in the sense that these operations can be properly explained only in terms of these contents. Just glancing through the 92 abstracts in *The Cognitive Neurosciences* (Gazzaniga 1994) reveals that virtually every paper could be dismissed on grammatical grounds as committing the grossest errors of attributing various cognitive functions to the brain which it could not (logically or grammatically) be said to perform. But I think we *can* understand the sense in which the brain might generate, say, a perceptual hypothesis about which face of the Necker cube is nearest the eye without supposing that there are little commit-tees of full-fledged thinkers debating the issue within the brain (a supposition that is itself ruled out by considerations of plausibility and explanatory usefulness but *not* by philosophical grammar). I rather doubt that there is a substantive discipline to be labelled philosophical grammar. There is theoretical linguistics and there are the linguistic intuitions of speakers.[30] These intuitions are valuable data, but it is danger-ous to suppose that they can be used to expose the ultimate limits of science (or language) without the bother of empirical investigation.

From the particular point of view of the generation problem of consciousness the attempt at dissolution is pretty clearly unsuccessful. Either it presupposes an implausi-ble behaviourism coupled with an unconvincing verificationism, or it simply accepts consciousness as a fact which it makes no attempt to explain at all. For example, Ryle's free use of the language of feelings, pains, twinges, tickles, starts, etc. would strongly suggest the latter 'failing', so much so that the problem of consciousness as I conceive it was simply irrelevant to Ryle's concerns (of course, Ryle does say much of interest about consciousness; but not, I say, about the generation problem). From our point of view, Ryle was perhaps most concerned to undercut the Cartesian dualist view of the mind–body relation. The generation problem transcends the debate between dualism and materialism however. Similarly we find in Wittgenstein an unremitting attack on the notion that there are two 'worlds': one of matter, one of mind. But accepting this does not dissolve the generation problem. Again speaking for Wittgenstein, Hacker asks 'is it really mysterious that specific brain-events should produce curious "facts of consciousness"?' (1993, p. 239) and he notes that there is a completely commonplace sense to sentences like 'this is produced by a brain-pro-cess' when, for example, after certain brain stimulations 'the patient might report . . . a flashing of light on the periphery of his visual field'. It would be unfair to read this as the behaviourist remark that brain stimulations cause *reports* (i.e. certain vocaliza-tions). But to the extent we accept 'flashings of light' in our visual fields we are just accepting what the generation problem seeks to explain: how do brain events cause conscious apprehension of flashings? The generation problem asks us to look below the now entirely uncontroversial fact that the brain causes states of consciousness to address the problem of just *how* this causal process works.[31] It does not dissolve this problem to restate the obvious causal facts.

A variant on the dissolution theme, roughly half-way between the 'pure concep-tual' approach just considered and the alternative, more empirical approach scouted above agrees that a reworking of our intuitive view of consciousness will be needed to bring consciousness into the scientific fold. But it does not claim that this rework-ing will end up providing an explanation of consciousness of the sort whose absence the generation problem laments. Rather, it asserts that the correct view of conscious-ness explains why it looks *as if* there is a generation problem when in fact there is none. For example, Brian Loar writes that 'what explains the "appearance of contingency" [i.e. the sense that experiential qualities and material substrate are *arbitrarily* linked in nature] is that a phenomenal conception of pain and a conception of P [i.e. the physical-functional property to be *identified* with pain] in physical-functional terms can be cognitively independent – can have independent cognitive roles – even while introducing the same property' (1990, p. 85). William Lycan asserts that 'the lack of tracings and explanations . . . is *just what you would expect* if the self-scanner view of introspection is correct' (1996, p. 64). Without going into the details of these philosophers' theories, the basic strategy is this. The first step is to identify consciousness with some physical (or physical-functional, or simply functional) property. Phase two involves showing that, given the view of consciousness that goes with this identification, the *appearance* of a mysterious link between the physical base and consciousness is unsurprising and even explicable.

Box 1.4 • Mere Appearance?

Is it possible that the generation problem is an illusion, not borne of conceptual incoherencies but stemming from some feature of our own cognitive nature? Some have argued that the *appearance* of an explanatory gap between matter and consciousness is a natural product of our epistemic position. However, while this may ease our fears that one could argue from the explanatory gap to the unacceptable conclusion that consciousness is non-physical, it does not dissolve the generation problem which is primarily a kind of epistemological worry – a worry about how we can properly fit consciousness into the scientific picture of the world.

Here it is important to distinguish two distinct aspects of the generation problem. The generation problem can be thought to point towards an *ontological* difficulty or to an *epistemological* worry. The dissolution variant under consideration is designed to ease our ontological scruples about identifying states of consciousness with certain physical states. As Lycan puts it, 'the lack of such tracings and explanations, only to be expected, do not count against the materialist identification' (1996, p. 64) and Loar is clear that his target is 'anti-physicalism'. But it seems to me that the generation problem is primarily epistemological, and though it possesses an inescapable ontological component, this component is secondary and is really about the distinction between physical states that do as opposed to those that do not count as states of consciousness. In fact, it is only because we embrace physicalism that the generation problem can loom as a serious worry; what we want to know is *how* consciousness resides in or arises out of the physical machinery of the brain (or whatever). So we can ask, of either Loar or Lycan, for both of their accounts essentially agree on how to account for the appearance of the generation problem,[32] *how* or *why* do certain physical-functional states, with just *this* sort of conceptual role, ground conscious

29

experience? This question is independent of the details of Loar's theory of 'phenomenal concepts' or Lycan's quasi-indexical account and is not addressed by them.

A peculiar problem arises here about functionalism, which is worth mentioning though it opens too vast a territory to explore in detail. It is, I believe, a very deep metaphysical question. What is the ground for restricting the functional state definitions at issue here to *physical* states? If it be admitted that there is a bare possibility of non-physical stuff or states, why wouldn't the appropriate functional organization of these things or states, also generate conscious experience (there are, after all, some functionalists that take the positive answer to this question to be a virtue of their view)? If the very possibility of non-physical stuff or states is denied then physicalism is not just true, it is *necessarily* true. In that case the weight of the argument should be directed at showing this necessity, not at details of the interaction of phenomenal (for Loar) or 'quasi-indexical' (for Lycan) concepts and physical-functional concepts. I don't know of any very convincing arguments that physicalism is necessarily true (i.e. that *every* possible world contains nothing but physical things and physical properties). It is not, in any way, a scientific issue. One might be tempted by the identity theory again here, for we know that identities are necessary even if they are discovered empirically (see Kripke 1980; Putnam 1975). I think this shows very little in this case however. For though it is true that *if* water = H_2O then there can be no *water* in any possible world that lacks hydrogen and oxygen, there seems to be no metaphysical principle which rules out substances that are phenomenologically just like water in such worlds (or even, for that matter, in the actual world).[33] If the same is true of consciousness then we face the difficult task of explaining why certain physical states *are* states of consciousness whereas phenomenologically identical states in distant possible worlds are not states of consciousness (even though these states are realized in the same way as real states of consciousness are, save that the states involved are not physical). The main motivation for a functionalist theory of mental states would seem to militate against such a use of the identity theory. It is rather as if we discovered that all can-openers in America were made of steel and decided to identify the property of being a can-opener with certain steel-functional states. Then, when we discover aluminium European 'can-openers' (functioning as such too), we *deny* that they are really can-openers at all! This is neither plausible nor in the proper functionalist spirit. So the upshot of identifying consciousness with physical-functional states and *accepting* the possibility of non-physical things or states (even if in distant possible worlds) is a super generation problem: why can't consciousness arise in these distant possible worlds?

In any event, perhaps the problem I see stemming from the under-appreciation of the distinction between the ontological and epistemological aspects of the generation problem can be clarified by comparing it to problems arising from the use of the so-called 'anthropic principle' in cosmology. This principle (in its basic form) states that we must expect to observe conditions in the universe which are such as to allow for the existence of observers. So it is no surprise to find that the Earth is at such a distance from the Sun that life can thrive upon it, for were the Earth either nearer to or farther from the Sun there would be no one to measure the Earth–Sun distance. But it should be obvious that this fact does not eliminate the need to explain why the Earth is 93 million miles from the Sun (presumably, there is, or could be, a good astronomical account of how the conditions leading to the formation of the Solar System led to Earth being at this particular distance from the Sun). Or again, the fact that the gravitational constant, G, is what it is can be anthropically 'explained' by noting that were G even a little bit stronger stars would burn out too quickly for life to arise near them, and were G a touch weaker galaxies and stars would not have coalesced out of the remnants of the Big Bang at all. Thus, it is no surprise that we find that G has its observed value. This does not answer the question of why G has the value it has (in this case, we may need to appeal to what is essentially a brute fact about our universe).

Similarly, in the case of consciousness. Though theories such as Loar's or Lycan's explain why we should not be surprised at the appearance of the generation problem, this does not relieve them of the responsibility of explaining how or why consciousness is subserved by the kinds of physical states these theories favour as the basis of consciousness. They will, then, run into the problems of providing such explanations outlined above (and to be seen in more detail below).

In the theories to be considered below, dissolutions of the problem of consciousness will nonetheless loom large. But they will be dissolutions of the second, more empirical, sort. These dissolutions proceed by transforming consciousness into something else which, it is hoped or supposed, will be easier to explain. Although I don't think such approaches succeed, I do think that they offer the best chance of getting rid of the generation problem. Since the generation problem looks utterly intractable, the prospect of just getting rid of it is very attractive. But before getting to the dissolutions, let us examine an identity theory, which at least seems to offer a more straightforward attack on the problem of consciousness.

Box 1.5 • Summary

Descartes offers an entrance into the problems of consciousness which properly emphasizes the two questions of the nature and generation of consciousness. Descartes in fact provides an example of a somewhat sketchy theory of consciousness: a theory that makes states of consciousness one and all representational and which regards the matter–consciousness link as a brute fact, entirely inexplicable. Strangely, Descartes's deplored dualism turns out not to be a very important component of his views. The generation problem looks so intractable that ways around it have been sought. One can try to *identify* consciousness with certain physical states, but it is unclear that this really

Box 1.5 • Summary (cont.)

solves the generation problem. Or one can try to dissolve the problem. Plausible attempts to do so require a rethinking of the nature of consciousness. Most of the theories to come aim for this. We shall see how they fare against the generation problem. But first, let's examine a clear form of an identity theory.

2

IDENTITY THEORIES
AND
THE GENERATION PROBLEM

. . . to determine by what modes or actions light produceth in our
minds the phantasms of colour is not so easie. I. Newton

Box 2.1 • Preview

Although it applies only to certain elements of consciousness, an interesting identity theory has been advanced by Paul Churchland. His views depend upon the theory of cognition that has come to be known as *connectionism* and which is currently extremely influential. Connectionist models begin with the idea of a network composed of very simple units whose individual outputs depend upon the set of inputs they receive from all the units feeding into them. In this, they are taken to be rather like the brain. It is possible to regard the whole network as defining an abstract space, within which each of its possible states forms a vector. Churchland's identity theory is that there are sub-networks of the brain, operating in an essentially connectionist fashion, which correspond to – in fact can be identified with – states of sensory consciousness (colours, sounds, smells, etc.). Thus the abstract space associated with these sub-networks is also a space of qualitative consciousness, and the vectors within the space correspond to particular sorts of sensory experience. The problem with this view is that it confuses the sources of conscious experience with conscious experience itself. That is, while we might agree that activation of the appropriate neural 'vectors' is required for conscious experience, this would not show that such activation was identical to experience. In fact, there are reasons to suspect that these activations can occur in the complete absence of consciousness.

Very early in the morning of May 24th, 1987, Ken Parks left his home in Pickering, Ontario, drove 23 kilometres to his in-laws' house, parked in the underground garage, went into his in-laws' house using the key he had taken from his kitchen table, went upstairs, and killed his mother-in-law and almost killed his father-in-law. The interesting thing is: he was not conscious through the entire episode. Later, he 'found himself' in a house he knew well, with severe injuries of his own, confronting a horrifying scene which he could not understand. He then managed to drive to a nearby police station where he declared that he thought he might have killed two people. This was not quite a confession, perhaps, but it was an open and shut case to the police.

The case of Ken Parks went all the way to the Canadian Supreme Court, but at every stage of the tortuous legal journey Parks was acquitted – entirely and unreservedly. It was found that he was not guilty, by way of the defence of *non-insane automatism*. He was a sleepwalker (as well as sleep-driver, sleep-killer) who was not conscious while he performed the most momentous and horrible actions of his life (for a gripping if somewhat lurid account of the Parks affair, see Callwood 1990; also see Broughton 1994). Ken Parks is certainly not the only person who while sleepwalking has committed gruesome violence. Within a legal context, such cases can be recognized at least as far back as the middle ages (see Hacking 1995, pp. 145 ff.). The common law legal concept of non-insane automatism has been formed under the pressure of a very rare but apparently compelling set of events.

Non-insane automatism raises a host of fascinating questions, about the law, about morality and responsibility, the nature of the self, and more. But what is striking for the project of explaining consciousness is that the sleepwalking killer is a real world case of what philosophers have come to call 'zombies': human-like creatures who at least superficially behave as if conscious without *really* being conscious. Philosophers like to go to extremes and so zombie thought experiments tend to involve creatures who are behaviourally entirely indistinguishable from their conscious counterparts. A sleepwalker – even one who can drive 23 kilometres of urban roadway – is not so perfect a zombie. Sleepwalkers are pretty unresponsive to speech, generally clumsy and not good at avoiding obvious but non-stereotyped obstacles in their paths (for example, Ken Parks seriously cut his hands during the attack, and these cuts seem to be the result of grabbing and pulling a knife firmly by the blade, probably to disarm his mother-in-law). But still, such sleepwalkers must enjoy an extremely rich sensory interaction with the environment, and an ability to perform complex chains of structured actions whose last link lies far from the first. This is the normal home of consciousness. How can an unconscious brain perform such feats?

But are sleepwalkers like Ken Parks really unconscious? They could, for example, be dreaming. An interesting fact about sleepwalking, however, is that it occurs during the deepest, slow wave, stages of sleep in which dreams are apparently very rare (as contrasted with the so-called REM sleep which is highly correlated with dreaming). In any case, dreams have nothing to do with the sleepwalker's ability to navigate the world and structure actions. So, sleepwalkers walk during the deepest stage of sleep and do not recall their somnambulistic adventures upon awakening. Nonetheless, could they not be conscious, but just forget, rapidly and completely, what has happened to them? Perhaps, but this is an exceptionally hyperbolic assumption. The sleepwalker evidently does not 'forget' what he is about *during* the episode, so it must be the awakening that suddenly erases the records left by conscious experience. There is no reason to introduce such an extravagant and mysterious process. And here too the fact that sleepwalkers are imperfect philosophical zombies is of some importance, for they do not really act like conscious subjects if their behaviour is looked at closely.

One phenomenon that I know of does involve something like this sort of mysterious agent of forgetfulness and this is the 'switching' from one personality to another suffered by victims of what is now called dissociative identity disorder (still more familiar as multiple personality disorder). It is common, but not entirely general, for one 'alter' to have no memory or knowledge of the actions, or perhaps even the existence, of another. The famous historical cases of double and multiple personality are tales of people rather suddenly transforming from one person to another with no memory of their alternative life. For example, William James relates the case – as an instance of *alternating* personality – of Ansel Bourne who one day in 1887 turned into a Mr. A. Brown with no memory of Bourne, although he apparently remembered some incidents that had happened to him while he 'was' Bourne, and it could hardly be coincidence that he took a new name with the same initials as his old. In the spring of '88 he just as abruptly turned back into Bourne, with no memories of the previous personality but with reclaimed Bourne-memories, and was rather startled, to say the least, to find himself in a strange town amongst strangers who did not regard him as a stranger (see James 1890/1950, pp. 390 ff.). But again, the case of multiple alternating personalities is quite unlike that of the sleepwalker. In the former, there is no question but that each personality is a conscious being (at least when it is 'out') and the behaviour of any of the multiple personalities is manifestly unlike that of the sleepwalker. It might be suggested however that the sleepwalker is similar to the multiple in that the actions of the sleepwalker are uncharacteristic or 'out of character', revelatory of some normally hidden state of mind or motivation. In fact, I think this is to characterize improperly even those sleepwalkers who commit the most horrific acts. There is no reason to think that they are acting out some unconscious desire. They may be reacting to some confused dream contents or, as seems more usual, the very attempt to arouse them is what engenders the unknowing but aggressive response (these two possibilities can coalesce if a fragmentary dream is generated by the attempted arousal).

The whole issue of sleep mentation is very unclear but it seems likely that sleepwalkers are truly unconscious even as they engage in reasonably complex – sometimes remarkably complex – interactions with the world. As it is often put these days, there is nothing that 'it is like' to be a sleepwalker; sleepwalkers enjoy no experience. In this respect they are less than animals. No doubt there are internal physical differences which ground the distinction between the consciousness of a normal human being during normal waking existence and the utter blackness of the sleepwalker. Amazingly, these differences are not sufficient to disable the sleepwalker's sensory 'awareness' of the environment and his ability to interact more or less successfully with it.

This does tell us something about possible identity theories of consciousness: they will be harder to construct than we might have hoped. The problems are general, but I think they can be highlighted best by examining a particular identity approach. This approach is based upon an idea of extremely wide applicability and indisputable utility, and one that takes us to the core of the currently fashionable connectionist approach to the mind. In fact, the idea at issue is so general that I have fears that it lacks real content in the absence of highly constrained, precisely specified versions of it. The idea is that of vector coding (to use the term favoured by Paul Churchland 1986, 1995, and Patricia Churchland and Terry Sejnowski 1992).[1] In relation to the problem of consciousness, vector coding is supposed to provide a plausible picture of exactly *what* is to be identified with the qualities of consciousness (the 'what it is like' part of the now familiar catch phrase 'what it is like to be a . . .').

To begin, imagine a neural network composed of ideally simple units which we may as well call neurons. Each toy neuron is capable of only two output states, which we may as well label 1 and 0. The output state of any particular neural unit is produced under well defined conditions, dependent upon the number and quality of incoming signals from other neurons to which it is connected, the weighting of these incoming signals and its own internal 'output function' (called its *activation* function). Here's a sketch of a 'generic' network showing some of the inter-unit connections, some of the connection weights between the units and indicating the existence of the activation functions 'within' each unit, as in fig. 2.1.

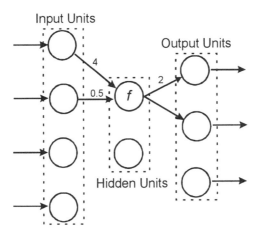

(Fig. 2.1)

However, we can ignore the complexities of the network in an explanation of vector coding and focus rather on the state of each element of the network. At any moment, the state of the network is specified by the states of all of its individual neurons; since there are but two possible states for any of our toy neurons, there will be 2^n network states if there are n neurons. The mathematical language of vectors provides us with an economical and powerful means of representing the network states, which for the simplest networks can readily be visualized. Let each neuron's set of possible output states be represented in one dimension (i.e. on a line) which will form an axis in an abstract Cartesian coordinate system. So a two neuron network will form a two-dimensional space (illustrated in fig. 2.2 below). This represents the network as it is when both of its neurons are in output state 1; obviously the other three states are equally representable as distinct vectors in this little space (one such state will be represented by the null vector $\langle 0,0 \rangle$). If we allowed our neurons to have more possible output states, the number of representing vectors would also grow, and grow pretty fast. If we added more neurons to the network, the dimensionality of the space would grow as would the number of possible network states (and this growth would be even faster than in the case of adding more individual neuron output states). In any case, *every* possible network state is represented by just one particular vector.

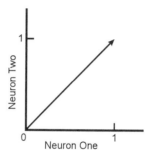

(Fig. 2.2)

We expect that over time the network will change its state as it goes about its business. Since each state is represented by a vector the changes in the network state will form a trajectory through the vector space. The exact properties of the neurons that form the network and their interconnections, along with any input to the network, will determine the nature of this trajectory. The most elegant example of how such determination occurs comes from an entirely different domain: classical mechanics.

In classical mechanics, instead of model neurons we have idealized mass points; instead of output states we have the basic properties of momentum and position (notice that momentum encodes both mass and velocity, so an obvious simplification is to suppose that all our mass points have identical mass). The simplest possible case is a single particle constrained to move in a single dimension (back and forth along the x-axis, say). This particle has only two sets of 'output' states: momentum in the x direction and position along the x-axis (both either positive or negative). A particle can have any position with any momentum, so these two output states are independent of one another and must be represented by distinct, orthogonal dimensions in the abstract 'output' space we are constructing. (This contrasts with the case of our model neuron whose two output states of 0 and 1 were obviously not independent – in fact they are co-definable – and thus were modelled as distinct points along a single dimension.) So the abstract representation of a single particle looks very similar to the representation of the states of our two-neuron network given above. If we suppose that, somehow, our particle can have but two momentum states and two position states, then the two representations are identical (in fact, of course, the particle is supposed to have a continuous infinity of possible momenta and positions).

The trajectory of the simple one particle system through this 'phase space' is determined by its initial position and momentum plus the laws of mechanics. This trajectory is trivial if we suppose that there are no forces acting on our particle, for in that case, as we know from Newton's first law (in the absence of forces, a body in motion maintains its state of motion), the momentum must be constant over time and the position is given by the simple rule: $x = vt + X$ where v is the velocity of the particle and X is the initial position. Perhaps we should regard velocity as a foreign intruder here, but it is a quantity definable in terms of momentum. Since momentum, p, is defined as equal to mv, v is just p/m and so our position rule should be $x = pt/m + X$. We can easily graph such a trajectory in our phase space if we adopt some convention about representing time along the trajectory; the graph will just be a straight line, as in fig. 2.3.

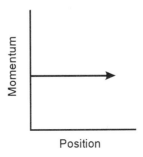

(Fig. 2.3)

Here, the arrow is taken to mean that the trajectory is formed by considering time to 'move' from left to right; each point on the trajectory is later than any point to its left. Much more interesting trajectories are formed if we imagine that our particle is subject to some force. Suppose our particle is attached to an idealized spring and it is set in motion with a specific push. Then the trajectory will form a closed loop in phase space that will be endlessly repeated.

The trajectory of a neural network is just as much determined by its own 'mechanics', but these are defined by the activation patterns of the neural units and the connection weights amongst them (plus any rules there might be for the dynamic alteration of these weights, a subtlety important for networks that can *learn*) as well as the intrinsic properties of the neurons which specify how they react to input from their fellows. Consider our two-neuron network. In order to define its dynamics (such as they are) we need to specify each neuron's *activation function*. In this case, each neuron will be functionally identical. Let's say that the activation function, f, is just this: If a unit is in state s (either 0 or 1) then $f(s) = |s - (1 - I)|$, where I is the input from its single connected unit. That is, the final state is determined by taking the absolute value of the original state minus 1 minus the input from the other unit. We'll suppose that the output of a unit is just equal to its current state and that the connection weight between the units is simply 1 (so if a unit is in state 0 (or 1), its output is 0 (or 1) and it passes that value along to its mate). This activation function has the stultifyingly simple consequent that both neurons will end up in state 1 and once they are in that state they will stay there forever (since once the input from the other unit is 1 we will be subtracting 0 from the original state value, but an original state of 0 must soon transform into a state of 1). However, if we redefine the activation function so that $f(s) = I \times |s - I|$ we find that *if* we start the network with the two units in opposite states then the system will oscillate between the two possible states in which the units have opposite values.

Box 2.2 • Connectionism I

The brain is composed of maybe a hundred billion neurons and each neuron is connected to perhaps ten thousand of its fellows. This is a staggeringly complex system. Connectionism is a simplification and idealization of the probable functional structure of the brain. A connectionist system (often called a neural network) is a set of 'neural units' interconnected in various ways. Each unit receives multiple input from several others, but produces a single output. The output is determined by the unit's 'activation function' (a simple example would be an activation function which summed the unit's input and then emitted output if this sum was above some predetermined threshold). But not all the connections to a particular unit are equally important; the value of an input is adjusted by the *connection weight* between the units in question (in the example above, some input values might be doubled, others halved before the activation function got to work on them). A network can 'learn' (i.e. adjust its output 'behaviour') by modifying these inter-unit connection weights, and various methods for doing this have been proposed and developed.

Every network will have its own state space in which all its possible states can be represented. And, according to the details of the units' activation functions, initial states, inter-unit weights and so on, the transitions from network state to network state will form a trajectory within this state space. If the units are confined to discrete states then these trajectories will be 'jumpy'. It is also worth mentioning that the trajectories need not be strictly determined by the details of the network because it is possible to have non-deterministic activation functions.

There is another, and very beautiful, way to regard the trajectories a network can follow through its state space. It is possible and in fact typical to regard a subset of the neural units as 'input units', whose values are taken to be the input to the rest of the network of which they are a part, and to regard a second subset of the units as the output units, whose values, considered as the consequences of the input units' values plus the workings of the network, are taken to be the output of the network (those intermediate units which are neither input nor output units are usually called the 'hidden' units – see fig. 2.1 above). The values assigned to the input units form a string of activation values: a vector. The network can then be seen as transforming this input vector into an output vector: the string of activation values which the output units end up in after the input percolates through the network. This way of looking at a network reveals that a common mathematical operation is being performed by the network: a matrix operation on a vector. Consider, as a simple example, the following matrix:

$$M = \begin{bmatrix} -1 & 0 \\ 0 & 1 \end{bmatrix}$$

M will transform vectors of the form $\langle x,y \rangle$, 2-D vectors, into other 2-D vectors. In particular, M will rotate an input vector 'around' the y-axis to form the mirror image of its input vector.[2] Thus, if the input vector is $\langle 1,0 \rangle$ then $\langle 1,0 \rangle \times M = \langle -1,0 \rangle$. Does this tell us anything about the network that could accomplish this simple task? Yes, the elements of M are the *connection weights* between the input and output units of a four unit network (with no hidden units – such a simple network is called a linear associator). The network would look like fig. 2.4.

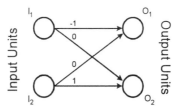

(Fig. 2.4)

Assuming that input and output units can take on the same range of values (to keep things very simple, we might suppose that each unit can have state values of –1, 0 and 1, although the net will work even for units that can take on any real number value), this network will perform the vector transformation encoded in M (the state value of an output unit is just the sum of its inputs, which are, one by one, the product of the value of the input unit times its connection weight with the relevant output unit). Of course, more complex kinds of networks require much more sophisticated analyses, but such analyses remain mathematical and can be expressed in the language of vector spaces and vector manipulation.

To me, this feels like one of those cases where we see an astonishing mathematization of the world, or a realization that certain aspects of the physical world are providing a real model of some range of mathematics. One might exclaim: so *this* is what neural networks are doing. It is hard not to be at least impressed with the possibility that vector transformation is the deep and rather abstract but mathematically comprehensible job for which brains were designed by evolution. It would be hyperbolic to compare the mathematization of the brain in these terms to Galileo's mathematization of motion and acceleration, but some of the fervency of connectionism's advocates surely does spring from this sort of revelatory experience which can radically transform one's perception of some domain.

Box 2.3 • Connectionism II

A connectionist network is normally divided into a set of input units which receive signals from the 'outside world', an optional set of hidden units connected to both the input units and the final layer of output units which transmit their signals back to the outside world. The whole network can be regarded as a machine that takes a set of input values, performs a certain mathematical function on them and finally returns a set of output values. We can also regard the state of the entire network, or any sub-network such as the input layer, at any time as a 'list' of the activation states of all the units. Such a list is a vector in an abstract space (the dimensionality of the space is the number of units). The operation of the network will involve it sequentially changing its overall state; that is, under the impact of the input to the system and the internal changes in activation induced by the propagation of the input through the network, the network will move from vector to vector. These changes will form a trajectory in the abstract space defined by the whole network. It is possible to find mathematical descriptions of these trajectories and, in general, of the dynamics of connectionist systems.

Several interesting facts about neural networks are highlighted in this viewpoint. Perhaps most important is that the network does not perform its matrix operation the way an ordinary computer (or a student of linear algebra) would. The ordinary way is to take each component of the vector and process it through the matrix to produce, one by one, each component of the output vector. Networks, however, work on all the components at the same time; the input vector kind of *flows* through the matrix deforming into the output vector as it goes. Obviously, this parallel processing is a very fast and very efficient way to proceed.

A second striking feature that emerges is the evident analogy between vector transformation and some kind of *categorization* process. If there are, as is usually the case, fewer output states than input states then the transformation of the input vector into the output vector is a sorting operation, and nets can be devised which solve a wide variety of recognition tasks based on this fact. The constellation of particular connection weights amongst the units which govern the input/output translation is a repository of information against which the input vectors are assessed. A simple, classic example can be drawn from logic: the exclusive-or function. This is an historically important case since it was once 'shown' that neural networks cannot realize this logical function. In fact, the x-or problem is one that requires a network with a layer of hidden units between the output and the input for its solution. Fig. 2.5 provides an elementary network that implements exclusive-or (adapted from Rumelhart and McClelland 1986, v. 1, p. 321).

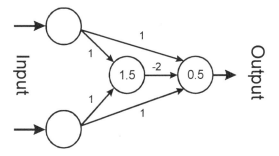

(Fig. 2.5)

The units of this network are, as above, capable of but two states, 1 and 0, which can also be thought of as the input and output of the units (we consider a unit which in fact produces no output as outputting 0). So the input vectors are exhaustively listed by $\langle 1,1 \rangle$, $\langle 1,0 \rangle$, $\langle 0,1 \rangle$ and $\langle 0,0 \rangle$. The net has only two possible output vectors however, which are $\langle 1 \rangle$ and $\langle 0 \rangle$. Thus the net can be thought of as sorting the input into two categories (in this case the categories are the *true* and the *false*). The activation functions for these units are set up so that a unit outputs its state value if (and only if) the sum of its inputs equals or exceeds its *threshold* (given by the number within the unit symbol on the figure). The input to a unit is, as above, the sum of the output values of its connected units *times* the connection weights (the number beside the arrows in the figure) between it and these units. (The possible ambiguity of this English formulation is eliminated in the formula: Σ (weight $\times$ output value).) Thus the hidden unit will give an output just in case it receives a 1 from both the input units. In that case, the hidden unit's output will act to shut down the output unit, so that the input vector $\langle 1,1 \rangle$ is mapped on to the output vector $\langle 0 \rangle$. Of course, the input vector $\langle 0,0 \rangle$, which is represented by no output from the input units, will leave the net entirely quiescent, and thus 'result' in the output vector $\langle 0 \rangle$ as well. Only in the case when exactly one of the input units is in state 1 will the output vector be $\langle 1 \rangle$. So this net does indeed implement the exclusive-or function.[3] This simple network exemplifies the primary requirement for categorization: the principled reduction of input information.

Another, somewhat but not extremely controversial, feature of such networks is their inherent similarity to actual neural organization. The brain is not really very much like the model networks that researchers have constructed so far, but there is a lot of evidence that the brain might well be set up to engage in a similar sort of activity, at least when viewed from a sufficiently abstract perspective. Abstractly speaking, the brain may very well be an engine of vector transformation in which such transformations are performed by systems which are closely analogous to the kinds of networks constructible from our model neurons. One can consider such transformative operations from various levels. At the absolute extreme is the austere view that considers the total human sensory apparatus as a vector input device. The immensely complex vector that the senses deliver is then transformed by the brain into an output vector which directs all the various motor (and perhaps visceral, endocrine, etc.) responses of which the body is capable. Such a view considers the brain, or the brain plus nervous system, as a single network of more than astronomical complexity. This is not a mere stimulus-response model since the network can embody a wealth of information within its vast multitude of variously weighted interconnections (and bear in mind also that the brain is not like the simple 'feedforward' nets of our examples but possesses instead an extremely rich feedback – or *recurrent* or *re-entrant*[4] – structure that continuously modifies the transformative operations upon the input vectors). This information can either be learned through experience or it can be, at least to some extent, inherent in the developmental processes that generate the basic architecture of the brain and nervous system. I hedge with the 'to some extent' since it seems that there just is not enough information in our genetic instruction set to wholly determine the brain's neural connectivity. Developmental contingencies must fix almost all inter-neuron connections. This fact may turn out to be surprisingly important for the identity theory solution to the problem of consciousness, as we shall see below.

A rather more practical viewpoint breaks the brain down into a myriad of sub-nets, whose vector transformation functions can be independently surveyed. This is not inconsistent with the grander outlook, since presumably a system of connected networks itself forms a network, but doubtless it is much easier to discern the structure and function of the sub-nets. From the modeler's perspective it is necessary to consider highly specific and constrained functions if any progress is to be made. In fact, at this stage of research, there is no very close relationship between model networks and brain structure, even in cases where one could argue that the brain must carry out the same task as the model network somewhere within its labyrinthine assembly of sub-networks.

Box 2.4 • Connectionism III

Two especially fascinating features of neural networks are their ability to store information in 'non-local' or *distributed* representations and their ability to process information in 'parallel'. A neural network computes some function which transforms input vectors into output vectors (see Box 2.2); such computations can often be interpreted as cognitive or proto-cognitive tasks, such as categorization, object or form recognition and the like. But the information which the neural network embodies and draws upon to complete its tasks is *not* stored discretely anywhere in the network. This information is rather all jumbled together in the full set of connection weights that govern the unit-to-unit inter-actions that, all together, determine what output the network will finally produce. This provides a concrete model for the heretofore rather vague ideas of non-local, non-symbolic and holistic representation. The way that information is 'scattered' throughout the network also means that all of the information can be processed at once, greatly speeding up whatever computational task the network is assigned. However, while neural networks might be faster than traditional serial computers because of their parallel processing abilities, it is perhaps philosophically significant that they are theoretically equivalent to traditional computers in their computational powers.

Despite our high level of ignorance and the fact that work within this paradigm is really only just beginning to get a hold on researchers, we have here an abstract theory of brain function which is compact yet fruitful, amenable to mathematization (which has always been a pretty sure sign of scientific advance) and which is comprehensible in the face of the brain's terrifying complexity. Still, I am sure the reader is asking, what does it have to do with consciousness? The bold answer: the vector coding/manipulation scheme tells us what, basically, consciousness *is*. This answer presupposes that the basic elements of consciousness are what philosophers now call *qualia*. Qualia are, for example, the visual qualities of colour, shape, texture, etc.; the auditory qualities of pitch and tone; the gustatory and olfactory qualities; the felt qualities of pain and pleasure, warmth, cold, pressure, etc. and etc. Qualia are what make up the way it is to be a conscious being. It is debatable whether qualia exhaust the range of possible states of consciousness. Some philosophers argue that conscious beliefs (as well as other intentional states) are conscious without any qualia – that it does not *feel* like anything to be conscious of one's beliefs and desires (see e.g. Nelkin 1989; the relation between consciousness and non-sensory intentional states will be examined more closely in chapter 8 below). It is even debatable whether there are any qualia; at least some philosophers say that they deny their existence (see Harman

1989, Dennett 1988, 1991b). However, this last debate is, I think, a debate about certain presumed conceptual features of qualia that are philosophically suspect. No one can seriously deny that, for example, the senses deliver information about the world in distinctive ways of which we can be aware (although, it would seem, being aware of qualia as such is a much 'higher level' sort of consciousness than that involved in merely having conscious sensory experiences which embody the qualia).

The vector coding idea is that qualitative features of consciousness are to be *identified* with certain vectors, or sets of vectors, within the vector spaces implemented by neural networks appropriately associated with the various sensory modalities (broadly construed to encompass proprioception etc.). This application of the vector coding idea has been most thoroughly explored by Paul Churchland (1986, 1995; see also Flanagan 1992). Let us see how it is supposed to work for the central case of visual colour qualia.

In the retina, there are three basic sorts of colour receptors (called cones, roughly after their shape as compared to the non-colour receptors which are called rods). These receptors vary in their sensitivity to light across the frequency spectrum, approximately illustrated by fig. 2.6.

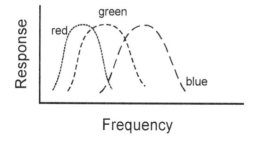

(Fig. 2.6)

Though the mechanisms which transform light into a neural signal are intricate and complex, they are functionally quite simple little machines. Their output is simply a rate of neural 'firing' – the frequency (or spiking frequency) of signals which they send down their output pathway. Interestingly, this output is *not* sensitive to the frequency of the incoming light falling upon the retina; the 'principle of univariance' says that the spiking frequency is entirely dependent upon the quantity of light energy absorbed, not upon its frequency (see Hardin 1988, pp. 26 ff.) although, of course, the efficiency of absorption is dependent upon frequency. For example, the detectors can't tell the difference between a little bit of light at their peak absorption frequency and a lot of light at a low absorption frequency. Thus the system would be unable to determine the frequency of incoming light if it were limited to a single receptor (unless, of course, the receptor itself was tuned to a single frequency or a very narrow band, but in that case it would deliver very little information indeed and often no information at all). By using three receptors, frequency information is regained as ratios of the outputs of all the receptors.

It is then natural to hypothesize that colour is coded in a three-component vector that sums up the activation level of each type of receptor and that the range of perceivable colours is given by the extent of the vector space in which the individual colour vectors can reside. The space that corresponds to this receptor activation model might look something like fig. 2.7 (adapted from Churchland 1986).

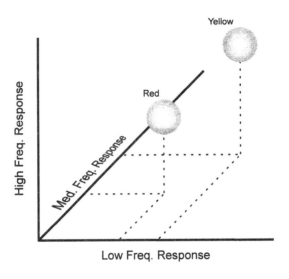

(Fig. 2.7)

All the vectors that correspond to the perceived colour red would have their endpoints in the sphere marked 'red', and similarly for perceived yellow. Of course, the diagram is highly idealized but perhaps 'paradigm bright red' would have such a circumscribed and nicely delineated region of colour space. Such a scheme is highly suggestive: it provides a nice picture, and a gesture towards a positive account, of colour qualia similarities and differences; it reveals a structure to colour qualia that lies behind, as it were, our experience of colour; it grounds colour qualia in a genuine physical property of our neural equipment (a property that of course directly embodies the previous features); and it provides a reasonable source for the intuition that the details of colour perceptual experience far transcend the linguistic resources available for their description. The 'linguistic colour space' is just not as rich as our neural colour space; linguistic categorization involves an extremely drastic information reduction.

Alas, this particular account is situated too far out on the sensory periphery; it is too closely tied to the states of the elementary colour receptors. The satisfying geometrical structuring of colour qualia which the model supplies is there because the modelers have drawn upon the well known three dimensional structure of *phenomenal* colour space. This is not to say that the vectors of this peripheral model are not an important part of the story of colour vision; there is no reason to suppose that they are not, or that some part of the brain is not forming them, transforming them and sending them on to other networks. But it is not a model suitable for explicating the conscious experience of colour vision. Obviously, receptor states themselves are insufficient to generate conscious experience. Nor are they necessary since we can imagine and dream colours. Proponents of this approach will deny any attachment to such a peripheral version of their theory. Churchland (1995) presents the vector coding story of colour qualia in terms now of the higher order processing of the colour-opponency system, in which we find two colour channels each of which is functionally defined in terms of the earlier receptor level representation (for example, the red–green channel is the difference between the output of the medium frequency and low frequency receptors, such that a positive difference of $L-M$ codes for red, and a negative for green). This opponency system is thought to reside in the visual cortex (see Thompson 1995). The vector story is much the same however: colour is still coded by three component vectors: the red–green channel component, the blue–yellow channel component and the achromatic, or brightness, component. Thus the match with phenomenal colour space is retained, and certain difficulties with the more peripheral account can be avoided, such as problems of explicating colour constancy as well as rather more philosophical problems of explaining why it is that, for example, red and green seem to be 'analytically' opposed to each other.

Still, the more sophisticated model fails to grapple with consciousness. The opponency systems operate below or outside of consciousness; they can, for example, be studied in operation within the brains of *anaesthetized* monkeys (see Thompson 1995, p. 77). Again, the champions of vector coding will charge us with over interpreting their theory, which is not a full-fledged theory of consciousness but rather an identity theory of qualia. Churchland, for example, says that 'a visual *sensation* of any specific colour is literally identical with a specific triplet of spiking frequencies in some triune brain system' (1986, p. 301, original emphasis) and, in a passage also approvingly quoted by Flanagan, Churchland deploys this identity theory to explain the apparent disparity between our linguistic resources for describing experience and the richness of the experience itself:

> The 'ineffable' pink of one's current visual sensation may be richly and precisely expressible as a '95 Hz/80 Hz/80 Hz chord' in the relevant triune cortical system. The 'unconveyable' taste sensation produced by the fabled Australian health tonic, Vegamite, might be

quite poignantly conveyed as an '85/80/90/15 chord' in one's four channelled gustatory system (a dark corner of taste-space that is best avoided) . . .

(1986, p. 303)

Evidently there is some confusion here. If qualia are so identified, then they can occur unconsciously. Yet qualia are *not* the ground, source or *cause* of conscious qualitative experience but the material of that experience itself. It is, to say the least, odd to suppose that qualia can occur independently of consciousness. Are we to say that the anaesthetized monkeys mentioned above are actually having visual experiences (more worrying: during surgery, under a general anaesthetic, does the patient still experience pain)? Or is it that while the monkeys are in fact *not* experiencing anything, nonetheless the visual qualia of consciousness are being realized in their neural systems? These absurd hypotheses can be eliminated simply by reducing the scope of our claims: the vector coding schemes are part of the neural machinery of qualitative experience; they are not to be identified with qualitative experience.

The problem here is that qualia do not exist in the absence of consciousness or, to put it another way, qualia are nothing but the *qualitative* 'part' of conscious experience. But any vector coding of sensory states of the kind under consideration could occur in the absence of consciousness. The identification thus fails. This does not impugn the usefulness of the vector coding schemes as theories of brain function, not even as part of the account of the underpinnings of consciousness. If we return to the case of the sleepwalker the problems of identifying qualia with these sensory coding vectors is clear. Ken Parks was able to drive, manipulate keys and locks, and generally get about the world quite effectively (e.g. as established during his trial, he would have had to obey many traffic signals on his drive). We can only suppose that his basic sensory-to-action system was functioning all the while despite his being unconscious. It is as if this system was acting in isolation from whatever it is in the brain that generates (or whatever the appropriate term might be) consciousness.

This suggests a rather abstract philosophical argument against this form of the identity theory. Nothing, in principle, prevents us from constructing, or growing, the sub-net which embodies the vector coding machinery which is to be identified with qualitative consciousness, or from excising that part of the brain intact and still functioning. Of course, practical difficulties consign this idea to science fiction for the present although some simple neural circuitry can be kept alive in culture and therein continue to function and even to be 'trained' – a step on the way to the 21st century nightmare of living brains in vats (see Rose 1993, pp. 216 ff.; and see Puccetti 1978 for an amusing philosophical development of the idea). Perhaps it is not provable that a system that does absolutely nothing more than code visual input into the hypothesized three-dimensional vector space of colour is *not* conscious, but it is certainly an extravagant hypothesis. If we entertain it, we have little choice but to allow that other, still simpler categorizing networks of the kind that have already been constructed are also enjoying conscious qualia. This would be to say that consciousness just is vector categorization wherever and whenever it occurs and this position has very little to recommend it. It would for example entail that our brains are awash in conscious experience of which *we* (or anyone else for that matter) have not the faintest awareness; our brains certainly do teem with ceaseless activity but it is a giant and unwelcome step to the conclusion that much, or perhaps all, of this activity is conscious. It would be natural to reply that only in the appropriate neural (or network) context are the relevant activated vectors conscious qualia. But this is to *deny* the identity theory not to modify it, for this new version really says that the relevant vectors are (part of) the ground of conscious experience, not consciousness itself (and, leaving aside worries about the particular vector coding system at issue, no one should have complaints about this).

Box 2.5 • Vector Coding Identity Theory

Connectionist networks can be regarded as encoding abstract vector spaces, with particular states of the network being represented by particular vectors in this space. If the brain is at all similar to our artificial networks then it, and its sub-networks, will define abstract vector spaces as well. It is then possible to hypothesize that there are qualia instantiating sub-networks – one, or several, for *each* sensory modality – whose associated abstract space is the space of qualitative experience. Visual qualia, to take a prominent example, could perhaps be coded in the three dimensional space associated with the three types of colour receptor in the retina (or, rather more likely, in some other 'triune' neural system much higher in the brain). The generation problem raises a typical difficulty here: amongst the plethora of neural sub-networks devoted to sensory processing and whose associated vector spaces more or less mimic the phenomenal consciousness of the sensory qualities in question, which are to be *identified* with the space of qualitative consciousness? It is not easy to give a principled answer to this question. Consciousness appears likely to escape the sub-nets and diffuse vaguely (and unidentifiably) throughout large regions of the brain. Nor does it seem unlikely that distinct neural networks will, so to speak, take over the generation of consciousness depending upon their specialized abilities and the needs of the circumstances.

It remains true that the details of the vector coding story could reveal a lot about conscious experience but this is hardly surprising even taken with the denial of the identity theory. Knowledge about the causal ground of anything provides a lot of information about it. It would be absurd to *identify* a plane crash with multiple engine failure, but knowing about the engines tells us something important about the crash. The vector coding schemes potentially reveal something about the 'structural' properties of visual colour qualia (I say 'potentially' since, of course, at the moment the vector codings are entirely hypothetical and their structural information is directly drawn from our pre-existing codification of phenomenal colour), but they cannot be identified with colour consciousness.

The strategy of the identity theorists is to search for a vector space that is both approximately isomorphic to some already structurally codified phenomenal space and also plausibly supported by some network functions found, or that could be found, in the brain. There are many difficulties with this approach. The most obvious is that it threatens to be vacuous: there is so much complexity in the brain that it is quite capable of reproducing any vector space that we could possibly imagine to represent the structure of some aspect of our conscious experience. So the issue of identifying some such neurally encoded vector space with conscious experience cannot be a matter of simply matching the neural vector space with some phenomenal space. Also, I suspect that it will be a general problem with such accounts that the neural machinery identified with consciousness will in fact be able to 'run' in the absence of consciousness. Our sleepwalker is one such example. Another is that of the anaesthetized monkeys alluded to above. The brain's job of processing the data (be it colours, sounds, smells or whatever) that somehow ends up in our consciousness is too important to be left solely within the domain of consciousness.

The issue is further complicated, and in ways that continue to tell against the identity theory, by more or less peculiar cases of colour vision. The honey bee, for example, possesses a highly evolved colour vision system, probably more highly evolved than our own, which employs a three receptor system and involves higher-order processors which exhibit opponency (see Hardin 1988, p. 151). Bee colour vision differs from our own at least to the extent that bees are sensitive to the low ultraviolet region of the spectrum, but their colour vision also exhibits many striking analogies with ours. As reported by Hardin (1988, p. 151), bees 'are sensitive to simultaneous contrast effects. Their colour mixing obeys Grassman's laws pretty nearly, and their spectral hue circle, like ours, is closed by an extra-spectral hue analogous to our purple and thus dubbed "bee purple"'. They seem to possess, that is, exactly the sort of vector coding machinery that is to be identified with colour qualia according to the sort of identity theory we are here considering.

Yet I must seriously wonder if bees are conscious and in particular if they are conscious of colour and other sorts of visual sensation. I don't think that the discovery that the brain mechanisms which subserve bee colour vision are analogous to our own settles the question of bee consciousness, but an *identity* theory, by its nature, ought to assert that it *is* settled once we see that the bee brain performs the appropriate vector codings. There are grounds to be sceptical about bee experience even while there is no doubt that bees extract and use colour information. We have, I think, general doubts about whether there is any sort of conscious experience for an organism as 'simple' as the bee. (The bee is not so simple really and I certainly don't think one can absolutely dismiss the possibility of bee consciousness or bee experience; I just want to emphasize that the matter is a delicate one, and one where intuition – at least my intuition most of the time – goes against asserting bee consciousness despite the vector coding machinery.) More specifically, bees seem to be strangely selective about when they bother to use colour; Hardin quotes Menzel (1979) as saying 'the bee discriminates colours in the behavioural context of collecting nectar and pollen and during orientation at the hive entrance, but is colour-blind during other behaviours' (Hardin 1988, p. 152). This suggests to Hardin that the bee is a 'highly modularized' creature, with the colour system rather isolated from many other neural systems, kicking in only when a certain quite delimited range of tasks is called for. Hardin wants to infer from such modularization a lack of experience; he says '. . . if one were able to account for the entire behavioural repertoire . . . by appealing entirely to a relatively small set of interconnected modules, one would have little reason for supposing the animal to have anything remotely like experience' (1988, p. 151). I confess I don't quite see the force of this inference, which involves a particular version of the generation problem: why can't a 'small' number of modules subserve conscious experience? But I agree that one can legitimately doubt whether bees do have any experience especially if this claim is made solely on the basis of colour coding neural machinery.

Evidence from the bizarre phenomenon of blindsight further suggests the complexities lurking within the neural representation of colour. Damage specific to the visual cortex, or deliberate excision in the case of experiments upon animals, can lead to a most peculiar form of blindness, in which visual information seems to be still represented in the brain but is not directly available to consciousness. In a famous case studied by Lawrence Weiskrantz (Weiskrantz *et al.* 1974, see also Weiskrantz 1986), a man had a large section of his right visual cortex surgically removed (for medical reasons) and as a result was, by his own admission, entirely blind in his left visual field. Studies showed however that he could nonetheless identify the location of light flashes within the blind field and could make shape discriminations within the blind field as well. More recent studies (see Stoerig and Cowey 1989) indicate that *colour* discrimination is also retained in blindsight. This suggests that there is a second brain mechanism devoted to the representation of colour. Is this secondary representation also a repository of *qualia*? It does the representational job required by the identity theory, and while it is always unconscious, so far as we know, this perhaps should not disqualify it since the nominal target of the identity theorists is at least *sometimes* unconscious (as in the sleepwalker or the anaesthetized monkeys). In fact, the blindsight colour representation simply strengthens the point that possession of a neural vector space which *represents* some perceptual feature is just not a ground for the *identification* of the relevant vectors with states of consciousness.

I suspect that there is a particular model of consciousness which lurks behind the advocacy of this sort of identity theory which I will call the perceptual model. According to this view, consciousness is the perception (or 'inner perception', 'quasi-perception' or 'introspection') of brain states by the brain itself. Such a model is entirely explicit in D. M. Armstrong's discussion of consciousness in 1968, where it is stated that: 'In perception the brain scans the environment. In awareness of the perception another process in the brain scans that scanning. . . . Consciousness . . . is simply awareness of our own state of mind' (1968, pp. 94–5).[5] Of course, this last statement is not a very good definition of consciousness since it would make it impossible for one to consciously see a tree unless one was *also* aware of one's seeing. And, since animals – at least *most* animals – are unlikely ever to be aware of their states of mind, it would entail that animals are never conscious. Identity theorists such as Paul Churchland do not make this claim about the nature of consciousness, but I think they do accept that consciousness is a kind of inner perception of one 'part' of the brain by another (see, for example, Churchland 1985). This in part explains why identity theorists would tend to identify qualia with brain processes that can occur independently of consciousness: the qualia are the *things* which are perceived (by consciousness) when we are conscious of, say, the colours and shapes before us. Thus, just as a tree can exist unperceived, so too a brain-quale can exist unconsciously.

This has the unfortunate consequence that it appears to be difficult to be conscious of anything *except* the brain, whereas one would normally expect that a brain process is one of the things in the world that it is most difficult to be conscious of. Worse, if we think of consciousness as a kind of perception of certain processes going on in the brain, we will face the question of how these brain processes *appear* to this faculty of inner perception. They certainly do not appear to be as they really are: neural activation patterns which realize 3-component vectors consisting of neural representations of brightness, red–green and blue–yellow values; they just 'look like' colours. The obvious question is, then, on which side of the appearance/reality division are the qualia of consciousness supposed to reside? The equally obvious answer is that colour qualia are, if they are anything in this ballpark, the *appearance* presented by certain brain states when we are conscious of colour. If they are the appearance, then they cannot be identified with the 3-component vectors which are the objects of these appearances. Consciousness is the home of appearance; the qualia we want explained live there, not in the vector spaces that carry colour information.

Perhaps Churchland would object to the claim that perceived colours don't 'look like' neural patterns (in particular, neural representations of the relevant 3-vectors), on the grounds that this presupposes a rather primitive view of perception (whether of the inner or outer variety). Certainly, Churchland is well known for defending the so-called theory-ladenness of perception or observation (see his 1979 or 1988a). And, in his paper on the so-called direct introspection of brain states, Churchland offers this analogy:

> Musical chords are auditory phenomena that the young and unpractic-
> ed ear hears as undivided wholes, discriminable one from another, but
> without elements or internal structure. A musical education changes

this, and one comes to hear chords as groups of discriminable notes.
. . . Why should it be unthinkable that sensations of color possess a
comparable internal structure, unnoticed so far, but awaiting our
determined and informed inspection?

(1985, pp. 26–7)

But it is surprisingly unclear whether Churchland really means to claim that the
application of new concepts to our visual experience will actually alter that experience. Earlier in the paper, where Churchland is discussing the acquisition of the ability
'to *feel* that the mean KE [kinetic energy] of [the summer's air] molecules is about 6.2
× 10^{-21} joules' (1985, p. 21, my emphasis), he wonders why we could not similarly
'come to know, by introspection, the states of one's brain'. He then goes on to make
this rather odd parenthetical remark: 'what would that feel like? It would feel exactly
the same as introspecting the states of one's mind, since they are one and the same
states. One would simply employ a different and more penetrating conceptual
framework in their description' (1985, pp. 21–2). So which is it? Does learning to
apply the new conceptual framework alter the experience or not?

If we can feel that p, then 'feel that' will be an intensional context. And it is
common for us to use 'feel that' in this way, as for example, if I say something like
'I feel that I'm getting a cold'. Then, for someone ignorant of statistical mechanics the
following argument is clearly invalid:

S feels that the air is about 21° C.
21° C = a mean molecular kinetic energy of about 6.2 × 10^{-21} joules.
So, S feels that the air has a mean molecular kinetic energy of about
6.2 × 10^{-21} joules.

It is ironic that Churchland should endorse an intensional fallacy on p. 21 of his paper,
seeing that he had spent the previous pages urging that an argument of Thomas
Nagel's falls victim to just such a fallacy. The existence of an 'intensional fallacy of
feelings' suggests that, after all, there is a conceptual dimension to feeling and
perceiving. And I think there can be little doubt that Churchland does accept the idea
that the thorough acquisition of new conceptual resources modifies both one's
thinking *and* one's experiencing: one begins to think, see and feel 'through' the new
conceptual system. For example, Churchland discusses the acquisition of new
conceptual abilities within sensory domains as a 'perceptual transformation' (1985,
p. 14). As Churchland puts it, 'the matured musician *hears* an entire world of
structured detail, concerning which the child is both dumb and deaf' (1985, p. 15). So
we are left with the conclusion that, at least before acquisition of the relevant neural
concepts, colour experience does not appear to be *of* neurological representations of
certain 3-vectors, even if the activation of such vectors is part of what underlies

colour experience. And, as noted in chapter 1, our current colour experience will *never* come to appear as revelatory of neurological mechanisms, for *that* would require a transformation into a different sort of experience. So, the argument from appearance advanced above cannot be evaded by appeal to the *conceptual* elements of perceptual experience.

Of course, we can chase the vector code higher or deeper into the brain, farther from the brain mechanisms whose specific function is the extraction of colour information from the environment. No doubt we have to. But then the pretty relationship between the vectors in the brain and the phenomenal structure of colour evaporates into something much more diffuse and complex, into nothing which is to be confidently *identified* with the elements of this phenomenal structure. This is a dilemma. The grounds for specific identification with *particular* qualia (like the ineffable pink of Churchland's example) stem from an analogy between the geometrical structure of a phenomenal and a neural vector space. But at the level of these analogies, the 'qualia' can occur without consciousness, i.e. they are not *qualia* after all, but, at best, an element of their cause, which cause happens, as is hardly unusual, to provide some structural information about its effect. However, moving into the brain in search of neural vector spaces more plausibly to be truly identified with the qualitative aspects of consciousness robs us of this structural homomorphism and leaves us in the rather trivial position we were in before all this began: there are brain processes responsible for consciousness.

A philosopher sympathetic to this sort of identity theory but who appears to be sensitive to the dilemma just sketched is Owen Flanagan. His distinction between 'informational sensitivity' and 'experiential sensitivity' (as discussed in Flanagan 1992, pp. 55 ff.) rests on the uncontroversial assertion that only certain rather limited ranges of vector coded information within the brain will be consciously experienced. No one could or would want to dispute this, but our difficulty is rather more particular; it is that the very same vector codings that are candidates for identification with qualia can be activated in the absence of consciousness. So unless one wants to embrace the possibility of unconscious qualia (and thus eliminate one's approach as a theory of *consciousness*) or the possibility of conscious experience which is detached from *experiencers* (which threatens to make consciousness extend rather too widely throughout the world), the theory must search for new candidates for identification. Until such candidates are advanced, we can't tell whether they will evade the possibility of 'unconscious instantiation'. But I think the prospects are dim; Flanagan himself sums up the informational/experiential distinction rather abruptly in this way: 'Some patterns of neural activity result in phenomenological experience; other patterns do not. The story bottoms out there' (1992, p. 58). Of course, as Flanagan hastens to note, there are plenty more details to be appreciated; we can, for example, explain why stimulations of certain retinal cells 'give rise to a sensation of red rather than green because of the length of the wave and the complex structure of the various channels involved in colour discernment' (1992, p. 59). Sure we can, but there is an ambiguity here in the statement of the explanation we seek, which is common throughout the realm of scientific (or, for that matter, any other sort of) explanation, but which can disguise the nature of the explanation on offer.

Suppose I request an explanation with the following question: why did Tom betray Mary so suddenly? Depending upon the context, I could be asking for several distinct explanations, which we can mark with italic emphasis: (1) why did *Tom* betray Mary so suddenly? (2) why did Tom betray *Mary* so suddenly? (3) why did Tom betray Mary *so suddenly*? We might call the particular feature of the situation which we want explained the 'focus' of the explanation. In any particular explanation, the facts surrounding the focus are presupposed. In Flanagan's example explanation, is the focus on the *difference* between creating a red versus a green sort of experience, or is the focus on the *creation* of the experience? If we assume that the explanation actually works, then clearly it is the former. What do we want a theory of consciousness to explain? Just as clearly, it is the latter. But when we ask the question with *this* focus, we are told that the story 'bottoms out'. It is just a fact that certain neural states 'result in' conscious experience.[6]

'Result in' is an odd choice of words for an identity theorist. Such a theorist presumably should say that the story bottoms out when we claim that certain neural states just *are* conscious experiences. Needless to say, we cannot say this about the retinal stimulation, nor, I have argued, about the higher vector codings of sensory properties where it *is* true that the most one can say is that they sometimes result in conscious experience (and, perhaps, that the abstract structure of the phenomenal field of experience will be mirrored by the vector space within the brain that encodes the sensory information – though this will be no surprise if we start with the phenomenal structure as our guide). Perhaps somewhere deeper in the brain and more spread out through the brain there are the vector spaces, whose activated vectors *just are* conscious experience.

In chapter 1 I tried to indicate that the identity option, in the pure and abstract form we have finally arrived at, does not solve (or dissolve) the generation problem. The fundamental problem, I think, is that there is no principled answer to the question of why a system that lacked the features we identify with conscious experience, but which nonetheless behaved *just like* a system that was conscious in virtue of possessing these features, would *not* be conscious. Compare this problem to a non-existent parallel problem about, say, water. We have discovered that water *is* H_2O; something that 'behaved' just like water but was not made of hydrogen and oxygen is not water because it is not made of the 'right' stuff. Similarly, two distinct sorts of brains, employing distinct vector coding machinery, might well be behaviourally indistinguishable but only one would have the 'right' machinery for consciousness. Why is only one the 'right' one? The scientists on the other side will likewise assert that they have consciousness and *we* are the ones who lack it but, we can be confident, their 'assertions' are just so many empty sounds backed up by no conscious understanding!

It is mathematically trivial to show that if some neural network embodies a function that transforms vectors in a certain way then there are innumerable distinct networks that instantiate the same vector input–output function. Consider the example network, with its associated matrix, M, given above. Obviously, if we interpose two matrix operations we can duplicate the original function in a network that is entirely distinct (if pointlessly so) from the original one. The new network could then be described as N × O, where N and O are as follows:

$$
M^* = \begin{bmatrix} 7 & 0 \\ 0 & 9 \end{bmatrix} \times \begin{bmatrix} -\frac{1}{7} & 0 \\ 0 & \frac{1}{9} \end{bmatrix}
$$

Mathematically, of course, this reduces to the simple original matrix M, but one could implement M* just as diagrammed, as a two step network. It would perhaps be natural for the identity theorist to reply that what matters is the resultant input–output function. This is, however, a dangerous reply. For the question will arise as to what the proper boundaries of the consciousness-instantiating networks are. In the face of problems of inequivalent input–output network correspondence, which correspondences do not at all have to be mathematically trivial, how can there be any principled boundary short of *behavioural* similarity? But then we don't have an identity theory any more.

Now, in fact, there is a serious question whether all human brains instantiate equivalent networks in any interesting sense (i.e. below the level of output behaviour). The work of Gerald Edelman on neural Darwinism suggests to me that it is actually quite unlikely that all brains use the same sort of networks, especially when we get above the level of sensory maps, to which the identity theorists have pointed, but which really won't do the job. According to Edelman's neuronal group selection theory (see Edelman 1987 or, for a brisker account, 1992), each brain develops its network structure as the result of competition between huge numbers of variously sized neuronal groups in the face of its own interactions with both the inner and outer environment. If this is so, we should not expect that each brain would end up with the same intrinsic network architecture even though we would, of course, expect that each brain would end up with more or less the same sort of behavioural capacities (but *only* more or less – the residual differences in behavioural capacities underwrite all of the differences in talent, personality, successes and failures in life, so evident and deeply significant in the human world). Wouldn't expecting all human brains to end up with isomorphic network architectures involve espousing a kind of evolutionary determinism, according to which, in the most general case, one would expect that all planets similar to the young Earth would produce the same set of species? (I take it that this is agreed to be very unlikely, see Dennett 1995, Gould 1989; for a brief but interesting debate on the probability of the emergence of intelligence, see Mayr and Sagan 1996.) Even with the simple nets and problems that researchers are investigating today there is no algorithm which reveals what network architecture will best solve the problem under study. Researchers just make (educated) guesses about the dimensionality of the network, constrained by the relatively weak hardware currently available (100 unit nets are hard to work with; the brain is, perhaps, a 100 billion unit net). Nor is there any algorithm for proper weight setting within a given network. Weights are set by the net itself by some form of training or learning, and the most popular form of training, the so-called back propagation of error, appears to be profoundly unbiological. All in all, it seems to me very probable that different brains could strike upon significantly different solutions to the ultimately constraining problem of effective organization of behaviour within a dynamic environment.

It is a trivialization of the identity theory if it ends up declaring that *any* neural network system that acts like a conscious being is a conscious being. For then – the other side of the coin I keep flipping – we need to know *why* it is impossible to produce an ersatz consciousness, a super version of our murdering sleepwalker. There might be answers to this question (for one attempt to dispel the threat of zombies see Dennett 1991b, Part Three) but they won't be answers stemming from an identity theory viewpoint, for that viewpoint is the one that naturally supports the possibility of zombies, just as chemistry supports the possibility of ersatz water. Note that this does not mean, in the case of chemistry, that ersatz water is really possible. Probably no other chemical combination could pass as water (nothing simple is going to do the job and any more complex form would, I think, be at the least either noticeably heavier or less dense than real water). The point is that just as chemistry finds 'within' water the structure that makes water what it is, and in terms of which water's macroscopic (behavioural) properties are explicable, so too an identity theory of consciousness should find within *us* the structures, processes or whatever that make us conscious. The water case is *easy* because once we find micro-properties that serve our macro explanatory purposes we can *declare* that we have found the essence of *water*; anything else that acted just like water can be ruled out by a kind of fiat and nothing is lost. Consciousness is not like this. If appropriate micro brain structures are found then, by right of the identity theory, creatures that lack them are *not* conscious, even if they act as if they are. And the problem with the identity theory is that this is profoundly unsatisfactory. It is fine to say that some hypothetical compound superficially like water is not really water because it is not made of hydrogen and oxygen; it is not fine to say that a hypothetical creature that acts as if it were conscious is actually not conscious because it deploys neural networks of type X instead of the requisite nets of type R. Surely we would want an answer to the question of just why only type R nets *are* conscious. Here the identity theory plays against itself for it *cannot* provide an answer to this question. This was supposed to be its virtue – that the generation problem would dissolve when we finally got down to the fundamental equation: consciousness = neural net structure R. But, ironically, the problem instead dissolves into just more problems centred on the generation problem itself – the question of exactly why only *certain* behaviour generating systems do or could 'support' consciousness.

If the identity theory will not ease the pains of the generation problem, are there other philosophical approaches to consciousness that might do better? If the identity theory founders upon the idea that there is some specific brain feature that directly embodies conscious experience, perhaps we could reject the presupposition that there are *brain* features which are directly responsible for consciousness. Since we are still looking for a theory of consciousness that remains properly physicalist, the rejection of this presupposition cannot be taken to mean there are non-brain features which can do a job the brain cannot. We could try instead to approach the problem of consciousness in the mood of philosophical *dissolvers* rather than *solvers* (as discussed towards the end of chapter 1, these will be dissolvers of the second kind who do not deny that there is a problem of consciousness, but think that it needs to be radically reconceived to be solved). The most prominent advocate of a rethought problem of consciousness is Daniel Dennett (see 1991b, 1993), and he is explicit in denying the presupposition of the identity theory, which he labels the error of Cartesian Materialism. But before getting to Dennett's theory I want to examine one of its close relatives, which in fact pre-dates the publication of Dennett's major work on consciousness. The theory I want to look at first is one that is rather more straightforward than Dennett's and involves a less radical rethinking of the nature of consciousness. This is the higher order thought theory of consciousness (or, for short, the HOT theory) which David Rosenthal has advanced in a series of papers over the last decade (see 1986, 1993a, 1993b, 1995). Can it do better than the identity theory on the problem of consciousness and, in particular, on the generation problem?

Box 2.6 • Summary

The connectionist approach to the brain and mind is fertile, promising and exciting. It may well mark a revolutionary change in our understanding of both the nature and function of the representations which inform cognitive processes (maybe, it will revolutionize the very idea of computation itself). The question is, insofar as connectionism provides us with a new kind of picture of how the mind might be implemented in the brain, does it yield any insight into the generation problem? Unfortunately, it is doubtful that it does. The brain is awash with neural networks handling every conceivable sort of operation upon sensory input (perhaps many *inconceivable* – at least for the present – operations as well). The vector coding identity theory provides no principled reasons for its hypothetical identifications; the condition that the abstract

---

Box 2.6 • Summary (cont.)

vector space of the proposed network be isomorphic (or approximately isomorphic) to the relevant phenomenal sensory space is far from sufficient to ground the identity claim.

3

HOT THEORY:
THE MENTALISTIC REDUCTION
OF CONSCIOUSNESS

Box 3.1 • Preview

The higher-order thought (HOT) theory of consciousness asserts that a mental state is conscious if it is the object of a thought *about* it. Given that we have some naturalistically acceptable understanding of thoughts independent of the problem of consciousness, HOT theory promises a mentalistic reduction of consciousness. Then, the naturalistic account of non-conscious mind – which is presumably relatively easy to attain – solves the whole mind–body problem. HOT theory makes substantial assumptions. It assumes that the mind's contents divide into the intentional (or representational) and the non-intentional (qualia, sensations). It assumes that consciousness requires conceptual thought, and what is more, requires apparently pretty sophisticated concepts about mental states as such. It assumes that no mental state is *essentially* a conscious state. It comes dangerously close to assuming that consciousness is always and only of *mental* states. Not all these assumptions are plausible, and they lead to many objections (e.g. can animals, to whom the ability to engage in conceptual thought may be doubted, be conscious; what is an unconscious *pain*, etc.). Some objections can be deflected, but problems remain that engage the generation problem and prevent the mentalistic reduction from going through successfully.

Philosophers have always been attracted by projects aiming to reduce consciousness to Something Else, even if this reduction might require a more or less radical reconception of our understanding of consciousness. They have been motivated by the hope that, as compared to consciousness, the Something Else would prove more tractable to analysis and would fit more easily into the physicalist world view (here it is perhaps encouraging that, compared to consciousness, almost *anything* else would possess these relative virtues). In the tradition of Descartes, consciousness was supposed to exhaust the realm of the mind, which itself thus became something immediately apparent and open to the mind's own self inspection (inasmuch as conscious states of mind were somehow essentially self-intimating). There is of course something intuitively appealing to such a thesis but we have long since lost any sense that it *must* be true and are now happy to countenance legions of unconscious mental states and hosts of cognitive processes existing beneath or behind our conscious mental states. As we saw in chapter 1, even Descartes ended up endorsing a form of the view that finds cognition, or cognition-like phenomena outside of consciousness. A second traditional idea, one stemming from the empiricist heritage, is that there are basic or 'atomic' elements of consciousness which are pure sensory qualities and from which all 'higher' states of consciousness are constructed, either by complex conjunction or mental replication, or both. Hume, for example, calls these atomic elements the simple impressions.[1] The impressions are the truly *immediate* objects of consciousness and their occurrence is supposed to be entirely independent of thought. The radical proposal of the HOT theories is to deny this last claim. What if consciousness were in fact dependent upon certain sorts of *thoughts* which themselves were part of the now admissible zone of unconscious mentation?

The appealing possibility is that consciousness is somehow a definable relation holding between certain *mental* states, where the latter do not already essentially involve consciousness and, of course, are in themselves less puzzling than consciousness itself. A mentalistic reduction of consciousness would have several virtues. The explanation of consciousness in terms of mentality would avoid the direct explanatory leap from consciousness to the physical, a leap which has always seemed somewhat to exceed philosophy's strength. If consciousness can be reduced to anything at all, it is evidently more plausible that it be to something already mental than directly to brute matter. Yet mental states which do not intrinsically involve consciousness can be seen as 'closer' to the natural, physical world, and so this sort of reduction promises to build a bridge across our explanatory gap, supported by intermediate mental structures which can be linked to both sides with relative ease.

In order to evaluate such a project we require a precise specification of, first, the relevant non-conscious mental states and, second, the relation between them that is to account for consciousness. One such reductive theory, distinguished by its clarity and detailed presentation, has been advanced by David Rosenthal, first in 'Two Concepts of Consciousness' (1986) and then in a series of papers that have appeared over the last decade (see for example 1993a, 1993b, 1995). My aim here is to review Rosenthal's theory and to argue that, in the end, it fails to reduce consciousness successfully. I will not claim outright that *any* theory of the sort we are considering must similarly fail, but I confess that the wide scope and extensive development of Rosenthal's theory makes me doubt whether there are other theories of this sort which differ significantly from it. Thus I hope my objections will possess a quite general applicability.[2]

Rosenthal begins by dividing mental states into the two traditional, and presumably exhaustive, classes: intentional mental states (e.g. beliefs, hopes, expectations, etc.) and phenomenal or sensory mental states (e.g. pains, visual sensations, etc.).[3] For now I'll follow Rosenthal in this distinction, but it is in fact a substantial assumption which I shall doubt for much of the rest of this book, and one that is curiously *unsupported* by the details of the HOT theory. Rosenthal understands this distinction in terms of a division of mentalistic *properties*, so:

> All mental states, of whatever sort, exhibit properties of one of two types: intentional properties and phenomenal, or sensory, properties. . . . Some mental states may have both intentional and phenomenal properties. But whatever else is true of mental states, it is plain that we would not count a state as a mental state at all unless it had some intentional property or some phenomenal property.
>
> (1986, p. 332)

The first demand of theory specification is then met by asserting that *no* mental states are intrinsically or essentially conscious. This sweeping assertion would appear to be necessary to ensure the *completeness* of the theory, for otherwise there would remain a species of consciousness – the essential, non-relational sort of consciousness – for which the theory would offer no account. The claim that mental states are not intrinsically conscious is most plausible for the intentional states and least plausible for the phenomenal states, but there are some intuitive grounds for both. It is undeniable that we frequently ascribe intentional states of which we claim the subject is not conscious, even as we also claim that these intentional states are part of the causes and explanation of the subject's behaviour. As for phenomenal states, Rosenthal offers this:

> Examples of sensory states that sometimes occur without conscious-ness are not hard to come by. When a headache lasts for several hours, one is seldom aware of it for that entire time. . . . But we do not conclude that each headache literally ceases to exist when it temporarily stops being part of our stream of consciousness, and that such a person has only a sequence of discontinuous, brief headaches.
>
> (1986, p. 349)

Of course, this is contentious, for one naturally wants to draw a distinction between the head*ache* and the persistent condition that underlies it. The ache, which is the mental component, is indeed discontinuous but we allow the persistence of the underlying cause to guide our speech, even though the underlying cause is occasion-ally blocked from having its usual effect on consciousness. One wants to say that the ache is a sensing of this underlying condition and this sensing is not continuous. By analogy, if we are watching a woodpecker move through a dense wood for an extended time we will not actually be seeing the bird throughout that time. We nonetheless say that we watched the woodpecker for an hour. However, on Rosen-thal's side, I should point out that in cases where the headache can be felt whenever attention is directed towards it we are, I think, rather more inclined to say that the headache itself persisted even during the time it was not being consciously experienced. This sort of neglected but continually accessible sensation is quite common. If, even upon introspection, nothing was felt we would be reluctant to say that the ache might still 'be there', whether or not the underlying condition persisted. Of course, such considerations do not sever the relation between certain mental states and consciousness, but they do make that relation more complex.

Box 3.2 • Essential HOT Theory

For α to be a conscious mental state, the subject must have a higher-order thought *about* α. But not just any sort of thought, brought about in any sort of way, will do. Roughly speaking, we can say that for α to be conscious one must have the 'properly' acquired *belief* that one is in α. So HOT theory *defines* consciousness as follows:

α is a conscious state of S if and only if (iff)
   (1) S is in the mental state α,
   (2) S has an 'appropriate' thought *about* α (we'll call having this thought 'being in the state T[α]'; the content of T[α] is something like 'I am in state α'),
   (3) S's being in α *causes* S's being in T[α],
   (4) S's being in α does *not* cause S's being in T[α] via inference or sensory information.

Each clause is necessary to avoid potential objections. It follows from HOT theory that to be conscious of anything is to be conscious of it *as* something-or-other. Every state of consciousness is 'aspectual'. This follows from the fact that every *thought* must be, so to speak, structured from concepts. But it does *not* follow from HOT theory that anything has an *essential* conceptual aspect under which one *must* be conscious of it. It also follows from HOT theory that one can't be conscious without having beliefs (i.e. the appropriate higher-order thought). But it does *not* follow that when one is conscious of a mental state that one is *conscious* of a belief. To be conscious of such beliefs requires yet higher-order thoughts about *them*.

In any case, I don't want to press this point since HOT theory may offer an explanation of why we tend to think that consciousness is intrinsic to certain mental states. This involves the second specification task, the delineation of the relation between non-conscious mental states that accounts for consciousness. Rosenthal explains it so:

> . . . it is natural to identify a mental state's being conscious with one's having a roughly contemporaneous thought that one is in that mental state. When a mental state is conscious, one's awareness of it is, intuitively, immediate in some way. So we can stipulate that the contemporaneous thought one has is not mediated by any inference or

perceptual input. We are then in a position to advance a useful, informative explanation of what makes conscious states conscious. Since a mental state is conscious if it is accompanied by a suitable higher-order thought, we can explain a mental state's being conscious by hypothesizing that the mental state itself causes that higher-order thought to occur.

(1986, pp. 335–36)

Thus it is possible to maintain that if we tend to think of certain sorts of mental states as essentially involving consciousness this can be explained as the mistaking of a purely nomological link for a 'metaphysical' one. It might be, for example, that pains are normally such as to invariably *cause* the second-order thought that one is in pain and that abnormal cases are exceptionally rare (and, needless to say, rather hard to spot). In fact, this does not seem at all implausible. The machinery of philosophical distinctions mounted above is then seen as merely a case of philosophical error forcing us into an unnecessarily complex view of pains. It is literally true, according to the HOT Theory, that a pain – in possession of its *painfulness* – can exist without consciousness of it, but in fact almost all pains will be attended by consciousness of them, in virtue of *causing* the appropriate state of consciousness. One might even hope to account for the strength and constancy of this nomological link by appeal to its evolutionary usefulness. Rosenthal comes close to making this point (while actually making another) when he says: '. . . people cannot tell us about their non-conscious sensations and bodily sensations usually have negligible effect unless they are conscious. So non-conscious sensations are not much use as cues to [bodily] well being . . .' (1986, p. 348). Nature would not likely miss the chance to entrench a causal connection between sensations, whether of pleasure or pain, and consciousness that is of such obvious biological benefit. Still, I believe that there remain serious difficulties with this view of the consciousness of phenomenal mental states, but it will take some effort to bring out my worries clearly.

Before proceeding let me introduce a piece of notation. We will frequently need to consider both a mental state and the second-order thought to the effect that one is in the former mental state. I will use Greek letters for mental states and form the second (or higher) order mental states as follows: the thought that one is in mental state α will be designated by $T[\alpha]$. If necessary, we can allow this construction to be iterated, so the thought that one is in the mental state of having the thought that one is in the mental state α gets formally named $T[T[\alpha]]$, and so on. This notation allows a succinct characterization of HOT theory:

For any subject, x, and mental state, α, α is a conscious state iff
    (1) x is in α,
    (2) x is in (or, more colloquially, has) $T[\alpha]$,

(3) x's being in α *causes* x's being in T[α],

(4) x's being in α does not cause x's being in T[α] via inference or sensory information.

Note that for α to be a conscious state, the subject, x, must be in T[α], but x will *not* normally be conscious of T[α] as well. This would require x to be in the still higher-order state T[T[α]]. Such higher-order thoughts are entirely possible but relatively rare; we are not usually conscious that we are conscious (of some particular mental state) and HOT theory's explanation of this is quite satisfying. HOT theory has many other virtues which are well remarked by Rosenthal himself.

Still, the definition as it stands fails to mark a crucial distinction the neglect of which can lead to confusion. We must distinguish between α's being a conscious state of the subject x and x's being conscious *of* α. Sometimes HOT theorists as well as objectors appear to be conflating the idea that the subject has a second-order thought about α which makes α a conscious state with the idea that the subject is conscious of α in virtue of having the second-order thought. I think it would be an unfortunate consequence if HOT theory entailed that one could be conscious *only* of mental states. Most conscious states have an (intentional) object; a conscious perception of a cat has the cat as its object and the subject in such a state is conscious *not* of his state of consciousness but rather of *the cat*, that is, the intentional object of the state of consciousness. In fact, it is very rare for anyone to be conscious of a mental state, at least if it is a mental state with its own intentional object, and despite the philosophical tradition it is entirely mistaken to define consciousness as an apprehension of one's own mental states. So in a spirit of improvement and to forestall confusion, we can emend the definition as follows. If α is a conscious state and the intentional object of α is ε then we say that the subject is conscious of ε (in virtue of being in the conscious state α). There may be, and Rosenthal assumes that there are, conscious states that have no intentional objects. In such cases, saying that α is a conscious state is equivalent to saying that the subject is aware of α. For example, if we suppose that pains are 'purely phenomenal' states with no intentional objects then to be conscious of a pain is just the same thing as the pain being conscious. But even here we must be cautious. To be conscious of a pain in this sense is not to be conscious of a pain *as such*. This is a much higher level affair demanding a state of consciousness whose intentional object is the pain, conceived of *as* a pain. We shall shortly see how attention to these distinctions can be important and can fit rather nicely into the HOT theory.

It is worth digressing here to consider a line of objection to HOT theory which I think ultimately fails. But the objection is interesting in at least three ways: it endorses its own radical transformation of our notion of consciousness and the reply to it reveals some subtle strengths of the HOT theory as well as bringing out certain features crucial for the defence of a representational view of consciousness. The attack is mounted by Fred Dretske (1993). Dretske's objections fundamentally depend upon a distinction between an experience's *being conscious* and someone's being conscious of that experience, and the claim that the former does not imply the latter. If Dretske is right about this we have not only a powerful challenge to HOT theories, but also a substantial and, I would say, very surprising extension of our knowledge about consciousness. However, I will try to show that Dretske's objections cannot be sustained, revealing on the way some subtle strengths of HOT theories of consciousness.

Dretske follows Rosenthal's use of some key concepts in setting forth his objections. Some states of mind are conscious and some are not: *state consciousness* is the sort of consciousness which conscious states enjoy. Conscious states are always (we think) states of some creature which is conscious: *creature consciousness* marks the difference between the conscious and the un- or non-conscious denizens of the universe. Creature consciousness comes in two flavours: transitive and intransitive. Transitive creature consciousness is a creature's consciousness *of* something or other; intransitive creature consciousness is just the creature's *being* conscious. Dretske allows that transitive creature consciousness implies the intransitive form, or

(1) S is conscious of x or that P ⇒ S is conscious. (1993, p. 269)

Furthermore, transitive creature consciousness implies state consciousness:

(2) S is conscious of x or that P ⇒ S is in a conscious state of some sort. (1993, p. 270)

A further crucial distinction is evident in (1) and (2) – the distinction between what Dretske calls *thing-consciousness* and *fact-consciousness* or the distinction between being conscious of an object[4] and being conscious that such-and-such is the case.

Dretske's basic objection to HOT theories, although articulated in a number of ways, can be briefly stated in terms of some further claims involving these distinctions. The most significant is that, in a certain sense, state consciousness does not require creature consciousness. That is, Dretske allows that states can be conscious without their possessor being conscious *of* them or conscious *that* they are occurring. Consider, for example, someone who is consciously experiencing a pain. By hypothesis, this is a conscious experience. Dretske's claim is that it is a further and independent question whether this *person* is conscious of the pain or is conscious that he or she is in pain, and one which need not always receive a positive answer. If Dretske is correct, then HOT theories would appear to be in trouble, for they assert an identity between a state's being a conscious experience of pain and the possession of the belief than one is in pain.

We must, however, re-emphasize a subtlety of the HOT theory here. The belief that one is in pain, which according to HOT theories constitutes one's consciousness of the pain, does not itself have to be and generally will not be a conscious state. One would be conscious of this belief only via a third-order state, namely a belief that one believed that one was in pain. Thus one cannot refute the HOT theory by claiming that it is possible for one consciously to experience pain without consciously believing that one is in pain, that is, without being conscious of a belief that one is in pain. HOT theories cheerfully embrace this possibility. This is important because Dretske does not seem sufficiently to appreciate this subtlety. He claims that HOT theories must make a negative answer to the following question: 'can one have conscious experiences without being conscious that one is having them? Can there, in other words, be conscious states without the person in whom they occur being fact-aware of their occurrence?' (1993, p. 272). But, plainly, HOT theories allow an affirmative answer to this question. To have a conscious experience is, according to the theory, to believe that one is having it but not necessarily to *consciously* believe that one is having it. To put the point more generally in terms of the notation introduced above, to be conscious of α is to be in the state $T[\alpha]$; this says absolutely nothing about whether one is in the state $T[T[\alpha]]$ or not, and it is the latter state that is required for $T[\alpha]$ to be conscious. So, according to HOT theories we have, roughly,

S is conscious of pain = S believes that he is in pain,

so the correct analysis of fact-awareness must be along these lines:

S is conscious that he is in pain = S believes that he is in f(he is in pain),

where f is some self-ascription function. I would suggest that f(he is in pain) should be cashed out as something like '. . . is in a state characterized by *I am in pain*'.[5] Of course, normally we are rapidly carried from the conscious pain to the fact-awareness *that* we are in pain but this is a feature of our cognitive machinery, not an analytic truth constraining HOT theories of consciousness. If one considers animal consciousness the need to separate these states is apparent. HOT theories must assert that an animal's being conscious of something is the animal's having an appropriate thought. While this is a real difficulty for HOT theories of consciousness, for there are many who would deny to animals the ability to have thoughts of any kind and even more who would deny that they have thoughts about their own mental states, this is not the difficulty Dretske advances.[6] It is natural to say that animals can be conscious of pains but that they cannot be conscious *that* they are in pain. However, given that animals can have *some*, perhaps quite 'primitive', thoughts (and the HOT theory simply *must* address animal consciousness in this way), the distinction is successfully accounted for within HOT theories by the above analysis.

The worry that Dretske may not be taking this subtlety into account is strengthened by his remark that: 'HOT theories . . . take an experience to be conscious in virtue of [its] being the object of some higher-order-thought-like entity, a higher-order mental state that . . . involves the deployment of concepts. My concern . . . therefore, was to show that conscious experience required no fact-awareness . . .' (1993, p. 279). Since HOT theories allow that experiences can be conscious in the absence of fact-awareness of these experiences, this line of attack is, strictly speaking, misguided. It may be that Dretske meant to assert no more by 'fact-awareness of p' than 'belief that p', without any implication that these beliefs are themselves conscious. Such an interpretation would not be foreign to common usage and would lead immediately to the objection against HOT theories considered below. But Dretske actually says that 'consciousness of a fact [which must surely be fact-awareness] . . . requires a *conscious* belief that this is a fact' (1993, p. 272, my emphasis). HOT theories do not require this, and would consider it an unnecessary leap to *third-order* thoughts.

Box 3.3 • Dretske's Objection

Since HOT theory makes every conscious state the object of a thought about it, every conscious state has an associated conceptualization of it, as given in the thought that 'makes it' conscious. Dretske objects that it is possible for there to be conscious experience without any of what he calls fact awareness. Fact awareness is consciousness of facts, which are conceptual entities; an example would be an awareness *that* snow is white. One can be aware of white snow without being aware that snow is white (one can even be aware of the whiteness of snow without being aware that snow is white). But HOT theory does not require any *consciousness* of facts for there to be conscious experience; it only demands that there be some conceptual categorization of the experience which is itself generally not conscious. Dretske's basic objection can thus be countered. Dretske can, however, further deny that every conscious experience requires some conceptualization of it. However, while one can plausibly argue that no conscious experience has a *mandatory* conceptualization, it is very difficult to show that some conscious experience has *no* conceptualization. HOT theory asserts rather that every consciousness is a *consciousness as of*. . . . Contrary to Dretske, this seems entirely plausible.

In any case, HOT theories do assert an intimate connection between conscious experiences and beliefs *about* those experiences. Dretske must show that some states can be conscious in the absence of any such beliefs. Put another way, he needs to show that states can be conscious in the absence of *any* conceptually articulated characterizations of them.

I do not find any explicit argument for such a thesis in Dretske's article. The nearest thing is his defence of the following principle:

(3) For all things x and properties F, it is not the case that, S is
conscious of x ⇒ S is conscious that x is F. (1993, p. 266)

It would be easy to produce an argument against HOT theories based on this principle if we could identify 'S believes that x is F' with 'S is conscious that x is F', but as we have seen this is an identification that HOT theories need not endorse in general. But there is a closely connected claim which *is* made by HOT theories.

HOT theories must endorse the transition from state consciousness to transitive creature consciousness. For suppose some state, α, is a conscious state (i.e. possesses state consciousness) of subject S. HOT theories analyse this as S's believing that he is in α (or, in the notation introduced above, having the thought T[α]). But this is identified with the state of S's being conscious of α.[7] Thus HOT theories identify transitive creature consciousness of α with α's being a conscious state. Thus Dretske's line of attack is indeed well motivated and he is right to say that HOT theories must deliver a negative answer to the question: 'can there be conscious states in a person who is not thing-aware of them?' (1993, p. 272). S's belief that he is in α, or S's consciousness of α, must then characterize α in some way via the deployment of concepts. I take it that this is HOT theory's way of claiming that, as well as explaining why, all consciousness is consciousness *as . . .*, where the '. . .' is to be filled in by the conceptual characterization of α occurring in S's belief. It is possible, then, to interpret Dretske's defence of (3) as a defence of a slightly different principle, namely the denial that a consciousness *of* is always a consciousness *as*. We could write this version of (3) as

(3*) For all things x and properties F, it is not the case that, S is
conscious of x ⇒ S is conscious of x *as* F.

If (3*) is correct we have the basis of a powerful objection against HOT theories of consciousness. However, this is a big 'if'.

In the first place, the exact import of (3*) (or (3) for that matter) is not altogether clear. Dretske's arguments for the principle may help to clarify it. He begins by noting the obvious truth that one can be conscious of x, which as a matter of fact is an F, without being conscious of x *as* an F (his example, which certainly rings true for me, is the possibility of (consciously) seeing an armadillo while having only the faintest idea of what an armadillo is). Such cases, however, only support a much weaker version of (3*), which would read as follows:

(3**) For all things x and *some* properties F, it is not the case that,
S is conscious of x ⇒ S is conscious of x *as* F.

Dretske then goes on to argue that there is *no* property, F, such that if one sees an armadillo one must characterize it as an F. This is also true but exposes a critical ambiguity in (3*).

To see this clearly we must note that a modal component lurks within our principles. The '⇒' in (3*) cannot be regarded merely as material implication on pain of the ridiculous logical consequence that S is conscious of everything. Dretske means to assert that it is *possible* to be conscious of x without being conscious of x as an F. The proper understanding of (3*) crucially depends upon the scope of this possibility operator.

Approaching this point somewhat obliquely, consider the following explicitly modal principle:

$$(EX) \quad (\forall x)(\exists F)\Box(Aw(S,x) \supset CON(S,x,F)),$$

where 'Aw(S,x)' represents 'S is conscious of x' and 'CON(S,x,F)' stands for 'S is conscious of x *as* F'. This principle asserts that there is at least one distinguished or essential conceptual characterization which any consciousness of x must ascribe to x. This principle is clearly false, as Dretske ably shows. Thus we can take it that:

$$(\forall x)\sim(\exists F)\Box(Aw(S,x) \supset CON(S,x,F)).$$

(Strictly speaking, this is stronger than the mere denial of (EX) but there is no reason to suppose that essential characterizations exist for *any* object.) After some logical manipulation, this becomes something close to (3*), viz.

$$(POS) \quad (\forall x)(\forall F)\Diamond\sim(Aw(S,x) \supset CON(S,x,F)),$$

or, equivalently,

$$(POS) \quad (\forall x)(\forall F)\Diamond(Aw(S,x) \& \sim CON(S,x,F)).$$

This states that for any characterization, F, of x, it is possible to be conscious of x but not to be conscious of x *as* F. This seems to be true. However, (POS) is not the correct rendition of (3*) for (POS) is compatible with a weaker version of (EX) stating only that it is necessary that *some* characterization apply to x whenever one is conscious of x. Precisely,

$$(EX^*) \quad (\forall x)\Box(\exists F)(Aw(S,x) \supset CON(S,x,F)).\text{[8]}$$

The arguments that Dretske offers for (3*) are all compatible with (EX*), for they are all to the effect that no particular ascribed characterization of x is necessary for one to be conscious of x in any given situation. Nonetheless, all these situations are such that x is characterized by *some* F. Thus, these arguments can only support the weaker principle. But it is fallacious to infer from (POS) the stronger form which *does* express the intended meaning of (3*), namely,

$$(\forall x)\Diamond(\forall F)(Aw(S,x) \, \& \sim CON(S,x,F)).$$

The fallacy here is the well known modal fallacy – here applied to attributes – of inferring from the fact that something is possible of each thing to the fact that something is possible of all things.

Since (3*) is unsupported, it cannot be used in an attack on HOT theories. What is more, the correct principle, (EX*), can be invoked to disarm Dretske's final objection against these theories. This objection begins from an unexceptionable premise, namely that experienced differences require different experiences. Dretske asks us to imagine attentively examining some complex scene and then shifting our attention to a second, very similar scene which we then also attentively examine (as in those common puzzles that ask you to spot the difference between two very similar pictures). One might not consciously notice that there was any difference between the scenes but nonetheless it may be true that one was conscious of every element of each scene. Thus the experience of scene 1 must have been different from the experience of scene 2 (for example, it could be that scene 2 lacks an element of scene 1 and so one consciously experienced *that* element when scanning scene 1 but of course had no such experience during examination of scene 2). Dretske concludes that we are thus committed to the 'possibility of differences in conscious experience that are not reflected in conscious belief' (1993, p. 275). Although we have seen that this is an infelicitous way to put the objection, Dretske wishes us to take his point to show that there can be 'internal *state* consciousness with no corresponding (transitive) *creature* consciousness of the conscious state' (1993, p. 275). This would clearly threaten HOT theories given their inescapable contention that state consciousness entails transitive creature consciousness.

But here, I think, Dretske is equivocating between what is, in essence, a *de re* and a *de dicto* characterization of consciousness. Would HOT theories demand that S be conscious of the difference between any two distinct experiences *as* a difference? Clearly the answer is no, for S may simply have never consciously compared them. In such cases – quite common I should think – S need not be conscious of the difference at all. Well, should HOT theories require that if any two of S's conscious experiences are different *and* S is actually conscious of the difference (i.e. conscious of what is different between the two experiences) then S must be conscious of this difference *as* a difference? This also calls for a negative answer. To say that S is conscious of the difference in this sense is to say that there is something different about the two experiences of which S is conscious; this puts no, or very few, restrictions on *how* that

71

experience will be characterized in S's belief about it which, according to the HOT theory, constitutes S's consciousness.

That is, to say that S is conscious of the difference is, on the HOT theory, to say that S believes that he is experiencing the difference. But in the case envisaged this is true only on a *de re* reading of this belief. A more precise specification of this belief that brings out its *de re* character is this: of the difference (between the two experiences) S believes of it that he is experiencing it. It does not follow that S is conscious of the difference *as* a difference. To find out how S is experiencing the difference (that is, how to fill in the relevant *as* . . .) one must discover the correct *de dicto* characterization of S's belief. Our principle, (EX*), guarantees that there is some such characterization but certainly does not demand that S should end up experiencing the difference *as* a difference. I can see no good reason to deny HOT theories access to *de re* characterizations of the beliefs that underwrite conscious experience. Of course, such characterizations do not help to specify the state of consciousness as it is to the subject himself but that is quite typical of *de re* belief constructions. They function, as illustrated above, to provide identification for outsiders of what a belief is *about* or, through the use of the HOT theory, to explain *what* someone is conscious of without a commitment as to *how* that person is conscious of that thing.

In short, the HOT theories of consciousness can admit the phenomena that Dretske points out without succumbing to the objections he believes they generate.

So, the HOT theory is surprisingly resilient and seems able to generate its own range of insights into the nature of consciousness. It is obvious that HOT theory is structurally similar to familiar theories of perception and thus it has certain affinities with other 'perceptual' theories of consciousness. By this, I do not primarily mean to connect HOT theory with those views of perception which explicitly make perceiving a kind of believing (see e.g. Armstrong 1968, chapter 10), though perhaps HOT theory could be mobilized to increase the plausibility of such views. More simply, one can see that the clauses of our definition of HOT theory quite naturally transform into a pretty conservative characterization of perception, rather as follows:

> S perceives O iff
> (1) O exists,
> (2) S has an experience as of O,
> (3) S's experience is caused by O,
> (4) S's experience is *properly immediately* caused by O.

With regard to consciousness itself, HOT theory is reminiscent of both David Armstrong's view of consciousness as one part of the brain physically 'scanning' another (see Armstrong 1968, pp. 92–94 and also chapter 15) and the early Daniel Dennett's view of consciousness as a content carrying brain state that gets access to the speech production centre (see Dennett 1969, chapter 6).[9] The relative advantage of HOT theory is that it does not link the theory of consciousness with any attempt to model the workings or structure of the brain and its cognitive architecture. It yet remains compatible with these attempts, which can be seen as physicalist efforts to delineate the mechanisms that would be required to make clauses (3) and (4) of our formal characterization of HOT theory true within a working brain.

The analogy between theories of perception and HOT theory also suggests that according to HOT theory consciousness will suffer analogues of the various forms of misperception that philosophers of perception have appealed to, postulated or discovered. These are occasioned by considering the effects of letting one or more of the clauses of the definition of HOT theory, as given above on page 64, become false while maintaining as many of the remainder as possible. Let us catalogue the possibilities without, for now, going into either the question of their *genuine* possibility or their consequences.

Box 3.4 • The Four Pathologies

For each clause of the HOT theory definition of consciousness (see Box 3.2 above) there is a possible corresponding pathology of consciousness. The pathologies are generated by denying one clause of the definition while maintaining the truth of as many of the rest as possible. These are test cases with which to explore the limits of HOT theory's plausibility. Deny clause (1) and we get an 'hallucination' of consciousness, e. g. one thinks one is in pain when one is in fact not. Deny clause (2) and we get a mental state that is not 'noticed' (this is not very pathological except in certain extreme cases, as when one fails to 'notice' an excruciating toothache). The denial of either clause (3) or (4) leads to interesting and problematic cases, which get to the heart of HOT theory. In both cases we have to ask whether it is in any more than at most a merely legalistic sense in which there is no conscious awareness of the lower-order mental state, α. If the subject gets into $T[\alpha]$, how can the subject or 'the world' tell how $T[\alpha]$ was brought about? If $T[\alpha]$ is the sort of state that 'generates' consciousness, won't an at least *as if* consciousness result whenever the subject gets into $T[\alpha]$?

First, let (1) be false. Then of course (3) and (4) must be false as well, but there is no reason to deny (2). This is a case of an hallucination of consciousness, the description of which is somewhat problematic, but whose possibility is a fundamental characteristic of HOT theory.

Second, let (2) be false. Again, it follows that (3) and (4) are false. This is simply the case of an unnoticed mental state, indubitably somewhat odd if the state is a pain or other highly distinct sensation. As we saw above, HOT theory can perhaps account for the sense of oddity we feel about such cases.

Third, let (3) be false. In such a case, while (4) must be false, (1) and (2) can remain true. The description of this case is also problematic, as we shall see.

Finally, let (4) be false. All the other clauses can nonetheless be true. Would this be another *hallucination* of consciousness, or in this case would there be no consciousness of α whatsoever? This is a tricky question, as we shall see below. It is also worth noting that clause (4) is unclear as to which *sorts* of inferences or sensory information are to be forbidden. Is *any* intermediary of this kind prohibited, or only *conscious* inference or sensory information? It could hardly be the latter for that would make HOT theory circular as an account of consciousness. As to the former, modern cognitive theories abound with hypothetical unconscious inferential, or quasi-inferential processes, particularly in the case of perception, the very case upon which HOT theory is largely modelled. Why couldn't the link between α and T[α] be a cognitive link in this sense: that the process connecting them can be usefully described in information-theoretic terms? To put the question another way, why would a 'cognitive link' as opposed to one of a different, perhaps more 'direct' sort, fail to produce consciousness? Intuitively, we know there must be some difference. Here, as so often in philosophical analyses we wish we could simply write 'a link of the appropriate sort . . .'. But even if we could get away with this in philosophy (which in truth we cannot), any empirical investigation into the physical differences between proper and improper linkages will bring us up against the generation problem.

We can, following Rosenthal, call these four ways of only partially fulfilling HOT theory 'pathological cases'. According to HOT theory they are all genuinely possible. As Rosenthal says:

> . . . since [the] higher-order thoughts are distinct from the mental states that are conscious, those thoughts can presumably occur even when the mental states that the higher-order thoughts purport to be about do not exist.
>
> (1986, p. 338)

Explicitly, this passage deals only with our first pathology, but the reason Rosenthal gives for *its* possibility supports that of the other pathologies as well (and, of course, Rosenthal independently goes to some length to support the possibility of the second pathology).

One thing we can say about the pathologies in general is that the causal link between α and T[α] is of a much closer and more intimate sort than the causal links in perception that mediate between literally distant objects and the brain. The mechanisms of HOT theory are presumably all within the brain and in fact they will generally form a part of the more complex and extended causal sequences involved in perception. This alone suggests one reason why we feel that the link between consciousness and the mental state of which we are conscious is so peculiarly intimate. According to HOT theory, it *is* an intimate link, but one that is at bottom causally 'ordinary', not metaphysically unique.

HOT theory's willingness to countenance these pathologies allows us to answer a subtle but very important question about the theory. The general dictum that to be conscious of α is to have T[α] does not resolve the question whether possession of T[α] *alone* is itself sufficient for conscious experience or whether consciousness depends upon the existence of the proper link between α and T[α]. The account of pathology 1 just given suggests that HOT theory claims the former: T[α] is by itself sufficient for consciousness. The other clauses serve to mark out how a certain T[α] is a consciousness *of* some other particular mental state, α, or confers consciousness on α. Again we see analogies with theories of perception, which always possess components that mark out what *object* is the perceived object but must also include other components to account, or at least allow, for the possibility of perceptual error and hallucination. Rosenthal provides more direct textual evidence that this is his understanding of HOT theory as well. The quote above from 1986, p. 338 makes the point reasonably clearly and during a discussion of the 'reflexivity' of consciousness Rosenthal says:

> The sense that something is reflexive about the consciousness of mental states is thus not due to the conscious state's being directed upon itself, as is often supposed. Rather, it is the higher-order thought that confers such consciousness that is actually self-directed.
>
> (1986, p. 346)

What is important here is the claim that it is the higher-order thought, in our terms, T[α], which *confers* consciousness. In addition, Rosenthal states elsewhere: '. . . we are not normally aware of the higher-order thoughts that, on such an account, *make* mental states conscious' (1986, p. 340, my emphasis) and more recently Rosenthal says: '. . . a mental state's being conscious consists in its being accompanied by a HOT' (1995, p. 26 n.). I also observe that in 1995 Rosenthal adds: ' . . . HOTs can presumably occur in the absence of the states they purport to be about. What would that be like subjectively? Since having a HOT makes the difference between whether there is or isn't something it's like to be in a mental state, it may be that having a HOT without the relevant state is, sometimes at least, subjectively indistinguishable from having both' (1995, p. 26 n.). One has to ask: how could it be only 'sometimes', if the appropriate HOT occurs?

I think we can also see that this reading of HOT theory is forced by considerations of plausibility. Suppose we maintained that consciousness demanded the fulfilment of all four clauses of HOT theory – that whenever anyone was conscious at all this consciousness would satisfy all four clauses of the HOT theory. This would directly entail that, for example, no one could be consciously mistaken about their own mental states. For example, it would be impossible consciously to take oneself to believe p while in fact one did not. For, on our present reading of the theory, one could not be conscious of the belief that p, or have the 'experience'[10] of believing that one believed p, unless one did believe p. Otherwise clause (1) would fail, contrary to our present supposition. Yet it is, I think, overwhelmingly plausible that people can consciously take themselves to believe, desire or hope for what they in fact do not (that people can have 'false consciousness'). This phenomenon is by its nature subtle and complex and it is difficult to trot out elementary examples. Freud offers many rather extreme cases and some are certainly quite plausible. But it is a common experience to find someone's self-image (that constellation of beliefs, desires, etc. that one consciously takes oneself to possess) at odds with what an outside observer would rightly take to *be* that person's beliefs, desires, etc. Nor is it uncommon for people to find out that they had mistaken the nature of, for example, a particular desire of theirs when suddenly confronted with its imminent satisfaction.

We might call this implausible interpretation of HOT theory the Fully Relational Reading and while it is unlikely to be correct we should note that it could immediately account for the sometimes presumed incorrigibility of our consciousness of our own mental states. If consciousness *were* necessarily the fulfilment of our complex of four clauses then it would indeed be impossible to be conscious of α via $T[\alpha]$ without being in the state α.

But the implausibility of the Fully Relational Reading of HOT theory stems from the implausibility of incorrigibility itself, and the alternative reading of HOT theory can obviously account for this failure of consciousness. Failure of self-knowledge stems from pathologies 1 and 2 (differing in the 'direction' of the failing). As befits pathologies, they are relatively rare, but their frequency could vary widely depending upon the type of mental state involved or the particular contents of those mental states. Such variance would be explicable in terms of the patterns of cause and effect between the relevant αs and $T[\alpha]$s. The Freudian style of psychological analysis can be seen as at least a model for such causal classifications of mental state inter-relationships.

We are thus driven to reject the Fully Relational Reading of HOT theory. HOT theory cannot retreat to it in the face of difficulty. This is important, since the objections I will raise stem from the acceptance that it is the higher-order thought, $T[\alpha]$, that *confers* consciousness, independent of the conditions under which $T[\alpha]$ is brought about. That is, should $T[\alpha]$ occur to someone (i.e. should someone get into the mental state designated by $T[\alpha]$), that person will be in a state of consciousness indistinguishable from that of being in state α whether or not they are in α. There will be nothing 'in' that person's consciousness by which to distinguish the veridical from the pathological cases. Again, this is analogous to the case of perceptual hallucination where there need be nothing 'in' the perceptual experience that could reveal an hallucination as such.

Nonetheless, there is nothing in HOT theory, nor in the case of perceptual hallucination, that precludes the *recognition* that one is the victim of a pathological state of mind. The Müller-Lyer illusion is a very simple perceptual 'hallucination' which illustrates this point. Even while we cannot help but *see* one line as longer than the other, we all *know* they are nonetheless the same length. Similarly, each of HOT theory's pathologies is compatible with the knowledge that one is suffering it. This suggests a variety of rather traditional objections to HOT theory, of which perhaps the simplest is the following.

According to HOT theory (via pathology 1), it is possible to be as it were conscious of pain while one is in fact not experiencing any pain. In such a case, that is to say, the phenomenal property of painfulness will not be exemplified at all even though the subject 'thinks' that it is. The objection is straightforward. There is no difference, to the subject, between this case and the veridical case of 'true' consciousness of pain because in both cases the consciousness-conferring thought, T[α], occurs. There is every bit as much *suffering* in the pathological as in the normal case, every bit as much reason to eliminate T[α] in this case as in the normal case. Since it is the presumed painfulness of pains that provides us with the grounds to attribute and sympathize with suffering as well as giving us the reasons to try to ease the suffering, this would strongly suggest that the relevant phenomenal property of pains – painfulness – occurs in both cases, contrary to what HOT theory appears to assert. One cannot reply here that the phenomenal property goes with T[α] rather than α. Since this is a case of consciousness, HOT theory would then require an appropriate third-order thought, T[T[α]] to account for the consciousness of this phenomenal property of T[α]. We could then invoke a second-order pathology from which, in strict accord with the foregoing, it would be evident that the phenomenal property of painfulness actually belongs to T[T[α]]. We would thus generate a viciously infinite hierarchy of thoughts about thoughts about thoughts . . . . The phenomenal property in question would forever remain one step *above* whatever level of the hierarchy was under consideration and thus could find a home at no level of the hierarchy and therefore would not belong to *any* mental state, which is absurd.[11]

Instead of chasing an ultimately imaginary phenomenal property up through this hierarchy one could reply that the pain – α – possesses its own sort of phenomenal property, but so too does T[α]. In fact, solely within consciousness, there is no discernible difference between the experience of either. Thus, in normal cases, the appearance of T[α] will be a consciousness of α and (or via) α's attendant phenomenal property of painfulness. In the pathological case, T[α] occurs without α but also, we may postulate, T[T[α]] occurs as well, and this latter will be a consciousness of the phenomenal property of T[α]. This reply is entirely *ad hoc* and endlessly multiplies essentially indistinguishable phenomenal properties, but it also suffers from a worse defect. T[T[α]] is a consciousness of the thought that one is in pain (i.e. in α). Even if we grant that the thought that one is in pain has its own phenomenal properties (somehow, conveniently and miraculously, indistinguishable from the phenomenal property of painfulness that α carries), T[α] carries propositional *content* as well. Yet in the pathological case, there need be no conscious awareness of the *thought* that one is in pain. Pathology 1 only requires that one think *and* experience, falsely, that one is in pain. It does not require that one also think that one think that one is in pain. Putative sufferers of pathology 1 would sincerely assert that they were suffering *pain* and there would in truth be no difference in the experience between the pathological and non-pathological cases. There is no reason whatsoever to suppose that whenever cases of pathology 1 occur there must also occur an additional, still higher-order, thought.

The danger here is that HOT theory cannot place the phenomenal properties of mental states in the proper location (and it is hard not to suspect that the reason is that phenomenal properties are in fact somehow tied intrinsically to consciousness and cannot be given a relational analysis). This difficulty is reinforced if we suppose a sufferer of pathology 1 to be informed of his condition. Let us further suppose that our sufferer is an ardent supporter of HOT theory and hence is happy to allow the possibility of pathology 1. It is pretty clear that despite the additional knowledge our subject will still report that he *feels* pain. In addition, he may say, in line with HOT theory, that he is not *really* feeling pain but he cannot deny that he is feeling *something* quite indistinguishable from it, for if pathology 1 were consciously distinguishable from 'true' consciousness then HOT theory would be falsified since in that case $T[\alpha]$ would not be what confers consciousness. HOT theory is thus faced with an unhappy dilemma. Either the phenomenal property of painfulness is not exemplified at all in this version of pathology 1, in which case there is no accounting for our subject's reports and evident suffering, or else it is not the pain which exemplifies the property of painfulness, which is not only obviously implausible, but it leads to the further implausibilities I have just outlined. In fact, it seems to me that if HOT theory can seriously countenance the idea that the phenomenal property of painfulness is not exemplified in this case, then there is no reason to admit the existence of phenomenal properties at all. Their *raison d'être* is to account for and provide the content of the consciousness of sensations. If this very consciousness can occur without any phenomenal input, no real role remains for the phenomenal properties, which become merely a gratuitous metaphysical extravagance.[12]

Focussing more closely on $T[\alpha]$'s ability to confer consciousness naturally brings us to pathologies 3 and 4. In both, the consciousness conferring state, $T[\alpha]$, occurs but, in pathology 3, α occurs but does not *cause* $T[\alpha]$ whereas, in pathology 4, α does cause $T[\alpha]$ though not immediately but rather through some inferential process or a process dependent upon sensory information. As we have seen above however, so long as $T[\alpha]$ does occur, there will be a consciousness 'as it were' of α. Pathology 3 is perhaps not particularly interesting – it is a case of an hallucination of consciousness, akin to pathology 1, but one in which, by some chance, the mental state which would make $T[\alpha]$ a case of what we might call *veridical* consciousness (i.e. of course, α) happens to occur alongside $T[\alpha]$. In the field of perception, it is just the possibility of such coincidences of perceptual experience along with what would make them veridical that drives philosophers to impose the condition that the perceived object *cause* the perceptual experience. HOT theory quite properly draws the same lesson from its analogous possibility.

Pathology 4 is much more interesting and leads to what I take to be the most fundamental objection to HOT theory. HOT theory grants that the state T[α] confers consciousness, that is, that anyone in the state T[α] will have a conscious experience that is at least 'as if' one were conscious of α which is, so far as the conscious experience is concerned, completely indistinguishable from a true consciousness of α. Given this, it is hard to see what is improper, from the point of view of T[α] being a state of consciousness of α, with any causal process whatsoever getting one into T[α], so long as it does get you into that state of consciousness.

One complication can be set aside. It is possible to imagine a causal chain from α to T[α] which includes, as essential links, other phenomenal mental states the conscious experience of (at least some of) which is indistinguishable from that of α. In such a case, a principle of causal proximity would seem to require that the state of consciousness be *of* the final such phenomenal state in the chain. This is again rather analogous to possible examples drawn from the field of perception. Suppose that you are in a dark room looking at the place where a small light bulb will be turned on. Unbeknown to you, a mirror angled at 45° lies between you and the light bulb, but a second light bulb has been strategically placed off to the side so as to be visible in the mirror. This second bulb lights only if the first bulb lights. So the first bulb causes your perceptual experience, which is a perception of a light bulb. The causal proximity principle correctly entails that you are really perceiving the second bulb. But if the second bulb is replaced by a suitable arrangement of two mirrors (or even video monitors), you will now perceive the first bulb whenever it is illuminated even though its light (or even a representation of its light) takes a somewhat devious route to you. The causal proximity principle applies only to causal intermediaries that 'satisfy' the resulting perceptual experience. Returning to HOT theory, we can legitimately prohibit *this* kind of indirect consciousness, but of course hardly any sort of inferential process or processes relying on sensory information will interpose the particular intermediate mental states required to rule out such processes. In what follows there will be no danger of inadvertently appealing to this kind of truly illegitimate mediated consciousness.

Consider first the possibility mentioned earlier that the inferential processes that, supposedly improperly, link α to T[α] are all unconsciously buried in the sub-personal realm of our cognitive architecture. Suppose, that is, there are functional units in the brain whose cognitive task is simply to bring certain states *up to* consciousness. It is not implausible to suppose that there is something of a competition amongst the myriad of brain states which underlie our phenomenal and intentional mental states, some signalling distant objects of perceptions, others important states of the body, still others potentially relevant intentional states. All these states will loudly clamour for 'consideration' by our hypothetical functional units but only a few will become conscious. The conditions for becoming conscious could well involve some form of hypothesis generation and testing at the sub-personal level. Such cognitive mechanisms depend on various sorts of information processing, some of which are closely akin to inference, as well as necessarily involving (sub-personal) sensory information.[13] This is a sketch of *how* the brain might get from α to $T[\alpha]$ and the fact that this process involves essentially inferential processes and a reliance on sensory information does not seem to threaten in any way $T[\alpha]$'s claim to be a consciousness of α, given that $T[\alpha]$ itself confers the conscious aspect of the experience, leaving only the identity of what $T[\alpha]$ is a consciousness *of* to be decided. The situation here is once again analogous to that in theories of perception, especially visual perception. Many of these theories are irredeemably inferential in nature (see, e.g. Gregory 1990 or Marr 1982). Whatever the faults of such theories, no one has ever suggested that they fail simply because the posited inferential properties of the sub-personal cognitive system *by themselves* preclude perceptual experience!

What really motivates inclusion of clause (4) in HOT theory is not the fear of a supposedly impossible mediated consciousness, but rather the evident fact that possession of just *any* second-order thought that one is in a certain first-order mental state will not, by itself, make one conscious of that mental state, even if the second-order state is caused by the first-order state. (Just as, in the case of perception, merely having the thought or belief that a candle is visible before one is not by itself sufficient for a perception of the candle, even if this belief is somehow caused by the presence of the candle.) In fact, HOT theory's acceptance of pathology 2 makes this very clear. Recall that the second pathology involves a subject being in state α unaccompanied by the consciousness conferring state $T[\alpha]$. To make the case as stark as possible and certainly pathological, let us suppose that α is the unconscious experience of a spot of white light in an otherwise jet black visual field (suppose the subject is sitting in an experimental chamber, utterly dark, in which spots of light at various locations can be turned off or on). Just as HOT theory allows that one can be in pain while not being conscious of the pain, one can have visual experiences without being conscious of them.[14] In such a case, α = *seeing a white spot*. We are supposing that, for whatever reason and, of course, atypically, $T[\alpha]$ does not occur. Now imagine that our subject is told both that in actual fact he is seeing a white spot and that, let us say for some technical and neuro-experimental reason, he is suffering pathology 2. It is given that our subject fully accepts HOT theory and its consequences, has trust in the experimenter and the brain theory she employs, etc. Thus the subject comes to have the thought that he is seeing a white spot and is suffering from pathology 2, i.e. $T[\alpha]$ plus an independent thought about mental pathology. It is clear that *this* $T[\alpha]$ will *not* confer the consciousness of a small white light against a jet black background, apparently contrary to the dictates of HOT theory. HOT theory is supposed to be saved, of course, by appeal to clause (4): our imagined case is blatantly a case of inference to $T[\alpha]$ via sensory information.

But notice that clause (4) *cannot* do this job. First of all, we have seen that mere appeal to inferential or sensory informational mediation will not necessarily rule out consciousness. And second, HOT theory already accepts that T[α] is the state that *confers* consciousness, in the sense of 'mere experience' independent of questions of *what* the experience is an experience of. So if our subject actually gets into T[α], he must be conscious 'as it were' of a white spot against a jet black background. It is clear that in our imagined situation the acquisition of T[α] will not confer this consciousness. So it follows that the possibility of pathology 2 along with the assumptions of our imaginary situation (all compatible with HOT theory) entail that one simply *cannot* get into a *suitable* T[α] in this sort of way.

Compare our hypothetical thought experiment with a kind of perceptual experience that actually occurs quite frequently. Say you are out bird watching; to be specific let us say that you and a friend are looking for the elusive spruce grouse, a bird given to freezing when startled, relying on its effective natural camouflage to escape detection. As you walk through the bush, you hear the tell-tale rustling sound and look in its direction. Your friend spots the grouse and quietly tells you that you are looking right at it, yet you still do not discriminate the grouse from the background. You *believe* your friend and thus you acquire the belief that you are looking at a spruce grouse but this belief does not yield the perceptual experience of a spruce grouse. Then quite suddenly, with no apparent change in anything else, you do see the grouse. You would not have spotted the grouse but for your friend's information, so this is a kind of inferentially and sensory informationally mediated perceptual experience, but of course it is nonetheless a perfectly genuine perceptual experience.

More 'scientific' examples can easily be given as well. A well known visual illusion involves what is called the 'transparency effect' (see Rock 1985, pp. 112 ff, 138 ff.). Consider fig. 3.1:

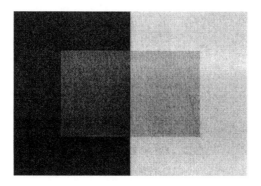

(Fig. 3.1)

At first glance this looks – to most people at any rate – like four distinct, variously shaded rectangles. But if one is told that it is a grey, transparent sheet placed over the two-colour rectangle underneath, one can come to see it *as* just that. It seems that the information about what one is looking at transforms the way it looks to one, and again we have a genuine conscious experience that is inferentially, informationally mediated.

We can extend our thought experiment, by analogy with such actual events, to show that of course one *can* get into a suitable T[α] in *all sorts* of ways. We can imagine that our subject is in a 'primed' state such that being told that he is seeing a white spot will causally release the subject from pathology 2, just as being told that a spruce grouse is hiding right before your eyes can actually trigger its discrimination from the background. Thus an inferential and sensory informationally mediated process *can* yield a suitable T[α]. The crucial question is: what is the difference between a suitable and an unsuitable T[α]?

My fundamental objection to HOT theory will now, I hope, be clear and clearly damaging. It is that there is no way to delineate the *suitable* T[α]s from the unsuitable ones except in ways ultimately equivalent to this: a *suitable* T[α] is one that confers consciousness. If this is correct, then HOT theory cannot be a reduction of consciousness or an explanation of consciousness, for one must appeal, tacitly, to the very thing one wishes to reduce and explain in order to characterize HOT theory in complete detail. This does not mean that HOT theory is wrong to link consciousness and higher-order thought. It is, indeed, pretty evident that consciousness does have some intimate connections with higher-order thoughts. But it does mean that one cannot explain consciousness in terms of, or reduce consciousness to, a relation between lower and higher-order thoughts.

We can go some way towards diagnosing HOT theory's failing. Ultimately, it lies in the acceptance that T[α] is a state which confers consciousness *along with* the characterization of T[α] as a content carrying higher-order thought to the effect that one is in the state α. Since HOT theory demands as well that T[α] be a separate mental state from α there is no way to rule out T[α] being caused by a wide variety of atypical causes (hence HOT theory's acceptance of the pathologies of consciousness). At the same time, it is clear that many states that would intuitively, and correctly, be counted as such higher-order thoughts do *not* confer consciousness, and so the suitable ones must be separated from the unsuitable ones. But this cannot be done by any appeal to the process which generates T[α], for the separateness of T[α] means that, bluntly speaking, any such process can produce, in the respectively proper circumstances, either a suitable or an unsuitable T[α]. In the end, the only possible characterization of this distinction that conforms to the dictates of HOT theory is one that appeals to consciousness itself, or the ability to confer consciousness. Thus HOT theory cannot succeed as a reduction or explanation of consciousness.

This objection cannot be made against what I called the Fully Relational Reading of HOT theory for on that construal, T[α] alone is insufficient to confer consciousness. This is no help however, for, as we saw, the Fully Relational Reading is extremely implausible on independent grounds.

Such objections reveal that the HOT theory will not face up to the generation problem any better than did the identity theory. Suppose that we accept the division of HOTs into the two fundamental groups: those for which, to use Rosenthal's words, 'a mental state's being conscious consists in its being accompanied by a [suitable] HOT' (1995, p. 26 n.) and those for which this is not true. Whatever manages to produce a HOT of the former sort (be it inference, causal mechanisms within the brain or even the direct will of God) will also produce conscious experience. Within HOT theory there can be no explanation of what this difference amounts to, for the occurrence of the appropriate HOT is by itself sufficient to 'generate' consciousness – the causal ancestry, or any other feature, of the HOT doesn't matter once it has come into being. So we are left with the usual question, which is the generation problem once again, of exactly what it is about the appropriate HOTs that allows just them to confer consciousness upon certain states?

Notice that for all my objections, there is a sense in which the HOT theory could still be *true*. I have tried to show that one cannot reduce consciousness to a kind of thinking or explain consciousness in terms of the HOTs. Nonetheless, it might be that consciousness is, as a matter of brute fact, precisely the kind of cognitive operation to which HOT appeals. So too, the neural vector coding theory could, as a matter of brute fact, be what consciousness is (the two theories could even collapse into one if we wanted or needed to identify the neural vectors with thoughts instead of the phenomenal qualities). I noted that, on the neural identity option, the question of just how come *only* those creatures with the appropriate vector machinery were conscious is pressing (to which the answer 'brute fact' is not very comforting in the face of behavioural evidence of consciousness). Similarly, while the HOT theory resides at a higher level of abstraction than the neural vector identity theory, it too faces an analogous problem. HOT theory must claim that beings without thoughts are without consciousness. This is problematic for animals. One might wish to argue that consciousness emerged *prior* to thought, rather than only after there were creatures capable of having thoughts, and, worse still, having the sort of complex thoughts that manage to be about other mental states. Much more radical versions of this problem arise when we couple the HOT theory to theories of thought and the contents of thoughts. Before getting to this issue however, I want to examine Dennett's views on consciousness, which are closely related to the HOT theory, though more radical in the reformulation of our notion of consciousness which they advocate.

Box 3.5 • Summary

HOT theory promises a mentalistic reduction of consciousness to non-conscious mental states in the hope that a naturalistic treatment of the latter will be relatively easy to find. HOT theory could then *explain* what makes a state conscious: a mental state, α, is a conscious state if it is the object of a thought with the content that the subject is in α.

Box 3.5 • Summary (cont.)

If such an explanation is successful, HOT theory might even solve the generation problem. But HOT theory suffers from several damaging objections, the primary one being the worry that HOT theory cannot distinguish those higher-order thoughts which can confer consciousness upon a mental state from the myriad of possible higher-order thoughts which do not. In the end, the only characterization of the 'suitable' higher-order thoughts is simply that they are the ones that confer consciousness. Unfortunately, this obviously leaves the generation problem untouched and, worse, makes the HOT theory explanation of consciousness covertly circular and hence no *explanation* at all.

DENNETT I:
EVERYTHING YOU THOUGHT
YOU KNEW ABOUT EXPERIENCE
IS *WRONG*

Box 4.1 • Preview

Dennett's project is to explain consciousness without explaining phenomenal consciousness. The explanation will be couched entirely in the language of content,
representation and intentionality. But, says Dennett, we need not draw any direct
explanation of phenomenal consciousness from these resources because there is *no such
thing* as phenomenal consciousness! Crudely speaking, we need only explain why
people *think* there is phenomenal consciousness. It looks like the generation problem
can be dodged, and consigned to the dustbin of misbegotten, purely philosophical
pseudo-problems (hence Dennett aims to dissolve rather than solve the problem of
consciousness). The first task is to undermine our conception of phenomenal consciousness. Dennett's attack is specifically directed at the notion of *qualia*: the 'what it is like'
to experience something, the colours of the sunset, a vivid visual memory of your
mother's face, the sound of an orchestra playing in your dreams. Dennett argues that
the very idea of qualia is subtly confused and incoherent. His approach is to display a
variety of ingenious thought experiments which are supposed to reveal the incoherence
lurking within the concept of qualia. The conclusions drawn from the thought experiments depend, however, upon certain exotic philosophical principles, especially
verificationism (the doctrine affirming that where one can't tell the truth about
something, there is no truth to tell). It is not clear that the cases Dennett considers really
suffer from serious verificationist problems; worse, it seems that Dennett's verificationism is a good deal less plausible than is an innocuous conception of qualia sufficient to
underwrite the idea of phenomenal consciousness.

Daniel Dennett shares with the HOT theorists the desire to explain consciousness in
terms of a set of mental states that are themselves non-conscious, whose nature is
already pretty well understood (at least supposedly), and which can take a place
within the natural, physical world with little or no discomfort. Dennett also agrees
with the HOT theory that the members of the explanatory set should be intentional
mental states, that is, mental states that in some way carry informational content (the
paradigm case is belief) without necessarily carrying any of what might be called
phenomenal content. But for Dennett, instead of aiming to spell out precisely *in what*

the occurrence of the phenomenal consists – as was the aim of both the identity and HOT theories – the idea is, roughly speaking and somewhat paradoxically, to somehow explain, or explain away, the *appearance* of phenomenal content in terms of informational content. Dennett also disagrees with HOT theories about whether such an account can be given simply in terms of the apparently rather ordinary thoughts about one's own mental states claimed by the HOT theory to generate conscious experience. The correct story, according to Dennett, involves much more complex interactions among a variety of content bearing states as well as a more circumspect analysis of just what the contents of the appropriate explanatory states might be. For example, the contents crucial to this explanatory project are likely to be entirely distinct from the contents of our 'highest level' intentional states, our own beliefs, desires, etc., and perhaps the requisite content cannot be specified in propositional terms at all.

It seems that there are three crucial hurdles that Dennett's theory must vault. The first concerns the nature of intentional states: the required account of them must not covertly involve or presuppose consciousness, must possess independent plausibility and should meet the naturalistic condition that the account avoid appealing to anything which cannot be reasonably viewed as smoothly fitting into the physical order. The second hurdle is to show that, despite intuition and appearances, the phenomenal aspects of consciousness are *not* intrinsic features of consciousness whose basic properties must be accommodated within any account of consciousness, which would naturally be thought to require a causal explanation and for which a *positive* explanation is a necessary part of any theory of consciousness. This is crucial for an assault on the generation problem. Any theory that explains consciousness in a form like: a system is conscious whenever condition ϕ is met, has got to face the question of exactly how ϕ manages to produce (underlie, ground, or be) conscious experience (as opposed to producing its popular surrogates: speech and/or behaviour). It is a radical step to deny the terms of this demand, to deny the intelligibility of the generation problem. To succeed in such a step, the phenomenal nature of consciousness must itself be radically rethought. Dennett is forthright on this point, though surprisingly reticent when it comes to spelling out the relationship between his views on 'phenomenality' and the generation problem. The final hurdle, of course, is to show how the proper deployment of the appropriate set of intentional states (and their dynamic interaction) can account for the reconceived domain of the phenomenal. This is a vast project, upon which Dennett has toiled for about 30 years. It would be hardly less vast a project to enter into a thorough critique of every aspect of Dennett's views, but I want to focus here only on the second two hurdles: Dennett's revisionary treatment of phenomenality and his account of how an appropriate appeal to the intentional mental states can deal with the radicalized domain of the phenomenal.[1]

Dennett approaches the problem of reforming our notion of the phenomenal indirectly, through a negative critique of what philosophers call qualia, by which is meant simply the phenomenal aspects of consciousness – the 'what it is like' part of Nagel's famous challenge to physicalism to provide an account of 'what it is like to be an x' (see Nagel 1974). Despite a disturbing diversity of views about qualia, most philosophers agree that some kind of non-eliminativist account of them is necessary. Such accounts range from the despairing claim that qualitative consciousness is simply inexplicable (McGinn 1989, 1991), through the straightforwardly optimistic identity theories, to the intentionalist constructive approach of the HOT theory, all the way to a pure representationalist view (to be examined below in chapters 6 and 7). It would be an understatement to say that no consensus has emerged.

It is indeed one possible explanation for this inability to reach any settled agreement about qualia that we simply don't understand consciousness, and our ideas and models of it, the primary one perhaps unfortunately being based on perception, reflect our ignorance. But another potential explanation for our difficulty is that we are the victims of an intellectual illusion. Perhaps our ways of speaking about consciousness, some of them almost exclusively philosophical but others common parlance, have mistakenly led us to the conclusion that there is a genuine phenomenon here when in fact there is little more than these disparate ways of speaking, whose lack of ground is revealed through the difficulties, puzzles and paradoxes which they engender. Acceptance of this eliminativist view could provide comfort. It would mean that there is simply no need to provide any sort of theory of qualitative consciousness; theorists could focus on somewhat more tractable empirical notions such as attention, attribution, feedback governed behaviour and speech mechanisms. Indeed, a large part of the burden of the problem of qualia seems to be the lurking threat that no *scientific* theory of them which could credibly tackle the generation problem is even so much as possible.

Few have dared seriously to offer this second explanation which seems to crown ignorance as the arbiter of what is and what is not. That there are ways that the world seems to us and that conscious beings somehow stand in a peculiar relation of acquaintance to *them* flatters intuition. Surely puzzles about them and this relation are the natural product of ignorance of which honesty demands recognition. How could one seriously argue for the *elimination* of qualitative consciousness? With great ingenuity – but also by appeal to exotic philosophical principles of his own – Dennett has found a way to mount an attack against the general notion of qualia (see Dennett 1988 and 1991b, especially chapters 12, 14). The basic idea, which Dennett had tried out before in a preliminary skirmish (see Dennett 1978), is to marshal conflicting intuitions about the putative phenomena via a series of thought experiments which, when taken together, reveal that the underlying conception of qualia is incoherent. Since an incoherent concept cannot have an extension, the phenomena, as conceived, cannot exist, though of course there may remain some acceptable feature(s) of the world which plays a role or roles somewhat like that of the now deposed qualia, and which can account for the intuitive appeal of our notion of qualitative consciousness.

The strategy is very dangerous. First of all, it is difficult to bring to a convincing conclusion since the presumed incoherence within the target concepts must be quite substantial. Otherwise it is reasonable simply to drop certain claims about the phenomena to recover consistency (for example, although Frege's original concept of a set was, so to speak, severely inconsistent it was still *sets* that he was talking about). Second, it trades puzzlement for ontological scruples, but sometimes one just ought to be puzzled. Think of the baffling properties of the quantum; one could wield Dennett's strategy against the electron with fair success (how can it be in two different places at the same time, as in the famous two-slit experiment, how can it know what other electrons across the universe are doing, as apparently evidenced by the Bell-correlations,[2] and so forth). One might say that the electron nonetheless presents a clear and robust set of phenomena which we must respect. It seems that one might in reply say the same, and with rather more rock bottom certainty, about qualia. Puzzles can be a sign of ignorance. The quantum world is baffling and strange and our best theories of it at least flirt with outright mathematical inconsistency. But I daresay that conscious awareness – a product or feature of the most complex entity in the universe (so far as we know) – is also the most bizarre, and perhaps the most rare, in the universe and thus it should not surprise us if we do not have a good grasp of it or that getting a grasp of it is exceedingly difficult. Of course, being a paradigmatically physical object the electron cannot trouble our physicalist inclinations whereas the problem of physicalism has always provided extra reason to fret about consciousness. But physicalism is not the central issue here, for one of the main puzzles about qualia is how they can be physical or be made acceptable to physicalism. That is, we can accept that qualia are physical, though the exact import of this claim and how it could be true remain a mystery. The generation problem gets its force exactly *from* the assumption of physicalism. We could exchange our fears about the truth of physicalism for the mystery of how qualia are generated by the physical (or just *are* physical) and there might be reasons for thinking this a good bargain (see Nagel 1986 and McGinn 1989).

All the puzzles about qualia remain and their very existence still hangs in the balance, for if the notion of qualitative consciousness is actually incoherent there most certainly is no such thing. 'Incoherent' is, though, an ambiguous term and we must be wary not to take oddity for logical inconsistency. It stands to reason that qualia are odd and Dennett's thought experiments might show this very well. It is another thing to show that the concept is logically inconsistent, which is what the argument needs strictly to guarantee the success of its assassin's job.

To fix our ideas, let us accept Dennett's basic four-fold characterization of qualitative consciousness or qualia as (1) Ineffable, (2) Intrinsic, (3) Private and (4) Immediately Accessible. These familiar features have all been subject to such close examination by so many philosophers that a review of possible interpretations is impractical. Instead, I want to provide a 'minimalist' interpretation of the four properties which I hope is broadly acceptable and use it to find a path through the thicket of thought experiments which Dennett sets in our track. I think that this minimalist view is almost neutral amongst almost all positive accounts of qualitative consciousness and simply maps out what needs to be explained about such consciousness (the caveats are most needed for certain forms of the representationalist accounts of experience and they apply, I think, only to the issue of whether qualia are intrinsic properties of experiencers). Here I will speak somewhat more positively and rashly than is truly justified, for I stress again that there are mysteries here that deserve respect. It is also worth re-emphasizing that physicalism is not the issue here. If Dennett is right there is no such thing as qualitative consciousness, whether or not physicalism is true.

1) *Qualia are ineffable.* I take this minimally to require that one cannot know what it is like to have a certain sort of experience except by having such an experience, but we can be quite liberal in 'typing' experiences. In particular, the required experience could be induced in many different ways. Although the usual model is perceptual experience, one can have the relevant experience by use of memory, imagination (as in Hume's famous case of the missing shade of blue) or even, presumably, direct neural stimulation.[3] We should remember that the sense experience model which philosophers commonly appeal to for convenience is somewhat simplistic. There are forms of consciousness that are not well modelled by the appeal to the senses. What is it like to be only moderately drunk? While this is a distinctive state of consciousness which possesses a definite qualitative character (as we would naively say) it is not a state much like 'seeing red'. Even visual perception itself presents a range of conscious experience rather more extensive than the basic example of colour perception reveals. Consider the experience of the river-boat pilot, as detailed by one who meets the subject's side of our condition of ineffability. The steamboat has just passed over what appeared, to the apprentice pilot, to be a deadly 'bluff' reef. The master pilot explains:

> 'Now don't you see the difference? It wasn't anything but a *wind* reef. The wind does that'. 'So I see. But it is exactly like a bluff reef. How am I ever going to tell them apart?' 'I can't tell you that. It is an instinct. By and by you will just naturally *know* one from the other, but you never will be able to explain why or how you know them apart'. It turned out to be true. The face of the water, in time, became a wonderful book – a book that was a dead language to the uneducated passenger, but which told its mind to me without reserve . . . .
> (Twain 1883/1961, pp. 66–67)

Obviously, the education referred to is not book learning. You can't get to *see* the river in the right way except by having the right sort of experiences and the initiated can extract information from the appearance of the river in a way not communicable in words. All experience, and particularly visual experience, is extremely rich and shot through with elements that are far from being the paradigmatically pure sensory qualities of a hue-brightness-saturation triple located at a point in the visual field.

The sort of ineffability enjoyed by qualia in this minimalist picture is quite moderate. There is no absolute stricture against *communicability* but communicability must be achieved by the production of an appropriate experience. This pacific brand of ineffability is accepted by several philosophers of physicalist persuasion (Lewis 1983a, 1988, Nemirow 1980, 1990, and, apparently, Paul Churchland 1985, and Patricia Churchland 1986, chapter 8,[4] see also Dretske 1995 who *almost* accepts it, as we shall see in chapter 6 below, and Tye 1995 who, from a perspective very similar to Dretske's, does accept it). Some of these philosophers are even convinced that the ineffability of qualia can be *explained* by the hypothesis that the channels that evoke (or 'realize') qualia are extremely rich in information – so rich that linguistic encoding of the information is impossible. Now in fact Dennett admits that the neural items that play roles somewhat akin to the traditional role of qualia – though from his point of view not close *enough* to permit identification – do possess what he calls 'practical ineffability' for much the reason just given (see discussion at 1988, pp. 541 ff.).[5] As Dennett puts it, the sound of an osprey's cry is 'a deliverance of an informationally very sensitive portion of my nervous system'. However, it is obvious that the information actually delivered can sometimes be very impoverished. For example, astronauts above the protective atmosphere occasionally see very brief flashes of light caused by energetic particles that strike and fire a few receptors in the retina. The sensory information gained from or transmitted by such a flash is very meagre, but of course it would be just as hard, if not considerably harder, to communicate what a flash of light is like to the permanently sightless than, as in Dennett's example, to communicate what an osprey's cry sounds like to one who has never heard that particular bird. If we are to find a rich source of information in cases where the world delivers little information we must look to the complex inner processing which even the simplest stimuli receives. Thus it must be the properties of the information channel itself and not the richness of the world that produce ineffability (whether 'practical' or some other sort). So qualia, or, for Dennett, somewhat qualia-like but acceptable items, turn out to be *internal* states (though they may *represent* external properties) just as we would wish. This is important for our next topic.

2) *Qualia are 'intrinsic' features of experience.* There is no hope of adjudicating the dispute about intrinsic vs. extrinsic properties here. But we can advance a modest proposal that will clarify the sense in which qualia are intrinsic which, after all, is our sole concern at the moment. The assumption of a very weak physicalism will help us here. I will assume that everything is physically *determined*, that is, that two worlds (somewhat more precisely: two nomically possible worlds, i.e. worlds that share their laws of nature) that are physically indistinguishable are indistinguishable *tout court*.

Further, I assume that the basic physical properties of objects, whatever they are, are intrinsic, however this might be analysed. Then, a property, F, of an object x is an intrinsic property if some basic physical change must be made in x in order for x either to lose or gain F. Another way to put this is in terms of possible worlds: F is an intrinsic property of actual-x iff in any world where possible-x is physically indistinguishable from actual-x, possible-x has F. Still another way to say this is in terms of local vs. global physical supervenience. A property, F, of object x locally supervenes just in case any change in F necessitates a physical change in x. F globally supervenes if a change in F requires merely a physical change somewhere or other. In these terms, an intrinsic property is one that supervenes locally on the physical state of the subject (for more detailed discussions of these notions of supervenience see Kim 1993 or Seager 1991a, chapter 4).

We can use some examples to test our criterion against our intuitions. Take the property of 'being an uncle'. This is not an intrinsic property. One can become an uncle without suffering any physical change. There are worlds where I (an uncle in actual fact many times over) am not an uncle but am physically identical to the actual me. Or we could say that 'being an uncle' does not supervene locally but only globally (for me to become an uncle there must certainly be a physical change in the world somewhere, though it could, in principle, be at any distance from me whatsoever). Dennett provides other examples: '. . . consider Tom's ball; it has many properties, such as its being made of rubber from India, its belonging to Tom, its having spent the last week in the closet, and its redness' (1988, p. 539). Our criterion obviously makes the first three of these non-intrinsic, just as it should. Whether the last property, that of 'being red', is intrinsic or not depends on whether there is a stable physical substratum for appearing red to normal observers in standard conditions (rather as there is such a sub-stratum for the temperature of a gas). Although Dennett dismisses this possibility, there are philosophers, the so-called objectivists, who accept it (Armstrong 1968, see chapter 12; Churchland 1986, see p. 300; see Hardin 1988 for a thorough discussion from the other, subjectivist, side). We need not resolve the issue here.[6]

We saw above that one fairly plausible ground for the ineffability of qualia reveals them (or, to retain a decent modesty, at least their causes) to be internal states in the sense that the physical information that qualia distinctively carry is in part about or at least conditioned by the workings of the channel from the world to consciousness, not simply about the world.[7] Thus qualia supervene locally and thus they are intrinsic by our criteria. Anti-physicalists will insist that qualia carry a distinctive sort of information in addition to the physical information about the world and their brain causes or correlates which is sometimes called 'phenomenal information' (see for example Jackson 1982 or Seager 1991a, chapter 5). We can bypass this worry so long as we retain our assumption of physical determination which is perfectly compatible with the intended sense of the hypothesis of genuine phenomenal information.[8] It is still the case that qualia are locally supervenient and hence are intrinsic properties of conscious beings.

As mentioned above, this is the least neutral element of my minimalist picture of qualia. The problem is that, roughly speaking, a representationalist account of consciousness, if it also accepted an externalist account of representation, would deny that qualia were intrinsic. For reasons to be discussed in later chapters, I still think that qualia are intrinsic in the sense outlined above. Of more importance here, Dennett's arguments against the intrinsic nature of qualia do not invoke the spectre of externalism, since they are aimed at eliminating the qualia rather than explicating them. So I aim to show here that at least Dennett's attack on qualia does not threaten their intrinsic nature. Later, we shall deal with externalism.

3) *Qualia are private.* The traditional problems of privacy revolve around incommunicability and privileged access so once we have separated ineffability and immediate accessibility from privacy, surely all the latter involves is the obvious metaphysical truth that distinct objects can share only state-types, not tokens or instantiations. Thus the privacy of qualia is no different than the privacy of any other property. The privacy of your qualia does not at all imply that others can't know what experiences you are having or what they are like. But of course they cannot know this by literally sharing your experiences.

4) *Qualia are immediately accessible.* The minimal explication of this notion is that we are non-inferentially aware of our modes of consciousness, of the way that things currently *seem* to us. In contrast, *both* the information about the world that these modes convey and the conscious state of mind that they betoken becomes knowledge via some sort of inferential process, although it is a process that is often, perhaps usually, unconscious (see Dretske, 1995, chapter 2, for more on the view of introspection hinted at here; see chapter 6 below as well). If one balks at the notion of unconscious inference then label the relevant process 'quasi-inferential' – the point is that acquiring knowledge of the world involves both the appearance of the world and some 'reference conditions' against which the appearances are evaluated. When one sees a cellular phone antenna on a car does one infer that there is a phone within? Although one may not spend any time thinking about this it seems very like an inference (surely one just *cannot* get such knowledge directly). We suppose that the knowledge is generated by an inference-like process since we know that there is no necessary connection between antennas and phones whereas there is an obvious *evidential* connection. But in truth the same goes for the phone itself (especially recently: I note that fake cellular phones are now available for the ostentatious but inexpensive adornment of your vehicle). We must not conclude from this that visual qualia, say, are limited to shapes and colours. There may be a qualitative experience 'as of a cellular telephone' which is produced by the concerted action of both the visual system and certain cognitive processes.

The ability to be non-inferentially aware of our modes of consciousness is not linguistic. We can easily forget the words that name our experience; these words are in any case inadequate to express the nature of the experience (since qualia are ineffable) and there is no reason to think that loss of one's linguistic abilities (through aphasia say) necessarily entails the disappearance of this sort of awareness. It may be though that possession of linguistic ability might actually *affect* the sorts of qualia that one can enjoy (it seems clear for example that utterances sound different to one who understands the language compared to one who does not).[9]

This special awareness of qualia extends only to those involved in our current state of consciousness. Memory is of course fallible, and our states of consciousness are only weakly and variably recoverable or composable from memory and imagination. It is easy to forget what something tastes like or looks like and the power of imagination varies considerably from person to person and from time to time (as noted by Hume in section 7 of the first *Enquiry*). What can be called 'immediate consciousness' just has the peculiar reflexive property of allowing an appreciation of both the information being conveyed and the mode of conveyance. These modes of conveyance are what we call qualia. It must be admitted that this is mysterious. This merely goes to show that indeed consciousness is not well understood but as we shall see below in chapters 6 and 7, a representational account can go some way towards explicating this facet of the mystery.

The customary question about immediate accessibility is whether it is infallible. Given the constraints above the question becomes: can one be unaware of one's 'real' qualitative state of consciousness during the time one is conscious of *some* qualitative state. Obviously not, since there is no viable distinction between real and only apparent qualitative states of consciousness. But this says very little. One can easily make a whole range of mistakes that involve qualia. Churchland (1988b, p. 77) gives a rather morbid example. After a series of burns a victim is touched with an ice-cube and, at that moment, the victim thinks he is being burned yet again (*that* is his mistake). Tendentiously, Churchland says that the victim thinks he is in pain when he really is not. But this is not very plausible. Suppose the victim's delusion persists; he winces, moans, complains etc. about the application of ice. We would, I think, be forced to accept that he was in pain, no doubt because of some peculiarity of his nervous system. Churchland's example depends upon our tacit acceptance of the 'fact' that the fleeting application of ice-cubes doesn't hurt. Another natural way to talk about this phenomenon is that upon the touch of the ice-cube the brain briefly interprets the stimulus as pain, because of some sort of 'priming' effect brought on by the earlier series of burns, and then corrects itself. The state of consciousness 'enjoyed' is the product of the brain's operation so in this case there was indeed a brief pain (with an unusual cause).

The knowledge gained through our acquaintance with our own experiences is not that of knowing the word to apply, or of recognizing that the experience is like some other that we have had before or of realizing that the experience matches something we were imaginatively prepared for. It is knowledge about *how* the world is being presented to us and the consciousness of the qualitative nature of our experience just is getting this sort of information. In my opinion, the apparent oddity of the doctrine of infallible access stems mostly from illicitly thinking of our awareness of our own modes of consciousness as a perceptual process with qualia on one side and conscious appreciation of them on the other (just like seeing). This perceptual model is not correct: it is in fact misleading and it makes infallibility seem extremely implausible or even manifestly absurd. No one has ever come up with a good alternative model of this process and it may be that we cannot, perhaps because there is nothing simpler or more familiar by which to understand it; in any case we don't need a model to appreciate the phenomenon.

Box 4.2 • The minimalist 3I-P picture of qualia.

We want an understanding of the core properties that qualitative consciousness is supposed to possess and we want it to involve a minimal number of assumptions about the nature of consciousness. The 3I-P picture asserts that qualia are: ineffable, intrinsic, immediate and private. Minimal ineffability is that one can't know what it is like to have an experience of a certain sort unless one has *had* an experience of that sort (one doesn't know what lobster tastes like until one has tasted lobster – or something else that tastes just like lobster). Minimal intrinsicness is the claim that states of qualitative consciousness are properties of the subjects who have them, depending only upon the nature of the subject. Minimal immediacy is the claim that subjects are non-inferentially aware of the way things seem to them (some delicate issues arise here, since there is no claim that subjects must have the concepts available for any *mentalistic* description of their own states of consciousness). Finally, the minimal notion of the privacy of states of consciousness is rather trivial. It is simply that only you can be in *your* states of consciousness (nothing prevents your neighbour from being in a *qualitatively* identical state of consciousness however).

Although the above account of the cardinal features of qualia is crude and no doubt has its difficulties it is reasonably minimal in its commitments. For example, it does not in itself tell either for or against physicalism, as is evident from the free assumption of weak physicalism in its development. It is compatible with a number of distinct treatments of qualia, especially including a representationalist account, save perhaps for a thoroughly externalist representationalist view, but, I will argue below, such an account is independently implausible. With it we can examine Dennett's attack on the notion of qualia and hopefully see that his eliminative conclusion is unwarranted, at least on the basis of the considerations he offers.

Let us begin then with ineffability. As was briefly mentioned above, Dennett admits there is a 'practical ineffability' about certain states that take roles somewhat like those of qualia. According to Dennett, this amicable sort of ineffability arises in the following way. Within us are certain 'property-detectors' which respond to properties extremely rich in information. Dennett's example is the characteristic sound of a guitar, a complex property that is in fact 'so highly informative that it practically defies verbal description' (1988, pp. 543–4). The response mechanisms of our property detectors act somewhat like traditional qualia and a kind of ineffability is 'carried through' the external property to the experience. But the astronaut example given above shows that this cannot be quite right. Some properties responded to are simply *not* very rich in information (as in the example when the information is just 'particle here'). We can easily say what property was responded to: an electron hits the retina. By rights then the subjective state associated with this response should be equally easy to communicate. But as noted above, the astronaut's experience of the flash of light is every bit as ineffable as any other subjective experience. Take another example. Suppose you are in a dark room with the task of reporting whether an electron has been fired on to the right or left half of the retina of your left eye (the other eye is well shielded). In those circumstances, the 'external' information responded to is worth exactly 1 bit, a pathetically *impoverished* amount of information. It is also easy to describe the two possible experiences which this experiment produces but that will not tell someone who does not already know what seeing a flash of light looks like what it is like to participate in the experiment.

Dennett's property detector model also seems rather incomplete as a guide to qualitative experience. Think again of the way it feels when one can just begin to notice the effects of alcohol. That delightful alteration in experiential tone (for want of a better phrase – ineffability is inescapable) surely counts as an instance of qualitative conscious experience. The operation of what property detector will count as the surrogate for this quality of experience? One's brain is indeed 'detecting' the dilute alcohol bath in which its neurons now swim. But this is not a case of information being transferred via brain mechanisms. A brain in a vat cannot be made drunk by feeding the right signals into its afferent nerve endings. The very functioning of the neurons is altering and with it our consciousness. (The importance of the nutrient bath has been unjustly neglected in brain-in-vat thought experiments. To do the job properly, the computer stand-in for the evil genius must not only be able to excite nerve endings but must also have an extensive array of chemicals ready to throw into the vat.)

Here one might follow the line presented in our initial discussion of ineffability. That is, one could claim that the information load is in the inner brain channel and not in the external event, but this is not Dennett's line since that would be dangerously near to 'stepping back into the frying pan of the view according to which qualia are just ordinary properties of our inner states' (1988, p. 542) no doubt being 'scanned' by some other neural mechanism.

Dennett seems to confuse the indescribable with the ineffable. Everything is describable, better or worse. An experience is ineffable when no description by itself yields knowledge of what it is like to have that experience. A description might permit one to imagine or remember the experience and thus to gain knowledge of what it was like to have it (the conditions under which this is possible are interesting and deserve exploring, although not here) but it remains true that an experience must be generated for one to gain this knowledge. Dennett discusses the increased ability to describe the sound of a guitar thus: [after simple training] 'the homogeneity and ineffability of the first experience is gone, replaced by a duality as "directly apprehensible" and clearly describable as that of any chord' (1988, p. 543). This appeals to and then threatens a kind of 'ineffability' that qualia need not possess. Once one takes up a suitably modest view of ineffability the growth in one's ability to describe experience does not say anything against the ineffability of experience.

Furthermore, it seems possible to have functioning property detectors while lacking the normal experience associated with them. David Armstrong's famous chicken-sexers are an example (1968, pp. 114–15).[10] More immediately relevant, those afflicted with blindsight can discriminate the location of light flashes with apparently no visual experience; some such patients can also discriminate colour without visual experience (see Stoerig and Cowey 1989). Something similar happens in blind-touch. One patient who, because of certain brain lesions, had no consciousness of sensation in her right upper arm but could nonetheless locate stimuli within this region is reported to have said about an experiment: 'you put something here. I don't feel anything and yet I go there with my finger . . . how does this happen?' (Oakley 1985, pp. 173–74). A fascinating, if necessarily somewhat conjectural, extension of this sort of case is considered by Nicholas Humphrey (1984, chapter 3). Humphrey reports that monkeys suffering from surgically induced blindsight can be retrained, over a considerable period of time, so as to once again employ the information supplied by the undamaged early visual system. So much so, in fact, that such a monkey cannot easily be distinguished from those who retain an undamaged visual cortex. Humphrey nevertheless believes that the 'cortically blind' monkey remains unconscious in the sense of not enjoying visual *sensations* even though it acquires knowledge through vision. It is possible to imagine a training so effective that blindsighted monkeys are behaviourally indistinguishable from their visually conscious associates. If discriminative abilities can occur independently of qualitative experience, as it seems they may, then it is hopeless to define qualitative states of consciousness or differences amongst such states in terms of them.

But who is to say that such monkeys have not, through the hypothetical training process, regenerated, as it were, their qualitative states of consciousness? If we think of a parallel example for a *human* suffering from blindsight, true indistinguishability would mean that our human subject would not only *act* normally but would even claim to be visually conscious. We might suppose we faced a most peculiar combination of blindsight with blindness denial completely masked by the special training which permitted some non-conscious functions of the brain to take over visual processing. How could we ever verify this peculiar hypothesis in contrast to the 'regeneration' hypothesis?

Of course, Dennett exploits our discomfiture here, but perhaps we in our turn should lament the unfortunately strong current of verificationism that runs throughout Dennett's treatment of qualia. Dennett would have us, on the basis of the empirical equivalence of our two hypotheses, deny that there was a difference between them. While it is my view that verificationist arguments have little bearing on metaphysical questions, this matters little for it is clear that empirical evidence could favour the no-consciousness hypothesis in some cases, the regeneration hypothesis in others. For example, suppose nine of ten trained blind-seers cannot make verbal reports about the visible world despite their manual dexterity and remain verbally adamant that they are unaware of visual stimuli. Further suppose that the tenth, perfectly trained, subject falls into verbal line with the rest of us and, in complete reversal of the case of the other nine, we find that the neural ground of this ability is activation, or reactivation, of brain regions we independently know to be intimately involved in consciousness. Perhaps this would not be utterly decisive but that should worry only the most doctrinaire of verificationists.[11]

Box 4.3 • Dennett's Verificationist Thought Experiments

VTE1: Colour Inversion. Suppose that some mad neurosurgeon performs an operation on you that systematically inverts your perception of colours. Tomatoes now look green to you, the sky appears to be yellow, etc. It looks like your qualia have been switched and so there must be some qualia to be switched. But wait. Contrast the above description with this: the surgeon has done nothing to your colour vision but has 'inverted' your memory based dispositions to classify colour experiences. After the operation, you just *think* the colours of things are wonky because your memory now, falsely and due to the operation, tells you that experiences of red should be *called* 'green'. A really thorough switch of memories and behavioural dispositions would, it seems, leave you unable to decide between these two scenarios. Verificationism suggests that then there is no fact of the matter, thus undermining the very existence of qualia.

VTE2: Inverted Taste. This is similar to VTE1, save that now we imagine that it is tastes that have been systematically inverted or shifted (sugar tastes sour, salt tastes bitter, etc.). A different lesson is drawn from this thought experiment however. The unverifiable difference is now between unchanged qualia plus *changed* memory versus the possibility that the memory change has produced *changed* qualia.

VTE3: The Taste of Beer. Most people don't like beer when they first taste it, but equally most people do eventually come to like beer. Is this because of an increased appreciation of *the* taste of beer, or is that with more experience the taste actually *changes* to one that is more likeable? If the taste of beer somehow depends upon one's reactions to it, then the claim that qualia are intrinsic properties might be threatened.

Box 4.3 • Dennett's Verificationist Thought Experiments (cont.)

VTE4: The Upside-Down World. It is possible to devise spectacles that invert vision so that everything appears to be upside-down. Experiments with such inverting glasses show that after some time, people can adapt to them, so that they once again interact fairly smoothly with the world. The question now is whether it makes sense to suppose that there is a genuine, substantive opposition between the claim that one merely adapts to an upside-down world and the claim that adaptation manages to de-invert one's vision so that things look upside-up again.

Dennett's primary employment of verificationist arguments is to undermine the notion of our direct access to qualia and, in particular, to deny that *intra-subjective* qualia inversion is possible. The typical account of this imaginary syndrome is that as the result of some complex neurosurgery, one's colour experience becomes systematically inverted (where you used to see red you now see green, blue is switched with yellow, etc.). The victim of the surgery wakes up one morning to find his visual experience radically altered. Dennett notes that there are (at least) two hypotheses that could account for this:

(I) Invert one of the 'early' qualia-producing channels, e.g. in the optic nerve, so that all relevant neural events 'downstream' are the 'opposite' of their original and normal values. *Ex hypothesi* this inverts your qualia.

(II) Leave all those early pathways intact and simply invert certain memory-access links – whatever it is that accomplishes your tacit (and even unconscious!) comparison of today's hues with those of yore. *Ex hypothesi* this does *not* invert your qualia at all, but just your memory-anchored dispositions to react to them. (1988, p. 525)

After the operation, at least if one is aware of the second possible hypothesis, one should, Dennett says, 'exclaim "Egad! *Something* has happened! Either my qualia have been inverted or my memory-linked qualia-reactions have been inverted. I wonder which". . .' (1988, p. 525). Dennett's point is that while it is presumably possible to invert a subject's dispositions to react to the various properties of the world about which we are informed via the visual system this is not equivalent to the inversion of qualia. If these are not equivalent and the only evidence we have for qualia are reactive dispositions (including verbal ones) then the nature of the qualia 'behind' the reactions is unverifiable. So, by verificationism, there is no 'fact of the matter' as to the qualia at all. Thus, at best, qualia lose their direct accessibility. As Dennett puts it: '*if* there are qualia, they are even less accessible to our ken than we thought'. Unspoken is the *modus tollens*, that since special accessibility is essential to qualia, there aren't any.

However, Dennett's thought experiment is about memory, not qualia; nor is it about the kind of access which our moderate interpretation advanced above. The kind of access Dennett attacks is one that claims that memory of qualia is infallible and few would want to hold this. It is obvious that one can forget what some experience is like; in fact it is hard *not* to forget the nuances of experience. I am quite sure that everybody misremembers the qualitative character of past experiences to a greater or lesser degree. For example, every year I am astounded at the taste of wild strawberries – my memory simply does not very well preserve the exquisitely fresh mixture of tart and sweet that strawberries evoke. Does such an admission only show that Dennett's problem is genuine and acute? No, because Dennett's dilemma is akin to those put forward in sceptical arguments that illegitimately try to undercut all sources of relevant evidence. The question should be: after the apparent inversion, do I have any reason to doubt my memory? If I was to be subjected to one of either I or II but did not know which, then of course I would have reason to wonder which was true, and I could not tell 'from within', even though in both cases I would enjoy equally direct access to my qualitative consciousness. On the other hand, if I knew that the inversion was occasioned by an operation *on the retina* I would have no reason whatsoever to suppose that my memory was at fault and I would have correspondingly good grounds for accepting that my colour qualia had been inverted.[12] Could qualia memory be disrupted by no more than a retinal operation? Perhaps, but only in the sense of possibility in which it might be that I should come to think I was Napoleon as the result of cutting my toenails.

The evident possibility of *misremembering* qualia permits Dennett to introduce a set of thought experiments that contrast alterations in qualia versus judgements *about* qualia. One such imagines a coffee taster who no longer likes the taste of his company's coffee. But there are two possibilities for explaining his new judgement: 1) the coffee still tastes the same but his feelings about *that* taste have altered; 2) the coffee simply no longer tastes the same to him (but there has been no change in his judgement about the taste of coffee – were he to taste the *old* taste again he would approve of it). It is because he cannot trust his memory with regard to the taste of coffee that he can entertain these as competing hypotheses.

The lesson we are supposed to draw from these examples is again verificationist. If there is no way to adjudicate between these hypotheses then there is no content to their putative difference, and we proceed as before to eliminate the qualia that are taken to underlie the empty distinction. But again, as Dennett admits, there are lots of empirical ways to favour one of these hypotheses over the other. We are left with the rather uncontroversial claim that there are certain situations describable in terms of qualia the actuality of which one could not verify. This is a very weak claim on which to found the complete elimination of qualia.[13]

Dennett attempts to strengthen the claim via still another thought experiment. Here we first suppose that our subject has suffered 'taste inversion' so that 'sugar tastes salty, salt tastes sour, etc.' (1988, p. 530). But then our subject adapts and compensates for the inversion so thoroughly that 'on all behavioural and verbal tests his performance is indistinguishable from that of normal subjects – and from his own pre-surgical performance' (1988, p. 531). As Dennett then notes, there are still two hypotheses that roughly mirror the two considered above (I and II), that is, it may be that:

> (I*)   our subject's memory accessing processes have been adjusted without any change in qualia to effect the compensation, or

> (II*) it may be that the memory comparison step which has been modified now *yields* the same old qualia as before.

Dennett then claims that there is no way to verify which of these two hypotheses actually accounts for the (putative) phenomenon of taste inversion compensation or adaptation. He says: 'physiological evidence, no matter how well developed, will not tell us on which side of memory to put the qualia' (1988, p. 531).

This both overstates and misstates the situation somewhat for we may not need to judge about this last claim before grappling with the dispute between I* and II*. This can be illustrated by a slight extension of our current thought experiment. Let us say that the original surgically imposed taste inversion was effected 'early-on' in the gustatory processes, thus giving us good reason to hold that we indeed had a case of qualia inversion when we take into account the subject's post-operative reactions. Now suppose that after the compensation we note a peculiar alteration in the subject's brain. He has grown a new (functional) unit which in effect takes our inverted signals and re-inverts them back to their original values and sends them on to substantially unaltered 'higher' systems. Such a re-inversion system is not impossible to imagine. In *this* case, would we not have good grounds for supposing that the qualia have been restored to what they were prior to the inversion? So physiological evidence *could* tell for or against one of these hypotheses as opposed to the other.

Even those with lingering verificationist yearnings should admit that their doctrine would take force only in situations where evidence is strictly irrelevant. It is an irrefutable lesson of the philosophy of science that *no* hypothesis can be absolutely confirmed but it would be absurd to infer from this that science is cognitively empty on verificationist grounds! Abstractly speaking, an unverifiable hypothesis pair is formed of two propositions, H and H* such that for any sort of empirical evidence,

E, the probability of H on E is equal to that of H* on E. This is a bit crude; to get fancier, we should perhaps include the precondition that we begin with the assumption, probably counterfactual, that the antecedent probabilities of H and H* are equal and we will not permit evidence that logically entails either H or H* to count (this should really be already covered in the demand that E be *empirical* evidence). But, however it is to be precisely spelled out, the apparent oddity of propositions which meet such a condition is at the core of whatever is plausible about the verificationist rejection of hypotheses. A classic, albeit primitive, example of such a truly unverifiable hypothesis pair is suggested by the famous contrast between 'The universe is billions of years old' and 'The universe is five minutes old but was formed so as to appear billions of years old'. Once we counterfactually assume that both of these hypotheses are granted equal prior probability, it is obvious that there can be no empirical evidence that can differentially affect the probabilities of these two hypotheses. But with regard to qualia inversion it has just been shown that the probabilities of (I*) and (II*) will respond *differently* to certain sorts of empirical evidence. So they are not an unverifiable pair and we cannot so much as hope to deploy verificationism (which, I recall, is in any case implausible as arbiter of truth) against qualia via this particular thought experiment.

Further consideration of (II*) leads Dennett in another direction towards an attack on the third feature of qualia, their intrinsic nature. The relevant thought experiment is about what we commonly call *acquiring a taste* for something, in this case beer, and the two hypotheses at issue in this case are (see 1988, p. 533):

(I**)   With experience, one's appreciation of the taste of beer matures and one comes to enjoy *that* taste.

(II**) With experience, the taste which beer occasions alters towards one that is enjoyable.

Although closely related to earlier imaginings this is subtly different. Now we are supposing that the qualia themselves can alter through increased experience and, while further questions of verifiability could easily be raised here which would, I think, suffer the same fate as earlier ones, the focus of Dennett's offensive is elsewhere. What Dennett says is that if II** is accepted then the intrinsicness of qualia is threatened:

> For if it is admitted that one's attitudes towards, or reactions to, experiences are in any way and in any degree constitutive of their experiential qualities, so that a change in reactivity *amounts to* or *guarantees* a change in the property, then those properties, those

'qualitative of phenomenal features' cease to be 'intrinsic' properties, and in fact become paradigmatically extrinsic, relational properties.

(1988, p. 533)

This is of course a tendentious interpretation of the phenomena. One can preserve the difference between (I**) and (II**) and accept the quite obvious fact that experience can alter the way things appear to us without acceding to Dennett's rather strong claim. It might be that increase of experience or maturation of judgement are, on occasion, *causal conditions* of qualia change. If the mere possession of causal conditions by a property makes that property a relational property then truly the distinction between the intrinsic and the extrinsic is utterly empty, for every empirical property has causal conditions for its instantiation.

We can recognize that the causal conditions of qualitative consciousness are mighty complex. Conscious experience is at the 'top' of all cognitive processing; we are aware of the world as made up of telephones, airplanes, people, animals, etc. Qualia are not bottom level aspects of the brain or mind (but this obviously does not entail that they cannot be affected by alterations of 'early processing'). 'Qualia' is a word that reminds us that conscious experience always has a specific content or mode by which information about the world is conveyed to us. Visual or colour qualia do not reside in the retina, but 'appear' as the visual system finishes its task and 'delivers' information to consciousness (the delivery metaphor is very poor here – better to say that it is the full operation of the visual system that underlies qualitative conscious visual experience). Qualia are not untainted by cognitive abilities, learning or maturation. Experience is altered by knowledge. But all this is extremely complex, since some sorts of qualitative experience are more and some less susceptible to cognitive penetration as well as many other subtle influences. For example, consider the famous Müller-Lyer visual illusion. It seems that the apparent difference in length of the two lines is a feature of our qualitative experience and one which is not cognitively penetrable (we all know that the lines are the same length). Yet the degree to which people are susceptible to this as well as other visual illusions is, in part, a matter of cultural milieu (see Segall *et al.* 1966). We need not consider the possible explanations of this – the point is that 'cultural penetration' on the effect of the Müller-Lyer does not make qualia extrinsic, as can be made clear by contrasting qualia with beliefs.

Recently several philosophers have propounded a view of the intentional psychological states which is called psychological externalism.[14] I will not detail this view here or defend it (for a sample of the literature see Putnam 1975, Burge 1979, Baker 1987, Davidson 1987 and Fodor 1987, chapter 2) but what it claims is that the contents of beliefs (or, in general, intentional mental states) are fixed, in part, by features of the environment, broadly construed. For example, on Putnam's infamous Twin-Earth (where what looks like, tastes like, feels like, etc. water is not H_2O but rather XYZ) people believe that XYZ is wet whereas people on Earth believe that water (i.e. H_2O) is wet. But the people in question could be physically identical in all relevant respects (it is a slight complication that the Twin-Earthers are mostly made of XYZ instead of water but presumably this is psychologically irrelevant). Whatever its merits, psychological externalism clearly makes 'believing that p' an extrinsic property rather than an intrinsic one.

And it makes it so in a way that exactly accords with our notion of intrinsicness as outlined above. That is, according to psychological externalism belief does not supervene locally; one can alter a person's beliefs without making any physical change to them (by transferring them to another linguistic community say, though this may be so only counterfactually since one may, so to speak, 'carry' one's linguistic community with one wherever one goes) or two people could be physically identical but differ in their beliefs.

It is extremely implausible that qualia fail to be intrinsic.[15] This is easy to see. For simplicity, suppose there was a culture totally immune to the Müller-Lyer illusion. We might say that when people from such a culture are presented with the illusion they immediately judge that the two lines are or at least appear to be the very same length. We *might* say this, but it would be inaccurate since only 'normal' members of the culture will meet this condition. For imagine that a child, Lyer, is raised so as to end up (somehow) a precise physical duplicate of one of us who has never happened to see the illusion. Lyer has never been exposed, as it were, to whatever it is that immunizes his people from Müller-Lyerism (I don't say it would be easy to meet this condition but it is, as philosophers say, possible in principle). I predict that Lyer will see one line as longer when first he sees the illusion. I think this is in fact quite obvious.

The reason for this is also quite obvious – it is that the features of experience are intrinsic properties. Physical duplicates share them. Recall we are supposing physical determination throughout, what we are arguing about here is whether qualia are *locally* determined. It seems that they are, and this is all we need to maintain that qualia are intrinsic. The fact that qualia have *causes* is neither surprising nor worrying to the view that they are intrinsic features of experience.[16]

Yet a further thought experiment bears on the question of intrinsicness. In it, Dennett tries to undermine the intuition that qualia *must be* intrinsic by exhibiting a kind of qualitative experience where intrinsicness is apparently quite implausible. The thought experiment has to do with true inverted vision. It is possible to wear specially rigged eye-glasses that make the world appear upside-down. If one wears these for some time one will eventually adapt to a greater or lesser extent so that some of one's behaviour, at least, returns to normal. Although philosophers like to talk about the 'in principle possible' complete adaptation, no real case comes even close to this (see Smith and Smith 1962, especially chapter 6). Again we can produce our pair of hypotheses about this phenomenon:

(I***) One's visual qualia remain upside-down but one has perfectly adapted (so much so, perhaps, that one has forgotten what the world used to look like).

(II***) Adaptation alters one's visual qualia so that they are again truly right-side-up.

But does this opposition make any sense? As Dennett says, 'Only a very naive view of visual perception could sustain the idea that one's visual field has a property of right-side-upness or upside-downness *independent of one's dispositions to react to it* – "intrinsic right-side-upness" we could call it' (1988, p. 535, original emphasis). If we admit that this aspect of qualitative experience is not an intrinsic property then, Dennett says, we are free to withdraw the claim of intrinsicness about all qualia.

It must be noted that Dennett is here covertly changing the target properties which are supposed to be intrinsic. In the above, what is putatively intrinsic is a certain property of some phenomenal object – the visual field. But qualia are properties of whole perceivers, they are the ways that people experience the world and themselves. They are intrinsic if physical duplicates share them.

It is not the visual field that we are concerned with but rather the experience of seeing. Thus we can pursue a slightly different line of thought about this case. Putting on inverting glasses alters the way the world appears. One can adapt to this and a natural question is whether after adaptation the world once again appears as it did before. My question is, what are we wondering when we wonder about this? Are we wondering whether adaptation will take place? Take my word for it, it will. How does it look after one has adapted? That I can't say (having never gone through the process). It seems to me that this is a legitimate question, as is borne out by the peculiar reticence and difficulties adapted people have in answering the question (see, again, Smith and Smith 1962, chapter 6). But if Dennett is right, there is no separate question of how it seems once we agree that adaptation has occurred. But I can imagine that after adaptation one would still say, if asked to reflect carefully, that the sky looked to be above the sea but this no longer bothered one and was easy to deal with (real subjects often report in just this way – when engaged in a task for which they are well trained they note that everything seems normal, but when asked to reflect they admit that things are still upside-down). Does the ability to take such a reflective stance about experience and to note a continuing difference compared to past experience reveal an 'incomplete adaptation'? We could *define* it so that 'adaptation' became a technical term roughly meaning 'totally indistinguishable from people not wearing inverting glasses'. The evidence we have suggests that no one has ever completely adapted in this sense to inverting glasses and thus the grounds for maintaining a qualitative difference in experience even after 'normal' adaptation remain.

I can imagine other responses however. Perhaps our subject would tell a story that included the claim that one day he just noticed that everything looked proper again whereas he could remember that for a time, the sky seemed to be below the sea. Or, again, perhaps he will be stumped at the phenomenon and be utterly at a loss for words. Or maybe he will claim that everything now looks exactly as it did before (and this is borne out by his perfect and unhesitating engagement with the world). In this last case we will face the same problems of verification as we have confronted in several thought experiments above. And it is pretty clear that empirical evidence could tell in favour of the hypothesis that our subject does now enjoy visual experience just as he did prior to donning the inverting glasses (for example, if as above the adaptation resulted from the development of a brain system that 'de-inverted' the appropriate signals at an early, near retina stage of processing).

The last remarks have not made reference to Dennett's starting point – the 'visual field' – but rather to the experience of seeing. This is because the visual field is a red herring. Dennett exploits, via a subtle shift in the supposed bearers of the intrinsic properties, the strong feeling that it is ludicrous to posit an intrinsic up-ness or down-ness to the visual field. But the reason for this is not the startling idea that (at least some) qualitative properties are extrinsic but the banal fact that spatial arrays have no intrinsic up-ness or down-ness. I take it that the visual field (which actually seems to me to be a purely theoretical entity not appealed to in ordinary descriptions of experience) is a spatial array of objects or coloured patches. As such it has no intrinsic orientation. However, our 'sense' of up and down is not only or even primarily a matter of vision (shut your eyes, stand on your head and you will know you are upside-down independently of vision). We experience ourselves as 'in' our visual field and this is a product of a very complex consciousness of spatial relations amongst objects, including parts of our own bodies, our expectations of the effects of movements (both of and on outer objects and our own limbs), our sense of balance and 'uprightness', as well, no doubt, as many other factors. Thus the plausible claim that the visual field carries no intrinsic orientation does not go very far towards showing that the conscious experience of 'up-ness' and 'down-ness' is not intrinsic in the same way that the consciousness of colours is.

So far the privacy of qualitative experience has not been mentioned. Given the extremely moderate interpretation of privacy that I outlined above which, in conjunction with the notions of immediate access and ineffability, provides us with a reasonable framework from which to view the phenomena of qualitative consciousness, there is no need to worry about it. The problems that Dennett raises for privacy are really directed at the combined notions of ineffability and immediate access and these have already been dealt with sufficiently. With privacy presenting no problems for the notion of qualia, it seems that Dennett's eliminativist strategy has failed. The various thought experiments can be accounted for without casting serious doubt on the coherence of our notion of qualia. Lucky for us, since if there were no qualia we would be entirely unconscious. The nature of qualitative consciousness remains mysterious and no light has been cast upon the generation problem, but it is comforting to know that our core conception of qualitative consciousness is at least coherent.

If successful, this chapter has shown that Dennett's arguments against qualia do not force us to abandon the notion and suggest that a positive account of qualitative consciousness is still necessary. However, a successful strategy which incorporates a radical transformation of our conception of qualitative consciousness could undercut these conclusions. Consciousness is mysterious, and a view which could do without a whole class of the seriously mysterious phenomena of consciousness would have much to recommend it. So even if Dennett can't show that we *must* give up – or at least very radically transform – our notion of qualitative consciousness, he could urge that the benefits of his approach, despite its radical tendencies, are so great that they justify a voluntary jettisoning of the notion. To see if this could be so, let's turn to Dennett's attempt to jump the third hurdle, that is, to his theory of how the proper deployment of the appropriate set of purely intentional states (and their dynamic interaction) can account for the radically reconceived domain of the phenomenal.

Box 4.4 • Summary

Dennett's attack on qualia is the first move in the demolition of phenomenal consciousness. If successful, an explanation of consciousness would require 'only' an account of mental content (or representation) and an explanation of why it *appears* as if there is phenomenal consciousness. The elimination of phenomenal consciousness proceeds by showing that there is nothing, and could not be anything, which satisfies the set of properties definitive of qualia. Dennett deploys a series of thought experiments aiming to show that putative facts about qualia dissolve into unverifiable pseudo-facts under pressure of philosophical investigation. These thought experiments all depend upon a very suspect doctrine about facts in general: verificationism. It appears, contrary to Dennett, that a minimal but sufficiently substantial notion of qualitative experience can withstand this first assault. This notion does not lead to seriously worrying verificationist problems. It remains to be seen whether Dennett's positive account of 'no-qualia consciousness' has so much to recommend it that we should accept it even in the face of the failure of his attack on qualia.

5

DENNETT II:
CONSCIOUSNESS FICTIONALIZED

Box 5.1 • Preview

Dennett's project is to 'intentionalize' consciousness and to 'explain' it by transforming phenomenal consciousness into an illusion (and a *non-phenomenal* illusion too). In a way then, Dennett's view is similar to a HOT theory *minus* the lower order target states! These become mere 'intentional objects', the imaginary correlates of the conceptual structure of 'phenomenal consciousness'. The first step of Dennett's project requires a theory of how the brain produces and operates upon meaning or content. The problem of the production of content is dealt with by Dennett's long developed and still developing theory of intentionality; the operations *upon* content stem from a fascinating 'cognitive pandemonium' model of thought. The second step – showing that phenomenal consciousness is, in a significant and entirely non-phenomenal sense, illusory – depends upon a series of verificationist thought experiments. These now aim to show that while 'there seems to be phenomenology', this is *mere* seeming. While these new thought experiments are ingeniously subtle and avoid some of the problems besetting those of the last chapter, they remain problematic and the verificationism is still implausibly strong. More positively, many of Dennett's ideas point towards the representational theory of consciousness to come.

Once upon a time Dennett allowed that his theory of the intentional states was essentially an 'instrumentalist' sort of theory (see, originally, Dennett 1971, and strong traces remain scattered through Dennett 1987). That is, whether it was correct or not to attribute intentional states such as beliefs, desires, etc. to any system was entirely a matter of the instrumental success gained by the attribution. If one was better able to predict and explain the system's behaviour by describing it from the *intentional stance*, then that was all that was required to ground the truth of the predictive and explanatory intentional state attributions. Within the philosophy of science, there have always been objections to instrumentalist accounts of theorizing. For example, it is not clear whether one can really explain any phenomenon in terms of entities which have no claim to any sort of 'existence' except their explanatory role. This seems perversely backwards: surely, for example, electrons explain things because they exist, it is not that they exist because they explain things, although, of course, it may be that we *know* that they exist because of how they can explain things (an early form of this sort of objection was raised in Cummins 1982). Nor does it seem quite correct to ground intentional state ascription *solely* upon the possibility of predictively and explanatorily successful ascription since, for example, it seems possible that such success could be grounded in features of a system irrelevant to, or even blatantly inconsistent with, the actual possession of intentional states let alone states of consciousness (for these sorts of objections see Peacocke 1983, pp. 203 ff. or Block 1978 or, for some interesting remarks on Dennett's irrealism, Block, 1993, or even, by inference, Searle 1980). From the point of view of explaining consciousness there seems to be a much more serious problem with instrumentalism about intentional states. Among other things, it is the *desire* for explanatory and predictive success, along with the *belief* that the ascription of beliefs and desires can yield that success, which drives our ascription of desires and beliefs.[1] These are conscious desires and beliefs and their existence does not seem to be merely a matter of the predictive and explanatory success that someone else (or ourselves) would gain by attributing them to us! The worry here is that the instrumentalist view of intentional states in fact presupposes unexplained instances of the things it purports to explain.

Perhaps because of such criticisms, Dennett no longer welcomes the label 'instrumentalist', but his professed realism about intentional psychological states remains somewhat less than whole-hearted. While the ascription of beliefs, desires, hopes and the like is needed to bring out the 'real patterns' in the behaviour of intentional systems, this does not license the inference to any definite and well disciplined set of brain-states which provide the neural home base of intentional psychological states. The inference is shakier still considering the presumably wide range of extra-biological physical systems that might provide the causal ground for the behaviour of intentional systems. Dennett would still embrace this tale about the way that intentional states relate to actions, drawn from *The Intentional Stance*:

> Tom was in some one of an indefinitely large number of structurally different states of type B that have in common just that each licenses attribution of belief that p and desire that q in virtue of its normal relations with many other states of Tom, and this state, whichever one it was, was causally sufficient, given the 'background conditions' of course, to initiate the intention to perform A, and thereupon A was performed, and had he not been in one of those indefinitely many type B states, he would not have done A. One can call this a causal explanation . . . .
>
> (1987, p. 57)

While I do not want to descend to what Dennett insults as 'slogan-honing', I do want to point out that Dennett's outlook remains fundamentally instrumentalist even

108

though he does not fully accept what I would call scientific instrumentalism. For one of the central features of instrumentalism, as I take it, is a principled resistance to the claim that the world provides a model of the instrumentalist's theory. The instrumentalist line on the Coriolis or centrifugal forces denies that the world *really* pushes things about by invoking forces that directly correspond to the theory's postulates, and this contrasts with the straightforwardly realist attitude towards those forces which are accepted as ultimately driving the world forward. Metaphorically speaking, it *looks like* a force or entity as described by some theory is at work but the instrumentalist denies that anything in the world demands full acceptance of *that* force or entity as an element of nature. The interaction of other forces, perhaps very difficult to describe, conspires to produce a world in which appeal to that force can become useful.

The Coriolis force, for example, at least comes close to picking out a 'real pattern', for it brings order into an otherwise bizarre collection of phenomena such as ballistic trajectories, wind patterns, ocean currents, errors in position determination made with a sextant from a vehicle in motion and the peculiar fact that northern hemisphere rivers, especially those that run predominantly north-south, scour their right (looking downstream) banks more severely than their left (and high latitude rivers exhibit the effect more than those at lower latitudes). In this case, however, there is a common factor, motion across the *spinning* Earth's surface, from which all these effects of the Coriolis force can be inferred and 'explained away' which satisfies us that the instrumentalist *denial* of the reality of this force is correct. Obviously, we have no similar prospects of replacing our ascriptions of intentional psychological states with brain talk. Sometimes it seems that the indispensability of our intentional idioms is Dennett's main support for his realism about intentional states, but I doubt whether an appeal to it is necessary. Given that the instrumentalist seriously does not expect the brain to provide a model of the set of intentional states, I don't see that a new and extremely effective brain theory that did not provide a model of the intentional states would be any kind of a threat.[2] My point is that the traditional controversy about realism is not the most interesting feature of instrumentalism. There are, according to Dennett, independent reasons for supposing that the intentional states are not modelled in the brain and these provide support for the core of an instrumentalist position irrespective of the realism issue.

Classically, instrumentalism in the philosophy of science is grounded on a presumed epistemological barrier to knowledge about unobservable entities and instrumentalists are thus driven to a quite general scientific anti-realism (although he is also somewhat uncomfortable with the label, Bas van Fraassen 1980 provides an illustration). Dennett is no anti-realist. He is happy to fill each of us with a myriad of unobservable functional cognitive systems all of which depend, ultimately, on the workings of the truly microscopic, scientifically posited, elements of the brain.[3] But he balks at the idea that the system of intentional states by which we all explain and predict the behaviour of our fellows is *modelled* in the brain. Yet this is the standard realist alternative to instrumentalism, and the primary source of the urge towards an identity theory of the mental. Consider: we have a theory, or group of theories, that posits an entity, say the electron. We aren't instrumentalists about electrons because we think there are literally elements of the world that provide a good model – in the sense of this term that comes from logic – of this theory (or theories), and, in particular, of the workings of this element of the theory. This kind of realism holds that the world is the semantics for our theories in pretty much the way we learned about semantics while studying first-order logic.

While no one would think that intentional psychological states are modelled by particular elements drawn from the scientific image of the world, that is, that psychological states are *physically* fundamental, it is not so implausible to suppose that such states can be seen as quite definite assemblies of scientifically posited elements, or as constituted out of specifiable assemblies of these elements. Such is the view of the traditional identity theory and, in a more subtle form, of functionalist theories of psychology.

What remains essentially instrumentalist in Dennett is the claim that this kind of scientific identification of the psychological with the physical commits what Dennett's teacher called a category mistake. It puts the ghost back in the machine, in what is still an objectionable sense of 'in'. It supposes a physical regimentation of the intentional states which is at odds both with the function of our attributions of such states and with the constraints which govern these attributions. As Dennett has emphasized in many places, our attributions of intentional states are constrained by such factors as the general canons of rationality, coherence of psychological character, 'normality' – in both a biological and social sense of this word – of human desire and belief and so forth. And their function is both to mark and pick out the real patterns of behaviour that legitimize them.

In light of our profound ignorance of the brain's inner workings, it might seem that a decent modesty would require the neo-instrumentalist to leave open the possibility of a future discovery that the intentional states are in the brain something like the way sentences are in books. It could still be maintained that such a discovery was, in essence, a kind of accident, perhaps rather like it was an accident that, until quite recently, telephone signals were all analogue electrical waveforms. As in this rather obvious technological case, a specific, let alone easily decipherable, brain coding scheme for the psychological states is not particularly to be expected and is by no means required for the fully successful use of intentional ascriptions in explanation, prediction and understanding. But Dennett is not modest.

I think it can be seen that the idea that there will be, or even could be, some kind of scientific identification of the intentional psychological states with particular sorts of neurological states is a species of what Dennett calls 'Cartesian Materialism' (discussed above in chapter 1). This is important for Dennett, since, one, he explicitly maintains that *consciousness* cannot be identified with particular types of brain states or processes, and, two, his strategy is, in a way, to replace conscious experience with *judgements about experience*, in which experience becomes an intentional object, and judgements, being content carrying states, naturally answer to the constraints of intentional state ascription. So if Cartesian materialism is false with respect to consciousness, it will have to be false with respect to at least some intentional psychological states. In fact, it will be false for all of them.

Box 5.2 • Cartesian Materialism

Descartes is famous for maintaining that there is an absolutely fundamental separation of mind from body. When faced with the obvious question of how two radically distinct kinds of substances could interact, as they so evidently appear to do, Descartes invoked the hand of God and posited a central locus of brute and mysterious interaction deep within the brain (see chapter 1). Few now espouse Cartesian dualism, but Dennett claims that many retain an allegiance to holdover Cartesian doctrines. Cartesian *materialism* is the view that there is a place in the brain where 'it all comes together' in consciousness, a place where the contents of consciousness reside and where, if we could but find it and break its neural code, the stream of consciousness would be laid bare, determinate in both its content and temporality. More generally, it seems that any view that asserts there is some property of the brain which 'fixes' one's states of consciousness and their temporal relationships is a kind of Cartesian materialism. On this understanding, Dennett is no doubt correct in his claim that there are closet Cartesian materialists lurking everywhere in philosophy, neuroscience and cognitive science.

Although the doctrine of Cartesian materialism is Dennett's *bête noire* throughout *Consciousness Explained*, just what it amounts to is not entirely clear. Sometimes it appears as the doctrine that there is a special place in the brain in which consciousness resides. Dennett says:

> Let's call the idea of such a centred locus in the brain *Cartesian materialism*, since it's the view you arrive at when you discard Descartes's dualism but fail to discard the imagery of a central (but material) Theatre where 'it all comes together'. . . . Cartesian materialism is the view that there is a crucial finish line or boundary somewhere in the brain, marking a place where the order of arrival equals the order of 'presentation' in experience because *what happens there* is what you are conscious of.
>
> (1991b, p. 107, original emphases)

The existence of such a place, plus a way of decoding its neural processes, would let us know what a person was *really* conscious of at any particular time, thus fixing a determinate temporal order in experience. The extension to intentional states is clear: such a place would be *the* place where we should take a decoded content, along with an 'affective index' marking the content as believed, doubted, feared etc., to be the genuine intentional state of our subject (this is, as it were, the place where you should take seriously what you find written in the brain's language of thought). Since any conscious experience is typically very closely tied to an apprehension of the nature and significance of 'it', if there was a way to decode, moment to moment, the really genuine beliefs of a subject, it would then also be possible to specify the subject's state of consciousness. And even if it was not guaranteed that the move from belief about experience to experience would always be correct, the move would have an obvious evidential value which would also be at odds with Dennett's views.

Note that this form of Cartesian materialism provides a straightforward way for the brain to model consciousness or intentional states – there will be definite events or processes in a definite region of the brain that correspond to states of consciousness or intentional states. We thus expect the instrumentalist to deny such a doctrine. But couldn't a realist deny Cartesian materialism as well? Dennett admits that hardly anybody would come out explicitly in favour of Cartesian materialism, as defined. Couldn't consciousness and intentional states depend more globally on the states of the brain? It turns out that in Dennett's eyes this, too, is a form of Cartesian materialism:

> There is, it seems, an alternative model for the onset of consciousness that avoids the preposterousness of Descartes's centred brain while permitting absolute timing [of conscious experience]. Couldn't consciousness be a matter not of arrival at a point but rather a matter of a representation exceeding some threshold of activation over the whole cortex or large parts thereof? . . . But this is still the Cartesian Theatre if it is claimed that real ('absolute') timing of such mode shifts is definitive of subjective sequence.
>
> (1991b, p. 166)

What Dennett wants to deny is that there is *any* feature of the brain that marks out by itself the determinate order of conscious experience, the real content of conscious experience or the genuine intentional states of a subject. A search for the grounds of his denial will take us to the heart of *Consciousness Explained* and vividly raise the particular issues I want to consider about Dennett's 'intentionalizing' theory of consciousness.

Dennett's background model of the brain is a thoroughly cognitive pandemonium, here meant in the sense, introduced by Oliver Selfridge, of a system composed of multiple relatively *independent* agents (for an example see Selfridge 1970). Within the brain reside a huge number of relatively independent, sometimes competing, functionally specified agents, each performing a restricted task but whose concerted efforts deftly manoeuvre the body through an exceedingly complex world. Many of these agents deal with *content* – this is why I label Dennett's view a *cognitive* pandemonium – although the kind of contents that they deal with may be far removed from the kind of content that we normally ascribe to systems (certainly, to *people*) when we take the intentional stance. There are agents, for example, whose job is to hypothesize about the external world based on the data sent them by various more basic perceptual agents and such data can be quite remote from our ordinary conception of the world, for example, as it might be: 'edge', 'moving edge', 'shaded region', etc. To speak picturesquely, bits and pieces of content are perpetually whizzing about the brain. Furthermore, these agents are vying for a say in what the entire system will *do* or how it will act in the world and it is no easy task to specify the conditions under which some agent will succeed in getting a piece of the action.

Box 5.3 • Cognitive Pandemonium

The primary job of the brain is to intercede between sensory input and motor output – to inject some *intelligence* into the gap between seeing and acting. This is rightly called a cognitive process because (or *if*) the gap is filled with information and operations upon information. Dennett's picture of the interactions and relationships amongst content carrying brain states is *cognitive pandemonium*. In computerese, a 'demon' is a process, or *agent*, which lurks in the background waiting for an appropriate (in a program, strictly defined) moment to grab control of the system (or at least to have its say). A system made up of such agents operating without any need for a 'top-level' controller is then a pandemonium. Now imagine that the brain is full of a huge range of distinct contents, not all consistent with one another, not all equally relevant to the current situation, but all 'fighting' for control of the system (or, more likely, the sub-system of which they are a natural part and in which they form and dissolve). It is quite possible for such a chaotic and rancorous system, lacking any sort of executive control, to display well coordinated, goal oriented behaviour. Maybe our brains do work this way. It is the relation between the cognitive pandemonium and consciousness that is at issue. According to Dennett, what makes a contentful state conscious is *cerebral celebrity*. This is nothing more than the temporary control of the whole system, especially the vocal output, or speech, sub-system and the memory sub-system.

Imagine that you are crossing a quiet street and notice that your shoe is untied. While crouched down to tie it up again you see an oncoming vehicle, give up your shoe-tying project and move rather quickly across the street. From the point of view of the internal agents orchestrating your behaviour a much more complex tale must be told. It is in the first instance a tale of conflict: the various agents who have currently taken control of the system and directed it towards shoe-tying might be just as insistent as ever that *the shoe must be tied*, others may side with them and deliver the 'claim' that there is plenty of time for the operation. But still others will deliver an opposite verdict and they will enlist on their side agents demanding that the shoe project be abandoned or temporarily set aside. As it becomes increasingly 'evident' to more of these sub-systems that the oncoming car represents a real threat, their ability to wrest control of the whole system will grow, until finally action ensues. From the point of view of the person involved this little battle will not take long and will usually be almost entirely unconscious.

Of course, this is a hopelessly crude version of what is a terrifically complicated, multifaceted cognitive process and it appeals to a kind of content ludicrously similar to the sort we are familiar with in consciousness. Still, the example is enough to make the point that as there is a myriad of content-carrying brain states participating in the multi-agent negotiations that lie behind any action, picking out the genuine intentional states of the subject will be impossible if one is restricted simply to current information about the brain, even if one is outright given a way to decode the represented content within that brain. The genuine intentional states of a subject will be determinable only via the processes of rational interpretation that form the basis of Dennett's intentional stance. In the end, what matters is what the subject will do (which naturally includes what the subject will *say*).

A philosopher would ask, might it not be possible, at least in principle, to predict which agents will emerge victorious in the struggle to direct behaviour? The genuine beliefs of a subject would then be whatever content will play a decisive role in behaviour generation. This question is in part engendered by the simplifying assumption used in the example – in reality the agents probably don't have to deal with the *same* contents as are ascribed to the subject. These agents are, after all, the elements of the ingenious 'hierarchy of harmonious homunculi' that Dennett has deployed in the past to avoid the absurdity of explaining intelligence by positing equally intelligent sub-systems; they are not to be thought of as fully fledged intentional systems in their own right on a par with the subject whom they constitute. (It is interesting that in *Consciousness Explained* we see that the hierarchy is not so harmonious. There are distinct, independent and sometimes competing hierarchies of homunculi. This is a natural and plausible way to marry the demand to 'discharge' intelligence in a hierarchy of ever more stupid sub-systems with the demands of the pandemonium model of cognition. But how typical of the late twentieth century to posit an essentially bureaucratic model of intelligence.) Even casting aside this bow to sub-psychological reality, the question reveals nothing but the possibility of 'predictive interpretation'. Of course it is true that if we could predict bodily motion on the basis of brain states – something which is sure to remain a fantasy for a good long time if not forever – we could couple this with our knowledge of the environment to produce psychological interpretations. The basis of the ascription of intentional states would nonetheless remain rooted in the canons of rationality, coherence and normality as applied to overt behaviour. It is also worth mentioning here that it is not implausible to suppose that there could be cases of genuine indeterminacy in the struggles between the cognitive agents, thus undercutting the presupposition of the question. In such a case, the intentional states of the subject would radically depend upon what the subject actually did.[4]

Thus it appears that Dennett's treatment of intentional psychological states fits very well indeed with the pandemonium view of cognitive processes presented in *Consciousness Explained*. In fact, this treatment is another significant battalion enlisted in the attack on Cartesian materialism in either its local or 'global' form. Perhaps ironically, it is when we turn to consciousness itself that things seem more difficult. It has often been observed that even though the intentional psychological states can be conscious, they do not presuppose or present any essential phenomenological aspect: there is no 'feeling' associated with believing that snow is white distinguishing it from the belief that grass is green (or distinguishing it from merely imagining that snow is white).[5] Thus the typical temporal continuity in a subject's beliefs does not require any phenomenological temporal continuity to underwrite it.

But surely when we turn to phenomenological continuity itself we cannot evade the demand that consciousness, when it is present, be temporally continuous and determinate. This is apparently at odds with the pandemonium model of consciousness, for if our consciousness is in some way the result of haggling amongst our subpersonal cognitive agents there will be times when our state of consciousness is, as it were, being formed but not yet decided. And the brain itself cannot know which agents will prevail. Certainly, as one who *is* conscious, I would want to say that my consciousness is temporally continuous and determinate – that is how it appears to me, and my consciousness is surely just what appears to me. Dennett's point is not to endorse the strange view that our consciousness is, unknown to us, 'blinking' off and on as the brain performs its consciousness producing feats of content juggling (something which cannot be ruled out by appeal to the way things seem for there are no seemings of sufficiently short time intervals), but rather to advance the even stranger view that our state of consciousness across some stretch of time is itself not determinate or continuous. Dennett's attempt to present this view illustrates three crucial features of his theory: the intentionalizing of consciousness, his adherence to the cognitive pandemonium model and his verificationism. With regard to the first two of these, consider this passage:

> We human beings do make judgements of simultaneity and sequence
> of elements of our own experience, some of which we express, so at
> some point or points in our brains the corner must be turned from the
> actual timing of representations to the representation of timing . . . .
> The objective simultaneities and sequence of events spread across the
> broad field of the cortex are of no functional relevance *unless they*

> *can also be accurately detected by mechanisms in the brain.* We can put the crucial point as a question: What would make *this* sequence [of brain events] the stream of consciousness? There is no one inside, *looking at* the wide-screen show . . . . What matters is the way those contents get utilized by or incorporated into the processes of ongoing control of behaviour . . . . What matters, once again, is not the temporal properties of the representings, but the temporal properties of the *represented*, something determined by how they are 'taken' by subsequent processes in the brain.
>
> (1991b, p. 166, all emphases original)

Although this passage deals explicitly only with the conscious representation of temporal order, I think it is safe to say that a similar story is to be told about all conscious representation, that is, all conscious experience.

Now, suppose we ask why we are never conscious of the workings of all those agents whose content involving efforts *fail* to be incorporated into the processes of behaviour control. The wrong answer would be to invoke some special, unknown (magical?) brain powers of the victorious contents which yields or generates consciousness. To answer in this way would open the door to all the difficulties of the generation problem. This would be, though, a relatively *comforting* interpretation of Dennett for it leaves conscious experience something real and really something like we tend to think of it, with a potentially 'normal' relation to its generating 'parts'. Consider this remark from the *New York Times* review of *Consciousness Explained*: '. . . from the collective behaviour of all these neurological devices consciousness emerges – a qualitative leap no more magical than the one that occurs when wetness arises from the jostling of hydrogen and oxygen atoms' (Johnson 1991). Philosophers will recognize the particular metaphor and the attempt to naturalize and demystify the relation between neural activity and consciousness, but it is not in Dennett. Johnson's review is generally astute but I think he falls prey here to the soothing hope that Dennett is offering a causal/constitutive explanation of consciousness which would be comfortably akin to the host of causal/constitutive explanations which science has already provided us.[6] But this issue is completely undercut by Dennett. According to him, to expect this kind of explanation of consciousness is to commit something like a category mistake.

Rather, consciousness is a kind of judgement about experience and our judgements just are, by the nature of the pandemonium model plus the interpretive workings of the intentional stance, the product of the winning cognitive agents, for it is these agents who, temporarily, direct the behaviour that ultimately underwrites the ascription of intentional states, including ascriptions of judgements about conscious experience. Experience itself, then, is a merely intentional object. Why 'merely'? Dennett says it with absolute directness: 'But what about the *actual* phenomenology?

There is no such thing' (1991b, p. 365). This *is* Dennett's claim, but there is nothing in the pandemonium model itself that requires such a treatment of conscious experience. This model sits well with Dennett's theory of intentional psychological states but the apparent consequence of the application of this theory to consciousness – the demotion of phenomenology to mere intentional object, strikes one more as an objection to rather than a verification of the theory. What prevents one from accepting the 'Johnson hypothesis' that a cognitive pandemonium of sufficient power is just the sort of machine that could generate, constitute, subvene or whatever actual phenomenology? Instead of avoiding the generation problem, could the model just face up to and solve it?

It is worth thinking about why refuting Johnson's hypothesis is so important to Dennett's project. As far as I can see, there are at least three fundamental reasons why the idea that consciousness is *generated* by the cognitive pandemonium that constitutes the functional architecture of the brain must be refuted – indeed, shown to be utterly wrong-headed. First, Dennett believes that conceiving of consciousness in this way is, in the end, to postulate unverifiable differences – putative differences that make no difference to the operation of the system. Dennett's verificationist tendencies refuse to permit such nonsense; in fact the unverifiability of certain hypotheses regarding conscious experience is not only a reason to refute them but is also, in a fine (but suspect) economy of thought, that very refutation. Second, if there was actual phenomenology it would be a bizarre sort of thing, so bizarre as to court incoherence. Since no genuine phenomenon in nature can be incoherent, any phenomenon whose putative properties *are* incoherent cannot be real. This is the line of argument dissected in the last chapter and which was, I think, found wanting but of course it remains a powerful motivator of Dennett's thought. Third, and by far the most important, if the cognitive pandemonium somehow generates actual phenomenology then Dennett's book is patently *not* an explanation of consciousness, for there is absolutely nothing in it which even begins to attack the problem of just how certain parts or aspects of a pandemonic system could manage to produce (cause, underlie or constitute) conscious experience. This would be left dangling as a 'mystic power' of such systems and Dennett would be guilty either of simply ignoring the very problem his book claims to solve or, perhaps worse from Dennett's point of view, he would be guilty of mysterianism by default.

None of these problems can be raised against what I take to be Dennett's true strategy. Instead, conscious experience is intimately tied to behavioural evidence, there simply is none of this bizarre phenomenological *stuff, process,* or whatever lurking around, and the problem of explaining consciousness reduces to the twin problems of accounting, first, for the genesis of our language of experience and, second, for the ascription of judgements, as well as other intentional states, couched in the terms of this language. These are hardly trivial problems but, unlike the traditional puzzles of consciousness – and especially the generation problem – they are not the sort that leave us looking for a place even to start. The former problem is, though not in any great detail, explained in terms of the evolutionary design of our brain's own systems of sensory discrimination, which can all be seen as potential agents in the pandemonic hierarchy. 'Qualia', says Dennett, 'have been replaced by complex dispositional states of the brain' (1991b, p. 431) which underlie and explain our discriminative capacities. In any real perceptual situation indefinitely many of these are active in (or as) various demons scattered through the cognitive pandemonium of the brain, but we will be conscious only of those that get to play a part in behaviour production, in particular in the production of discriminative behaviour that gets taken up into a judgement about the experience intentionally correlated with, if that is the right phrase, this behaviour.

I believe there is also a second component to the story of the genesis of our language of experience which might help account for our firm belief in the reality of phenomenology but which would have to be fleshed out considerably before Dennett's strategy could lead to victory. This is that one role of experience-talk is to find a subject for the reports of features of the world that we feel urged to make even when we know or find out that these features do not correspond to anything in the 'external world'. Truly ancient versions of the problems of illusion must have led to our talk of 'seemings' and 'appearances'. The division between primary and secondary qualities gave a scientific sheen to talk of 'mere appearance'. But once we succeeded in constructing a fragment of language with such subjects, it necessarily possessed the attributes of normal talk about 'things', with their perceptible properties, and, as we developed this aspect of our language and perfected our abilities to deploy it (especially the apparently non-inferential application of this language to ourselves), we naturally came to the conclusion that there *was* such a subject. Thus, it would have to be argued, experience (actual phenomenology) is really just a kind of linguistic artifact. On the other hand, the very success of this language counts in its favour. It is a disagreeable as well as formidable task to dump the language of experience into the same dustbin we use to scrap rejected theories (e.g. phlogiston theory). And since the candidate for elimination aims to refer to conscious experience itself, the eliminativist's task is much harder than that facing those (like the Churchlands as I understand them) who merely harbour doubts about the language of intentional psychology.

The solution to the latter of the twin problems is, of course, the story of intentional systems over which Dennett has laboured long and hard, and for which he has by now quite a detailed story that some, I among them, find reasonably plausible in many respects.

Nonetheless, Dennett's strategy is clearly one of explaining consciousness *away*. To be successful this requires much more than the presentation of an alternative picture. What seems to be the case always has a *prima facie* claim on us and Dennett admits that there seems to be actual phenomenology: 'Exactly! There *seems to be phenomenology.* That's a fact the heterophenomenologist enthusiastically concedes. But it does *not* follow from this undeniable, universally attested fact that *there really is* phenomenology. This is the crux' (1991b, p. 366, original emphases). Nor, of course, does it follow that there isn't. Right now I can say that there seems to be a pen on my desk. This is mere seeming if further experience, and not just my own, is incompatible with a real pen's existence and, in the clearest cases, when there is a story about the perceptual circumstances that accounts for my misjudgement.

The world conspires nicely to divide my experience into aspects that are simply mere seemings and other aspects that provide solid information about the world. Yet what *experiences* do we have or could we have that are incompatible with there (or their) being actual experience? Obviously, perhaps logically, all my experience conspires to confirm the judgement that there is experience. Thus it is that Dennett must ascend to a more abstract attack upon experience. This attack is two-fold, as noted above: the first line of attack involves his verificationism, the second the 'bizarreness' or, what would be better, the outright incoherence of our picture of experience. As we saw in the last chapter, verificationist premises are required for Dennett's attempt to impugn the coherence of our notion of qualitative consciousness, but we could disarm Dennett's attack without challenging outright his verificationism. It is interesting that as Dennett pursues the intentionalization of consciousness, verificationism again takes a surprisingly central role. This still stronger dependence on verificationism is what I want to deal with here. For I believe Dennett can be placed in a dilemma: either his verificationism must be so strong as to yield extremely implausible claims about conscious experience, or it will be too weak to impugn the reality of actual phenomenology.

Let us begin by examining how Dennett uses verificationism to discredit certain apparent features of experience. In chapters 5 and 6 of *Consciousness Explained* there is a sustained attack on the notion that there is a determinate temporal order to experience at all temporal scales. Recall that the doctrine of Cartesian Materialism would entail that by observing the putative centre in the brain in which consciousness arises one could determine the temporal ordering of conscious experience. Dennett then argues like this:

> If Cartesian materialism were true, this question [as to temporal order
> of conscious experience] would have to have an answer, even if we
> – and you – could not determine it retrospectively by any test . . . .
> But almost all theorists would insist that Cartesian materialism is false.
> What they have not recognized, however, is that this implies that there
> is no privileged finish line, so the temporal order of discriminations
> cannot be what fixes the subjective order in experience.
>
> (1991b, p. 119)

This confusing passage raises several questions. Is Dennett denying the antecedent? If not, where is the proof that only Cartesian materialism allows that temporal order of discriminations fixes subjective order? Or is there an identification of Cartesian materialism with any view that has this consequence, in which case, isn't the argument simply begging the question? Also, the last phrase suggests that the temporal order of experience is fixed by something, though not by the order of discrimination. But the ordinary conception of experience only requires that this order be fixed. It surely does not have anything to say about the brain mechanisms which do the fixing.

Box 5.4 • The Phi Phenomenon

Apparently, it is a basic feature of our perceptual mechanisms to search for object continuity across changes in the visual scene. A striking example is the phi phenomenon. If a subject watches a blank screen, sees a dot of light at one location blink on and off but then sees a second dot of light blink on somewhat to the right, say, of the first, then the subject will quite literally see the dot *move* from one location to the other (you can easily program your computer to make the experiment on yourself). The more interesting, and perhaps contentious, extension is the *colour* phi phenomenon. In this variant, the first dot of light is green, the second red. It is reported that subjects see the moving dot change colour *half-way* across the gap between their true locations. If you think about it, this means that either we have a verifiable case of precognition (not very likely) or else there is some kind of temporal back-reference within our conscious experience. Actually, the ordinary phi phenomenon displays this characteristic, since it matters not where the second dot occurs – continuous movement will still be seen. Since the experiment can be set up so that the subject can't know where the second dot will appear we have a strict analogue to the peculiar features of the colour phi phenomenon.

Dennett would admit, of course, that generally speaking the temporal order of experience *is* fixed and determinate, but the fixing is the product of cognitive processes which produce an interpretation or, in Dennett's words, a narrative which incorporates a subset of the discriminations, and other contents, currently loose in the pandemonic network, a narrative that by and large obeys global constraints of reasonableness and conformity with earlier parts of the on-going narrative. This narrative is sensitive to the temporal order of the various contents it might incorporate, but it is not bound by them, and it may 'invent' events that would 'make sense' of otherwise improbable sequences of discriminations (as in the case of the colour phi phenomenon – discussed further below – where an intermediate colour change is 'interpolated' as the best guess about when the moving dot would change colour). All this is blatantly a tale of and at the sub-conscious level, so what prevents us from taking Dennett's story as outlining or sketching the conditions under which conscious experience, real phenomenology, is produced? Dennett allows that conscious experience is temporally determinate 'so long as we restrict our attention to psychological phenomena of "ordinary", macroscopic duration' (1991b, p. 168). Problems arise when we consider special circumstances, psychological experiments, whose temporal duration experience is of the order of just a few tenths of seconds. Dennett says that 'at this scale, the standard presumption breaks down' (1991b, p. 168).

What this would show is that at least one aspect of our 'seeming phenomenology' could not stand up to objective scrutiny. It would reveal that at least this aspect of our experience was a *mere* seeming and, Dennett expects, this would be a very liberating experience with regard to consciousness in general for it would open the door to the idea that all qualitative consciousness is really a kind of judgement about a merely putative phenomenology. But how is this breakdown accomplished? Obviously, we are aware, or seem to be aware, of temporally continuous and determinate experience over time spans of a few tenths of seconds. If we were not, there would be no seeming to explain away, and the experimental facts Dennett presents would be strictly irrelevant. So this feature of awareness (and indeed any feature of awareness) cannot undercut itself directly. Thus Dennett *must* appeal to verificationism in the attempt to show that there simply is no fact of the matter as to the temporal order of experience at these 'micro-time scales'. This will do the job since, again, it certainly seems that there are such facts about conscious experience.

The verificationist line that Dennett takes here depends upon opposing experience against memory of experience, but the opposition is here rather more subtle than when Dennett deployed it against qualia (and as considered in the last chapter). In the colour phi phenomenon – one of Dennett's prime examples – a green dot is displayed very briefly and then a red dot is similarly displayed, but displaced slightly in location. According to Dennett, subjects report that the dot moves across the space and changes colour about half-way across its trajectory.[7] Needless to say, the experiments were carefully structured so that the subjects had no way of knowing what colour the dot would 'become' on its second presentation, so – barring precognition – they couldn't literally perceive the reported colour change, at the time they report perceiving it, any more than they could literally perceive the non-existent motion. Yet in the case of the colour change, experience seems to be, as it were, projected backward in time, putting the colour change before any data specifying it are available to the subject. Two hypotheses suggest themselves:

(H1) Experience is generated by the brain after the second dot is presented. This experience includes the colour change and temporally 'marks' it as intermediate in the dot's motion. (This is what Dennett calls the 'Stalinesque' hypothesis (see 1991b, p. 120).)

(H2) Only the experience of the two distinct and motionless dots occurs, but the brain quickly lays down the memory of motion and intermediate colour change and this memory blocks any memory of the 'actual experience'. (This is the 'Orwellian' hypothesis.)

The colour phi phenomenon is undoubtedly fascinating and puzzling, but we must focus on the tactics of verificationism here. H2 claims that there is no experience of motion or colour *change* but the memory of such is laid down so quickly that no behavioural test could threaten it. Dennett expands H2 so:

> . . . shortly after the consciousness of the first spot *and* the second spot (with no illusion of apparent motion at all), a revisionist historian of sorts, in the brain's memory-library receiving station, notices that the unvarnished history in this instance doesn't make enough sense, so he interprets the brute events, red-followed-by-green, by making up a narrative about the intervening passage. . . Since he works so fast, within a fraction of a second . . . the record you rely on, stored in the library of memory, is already contaminated. You *say* and *believe* that you saw the illusory motion and colour change, but that is really a memory hallucination . . . .

> (1991b, p. 121, original emphases)

Box 5.5 • Micro-Verificationism and New Thought Experiments

The verificationist attack on qualia examined in chapter 4 did not fare so well. Dennett modifies his verificationism somewhat here, restricting its clear application to relatively short periods of time (a few hundred milliseconds), thus doubtless increasing its plausibility. The new verificationist thought experiment, adapted to micro-verificationism, involves the colour phi phenomenon and a distinction without a difference (supposedly) in possible models of the fixation of conscious content. There are at least two possible explanations of the colour phi phenomenon. One is that there is no consciousness at all until the second dot is seen, whereupon the brain generates the conscious experience of seeing a green dot move to the right, transforming to red half-way through its trip. This is called the Stalinesque model. Or, one can suppose that there is a consciousness of the motionless green dot and then a consciousness, at the appropriate time, of the equally motionless red dot. But these states of consciousness lack sufficient access to the memory sub-system; another demon, striving for object constancy and a smooth world, writes into memory what 'must have' happened: a single object moving from left to right, changing colour half-way across. This is labelled the Orwellian model. Micro-verificationism asserts that there is simply no way to distinguish these models and hence there can be no fact of the matter; no real difference between the models. But perhaps micro-verificationism is also too strong to be plausible.

According to Dennett there is no actual phenomenology but rather a series of judgements couched in the language of experience that account for the fact that there seems to be actual phenomenology. These judgements are the product of the pandemonic construction of our personal narrative which will generally abide by strictures of relevance, plausibility and 'making enough sense'. So it seems that Dennett ends up embracing H2, more or less. But this would not be for reasons of experimental confirmation, but rather that this version of events is in accord with a theory which, Dennett hopes, has sufficient independent grounds for acceptance.[8] Thus we have the intriguing conclusion that the only 'unverifiable' part of H2 is that there is consciousness of non-moving dots which is overwritten by the historian.

Which brings us to the second interesting feature of the passage: its modesty. Given such a speedy sub-personal revisionist historian, there is no need to posit consciousness at all. *There* is the difference between H2 and Dennett's own theory – H2 allows that there may be conscious experience which is unfortunately almost instantly erased from memory (or perhaps is never permitted to enter memory). Dennett's theory does not require consciousness at all, in the sense appealed to in our quoted passage at any rate (i.e. actual experience/real phenomenology).

I confess to finding this a very disturbing feature of Dennett's account. A consequence of Dennett's view, I fear, is that all is darkness within. The darkness is masked, however, by the brain's continual production of false memories and judgements about this completely illusory 'thing' we call experience. Thus we can sharpen our unverifiable distinction considerably while remaining within Dennett's framework. The ultimate opposition, put as starkly as possible is:

(H3) There is conscious experience.

(H4) There is *no* conscious experience, but (false) memories of conscious experience are being formed continuously, a tiny fraction of a second after the external (or internal) events against which we could, and normally do, check for conscious experience.

How could you tell whether you were conscious of, say, the taste of your present cup of coffee as opposed to being utterly unconscious of it *but* having an almost instantaneously implanted false memory of that taste? This immediately suggests a further question, the answer to which is crucial for Dennett's project: don't memories (some of them at least) require a phenomenology of their own (in fact, a phenomenology very closely similar to perceptual, emotional, etc. phenomenology)? If so, Dennett's strategy is hopeless, for the unverifiable difference between H1 and H2 would then have nothing to say about the existence of actual phenomenology, but would at most bear on a novel and rather bizarre debate about what *kind* of phenomenology was present in conscious experience: does conscious perception involve a kind of perceptual phenomenology or just some kind of memory phenomenology, or even some hybrid form of experience? Little of importance to us would hang on this debate. Indeed, the friends of actual phenomenology would not balk, I think, if phenomenology turned out to be in some way a function of memory plus perceptual discrimination rather than being in some appropriate sense 'directly' or 'purely' perceptual, especially when it is considered that this kind of memory is fixed in fractions of a second, is, apparently, spectacularly vivid and functions as director of behaviour. In fact, a well known psychological study undertaken in 1960 suggests a strong link between experience and a kind of evidently phenomenologically charged memory (Sperling 1960). The experiment involved, as phase one, flashing a set of rows of letters for the very short time of 50 milliseconds, then asking the subject to recall as many of the letters as possible. Subjects could recall about 5 letters. Phase two had the subjects recall letters from just a single row but the crucial feature was that the tone which indicated which row to recall was given just *after* the display had been turned off. Subjects could generally recall three of the four letters on the target under these conditions.

This is odd. It suggests that the subjects could focus on the target row *after* it had ceased being displayed and so gather more information than they otherwise could. The natural inference is that they were reading information off some kind of visual memory 'buffer'. According to Crick (1994, pp. 68 ff.), the effectiveness of this hypothetical buffer is greatly affected by what is displayed after the letter display is switched off; a bright 'mask' degrades the buffer very quickly, a dark mask rather slowly. But it is interesting that the relevant time periods are precisely within Dennett's window of verificationist victory, and this might suggest that there is after all a memory/experience fact of the matter even at these time scales. I don't know if the phi phenomenon has been integrated with Sperling type studies or with the masking effects; results of the combined experiment would be interesting. It is also worth noting that the grip of the puzzles arising from the phi phenomenon is naturally relaxed somewhat if we think of actual phenomenology as being a product of the rapid fixing of *memory*, which is recognized to be a shifty sort of thing, prone to unconscious construction which is by its very nature invisible to the subject.

Perhaps this move requires a little more discussion, since the issue that H1 and H2 address directly is that of the temporal determinateness of experience. But if the kind of memory phenomenology we are discussing lacks temporal determinateness (while nonetheless seeming to have it) then it too will be explicable without appeal to phenomenology, in just the way that temporal judgements about colour change in the phi phenomena can be accounted for without appeal to experience. Dennett's strategy is strong enough that the destruction of the temporal determinateness of experience leads to the destruction of experience itself, and this will hold no less for any putative memory phenomenology than for perceptual phenomenology. And if memory phenomenology has real temporal determinateness then phenomenology is just the way it seems and Dennett's undercutting strategy fails.

Now, of course, there is a kind of memory which does not involve phenomenology. This is the kind of memory that underpins, for example, our knowledge of the meanings of words, the location of familiar objects and a myriad of other kinds of stored information as well. Psychologists label this *semantic* memory, but they oppose it to the richer notion of experienced memory – the ability to recall and relive an episode of our own lives. Some of these memory experiences seem, if nothing else, to be phenomenologically exceptionally vivid and powerful. This second kind of memory is termed episodic memory (interesting connections between these types of memory and consciousness are drawn in Tulving 1985). The difficulty would be to show that, despite appearances, episodic memory itself does not really involve any actual phenomenology. I don't see how Dennett's arguments against perceptual phenomenology could be adapted to this case without begging the question. Nor do I see how a separate argument for this conclusion, based on different principles, could be mounted.

However, if we grant to Dennett the dubious claim that memory itself does not involve any real phenomenology then the apparent opposition between H3 and H4 is unverifiable. By Dennett's brand of verificationism, there is no fact of the matter whether we are conscious or not. Of course, Dennett cannot come right out and actually endorse this conclusion; instead he offers a new conception of what it is to be conscious. He says 'consciousness is cerebral celebrity – nothing more and nothing less' (1993, p. 929). He means by this to define state-consciousness (see chapter 3 above for this notion). 'Those contents are conscious that persevere, that monopolize resources long enough to achieve certain typical and "symptomatic" effects – on memory, on the control of behaviour and so forth' (1993, p. 929). Again, we must heed the warning that this is not a story of how the brain generates consciousness, or experience, or phenomenology. There is *nothing* of this sort for the brain to generate (and, if we think otherwise, no hint in Dennett's account of how such generation would be accomplished). Such a view denies that consciousness is an intrinsic feature of us, or our brains. As Dennett explicitly notes, on his model 'an instantaneous flicker of consciousness is . . . an incoherent notion' (1993, p. 930). I take it that Dennett will not insist upon an absolutely literal understanding of 'instantaneous' (as meaning a time with absolutely no extension, a temporal point).

The mechanisms of cerebral celebrity actually require some real duration of time to promote and publicize any candidate content. Experience itself *seems* to take up time; there are no experiences devoid of temporal extension, so perhaps everyone could agree that there are no literally instantaneous flickers of consciousness. Dennett's claim has real content when we specify the normal length of time required for a state to achieve cerebral celebrity. Call this time τ, though presumably τ is relative to the cognitive mechanisms available to the system and is constrained by the intrinsic speed of the fundamental constituents of these mechanisms.[9] Then we can make the claim that it is impossible for any system (of the appropriate sort) to be conscious if it exists for a time less than τ. The time that Dennett mentions as the zone of indeterminacy with regard to conscious experience is several hundred milliseconds (see, e.g. 1993, p. 930 n.). Obviously then, τ is greater than several hundred milliseconds. Let us say that it is 501 milliseconds or a touch more than half a second. So no system (with a brain like ours) could exist for half a second or less and be conscious. This is surely the place for an extravagant philosophical thought experiment: imagine God creating a universe atom for atom and law for law identical to our universe right now, but God permits this universe to exist for but half a second. Since this universe exists for a time less than τ the creatures on the 'Earth' of this short-lived universe are entirely, one and all, unconscious, even the ones that are attentively watching the sweep second hands of their wristwatches advance through half a second. This strikes me as entirely implausible.

Dennett claims that at micro-time scales the presumption that experience is temporally determinate breaks down, an idea which runs counter to the way conscious experience 'appears' to us. But another response, prompted by reflection on the opposition between H3 and H4 as well as that between H1 and H2, is that at micro-time scales the distinction between conscious experience and memory, or rapid memory formation, breaks down. Since both memory and, say, perceptual experience, at least appear to have a phenomenology, this response need not threaten our ordinary views about conscious experience, although it does of course create a certain healthy tension in our understanding of ourselves. We had, perhaps, thought it was always easy to distinguish the phenomenology of memory from that of perceptual experience (though data like Sperling's mentioned above already called this into question).

In any event, if the foregoing is a fair extension of Dennett's strategy and if the previous chapter showed that we need not concede that the idea of qualitative experience is incoherent, then Dennett's strategy is revealed to be, at bottom, a brand of philosophical *scepticism* (in this case about conscious experience) which, while always deserving respect and consideration, could not have enough force to overturn what universally seems to be the case. Dennett's sceptical view about consciousness is a peculiar inverse of Santayana's solipsism of the present moment: the view that all that is certain is the present moment of conscious experience (see Santayana 1923, chapter 1). For all that can be known, according to this view, the world is nothing but *this* momentary state of consciousness without past, future or external world, of temporal duration equal to what used to be called the specious present. It is a dizzying and philosophically liberating experience to realize that the apparent temporal 'depth' of experience, no more than the appearance of external objects, does not all by itself directly refute Santayana's hyperbolic hypothesis. Dennett's sceptical position reverses Santayana's: the unknowable component of the world is the *present* episode of consciousness, conceived of as 'actual phenomenology'. Although it is, perhaps, also a philosophically liberating experience – an ecstasy of eliminativism – to recognize the potential coherence of Dennett's view, the moment of insight is no more convincing than the appreciation of the force of any sceptical hypothesis. Dennett's mode of argument, once we draw it out, shares a paradoxical feature with other sceptical arguments: it is too powerful to be convincing.

Box 5.6 • Verificationism and Scepticism

There is a curious relation between verificationism and scepticism. Sceptics shock us with their denial that we can really *know* various familiar beliefs of which we thought we had a perfectly secure grasp, such as the existence of the 'external' world, the reality of the past, the existence of minds other than our own, etc. Strangely, if we follow verificationism to its limit we end up with essentially sceptical conclusions. This happens when verificationism leads to the denial that there is any fact of the matter about something which commonsense is happy to believe must be reasonably determinate. Dennett's micro-verificationism ultimately leads to the verificationist conclusion that there is no fact of the matter whether one is conscious or not, since a non-conscious, continuous, false memory implantation could yield the belief that one was conscious, and there would be no way to tell which of these 'hypotheses' was true (since the memory implantation occurs at time scales appropriate to micro-verificationism). This is equivalent to the sceptical hypothesis that you can't *know* whether you are conscious or not (even granting there is a fact of the matter), since this is a claim about the (very) recent past and there could be a continual false memory implantation of the belief that you are conscious. Though as intriguing and puzzling as all sceptical assaults on common knowledge, Dennett's verificationist version of the no-consciousness position is no more acceptable than the sceptical one.

I have just attempted what might be called a 'methodological *reductio*' of Dennett's position, but I want to conclude this chapter with consideration of an additional worry spawned by Dennett's verificationism about conscious experience. It can be approached by considering the restricted generality of my own *reductio*. I cannot claim that every verificationist argument degenerates into a sceptical one once we properly appreciate the strengths of realism. I maintain at most that in cases where the verificationist attack is directed at what appears to be evidently true, a sceptical attack will lurk behind the mask of verificationism. On the other side, the boundaries of legitimate verificationist argument must be drawn by Dennett. The difficulties this task presents can be easily illustrated by several examples. Notice that Dennett himself does not seem always to abide by his own verificationism. Consider his treatment of the classic example of unconscious action: driving a long distance without, apparently, being aware (at least consciously aware) of the road. What he says is this:

Many theorists . . . have cherished this as a favourite case of 'unconscious perception and intelligent action'. But were you *really* unconscious of all those passing cars, stop lights, bends in the road at the time? You were paying attention to other things, but surely *if you had been probed* about what you had *just* seen at various moments on the drive, you would have had at least some sketchy details to report. The 'unconscious driving' phenomenon is better seen as a case of rolling consciousness with swift memory loss.

(1991b, p. 137, original emphases)

According to Dennett's usage, a *probe* is anything which will elicit a report of one's current experience. But consider what Dennett says on the page before: 'what we are conscious of within any particular time duration is not defined independently of the probes we use to precipitate a narrative about that period' (1991b, p. 136). This does not seem compatible with Dennett's appeal to probes in his description of 'unconscious driving'. Could it be that what we are conscious of at a time is counterfactually defined as what we would report had we been probed at that time? I think not, since such probes can direct attention, hence consciousness, to contrary states. For example, while driving around a curve I could probe you by asking 'do you see the bend in the road?'. You will reply 'yes'. If I instead probed you by saying 'do you remember the eclipse in Hawaii?', you would also reply 'yes', but no one would want to say that you were therefore 'in some sense' conscious of eclipse-memories during the actual drive. How could we tell the difference between a probe making you conscious of something versus telling us what you were already conscious of? One could reply that such a probe will elicit memory reports covering the last few minutes of the drive (but not too many minutes back or else you weren't driving, as we say, unconsciously). But we have just seen that there are verificationist problems about such memories that undercut this reply.

The very notion of a 'rolling consciousness with swift memory loss' that is supported by consideration of counterfactual probing seems fundamentally at odds with Dennett's outlook. Another of Dennett's beautiful examples is the 'cutaneous rabbit', a psychological experiment in which a subject's arm is tapped a certain number of times at a few locations along the arm (discussed by Dennett 1991b, pp. 142–3). The taps are delivered at intervals of between 50 and 200 milliseconds. If a subject is tapped five times at the wrist, twice at the elbow then three more times on the upper arm, the report will be of a *regularly spaced* set of taps moving up the arm. This raises problems akin to those in the colour phi phenomenon, but we are interested here in what Dennett says about *probing* in this example. He describes how his model deals with the cutaneous rabbit so:

The shift in space (along the arm) is discriminated over time by the brain. The number of taps is also discriminated. Although in physical reality the taps were clustered at particular locations, the simplifying assumption is that they were distributed regularly across the space-time extent of the experience. The brain relaxes into this parsimonious but mistaken interpretation *after* the taps are registered, of course, and this has the effect of wiping out earlier (partial) interpretations of the taps, but the side effects of those interpretations may live on. For instance, suppose we asked the subjects to press a button whenever they felt two taps on the wrist; it would not be surprising if they could initiate the button-press before the forearm taps had been discriminated that caused them to misinterpret the second tap as displaced up the arm . . . . We must be particularly careful not to make the mistake of supposing that the content we would derive from such an early probe constituted the 'first chapter' of the content we would find in the narrative if we were to probe the same phenomenon later.

(1991b, p. 143, original emphases)

Why not say the same about the case of 'unconscious driving'? True, the time scales are different, but how does, or why would, that affect the problems of verification that Dennett raises about probing? If we accept the story according to which counter-factual probes fix experience, why not say that subjects were conscious of the taps as being on the wrist and this was swiftly overwritten by memory (rolling consciousness of tap location rapidly followed by memory overwrite)? This would be to side with the Orwellian, which, we know, is to sin against verificationism. I don't see any difference that makes a difference between this case and the driving case.

Finally, consider the philosophical problem of dreaming, a topic which is noticeable by the remarkably scant attention it receives in *Consciousness Explained*. In 'Are Dreams Experiences?' (1976), Dennett entertained the suggestion that dreams, as conscious experiences, do not exist, but rather that the brain generates certain false memories of experiences upon awakening.[10] This sounds familiar, and indeed the paper does prefigure much of Dennett's elaborated view. We can see now that *all* experience is to be analysed in essentially the same way that the early Dennett treated dream experience, which is, I think, implausible. Dreams raise other problems having to do with verifiability as well. We are told that most dreams are forgotten and this seems likely to be true, and certainly likely the kind of claim that *can be* either true or false. Yet how could we ever verify that most dreams are forgotten? Here is Dennett: 'Opposition to this operationalism [= verificationism] appeals, as usual, to possible facts beyond the ken of the operationalist's test, but now the operationalist is the subject himself, so the objection backfires: "Just because you can't tell, by your preferred ways, whether or not you were conscious of x, that doesn't mean you weren't. Maybe you were conscious of x but just can't find any evidence for it!" Does

129

anyone, on reflection, really want to say that?' (1991b, pp. 132–33). Yes, I would want to say it about forgotten dreams. Dennett goes on to finish the quoted passage thus: 'Putative facts about consciousness that swim out of reach of both "outside" and "inside" observers are strange facts indeed'. This sounds like something different: as if something could be conscious without us being aware of it at the time we were conscious of it. Forgotten dreams are not like that, yet they surely meet the condition that no test could reveal whether we had had one or not.

One might appeal to brain science here and claim that whether one was dreaming or not could be verified by EEG records of the so-called REM sleep associated with dreaming. But not everyone awakened from REM sleep reports a dream, and some wakened from non-REM sleep *do* report dreams. Still, it would be *evidence*. But no, that would be to fall back into the Cartesian materialism anathema to Dennett: the idea that certain specifiable states of the brain (or of a centre in the brain) could reveal one's current and true state of consciousness. Dennett cannot appeal to the findings of sleep researchers to remove forgotten dreams from the realm of the unverifiable. Thus it seems that there is no fact of the matter whether we ever forget dreams before reporting them (even to ourselves) at least once.

This is hard to swallow, for two reasons. On Dennett's view, dreams are not conscious in the sense that they present no actual phenomenology. But that is simply because there is no actual phenomenology. Worse, forgotten dreams aren't even conscious in Dennett's replacement sense which makes conscious experience the intentional object of judgements about experience. On the face of it, it seems intelligible to suppose there could be episodes of 'narrative spinning' carried on by myself in complete isolation with no associated overt behaviour. Such an episode could be the Dennettian stand-in for dream experience (or any other episode of 'private' conscious experience). Unfortunately, there is no way to verify that such episodes occur. If we look to the brain itself, we are appealing to the view Dennett dismisses as Cartesian materialism. Since such episodes are cut off from behavioural control (we are, in fact, more or less paralysed during our dreams) they fail Dennett's crucial condition for admittance into the charmed circle of consciousness: 'What matters is the way those contents get utilized by or incorporated into the processes of ongoing control of behaviour . . .' (1991b, p. 166).

One could look more closely still into these and other matters, but I hope it is clear that Dennett's verificationist strategy can be revealed as far too radical to be successful. Put bluntly, what emerges is an almost classical kind of *sceptical* attack on the notion of conscious experience. Dennett's attack carries no more conviction than the various species of classical scepticism. The cognitive pandemonium model is beautifully articulated in *Consciousness Explained*; it is fascinating, plausible and able to explain many puzzles locked within the psychology experimenter's treasure chest. However, the rejection of conscious experience does not follow from this model. It is a rather extravagant appendage mostly motivated, I suspect, by the common desire to fit consciousness into a pre-existing theoretical mold (intentional psychology in Dennett's case) and a fear of the generation problem that will not permit the admission that we just don't have a clue how the brain produces or supports actual phenomenology.

Box 5.7 • Summary

Dennett's cognitive pandemonium model of the brain and mind is intriguing and quite possibly correct. Such a model dovetails with connectionist views of cognitive function as well as the results of many psychological experiments on perception and cognition, and it would fit well with a representationalist theory of consciousness. The model also nicely allows for reasonable extensions, such as a rich influence of culture and learning upon the structure of consciousness. But as it stands, the generation problem would remain unsolved: exactly how and why, we should ask, does the appropriate pandemonic architecture generate real phenomenology? In the attempt to sidestep this issue and dissolve the generation problem, Dennett resorts to micro-verificationism, which persuades him to maintain that there just isn't any real phenomenology to be generated. But the micro-verificationism required for this conclusion is too strong to be plausible; the existence of 'real-time' consciousness too clear to be denied.

6

REPRESENTATIONAL THEORIES
OF CONSCIOUSNESS,
PART I

Box 6.1 • Preview

Traditionally, the contents of the mind, and so also the contents of consciousness, have been divided into two broad categories: the intentional mental states and the non-intentional phenomenal mental states. Intentionality is the property of 'being about' something or having an object. Franz Brentano hypothesized that *all and only* mental states have intentionality (he thus claimed that any non-mental state that appears to carry content must do so in virtue of some mental state carrying that content, which leads to the distinction between *original* and *derived* intentionality). Approximately, we can identify intentional states with representational states since, for example, the sense in which my belief that snow is white is *about* snow seems very close to the sense in which my belief *represents* snow. By contrast, the non-intentional states have, in themselves, no representational content, they are purely phenomenal; this is what *qualia* are usually taken to be. The representational theory of consciousness breaks with tradition and sides with Brentano; it asserts that all states of consciousness are representational. It thus immediately faces the problem that many states have been thought to be rather obviously non-representational (states such as pains, moods, emotions, tickles, twinges, etc.). Should it pass this obstacle, as I think it can, it still needs to develop a distinctive representational account of qualitative consciousness. This it can do in a most interesting way.

We have seen that there is currently a desire amongst philosophers to deal with consciousness through some kind of appeal to the notion of representation or intentionality (an appeal that can ultimately be traced all the way back to Descartes). The HOT theory wants to claim that consciousness is somehow constituted out of *belief* states (of the appropriate sort); Dennett wishes to replace qualitative conscious-ness with *judgements* about an ultimately fictitious phenomenality. Even the vector-space identity theory wants to link consciousness to the neural properties of the brain systems that represent the world and the self (it is, after all, a theory of vector *coding*). As we have seen, all these approaches face severe difficulties getting to grips with consciousness and, in particular, have a hard time dealing with the generation problem. Yet another approach is possible; one that makes a more direct appeal to the notion of representation. Crudely speaking, one might attempt to identify consciousness not with the neural substrate of representation but with representation itself. On this view, conscious states are not conscious because of some mysterious intrinsic causal power of the brain or via a special relation to other representational states; they are conscious because they are themselves representational states. Qualitative consciousness is quite real on this view and does not stand in need of any judgements *about it* in order to exist, or to appear to exist.

Of course, one cannot simply identify consciousness with representation since there are obviously many representations that are not conscious, e.g. the words on this page. So we need a theory which specifies just which representations are conscious, and we would also like this theory to tell us *how* these distinguished representations (or types of representations) become conscious and *why* it is that just this class of representations become conscious (we see our old friend the generation problem in the latter questions). There are various ways to develop such a theory but I think a sharp focus on a particularly well worked out version is the best way to explicate the theory and reveal its strengths and weaknesses (certain especially salient 'choice points' in the construction of a representational theory of consciousness can be highlighted on the way). In *Naturalizing the Mind* (1995), Fred Dretske outlines and vigorously defends a representational theory of consciousness as part of a still larger project of presenting a thoroughly representational theory of mind; it is upon this version of the theory I wish mainly to concentrate. Another lengthy development of a representational theory of consciousness is in Michael Tye (1995).[1] Tye's treatment will occasionally be contrasted with Dretske's although, despite being independently arrived at, they are in very many respects extremely similar. This is interesting since it suggests that there are some fairly strict constraints upon the development of a representational theory of consciousness which is, I think, a virtue of the view. It is also worth pointing out that arguably the first representational theorist of consciousness was Descartes himself (see chapter 1 above), who maintained that every element of consciousness was or involved an *idea* and that every idea was a representation.

What is a representational theory of consciousness? In the first place, it is a theory that dispenses with the widespread philosophical conviction that the mind's contents divide into two natural categories: the intentional states, or the states that are explicitly representational (the paradigm examples of which are such mental states as beliefs, desires, intentions, hopes, etc.) and the supposedly more purely mental, non-intentional 'feelings', which term is meant to encompass perceptual experience (conceived of as devoid of representational content), pains and other bodily sensations, moods, emotional tone, etc. According to the representational theory, everything in the latter category is to be somehow included within the first. This will seem implausible to many, at least with regard to some features of conscious experience. Yet it is not odd to view perceptual experience as inherently representational for surely perception does present a way the (or *a*) world could be, even in cases of illusion, dreams or outright hallucination. Even the vaguest, least informative perceptual experience, such as the coloured, swirling blobs experienced when – with closed eyes – one looks towards the sun presents coloured 'objects' as arranged and moving about in a spatial configuration centred on oneself (this example, originally, if unsuccessfully, presented as an objection to the representational theory by Christopher Peacocke, is discussed by Tye 1995, pp. 158–9). Nor is it difficult to regard bodily sensations, pains, twinges and the like as representations of one's body and its current condition. Such sensations always have a more or less well specified bodily location, which is, as phantom limb phenomena demonstrate, an *intentional* location, and obviously at least carry information about the state of the body.

To my mind, the claims of the representational theory of consciousness are in fact phenomenologically verified. I irresistibly regard perceptual experience as informing me about the local environment, I regard my 'inner experiences' as similarly informing me about my body and, of course, my conscious thoughts are always *about* something. Emotions normally have an intentional object but even objectless emotions such as diffuse depression or elation can be regarded as representational 'colourings' of our view of the world. No doubt this will remain controversial for many,[2] but if one can force oneself to swallow the universal representational character of all conscious experience, there are great benefits to be gained from this approach to consciousness. Some of these benefits are abstract or theoretical. If a representational theory is the right way to go then we can help ourselves to the vast and ingenious efforts which philosophers have put into understanding representation (more broadly, intentionality) itself. Such theoretical economy and unification is always welcome. On the other side of this coin, the representational view allows us to use what we know about consciousness in the development of our theories of representation, which certainly remains a deeply puzzling topic.

These theoretical benefits are to some extent shared with the HOT approach and Dennett's eliminativism,[3] but the representational theory has more particular benefits as well. Rather than trying to show a hidden incoherence in our talk about the phenomenal character of experience or claiming that when we are talking about experience we are really talking about a certain rather exotic class of beliefs, the representational theory can go a long way towards accepting, underpinning and explaining this talk. The minimal analysis of qualia given above (chapter 4) is more or less supported by the representational theory (whether *more*, or *less*, depends upon which version of the theory is under consideration). The representational theory can agree that qualia are ineffable in the sense that to know what it is like to have a certain sort of experience one must actually have that sort of experience. It can allow that we have a special sort of access to our own experience, which is quite distinct from anyone else's access to our experience (but it does not claim that our self access is 'incorrigible').[4] In fact, the representational theory allows us to formulate what is, I think, the most plausible theory of introspective knowledge yet devised. Furthermore, the representational theory allows and can account for the immediacy of our self access. The most vexed question is about the intrinsic nature of qualitative consciousness. Here the choice of one's underlying theory of representation forces the representational theory either towards or away from accepting intrinsicness.

Some caution is in order at this point. It has seemed to some that a representational theory of consciousness is forced to deny outright the existence of qualia. But the most the representationalist needs to deny is that there exist non-intentional or non-representational properties of mental states to which we have immediate access in consciousness. This hardly prevents the representationalist from talking about experience in completely non-eliminativist ways. In fact, as we shall see shortly, the representationalist has something of an argument for *identifying* the qualitative nature of experience with the perceptible properties of objects *as* represented. The representationalist view retains a kind of immediacy, special first-person access, privacy and, I will argue below, had better accept a version of intrinsicality as well. So if there is an issue here it comes down to the question of whether there is any need to posit non-intentional or non-representational features of experience to which we have immediate access in consciousness. The caveat of the last phrase is crucial, for whatever states of consciousness are at bottom they will of course have many non-representational features (just as tokens of words have non-semantic features, such as the kind of ink of which they are composed; this is Descartes's distinction between objective and formal reality again). Perhaps the most vigorous and persistent defender of *this* sort of qualia – rather tendentiously labelled, by Lycan (1996), 'strange qualia' – is Ned Block (see 1978, 1990, 1995). So let's call these hypothetical non-representational features of mental states to which we have consciousness access *Block-qualia* or *B-qualia* for short.

The B-qualia defender's basic line of argument against the representational theory is to imagine a case in which the representational properties of two mental states are identical but the experienced quality of the states are distinct, so that it would be impossible to identify the experienced quality with a representational feature of the state. The classic example of such an argument is the inverted spectrum thought experiment, in which we imagine two people who have their colour vision 'reversed' relative to each other, so that where one sees red the other sees blue and so forth throughout the colour spectrum (the one sees the 'colour negative' of the other's experience so to speak). However, the representationalist has, in principle, no difficulty dealing with and indeed accepting the possibility of the usual sort of inverted spectrum thought experiments (see Dretske 1995, p. 72 for example). Consider the case of 'Nida-Rümelin inversion' mentioned above in chapter 4. Recall that Nida-Rümelin 1996 reports that a rare genetic condition of 'double' colour blindness could result in the mutual replacement of the 'green' and 'red' cones in the retina in a tiny fraction of the male population. Such males therefore *might* suffer a sort of colour inversion. Since – arguably – the representational function of the colour receptors persists despite the retinal switch-over, the representational theory of consciousness predicts that, as described, this would indeed be a case of at least partial spectrum inversion. To get more of a flavour for how these thought-experiment arguments go, here's another example, this time from Block himself: 'imagine genetically identical twins one of whom has had color inverting lenses placed in its eyes at birth' (1990, p. 60). Block notes that one reply to the apparently pro B-qualia consequences of this thought experiment, which he ascribes to Gilbert Harman, is that we have here a case of the multiple realizability of colour experiences. That is, both twins see *red* when they look at ripe tomatoes. But as noted above, the representationalist can also say that, when gazing upon ripe tomatoes, the twin fitted with the inverting lenses gets into a state whose function is to represent *green*. So that twin still sees *green*, though he may well think that he is experiencing colours the same way that everyone else is and be behaviourally indistinguishable from his twin. I prefer the second line of reply, and have some worries that pursuing the multiple realizability reply would lead to very dangerous territory. But, in principle, either sort of reply is adequate to repulse the B-qualia defender's attack.

Box 6.2 • Spectrum Inversion Thought Experiments

Imagine that your friends see colours systematically different than you do. If you could see the world the way they do, it would look like a colour negative. But it is not so easy to spot the victims of spectral inversion for they have been trained to call tomatoes 'red' and grass 'green' no matter how such things might look to them (this is an old idea, going back at least to John Locke). Worse, their mental state of 'phenomenal red' does the same job within their cognitive system as your state of 'phenomenal green' does within your system. So functionalism seems to be false. It can also seem that their state of 'phenomenal red' and your state of 'phenomenal green' both represent the colour *green* and so, on a purely representational account of consciousness, you and they are in the *same* state of consciousness. This problem is highlighted by the Inverted Earth thought experiment. Inverted Earth has a double switch: everything has, compared to Earth, the inverted colour of its Earth counterpart but everyone speaks a language in which the colour vocabularies have also been inverted. So although the sky looks and is *yellow* on Inverted Earth, everyone calls it 'blue'. Now, imagine a normal Earthling secretly taken to Inverted Earth, but wearing special ocular implants that invert all colours! Such an Earthling will see the yellow sky as blue, and call it blue, and so fall into line with the inhabitants of Inverted Earth. But peculiar problems arise for the representational theory of consciousness as our Earthling 'semantically' adapts to his new home.

A more powerful argument is needed to assail the representationalist, and Block attempts to provide one in his paper 'Inverted Earth' (1990). This bizarre place has the convenient dual properties of switched colours and switched colour vocabularies. As Block describes it, 'everything [on Inverted Earth] has the complementary color of the color on Earth . . . [and] the vocabulary of the residents of Inverted Earth is

also inverted: If you ask what color the (yellow) sky is, they (truthfully) say "Blue!"'
(1990, p. 62). Next imagine that unbeknownst to you, you are taken to Inverted
Earth, after your body has somehow been given its complementary colour and with
your eyes fitted with colour inverting lenses. So when you arrive everything looks
normal to you and you look normal to *them*. You can apparently talk to the inhabitants about colours with no difficulty. But, says Block, after a while your word 'blue'
comes to mean 'yellow' as it falls into line with the local meaning. Let's grant that.
But of course (says Block) the sky still looks *blue* to you. The obvious reply is, once
again, that your inner state still has, and always will have, the job of representing *blue*
and so, yes indeed, the sky does still look blue to you (see Lycan 1996, pp. 113–14;
Tye 1995, p. 207). But then what colour does the sky look to the inhabitants of
Inverted Earth? It looks *yellow* of course! They are in the internal state that you get
in when you are seeing yellow things and, we may suppose, that state's job is to
represent *yellow*. If they put on the inverting lenses then the (yellow) sky would look
blue to them; you *are* wearing inverting lenses so it is hardly a surprise that the sky
looks blue to you. Now, there is something wrong with you, so to speak: you don't
notice that your colour *words* have (gradually?) changed their meanings over the years
you have spent on Inverted Earth. This has a few odd consequences in special
circumstances. For example, if you say to someone 'the sky looks the same to me
today as it did on December 24th, 20__' (that being the date you woke up on Inverted
Earth) you speak the truth, whereas if you say 'the sky looked *blue* to me on December 24th, 20__' you utter a falsehood, because when you make the utterance you are
no longer speaking ordinary Earth English (though false, your utterance will pass for
true amongst your acquaintances unless some happen to know of your peculiar travel
history). If we grant that your words change meaning over the years then, after the
semantic switch, the sky never looks *blue* to you again, it looks *yellow* (here using the
Inverted Earth language's words 'blue' and 'yellow'). However, this is merely odd
and says nothing against the representational theory. In fact, the oddity can easily be
duplicated on ordinary Earth; suppose that, unbeknownst to you, two of your friends
– John Smith and Bill Jones – legally switch their names (don't ask why they wanted
to). Now if you say of the person who used to be named 'John Smith', '*he* owes me
ten dollars', you speak the truth, but if you say 'John Smith owes me ten dollars' you
do not.

The Inverted Earth argument could, perhaps, be defended against this sort of reply
(see Lycan's discussion for example, 1996, pp. 113 ff. though Lycan agrees that in the
end the argument fails to persuade). Valuable insights could emerge from its defence.
But I think Block's pro B-qualia stance is undercut by a more fundamental methodological problem. Though Block wants to defend the existence of B-qualia, he also
accepts – as I believe everyone must – the existence of 'intentional consciousness' or
the awareness of intentional content (see Block 1995). Thus the B-qualia theorist has
to add an account of intentional consciousness. But since the representational theory

of consciousness does a good job of handling the issue of qualia within the confines of a theory whose primary aim is to tackle the awareness of intentional content, parsimony favours the representational approach. At the very least the burden of proof is on the defender of B-qualia, and Block's arguments, being subject to plausible replies, do not shoulder this burden.

Block's recognition of the existence of conscious intentionality makes his burden heavier. Not only must Block explain the nature of conscious intentionality (everyone has to explain that), he must tell us what the relation is between the consciousness of B-qualia (what he calls 'phenomenal consciousness') and the consciousness of representational content. It is very unclear what this relationship might be. It cannot be that intentional consciousness is constituted out of phenomenal consciousness. When I am aware of something *as*, for example, a computer, I am not simply aware of a certain set of shapes, colours, expectations. When I talk to myself I am not aware simply of the 'inner sounds' of the words. There is no *reduction* of conscious intentionality to phenomenal consciousness.[5] Could one then suppose that we are primarily or in the first instance aware of B-qualia and from that awareness we infer the representational qualities of our mental states? The product of this inference would be consciousness of content. Philosophers will recognize this story as the 'myth of the given'; I leave to Block the task of reviving this justly extinguished doctrine if he wishes. So it seems that the consciousness of B-qualia and conscious intentionality have to be given independent accounts. This makes the awareness of B-qualia still more mysterious.[6]

It would seem rather obvious that the – at least *a* – role of consciousness is to inform us about the world and ourselves. B-qualia consciousness would seem to be of no use for this. Awareness of states which represented the properties of the world and ourselves would, on the other hand, be eminently suited, exactly designed, for informing us about those properties. We need the latter, but the former are useless. Once again, the idea of B-qualia seems to sin against parsimony. And so many of our states of phenomenal consciousness so obviously do inform us about the world (or purport to) that the general representationalist thesis seems to deserve our support in the face of what is at best a very small zone of experience where intuition (but no unassailable arguments) might lead us to accept B-qualia.

In many ways the representational theory respects our intuitions about conscious experience and this must surely count in its favour. The representational theory also faces many difficulties, but before turning to these I want to expand upon its virtues. Curiously, there is an extremely simple yet powerful argument in its favour. It begins with a sub-argument (which I'll label 'the sub-argument'):

(P1)   The qualitative nature of conscious experience consists in the properties that things appear to have (or, qualia = appearances).

(P2)   Sometimes conscious experience is veridical (or, sometimes things are the way they appear).

(C1)   So, sometimes the qualitative nature of conscious experience consists in the properties that things actually have. (This argument is from Dretske 1995, pp. 83–4.)

We experience objects as having a variety of perceptible properties and the qualitative nature of our experience, and – very significantly – our introspective awareness of our experience, is exhausted by these properties (though of course the field of experience is complex and our own bodies are usually one of the experienced objects). What is the relation between us and these properties? Abstractly speaking, there seem to be only three possibilities. The first is that we, in our experience, *exemplify* these properties. The second is that we, in our experience, *exemplify* some *other* properties that bear a special relation to the perceptible properties. The third is that we, in our experience, *represent* these properties, or represent objects as having these properties. Although the first possibility has a long and distinguished tradition going all the way back to Aristotle and Plato, in light of our current knowledge about the brain and a constant background desire to naturalize the mind (i.e. show how the mind is no more than one more part, albeit a very special part, of the natural, physical order) it is not a very plausible model of consciousness. Experiences are *not* themselves red, or audible, tasty or smelly. At least, if we want to insist that experiences are, say, really coloured then they are certainly not denizens of the natural world (no little red Canadian flags – or rectangular, red and white images of the flag – appear in my brain, or anywhere else in the natural world, when I imagine the flag).

The second possibility is, I think, merely a technical or philosophically contrived one. The theory which exploits it is the so-called adverbial theory of experience, in which the claim to be experiencing, say, a red afterimage is rewritten as the claim to be experiencing *redly*. The adverbial theory, in effect, introduces a set of phenomenal properties of experiences (or 'experience events') which (by wonderful good fortune?) perfectly correlate with the perceptible qualities of objects. There are great difficulties with such an approach. One technical example from Tye (1995, p. 78): The two claims 'I see four pink afterimages' and 'I sense quadruply pinkly' are clearly not equivalent (how could the special predicate in 'sensing quadruply pinkly' underwrite the entailment to the equally special 'sensing triply pinkly'?). More important, once one sees the representationalist option, the adverbial theory seems rather *ad hoc*. The perfect dovetailing between these entirely contrived adverbs of experience and perceptible qualities is suspicious. So one is tempted to read a phrase like 'sensing quadruply pinkly' as something like 'sensing *as of* four pink objects', but this just *is* a version of the representational theory. And, unless one does read the adverbial theory in something like this way, it is hard to see how the adverbialist could render the sub-argument given above so as to capture what is undeniably correct in it.[7]

We are then left with the representational theory which requires neither peculiar phenomenal objects (e.g. sense-data) nor peculiar phenomenal activities possessed of their own set of peculiar properties. Let's consider, more closely now, how the representational theory handles some of the traditional features of qualitative conscious experience. Begin with introspective access to our own mental states. Dretske shows (1995, chapter 2) that the representational theory can provide an entirely plausible account of introspection in which an acceptable form of privileged access is coupled with a denial of any incorrigibility. Introspective knowledge is, of course, a kind of *knowledge* and must therefore require a set of concepts in which that knowledge can be expressed. What concepts? Roughly speaking, the family of concepts which makes up the general notions of sensory experience and mental representation. Once we have these concepts we can apply them to our experience and thus come to know *that* we are experiencing, and to know *how* we are experiencing. Thus, one has to know about the *mind* before one can introspect. This suggests that, for example, animals and young children, who lack any or a sufficiently rich conceptual characterization of the mind, cannot introspect even though they can have conscious experiences. Just when children can begin to introspect thus depends upon their conceptual development, and in particular it depends upon when they acquire some understanding of the nature of the mind, especially its representational nature. There is evidence that at least a basic form of such an understanding is acquired around the age of three to four years (see Perner 1993, Gopnik 1993). Admittedly, this view of introspection is contrary to a powerful philosophical tradition perfectly exemplified by the passage in Locke where 'consciousness' is defined: '[c]onsciousness is the perception of what passes in a man's own mind' (1690/1975, bk. 2, chapter 1, p. 115). But surely this is at best an attempt at a definition of self-consciousness or introspective consciousness rather than consciousness itself. Locke's definition would seem to imply that animals, for example, are not only incapable of introspection but are utterly unconscious, which is extremely implausible (but see Carruthers 1989 for a modern defence of a version of this Cartesian doctrine). It is, however, reasonably plausible to assert that animals are entirely unselfconscious. The representational theory accounts for this distinction very nicely.

This account of introspection also entails that given that one has the requisite conceptual resources, conscious experience alone is sufficient to ground introspective knowledge. This is a kind of privileged access, for *I*, but not *you*, am the one undergoing the experiences which engage these conceptual resources. Notice how this contrasts with the 'self-interpretation' view of introspection, defended, for example, by Ryle (1949), Dennett (here and there, especially 1987) and Lyons (1986). The Rylean view is distinguished by the claim that we know our own minds in just the same way we know the minds of others, via, first, the observation of our own actions and utterances and then, second, the creation of an intentional account or interpretation of these. While such a proposal has the advantage of denying any 'magical' kind of self access, it suffers from the rather grave disadvantage of applying very poorly, if at all, to the majority of our claims to self knowledge. Dretske's view shares this advantage but quite naturally avoids the disadvantages. Since experience is of the world *as* represented thus-and-so, and since representations can be in error, my introspective knowledge is not dependent upon the world being as I take it to be and remains valid even in the face of gross external error.[8] While Dretske's account is limited insofar as he explicitly deals only with introspective knowledge of perceptual experiences I believe that the theory can be extended to a complete picture of introspection.[9]

Perhaps it is also worth mentioning that this view of introspection connects to a number of problem areas in the study of the mind. If it is correct then the ability to introspect is coupled to the possession of a theory of mind. Some speculation about the characteristics which distinguish modern *Homo Sapiens* from our Neanderthal cousins suggests that the ability to introspect, to be self-conscious, was one of the crucial differences leading to our success (see Shreeve 1995). Given that we could somehow verify such speculation, we could give an approximate upper limit on the *date* of the creation of our folk theory of the mind, to roughly 50,000 years ago! Conceivably, it is much older, if current studies on the abilities of certain animals to engage in intentional deception support the view that such deception involves the ascription of intentional mental states to others (see Humphrey 1984). Since such animals do not seem to be capable of introspection, this would show that the theory of mind really did develop as a field of concepts which are properly applied to *others* with the self-ascriptive function arriving perhaps much later (maybe, again, about 50,000 years ago). Thus we could go some way towards verifying (at least parts of) Sellars's (1956) famous 'myth of Jones'.[10]

On a considerably less speculative note, there is a connection between this account of introspection and a lively current debate amongst philosophers, psychologists and cognitive scientists about which of the so-called theory-theory or the simulation theory gives a better account of our knowledge of the mental states of other people (see Goldman 1989, Heal 1986). Roughly speaking, the theory-theory asserts that we ascribe mental states to others by the application of a theory of mind (a folk theory, that is) to their observed behaviour and utterances. So long as we don't put too much weight on the term 'theory', a lot of philosophers would seem to line up on the side of the theory-theory. For example, Gilbert Ryle is famous for a view of mental states in which 'our knowledge of other people and ourselves depends upon our noticing how they and we behave' (Ryle 1949, p. 181). Obviously, the Rylean view is a version of the theory-theory insofar as it admits and requires the existence of an articulable set of principles by which we attribute mental states to others and ourselves on the basis of behaviour. The distinct versions of interpretation theory put forth by various philosophers are also versions of the theory-theory, in which the primary principles of the theory are those that maximize the rationality of our fellows' behaviour and mental life. Opposed to the theory-theory, the simulation theory asserts that we ascribe mental states to others by a process of internally modelling the situations other people find themselves in, 'reading off' the mental states *we* would be in if we were in those situations and ascribing these states to others.

This is not the place to attempt a survey of this debate. But I will note that the view of introspection offered by the representational theory could usefully add to the resources of the theory-theory, which seems to be somewhat mired in a basically, though more 'scientized', Rylean picture of self-attribution (see for example Gopnik 1993). More important, if the view of introspection under discussion here is correct then the status of the simulation theory becomes rather complex and somewhat precarious. The simulation theorists rely upon the fact that we know what our own mental states would be if we were in the simulated situations we take others to actually be in. But we know our own mental states because we know a theory of the mind. So the simulation theory presupposes the use of a theory of the mind after all. However, the simulation theory could still be correct if in our attributions of mental states to others we needed to go through the self attribution process in an imaginary situation. This is not particularly implausible. In fact, since in the representational theory's view of introspection, self attribution does not stem from self observation of our own behaviour or utterances but rather springs from a conceptual appreciation of certain 'elementary acts' of the conscious mind, putting ourselves in an imaginary situation could give us a new set of such elementary acts to use in our simulated self attribution. The situation is murky, since, after all, even Ryle could allow that we imagine how we *would* behave in imagined situations as we try to figure out the mental states of those who are really in such situations. The point to stress here is simply that, contrary to the professions of the simulationists, there is no escape from the need for a theory of mind in the simulationists' view, since their reliance on self-knowledge in fact presupposes just such a theory.

Qualitative consciousness is supposed to be knowable by introspection, but also to have the more peculiar property of being *ineffable*, in at least the sense discussed above in chapter 4. That is, one cannot know what it is like to taste strawberries, say, unless one has had that taste experience (needless to say, one need not get the experience from strawberries – someone with a good gustatory imagination and a knowledge of similar fruits could perhaps conjure up the taste, or even a suitably, science fictionally, equipped neurosurgeon might suffice). This is an unavoidable but also a very delicate issue for any naturalistic theory of consciousness. There are famous philosophical arguments from the claim that experience generates a special kind of knowledge unobtainable from any other source to the unpalatable conclusion that physicalism is false (see Jackson 1982, 1986, Nagel 1974). Here there is but the narrowest of rough straits between the Charybdis of supernaturalism and the Scylla of a blinkered reductionism. The representational theory may yet be able to navigate this passage. Here is how. The sub-argument given above shows that to know the perceptible properties of things is to know the qualities of conscious experience. But, it seems, anyone could know what properties are represented in experience, given a sufficiently deep investigation into both the world and the sensory capabilities of the target experiencer. Dretske is pretty much content to stop here. Consider Dretske's example of the extremely impoverished qualia of a hypothetical, very simple species of parasite that requires hosts to be at 18° C and thus has evolutionarily acquired an acute temperature sense. Ignore for the moment the doubts you might have about whether such simple creatures really have any sort of experience – that doesn't matter to the point being made here. The point, as Dretske states it, is: '. . . anyone who knows what 18° C is, knows what this property is, knows what quale the parasite's experience has. They know, with respect to this single quale, what it is like to be that parasite' (1995, p. 84). Dretske admits that, to many, this will seem preposterous.

Surely Dretske has been caught by Scylla here. Do we really want to say that because we know that bats – to take the mandatory example – can discriminate details of their prey through the neural analysis of high frequency atmospheric compression waves (in some species of bat, as high as 150 kHz) we therefore know what it is like to be an echo-locating bat (even just qua *echo-locating*). Bat sonar is evidently a spatial sense in that it presumably represents objects as located in space in front of the bat, but it does not, obviously, represent colour. So how are we to imagine or conceive a non-coloured (not even black, white and grey; not transparent either) array of spatially extended and located objects? Bat sonar is also a short range sense; the echoes from objects more than a few metres from the bat are too weak for it to perceive. What should we think of the 'perceptual field' between perceivable targets? One is tempted to imagine a kind of blackness but that is to appeal to a visual system attuned to the properties of light. Perhaps bat perception is purely mathematical, with the set of perceivable targets represented as nothing but a set of ordered values representing, say, distance and orientation from self and likely nature of target (the way radar data might be stored in a computer). Such a representation would contain the information the bat senses can deliver; it would specify the properties to which the bat is sensorily attuned. It is in fact perhaps the most direct way that these, and only these, properties could be represented (maybe to a computer the output to the CRT display *looks* like an array of numbers). Bats also vary the number of sound pulses emitted depending upon the circumstances: emitting only a few per second while on patrol but increasing this to maybe 200 per second during the final assault upon their prey. Does this mean that the bat's perception of the world flickers because of an inadequate 'frame rate' under the former conditions but smooths out into a continuous display as more pulses are emitted per second? We know this happens to humans, for visual spatial displays, at around 30 frames per second. For the bat the situation is more complex, since the echoes from various targets will not arrive at the same time, so the very notion of a 'frame' does not make full sense. Whether or not the bat's experience flickers is not explicable in terms of *what* it is representing (there is no sense in supposing that the bat's sensory system is, as it were, trying to represent a world flickering into and out of existence). But it nonetheless seems to be a real feature of experience which bat experience might or might not exemplify.[11]

Box 6.3 • Representational Theory and Qualia

According to the representational theory, consciousness is representational through and through. Consciousness of colour is an awareness of how the world is represented by our visual system. This is not implausible: sometimes the way things look is the way things *are*, so the way things look involves the properties things have. It is natural to interpret this as involving a representation of the way things are (or of the properties things have). So seeing a red flag requires no 'redness' in the brain, or any ersatz, mysterious *phenomenal* redness. Is this too easy? Doesn't it mean that simply by knowing what property a perceptual system represents we will know what it is like to have those sorts of perceptual experiences? Yes and no. Representation does not have to be veridical; it is possible to represent what is not the case. Furthermore, for any target, there are many ways to represent it. Knowing what it is like to be some kind of conscious creature (such as a bat, for example) does involve knowing what it is representing and how it is representing it. It may be that some representational machinery is available only by way of having certain sorts of experiences. Thus, it may be that one couldn't know how strawberries taste – what the gustatory system is representing – unless one had the experience of tasting strawberries. So it seems that the representational theory can accommodate the *ineffability* of qualia within a potentially naturalistic framework.

Would it not be preferable if we could somehow avoid Dretske's bold claim that knowing what property is represented in experience simply *equals* knowing what the experience is like while remaining within the representational theory? I think there is a way. Consider how we know what it is like to undergo our *own* experiences, or how we know what it is like to be a (conscious) human. If we know what it is like to experience anything, we must surely know what our own experiences are like. This is a kind of introspective knowledge and so, by the above analysis of introspection, will require some conceptual tools for its expression. To know what it is like to taste strawberries you will need to have a concept of the taste of strawberries, which you can apply to the experience that occurs when you eat a strawberry (usually, or under normal conditions, and, of course, which you might apply to ersatz strawberries or, as we say, strawberry-flavoured things). The problem is that it is all too easy to get a concept which is properly labelled 'the taste of strawberries'; before I've ever tasted a strawberry I have this concept if I can understand what it means to say that someone is now experiencing the taste of strawberries, and this is not much of a feat. What we need in order to know what strawberries taste like is what might be called a 'substantial' concept of *how strawberries taste*. What is a substantial concept? A possible approach – though one that I think ultimately asks too much of these concepts – is to say that a substantial concept is one that allows the recognition of the taste when reencountered. In general, an important, perhaps the primary, role of concepts is just to store information in a way that permits re-identification of the same sort of things as we reencounter them in all their various ways of being in the world. There certainly are such sensory concepts, for they underpin our knowledge that we are tasting the *same* sort of taste that we have tasted before. But, as Dretske admits, someone who just knows the property which is detected when one tastes a strawberry will not, simply in virtue of possession of this concept, be able to recognize a strawberry by taste.[12]

Now, I suggest that the normal, and practically speaking the *only*, way to get a substantial concept is by having the corresponding experience. Looking at things this way, it seems evident that our sensory plus cognitive machinery is in fact set up to generate such concepts from experience. There are, perhaps, also abnormal ways to get such concepts. Maybe a neurosurgeon could implant one into your brain or, to be more circumspect, could prepare your brain in a state which subvenes possession of a substantial concept. Furthermore, I want to say that the appropriate substantial concept is one that represents a taste in the same way that the experience represents the taste. In fact, this condition is a better characterization of the notion of a substantial concept than that of allowing recognition suggested above. Under the representational theory, experiences one and all represent objects as having certain properties (in our example, certain taste properties). Of course, these are properties that we can experience objects as having. We can also have concepts of these properties and to *know* that we are experiencing an object as having one of these properties we need to have the concept of that property (as well as much other conceptual machinery). Note that substantial concepts are not tied to language, at least not in the sense of requiring a *name* for the experiential quality corresponding to each such concept. It is often argued that the rich and fully determinate detail of experience outruns our conceptual resources. Certainly the richness and depth of actual experience exceeds our fund of names for the qualities we can experience, but the fact that we have indexical concepts for experienced qualities entails that experience cannot overreach our conceptual resources (see Tye 1995 and McDowell 1994 for curiously disparate discussions of this point).

The idea here is that when we experience something we can gain introspective knowledge of the experience by application of the concept of *that* . . . where the ' . . .' is to be filled by some determinable, such as colour, sound, feeling or whatever.[13] This can happen without any concept of how the experience represents things being permanently laid down in one's cognitive system. For example, one can be conscious of the taste of a fine wine, and thus know what it tastes like, without thereby gaining the ability either to recognize it when reencountered or to recall it to one's mind in imagination. This is a common occurrence but it seems in fact to be a decisive objection against the ability analysis of 'knowing what it is like'. However, it is also possible and hardly less common that such a concept will be added to one's permanent conceptual repertoire, in which case, at least normally, one will be able to know *that* . . . *again* the next time one has the experience. Sometimes one gains or even makes up a name for what the experience represents, if and as one learns, e.g., what 'azure blue' or 'Middle C' are.

There is some affinity between my notion of a substantial concept and Brian Loar's 'phenomenal concepts' (Loar 1990; a viewpoint similar to Loar's can be found in Rey 1991, 1993), but there is a crucial and instructive difference. Loar's phenomenal concepts are concepts which apply to mental states; they are the direct conceptual correlates of qualia conceived of as experiential features of mental states. They are, to speak crudely, ways of representing and classifying mental states.[14] Substantial concepts are ways of representing and classifying non-mental features (it is of course possible that some substantial concepts might apply to mental states though I can't think of any examples).[15] Knowing what strawberries taste like is knowing something about the world (about strawberries in fact). One can also talk about the mental state of 'experiencing the taste of strawberries'. According to such talk, when one is (consciously) tasting strawberries one is experiencing the taste of strawberries. I think it is obviously correct to say that there is 'something it is like' to taste strawberries (and most of you know what that 'something it is like' is). But I think it is very strange, almost incomprehensible, to imagine that there is 'something it is like' to *experience* the taste of strawberries if this is to mean anything more than that there is something it is like to taste strawberries (perhaps the oddity is enhanced if we ask what it is like to experience the *taste-experience* of strawberries). What would this quality of the experience itself (as opposed to the *taste*) be like? For myself, I can find nothing in my experience to answer to it.

However, Loar's main point is that the fact that there are two quite distinct kinds of concepts (in his case, phenomenal and physical-functional) does not present any metaphysical barrier to identifying the referent of the two sorts of concepts. Recognition of the very different roles of these sorts of concepts can also explain why there is an appearance (but *mere* appearance) of an ontological divide between the mental and the physical. Within limits, this is correct. I think it does ease a purely ontological worry but, as noted in chapter 1 above, does not ease the epistemological worry of the generation problem (and if one seeks to avoid mysterianism the epistemological worry alone can still fund some uneasiness about the nature of the mind–matter relation; this is to be explored in chapter 9 below).

The need for something like substantial concepts of *how* things are represented can be seen from another direction. Dretske claims that knowing what property is represented in x's experience will give us knowledge of what it is like for x to experience (an object with) that property. Is there another way to get this knowledge?

One might think that having the experience would do the trick (given the conceptual apparatus necessary for knowledge – we do not expect that bats, for example, know what it is like to be a bat simply because they have, first-hand, bat experiences; in all probability, they know nothing of the sort). But, of course, the fact that our ancient ancestors (say, to be safe, of 2000 years ago) knew what it is like to see red did not mean that they knew which property of things was represented in their experience. They had not the slightest idea that our colour vision represents ratios of reflectance triples. Nor do *we* know that this is the final and correct theory of colour vision (there is a lively debate about the nature of colour right now, see e.g. Hardin 1988, Thompson 1995) so in this sense even *we* don't know what property is being represented in our colour experiences. It hardly follows that we don't know what it is like to experience red! What follows is that we know the property at issue by way of a concept entirely distinct from the concept of 'ratios of reflectance triples', by way of a substantial concept of *how red looks*. And, while one can get the former concept from book learning, one can't get the concept of experienced red this way.

There is nothing startling in this; it is no more than the intensionality of knowledge. It does not follow from the two premises (1) I know what it is like to see red *as* red and (2) redness is such-and-such a reflectance property, that I know what it is like to see red *as* such-and-such a reflectance property. I suspect Dretske would prefer to say that the correct argument is somewhat simpler:

(1) I know what it is like to see red.
(2) red = such-and-such a reflectance property
(C) So, I know what it is like to see such-and-such a reflectance property.

This argument is obviously valid but won't get us what Dretske wants, which is a purely objective route to the qualities of experience. Consider Dretske's dogfish example (1995, pp. 86 ff.). Dogfish can, apparently, sense electric fields. Of course, as Dretske notes, the dogfish does not represent the field *as* an electric field of such-and-such form but rather 'what the fish represents about the electric field is its configuration, its geometry, its shape' (1995, p. 86). So if we know what it is like to represent geometry we know what it is like for the dogfish to experience an electric field. But, obviously, we know that there are lots of ways to represent geometry or shape. Here is one way to represent a circular shape: $x^2 + y^2 = a$. Here is another: O. Which way does the dogfish represent it? As in the bat example above, *not* the latter, since that is a visual representation in which the circular shape is represented by the essential use of colours (just black and white in this example but that is enough). The dogfish, I think, does not represent colour with its electric field sense. Of course, to the dogfish there might be 'quasi-colours' in which shapes are rendered, but the point is just that we don't know about that. On the other hand, I very much doubt that dogfish sense mathematical equations or represent via mathematical equations.

It's worth looking a little closer at how electric fields are sensed. Dogfish and other sharks are merely passive detectors of electrical discharge; they have a series of specialized receptors horizontally spaced along their bodies which are highly sensitive to electric current. A much more impressive electrical sense can be found in a rather odd fish, *gymnarchus niloticus*, a Nile fish for which there is apparently no popular name, which inhabits turbid fresh water, is about 20 inches long and is entirely nocturnal in its habits – in fact its eyesight is so poor that it serves only to tell night from day.[16] Gymnarchus can produce rapid electrical pulses (about 300 per second) with a special organ in its tail, like an electric eel though the discharges are very much weaker, and with each pulse the fish becomes the source of an electric field with the current lines running from tail to head, wherein we find lots of the electrical detectors. The basic structure of the generated field can be pictured as in fig. 6.1.

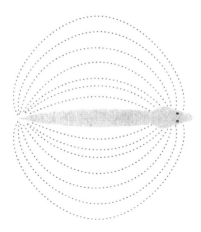

(Fig. 6.1)

In the absence of any object in the water around the fish and in the absence of any movement by the fish the field is constant and symmetric. But fish need to move and so Gymnarchus has evolved a most peculiar method of swimming. It propels itself, with equal ease either forward or backwards, by gracefully undulating its long and large dorsal fin while keeping its spine quite rigid. This helps to reduce noise in the generated field. Objects near the fish will alter the shape of the field according to their electrical conductivity. Field lines will diverge around relative insulators and converge through or towards conductors. In fact, the special electric detectors depend on this. Gymnarchus has a particularly thick and highly insulating skin but the electrical detectors reside at the bottom of pores filled with a jelly-like conducting material.

Thus the field lines will naturally converge towards the detectors. A nearby conducting object might alter the field something in the way shown in fig. 6.2.

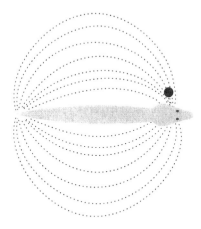

(Fig. 6.2)

The fish will 'notice' the concentrations of current along its skin from these deformations in the field. What the fish is measuring is the distribution of electric potential over its surface. Gymnarchus is remarkably sensitive and can perform feats that, relative to human senses, are very impressive. These fish can electrically 'see' through objects. Lissmann's experiments involved putting various objects within porous ceramic containers that were soaked with water (hence making them invisible or transparent to the electric sense). The fish could discriminate a container holding just water from one containing a glass rod of diameter less than 2 millimetres.

But are these fish sensing the 'shape' of the local electric field? Familiar questions arise about where to place the target of the representation: is it potential gradients on the fish's skin, is it the contours of the electric field, or is it the object, or certain properties of the object, which is creating the distortion in the electric field? It doesn't matter to the fish how *we* assign representational function but Dretske's theory requires that there be a *correct* answer. Otherwise these fish, and all sensing creatures for that matter, fail to have determinate qualitative conscious experience. If there is no fact of the matter about what a system represents then there is no fact of the matter about what the system's experience is like (note that to deny that there is such a fact is *not* to endorse a disjunctive representation). I think that we would normally take – and in other contexts Dretske himself is keen to take – the representation to be of the object (or certain properties of the object) causing the deformation, just as we want to claim that we see objects rather than the light reflected from the objects. Perhaps

149

we should say that we see objects in virtue of systems that detect reflected light; similarly in the case of the fish, they sense objects in virtue of systems that detect variations in electrical potential on their skins. I am sure that we would not want to say that the fish are *inferring* information about the objects from the sensory information about the fields (or skin potential gradients).

For these fish, what property is the object represented as having? The actual property detected is fascinatingly complex. Notice that for objects of identical form and location, field variation is caused solely by conductivity (ideally, ignoring the movements of the fish itself, variations in frequency and magnitude of the electrical pulses and the possible effects of other nearby Gymnarchuses).[17] For objects of identical form and conductivity, it is location that causes field variation. Finally, for objects of identical location and conductivity, it is form that determines the field variations. The property being detected is apparently an extremely complex amalgam of these three variables which in themselves each admit of further complexity. Imagine what odd sets of things (i.e. locations + conductivities + form) will generate stimulus equivalence classes! While it would presumably be possible to give a mathematical description of the function which specifies these classes (or at least an idealized relative of it), it is ridiculous to suppose that this function tells us what it is like for Gymnarchus to use its electrical sense.

We can avoid positing such a staggeringly complex property by invoking the aid of Mother Nature. As we shall see, this is entirely in line with Dretske's version of the representational theory. It is possible to suppose, and would even be testable to some extent, that evolution has given Gymnarchus some 'default' assumptions about the world that discipline the stimulus equivalence classes just mentioned. The set of locations can be assumed to all be very near the fish. And given that other fish (potential prey and predators) all have roughly the same electrical conductivity, and in some sense pretty much the same form as well, we can reduce the represented property to a more reasonable combination of constrained form and nearby location. Nonetheless, the property represented is *not* form and it is *not* location, but, to us, a completely mysterious *combination* of these two properties. What would this kind of sensing be like? Try to imagine two visually perceivable spatial configurations, each involving but one object at one location, that are indiscriminable from one another even though the shapes of the two objects are clearly discriminable and the positions of the two are also plainly discriminable! It is no wonder that Lissmann writes at the beginning of his article that 'Gymnarchus lives in a world totally alien to man' (1963/1974, p. 56). Because we lack this peculiar sort of sense, we cannot attain the conceptual machinery needed to understand what it is like for Gymnarchus to electrically sense the world (again, like Dretske, I skate over the worry that Gymnarchus is not sufficiently advanced to have *any* kind of experience with the claim that this possibility does not matter to the point of the example).

If the appeal to substantial concepts gets us by Scylla, does it send us back perilously near the Charybdis of supernaturalism? That is, does the appeal to and acceptance of substantial concepts mean that there is something left out of the naturalistic picture of the world? This remains a delicate matter. But arguably the answer is 'no' since all we have claimed is that the possession of complete physical knowledge about the physical basis of experience will not grant one the *possession* of all possible concepts. Why should it? Tye, for example, tackles this problem by devising a metaphysics of *facts*, in which some facts are substantive and some are 'merely conceptual', that is, they involve or are about the way things are conceived (see 1995, pp. 172 ff.), or, I might add, are represented. According to Tye, physicalism is the claim that all substantive facts are physical facts. Knowledge of the conceptual facts requires one to possess the relevant concepts and knowledge of the substantive facts will not necessarily generate these concepts. Dretske comes close to implicitly endorsing this sort of view in his deployment of the notion of 'knowing what it is like in the fact sense' for he notes that: 'if I know what a change of key is then in the fact sense, I know what it is like to hear a change of key. It is like *that* where the 'that' refers to what I know to be a change of key' (1995, p. 86). The question we should worry about is whether we should feel some metaphysical scruples in admitting that physical knowledge does not give *us* access to all of the conceptual facts for the simple reason that it does not give us all of the concepts. I don't see why we need to entertain such scruples.

Let's assume that our cognitive/sensory machinery is such that we cannot acquire the appropriate concept in which to formulate knowledge of what it is like to experience the bat's echo-location sense or Gymnarchus's electrical sense. So, for example, if there were intelligent bats, bats capable of introspective knowledge of their own experiences, they would know something that we cannot know no matter how much we knew about their (and the world's) physical constitution. This does show that physicalism is epistemically incomplete but it does not show that it is metaphysically incomplete. Is it not asking too much of physicalism that it not only encompass everything in the world but also every way of knowing everything in the world? But a 'way of knowing something' is a part of the world. Yes, and a physical part of it too, and *as* a physical part we can know it. We just cannot 'have' it as part of our way of knowing things (this line of argument is similar to one developed by Gilbert Harman 1990 as well as Tye 1995).

One last point on this topic. Compared to a non-representational view, the representational theory *must* have an easier time dealing with the 'incompleteness objection'. For it does not postulate the existence of any entities with odd phenomenal properties. It contents itself with positing entities that *represent* the sensible properties of things. To speak crudely, if I suppose that in imagining a unicorn there must actually be a little unicorn somewhere then I face the difficult task of explaining how unicorns can exist within the physical world (the problem is hardly made easier when we discover that *these* unicorns are somehow, exclusively, 'in the mind'). But if I suppose only that something *represents* a unicorn, then I am supposing nothing new. If the reader nonetheless senses some uneasiness on my part, a somewhat over assiduous attempt to convince myself, the reader is not mistaken, but I can't define a real problem here. And thus I think we *may* have navigated the dangerous channel.

Despite the strengths of the representational theory, it does face some serious objections. I want to turn to these now, focussing on ones that I think are not only problems for the representational theory but also raise important general difficulties in our understanding of consciousness. It is another merit of the theory that its engagement with the problems of consciousness reveals new and interesting aspects of these problems and sometimes highlights their most crucial features.

Box 6.4 • Summary

The representational theory of consciousness asserts that all states of consciousness are representational, and this allows for a parsimonious, unified and interesting account of consciousness within a representational philosophy of mind. The theory can be developed in ways that more or less respect the intuitions behind our notions of qualitative or phenomenal consciousness, despite the denial that there are any phenomenal *properties* of experiences. The 3I-P account of qualia (see chapter 4) can be pretty well translated into the representational idiom. Ineffability and immediacy can be integrated into the theory. An especially agreeable theory of introspection stems from the representational theory that has interesting connections to some problems about self-knowledge and our implicit knowledge of the nature of the mind. The issue of whether qualitative consciousness is an *intrinsic* feature of mind looms as troublesome however.

7

REPRESENTATIONAL THEORIES
OF CONSCIOUSNESS,
PART II

Box 7.1 • Preview

A representational theory of consciousness requires a theory of representation. At the moment there are lots of these on offer but they all seem to lead to real difficulties when coupled to the theory of consciousness. The two most worked out versions of the representational theory (by Dretske and Tye) differ in their underlying theory of representation but both suffer from similar objections. Some of the crucial issues that arise here: what is the relation between representation and *function*, how does evolutionary history affect the content of representations and hence affect particular states of consciousness, what is the relation between the acquisition of new representational functions and states of consciousness? Finally and most crucially, is the question of how the representational theory can deal with the problem of 'rogue consciousness', that is, creatures who lack the requisite features to count as *representing* (according to the favoured *theory* of representation of course) but who seem nonetheless to be capable of conscious experience. These are particular worries about how the representational theory of consciousness will *integrate* consciousness with the chosen theory of representation. The representational theory will also have to face the generation problem. What is more, the representational theory brings to prominence a problem that has been lurking in philosophy ever since Descartes although it is seldom noticed. It is a curious fact that in consciousness we are aware of what certain of our states – brain states no doubt – represent but we are never aware of what features of these states 'carry' the represented information, never aware of what we might call the *vehicle* of the representation. No other representations have anything like this feature and it is another deep mystery of consciousness.

The overriding worry is that the representational theory of consciousness is a hostage to the fortunes of its underlying general theory of representation. In itself, pointing out that consciousness now depends upon certain features of representation is no objection. However, the particular theory of representation appealed to might create serious problems. Dretske endorses, without argument in *Naturalizing the Mind*, a bio-functional theory of representation.[1] Roughly speaking, representations represent what they are *designed* to represent. The threatening circle or regress is broken by appeal to the possibility that evolution can 'design' representing systems without itself having any designs (without having, that is, any representations of its own). Recently, bio-functional theories of representation have been developed in great detail, especially by Ruth Millikan (primarily 1984; further developments of her views can be found in Millikan 1993; see also Papineau 1987, Godfrey-Smith 1994). This is not the place to discuss the general merits and demerits of 'biosemantics', as Millikan labels it; I will restrict myself to the interaction between this theory of representation and consciousness. Dretske's representational theory of consciousness thus asserts that the properties represented in states of consciousness are properties which have been assigned to those states either by evolutionary or, possibly, genuinely intentional design. This leads to a variety of problems.

Box 7.2 • Theories of Representation – Some Sample Sketches

Similarity. This very old, rather intuitive view, holds that S represents O just in case S is similar to O. There must be something right about this, but it is hopeless as it stands. Everything is similar to everything else, more or less. What matters is precisely which aspects of similarity make for representation and there is no good answer to this question. Furthermore, similarity is a symmetrical relation; if S is similar to O then O is equally similar to S, but the relation of representation goes only one way.

Causal Covariance. S represents O just in case S causally covaries with O. This is far too unconstrained as it stands and it is hard to see how exactly to make it more precise without losing clear cases of representation or making the account circular. Magnetic and electric fields causally covary with each other, but neither represents the other. The symmetry problem also appears to loom.

Functionalism. S represents O just in case it is the function of S to represent O. While this may be correct, it is blatantly circular and cannot be thought to give any sort of *account* of representation. But hope returns if we imagine some kind of naturalistic, 'reductive' theory of representational functions. (Note that functionalism forms the basis of a reasonable account of *derived* representation, that is, representations which depend for their representational power on other representational states.)

Bio-Functionalism. S represents O just in case S has been evolutionarily designed to represent O. Again, this is circular, but perhaps it can be married to a properly naturalistic account of representational function (this hope springs from the idea that it is proper, if metaphorical, to speak of evolution as a 'designer' without threatening evolutionary theory's status as a fully naturalistic doctrine). For example, we might say that representational function is a matter of causal covariation between S and O being created by evolutionary selection. Suppose it was the case that the covariation between S and O was maintained because this very covariation increased the chances of survival of some creatures. If it was the fact that S carries information about O that explains the evolutionary success of the systems which use the S–O covariation we might be close to a non-circular account of the origins of representation.

The classical version of the well known puzzle of the inverted spectrum stems from the idea that two people could have systematically inverted colour perception with no external behavioural indication of the difference and no internal functional difference either. While the representational theory offers a nice treatment of this issue, difficulties lurk over the horizon. Dretske accepts that two people could have identical discriminatory powers but differ in the qualities of their experience (1995, p. 72). But they would nonetheless have to differ in some objective way. Speaking abstractly, there seem to be only two possible objective differences available within the confines of the bio-functional version of the representational theory. Either the two could differ in the *functions* of the sensory systems that ground their discriminatory abilities or the two could differ in the *implementation* of systems with the same sensory functions.

Dretske's example of two speedometers is instructive here (see 1995, pp. 75 ff.). One speedometer, call it J, is a high precision instrument, initially and by design capable of discriminating speeds down to a hundredth of a mile per hour. It has the function of telling the difference between 78.00 mph and 78.01 mph. A second speedometer, K, is a relatively low precision instrument capable of discriminating only integer values of mph. Metaphorically speaking, 'J is a speed connoisseur. He can tell a 77.92 speed from a 77.98 speed. All these speeds "feel" the same to K. J has speed "quale" that K never "experiences". . .' (1995, p. 75). We can take the metaphor completely seriously; when we consider systems that – unlike speedometers – really can consciously experience things it is just such differences in functional capability that ground differences in the qualities of their experiences.[2] Now, functions can persist through the loss of discriminatory sensitivity. Dretske notes that even if J loses sensitivity so that it becomes equal in discriminatory power to K it still retains the function of discriminating speeds down to the hundredths ('the fact that J no longer delivers the information it is its function to provide does not mean that it loses the function of providing it' (1995, p. 77)). We can infer that two systems that provide information from the same domain but with distinct degrees of precision enjoy 'qualia-spaces' that are *entirely* distinct. This follows from the two premises that the systems represent distinct sets of properties and represented properties are the qualities of conscious experience. So if K registers '78 mph' and J '78.00 mph' these would correspond to distinct qualia, even when J and K are identical in discriminatory power (and, of course, this will apply to *every* speed they can discriminate).

This leads to rather odd consequences if we entertain a certain empirical possibility. Is it possible that evolution can select for systems that can *alter* their functions over time? I suspect that the increased fineness of sensory discrimination that humans (and other animals as well) can develop by extensive and intensive use of their senses can alter the *functional* precision of these senses. It seems that we can turn ourselves from a K-type sensory system into a J-type with practice. So it is with the accomplished wine taster, so it is with the visual artist or the musician and the formula one racing car driver, so it is, perhaps with those dogs trained to detect contraband drugs.[3] At least, so it seems. But if so, then the taste qualia of the wine taster become *entirely distinct* from the taste qualia of the more normal, less discriminating taster.[4] If this is correct then it is impossible for any wine to taste to me like it tastes to the wine taster (whereas we might have thought that the taster's set of taste qualia was a superset of mine). And since our taste spaces are entirely disparate it is unclear whether any sense can be made of cross-space similarity judgements. While I and the taster might agree that wine X is more like wine Y than it is like wine Z, there is no easy answer to the question of whether my taste of X is more like the taster's taste of Y or X or Z. This result is highly counterintuitive, and would suggest that the hypothesis that leads to it must be rejected. But the question whether evolution can select for function-changing discrimination devices cannot be answered in such a blatantly a priori manner[5].

Box 7.3 • Systemic and Acquired Representations

There are a large number of kinds of representations within any cognitive system, but Dretske draws a major division between systemic representations (representations$_s$) and acquired representations (representations$_a$). Roughly speaking, representations$_s$ are representations whose production is the (or *a*) basic representational function, underwritten by evolution or intentional design, of the system. If the representational functions are the product of evolution (though we might perversely wonder if this must be an evolution undirected by intelligent agency) then these representations$_s$ are called *natural* representations. Since it is the function of a tachometer to indicate an engine's revolutions per minute, when the dial points to '6000' that is a representation$_s$ of 6000 rpm. Acquired representations are systemic representations which have had their representational function altered, through learning or design. If I mark on to the tachometer in my aged car a red arrow at '6500', meaning to indicate that it is dangerous to exceed 6500 rpm, then the mark '6500' has taken on an acquired representational function of indicating *danger* (it still represents$_s$ 6500 rpm as well). The world is full of representations. Which ones are mental representations? Which are *conscious* mental representations or experiences? Dretske suggests that experiences are natural representations$_s$ that help in the construction of representations$_a$. Here one can see the generation problem looming, for there are myriads of representations within any cognitive economy, constantly forming, dissolving and interacting and a great many of them have a role to play in the construction of representations$_a$. But it seems that very few of them are conscious experiences.

Can Dretske avoid this result without engaging in a priori evolutionary theory? Dretske distinguishes what he calls representation$_s$ from representation$_a$ where the former is the *systemic* representational function and the latter the *acquired* representational function. The distinction also corresponds to the distinction between what Dretske calls the *phenomenal* versus the *doxastic* sense of experience terms (1995, pp. 67–68). Doxastic experiences require the backing of some concepts in that, to take 'looks' as an example, something can doxastically look ϕ to S only if S has the concept of ϕs. The phenomenal sense has no such conceptual requirement.[6] Dretske identifies experiences with representations$_s$ that 'service the construction of representations$_a$' (1995, p. 19) and goes on to explain this by adding that experiences 'are the states whose functions it is to supply information to a cognitive system for calibration and use in the control and regulation of behaviour' (1995, p. 19). It is possible, then, that the changes in sensitivity exhibited by the wine taster etc. are the result of changes in representations$_a$ built upon a stable base of representations$_s$. In effect, this is to say that the wine taster acquires a greater conceptual repertoire for classifying taste experiences but does not undergo any change in qualia. This interpretation is supported by Dretske's brief discussion of the *macula lutea*, the yellow spot on the retina directly behind the pupil over the fovea. Dretske reports that: 'as we age, there is gradual yellowing of the macula . . . that changes the signals sent from the retina to the brain about the wavelength of light . . . Despite this constant change in the information representational$_s$ states carry, there is no corresponding representational$_a$ change: we still see blue and yellow, red and green, *as* blue and yellow, red and green' (1995, p. 21, original emphasis).

The wine taster case is the inverse, where we have representational$_a$ change without representational$_s$ change (the change presumably being brought about by the increasingly sophisticated conceptual machinery being brought to bear *upon* the unchanging representational$_s$ states). But this does not avoid the problem. Dretske still has to *assume* that there is a stable sensory function to make this reply and that requires the assumption that evolution cannot make sensory systems that alter their function, even if just in what I've called their precisional function, through specialized use of these systems. The yellowing of the macula is obviously not 'meant' to initiate a change in the function of the cones of the fovea, let alone to cause functional changes higher in the vision system, but that goes nowhere towards showing that other changes are not truly functional. There is lots of evidence that the brain alters its representational capacities of a domain with use of, or attention to, that domain. For example, it is well known that motor and sensory cortical maps are continually being reconfigured reflecting behavioural contingencies; it is possible that these reconfigurations alter functional aspects of sensory representation (for discussions of a host of diverse mechanisms of cortical plasticity see Rose 1993 or Petit and Ivy 1988). On balance, I would guess that it is more likely than not that our sensory systems can adjust their functions or, at least, their functional precision across a variety of perceptual domains.

One could regard it as an advantage of Dretske's theory that it endorses the possibility of such genuine alterations in qualitative experience. Nonetheless, the fact that these changes would send the subject into an entirely distinct qualia-space is a radical and counterintuitive thesis. We are driven to it by the appeal to the identification of qualia with sensory *function*.

More problems stem from this identification. There is a chemical, phenylthiourea (henceforth designated simply as PTU), which is entirely tasteless to between one-third and one-quarter of us (non-tasters cannot discriminate its occurrence in anything from its non-occurrence); it is distinctly bitter tasting to the remaining two-thirds to three-quarters of the population. (For more on this odd chemical see Kalmus and Hubbard 1960.[7]) We can infer, on Dretske's theory, that either the sensory representational functions of the two sub-populations differ or that one sub-population has a defectively implemented sensory system. Neither of these possibilities is very plausible.

It is very unlikely that those sensory systems able to detect PTU have an explicit, evolutionarily explicable, function of representing the taste of PTU (shorthand for representing the property of PTU which their taste systems are able to detect). This must then be a case of what Dretske calls 'implicit representation' (1995, p. 21). This is a legitimate and useful notion. After all, we would not expect there to be a 'distinguishable evolutionary process' by which we can directly show that for *each* colour that we can see, or taste that we can taste, it is the function of the system to indicate *that* colour, or taste. (Dretske's example of an implicit representational function is a clock face upon which we put a '12' – all other hand positions now acquire an implicit indicator function.[8]) But in order to show that a system has the implicit function of indicating ϕ we must show that it is *because* a system has the explicit function of indicating x, y and z that it also can indicate ϕ. An accidental correlation between system states and ϕ is not sufficient to show that those states indicate or represent ϕ only a correlation based upon the explicit representational functions of the system can suffice. We can make up a speedometer example of our own to illustrate the point here about implicit representation. Suppose a factory makes speedometers. It needs to make them so as to represent speeds between 20 and 140 km/h. The space on the speedometer between 0 and 20 is not designed to represent any speed accurately and generally the pointer jumps around or moves erratically until a speed of 20 km/h is reached. Nonetheless, let us suppose, for a small percentage of speedometers, as an accidental feature of their manufacture, there is an 'accurate representation' of 10 km/h (that is, unlike the normal speedometers, there is a spot on the dial of these metres that the needle always hits at 10 km/h so you could use them to measure 10 km/h – you could even put a mark on the dial, though the machines are not generally reliable from 0 to 10, nor from 10 to 20). Does this subset of speedometers have the (implicit) function of indicating 10 km/h? Pretty obviously not.

The statistics of PTU tasting suggests that the ability to taste PTU stems from the possession of a dominant allele from a pair acting at a single locus (see e.g. Jones and McLachlan 1991). In order for this ability to be classed as an implicit representational function, we must show that there is an evolutionary account of *some* sensory representational functions which differ between the two populations *and* which explain why one can represent PTU while the other cannot. However, it is entirely possible and rather more likely than otherwise, that the ability to taste PTU is a merely accidental concomitant of genetic changes that have nothing whatever to do with the taste system's ability to discriminate other flavours. The fact that most of us are tasters is then nothing but a statistical effect of the dominance of the taster gene (according to Kalmus and Hubbard 1960 the non-taster gene is actually the more common in the population). That is, there is no selectional story which essentially depends upon the fact that there are some systems that happen to be able to taste x, y and z *and* PTU (what the tasters can taste seems to be a bitterness that depends upon certain molecular combinations of carbon, nitrogen and sulphur, what Kalmus and Hubbard label the 'NC=S group', see Kalmus and Hubbard 1960, pp. 42 ff.) and some that cannot, which explains why such systems come into being. It is like the speedometer story above. Of course, this is empirically controversial; it is certainly possible that there is a selectional tale which makes tasting this form (or source) of bitterness important for survival. But there is little evidence for this. There is some statistical evidence that non-tasters are 'slightly more prone to develop adenomatous goiter than tasters' (Kalmus and Hubbard 1960, p. 45). On the other hand, 'toxic diffuse goiter is more prevalent among the taster genotypes' (Kalmus and Hubbard 1960, p. 45; see also Mattes and Labov 1989). This is a fascinating issue and it is most interesting (and in a way very encouraging) that the genetics of taste abilities should be important to the evaluation of a theory of consciousness. The point here is that a theory that makes it impossible that any taste ability be selectionally accidental strikes me as implausible.[9]

And there is a general point here of crucial importance. Sensory sub-systems acquire new representational functions by acquiring new discriminatory abilities which enhance the super-systems' fitness. Now, in the first place and as I have noted, there is no concrete evidence to suggest that the ability to taste PTU is either directly or derivatively an enhancement to fitness. That is, there is nothing to suggest that the sensory systems of those who can taste PTU have, or have had, *any* fitness advantage over the rest of us in virtue of the system having some representational functions which, among other things, account for the ability to taste PTU. If so, there is no function (explicit or implicit) of representing PTU and so, in fact, no taste qualia of PTU. This is of course ridiculous. But more important, suppose that there had been some definite advantage to being able to detect PTU (as, no doubt, there really were advantages to being able to detect other chemicals or chemical concentrations). To make things as stark as possible, imagine a single mutation that confers the ability to discriminate PTU and imagine that this was beneficial. So those who receive the mutated gene do better. But I urge you to notice that this is *not* because they can taste PTU! They cannot taste PTU – have an experience of the taste of PTU – unless and until it is the *function* of their sensory systems to indicate PTU. But this function is acquired in virtue of being able to detect PTU. Normally, I think, we would say that survival was enhanced by the fact that those receiving the mutated gene could *taste* PTU. In fact, according to Dretske's theory, this is dead wrong. These creatures couldn't taste PTU *until* the function of detecting PTU was in place and this happens after the discriminatory ability is in place and then manages to account for the proliferation of the ability (see note 5 above for Millikan's account which makes this perfectly clear). The general point here is that no change in sensory discriminative abilities provides for a change in experience until it becomes a function of the system to make these new discriminations. It is natural to suppose that it is *because* we come to be able to taste new tastes that our taste-systems can fulfil new functions (discriminatory or otherwise) but now, it turns out, it is because our systems fulfil new functions that we can taste new tastes.

Box 7.4 • Representation, Function and Consciousness

Suppose we endorse some kind of bio-functional theory of representation. Then what a state represents is a matter of its evolutionarily selected and 'designed' function. Both the *how* and *what* of this function are matters of evolutionary history. In particular, there is no representational function until after there begins to be exploitation of the informational link between a sign and its object. The picture is that first there is the informational link, put into the world perhaps by luck or chance, ready to be exploited by creatures that are smart enough to use the link (this does not require a great deal of intelligence – think of the dance of the bees as well as other, simpler, insect signal systems). It is the evolutionary selection of the use of the link that confers the representational function on the preexisting covariation. Now couple this picture to the representational theory of consciousness. Until there is representation of a property there is no possibility of consciousness of it, for the consciousness of a property requires, by hypothesis, its representation. It seems to follow that consciousness of new sounds, smells or colours, or the ability consciously to discriminate more finely among sounds, smells, or colours cannot be what accounts for evolutionary advantage. It is rather the reverse – evolutionary advantage accounts for the consciousness of new sensory features. On the face of it, this seems backwards.

Before taking this aspect of the PTU problem to its logical and extremely perplexing conclusion, there is another issue I would like to raise. I call it the 'resolution of function' argument. Most functions of complex entities are fulfilled by sub-systems that fulfil sub-functions. The ability of any complex system to fulfil a high-level function stems from its deployment of a host of sub-systems with the ability to fulfil a myriad of much simpler, lower level functions. Potential problems for the representational theory arise from following such functional hierarchies in either direction. Let's go up one first. There seems to be a special 'module' in the human visual system for recognizing human faces. It has been known for a long time that almost from birth children discriminate between face-like and non-face-like stimuli (see for example Fantz 1958, 1961; for a discussion of a variety of very early cognitive abilities relating to facial and emotional recognition see Perner 1993, pp. 126 ff.). Breakdowns in the ability to recognize faces occur without the loss of the ability to see that one is looking at a face (or the parts of a face: eyes, mouth, nose etc.) and so presumably arise from some inability to 'parse' faces as such (see Young and De Haan 1993). If there is a built-in ability to represent faces then faces are represented$_s$ and thus, on Dretske's theory, there is a set of particular 'face-qualia', distinct from colour, shape, motion and other, 'purer' visual elements of experience. Is this plausible? We might wonder whether Dretske's double identification of experience with both *systemic* representation and with non-doxastic representation was over hasty. As Dretske presents it, the situation is this:

	Systemic	Acquired
Phenomenal	✔	✘
Doxastic	✘	✔

In fact, if our conceptual resources can affect the nature of our conscious experience then there will be a category of 'acquired phenomenal' states.[10] Dretske focusses almost entirely upon relatively low level perceptual experience and thus fails to discuss this important possibility. The fact that there might be a layer of conceptually uninfected experience common both to systems endowed with a conceptual component and those without does not show that there is not also a distinctive experiential difference between the two sorts of systems (this question will be examined in more depth in chapter 8 below). It also does not seem impossible for a cognitive system to come with built-in conceptual resources – innate ideas we might call them – so that the system could enjoy a number of systemic doxastic representational states that might, or might not, be phenomenal states as well.

On the other hand – going down a hierarchy – we know that the visual system's abilities rest on a set of quite primitive representational abilities: ratios of wavelength receptor strengths (for colour vision) and a variety of primitive geometrical representations: lines, edges, moving lines or edges, illumination contrasts of various sorts (e.g. light centre/dark surround, etc.). It seems quite certain that our visual systems represent$_s$ all these features. Are there qualia for all these as well? Generally, in our experience we don't *notice* such details.

In fact, our perception of the world is conditioned by a range of what might be called, somewhat paradoxically, visual illusions. We are subject to colour constancy which seems to adjust the perceived colour of objects somewhat in defiance of the actual reflectances we are subject to. Perceived illumination is also the product of extensive processing, as is the perception of form and motion. Consider the famous illusion in fig. 7.1 below. It is impossible not to see a distinct and comparatively bright circle from which the lines radiate, although we know that there is none and that there is no difference in illumination between the 'inside' and 'outside' of the illusory circle.

Presumably, the source of such illusions lies in the constructive details of our visual system in which a host of features and sub-features are represented$_s$ but of which we have no conscious awareness.

(Fig. 7.1)

Further problems stem from such considerations. One is the worry that there may not *be* the experiential qualia of which we seem to be aware. According to Dretske, we experience 'red qualia' only if our sensory-cognitive system represents$_s$ *red*. It will do this if it is the (or a) function of the system to represent *red* (either implicitly or explicitly). But it is entirely possible that there is no such function but rather a set of sub-functions of representing frequency ratios, illumination levels, etc. In other words, there may not be any stable property of objects which can be identified with 'being red'. Thus the representational theory seems to demand an objectivist account of colours.[11] At least, the bio-functional version of the representational theory has this burden. A more liberal representationalism carries a lighter load, for while it seems highly unlikely that evolution can select for the sensory representation of non-existent features of the world[12] there is, of course, nothing in general preventing the representation of the non-existent. Once again we see that it is the particular background theory of representation which leads to trouble within a theory that has the intrinsic resources to escape it.

Since Tye's version of the representational theory does not employ the bio-functional theory of representation, this is perhaps a good place to examine his alternative. Unfortunately, Tye devotes very little space to discussing the account of representation which underlies his theory of consciousness. He opts for a *causal covariation* theory of representation which he characterizes as follows. A state, S, of subject x 'represents that P =$_{df}$ If optimal conditions obtain, S is tokened in x iff P and because P' (1995, p. 101). There are two very different ways to understand this definition. The first is as a definition of *what* S represents *given* that S is a representation. The second is as a simultaneous definition of both what *makes* S a representation *and* of what it represents. It is simply not clear how Tye intends us to read the definition. On the face of it, the first, weaker reading is more plausible since the definition by itself does not seem to present any general theory of representation at all, inasmuch as it appears to let in far too many states as representations.[13] Tye himself claims that 'intuitively, the number of rings on a cross section of a tree *represents* something about the tree, namely, how old it is' (1995, p. 100). Here, since I can think of no reason to say that the number of rings *represents* the age of the tree *except* for the covariation between number of rings and age, I am drawn to suspect that Tye intends the stronger interpretation of his definition. Although I realize that one can tell how old a tree is by counting the rings, I don't find it at all plausible to say that this is representation. Another way to date trees (really old ones anyway) is by the ratio of carbon-12 to carbon-14 in the tree's substance. Does this ratio also represent the age of the tree? And the world is full of information-laden causal connections – in fact, by their very nature causal connections carry information no less than energy. Does the presence of the Earth's gravitational field *represent* its mass? Does a display of the Northern Lights *represent* high energy particles in the upper atmosphere? Does the depletion in the Earth's ozone layer *represent* the presence of CFCs in the atmosphere? Does the direction of a bar magnet's field *represent* the spin orientation of the electrons within it? Note how the bio-functional theory disarms such suggestions by the demand that the representational function account for the persistence of the relation between the representations and what is represented. It is not *because* mass is correlated with gravity that this relation persists (similarly for the other examples), whereas, for example, it is because the bee's dance is causally correlated with the presence of nectar that this correlation persists.

If consciousness is to be explained in terms of the representational states of systems, it is a crucial first step that we be able to pick out the genuine representations from the vast set of non-representational causal covariations exhibited throughout the world. For our bodies and brains too are home to any number of states which causally covary with other states without their being representations and without their being candidates for states of consciousness, even though they have a role to play in the production of mental states. Since Tye agrees with Dretske that *experiences* are to be identified as representational states which can and normally do figure in the production of beliefs and desires, his theory shares with Dretske the problems of inflation and deflation of function advanced above.[14] To the extent that there are many more apparently representational states within our cognitive economy under Tye's theory, the theory will have a worse time dealing with these sorts of problems.

We should also worry about the 'optimal conditions' clause in Tye's definition. If we pack into this clause the demand that the system be in conditions which are (or which are sufficiently similar to) the conditions under which it *evolved* or for which it was *designed* then it appears that Tye's view collapses into Dretske's bio-functional theory. Yet some independent specification of optimal conditions (for a system) is needed to avoid the ever present worry that the definition is vacuous: optimal conditions are the conditions under which S and P covary because of P, so every state of anything will represent anything it *can* covary with under some conditions (so, e.g. the weight of the morning paper represents yesterday's Dow Jones average since there are *some* – doubtless rather bizarre and of necessity difficult to specify – conditions under which the average would cause the weight). The problem is real. Take another of Tye's examples, a thermometer. The height of the mercury column in the thermometer covaries with the temperature, but it equally, if not actually more reliably, covaries with the volume of mercury in the tube. Tye's solution here is to invoke the intentions of the designers to specify both what is represented and, implicitly, what optimal conditions might be. But a perfectly analogous problem arises for the tree ring example. Is it the age of the tree or the number of growth spurts that is represented? The latter is likely to be the more 'accurate' representation since in a really bad year no ring will be laid down. And, obviously, there was no design, not even an evolutionary 'design' that makes tree rings into a representation of tree age (or number of growth spurts) which could adjudicate this question.

At bottom, one is inclined to suspect that representations covary with what they represent (to the extent that they do) because they are representations of that thing, rather than that they represent it because they covary with it. If this suspicion is correct then the optimal conditions clause should be read as 'x is the kind of thing which represents and is in the conditions suitable for fulfilling its representing function (and now I'll tell you what it represents) . . .'. But then we are owed an account of what makes something the kind of thing which represents and an account of its representing function. Tye provides no such account; obviously it is tempting to turn to biosemantics, but then any usefulness of the covariational part of the definition drops away. In any case, Tye's theory does not eliminate the problems we have so far been pressing on the representational theory.

Now back to Dretske. Another problem is deeply worrying. Sooner or later, any theory of consciousness will have to face the generation problem. According to Dretske, conscious experiences are those representations$_s$ that 'service the construction of representations$_a$' (1995, p. 19) or 'are the states whose functions it is to supply information to a cognitive system for calibration and use in the control and regulation of behavior' (1995, p. 19). But the deflation/inflation of function argument we've been considering shows us that there is an extremely extensive hierarchical range of representations$_s$ of which the huge majority, perhaps all, fulfil the condition for being conscious experiences. Although Dretske is notoriously willing to allow for conscious experiences of which no one is conscious (see his 1993 and for problems with this approach Seager 1994 or chapter 3 above), it stretches credibility past the breaking point to allow for a huge set of such experiences which occur in every act of sensory awareness and of which we are in fact completely *incapable* of becoming conscious. Our cognitive systems are hives of representational activity (certainly no representational theory of mind, such as Dretske espouses so fervently, can deny this) but surely consciousness is conferred upon only a tiny subset of the representations$_s$ buzzing about within the system. Yet they all play their part in servicing the 'construction of representations$_a$'. One demand of the generation problem is to explain why only some of a group of otherwise similar entities become conscious.

The simplest example of this problem that I can think of arises in something as common as stereo vision. Hold up a bookmark before you at arm's length in front of a patterned background. Shut your left eye and look through your right eye alone; now do the reverse. The two views are distinctly different and they are different again from the combined stereo view provided by both eyes. Of course, there is a sense of depth in the latter view missing from either view from a single eye but the views are different in more basic information content. A schematic example is given in fig. 7.2.

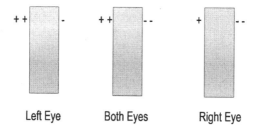

Left Eye   Both Eyes   Right Eye

(Fig. 7.2)

Each of these is a distinct representation$_s$, each of them can enter consciousness and the representation provided by both eyes is evidently some kind of combination of the representations from each eye. Note how the information about the background is integrated into a view containing information which neither eye can provide by itself. There is every reason to think that the representations from each eye remain active within the system during stereo vision, but they are no longer conscious representations. It is equally obvious that these representations continue to service the construction of representations$_a$, i.e. beliefs about the world. So Dretske owes us an account of what makes only some of the representations$_a$ which serve to construct representations$_s$ conscious while others remain non-conscious. This is a particular form of an extremely general problem of consciousness which no theory has successfully solved and upon which it seems the representational theory achieves no advance. With no answer to this question, the pure generation problem remains inviolate. What makes representations conscious? This mystery remains as deep as ever.

There is no end to these mysteries. Consider that, once a representation 'makes it' into consciousness, it will present to us a feature of the world as our cognitive system represents the world. As Dretske says, there is no problem in 'knowing *what* you believe and experience' (1995, p. 54). There is nonetheless a problem, as the passage continues: 'the problem is in knowing *that* you believe and experience it'.

Dretske then goes on to consider relatively benign instances of this difficulty. But there is a huge problem lurking here, which Dretske does not address until much later, in the very last chapter of his book.

Box 7.5 • Introducing Swampman

According to bio-functionalism (and many other theories of representation too), whether a state *is* a representation or not depends upon its standing in certain crucial relations to things entirely external to the representational system. According to the representational theory of consciousness, all consciousness is representational in nature. A system that was incapable of representing anything could not be, even to the slightest degree, conscious. This suggests a variety of 'rogue consciousness' thought experiments, in which are posited creatures that seem to be conscious but who do not stand in the appropriate external relations required to underwrite representation. The most extreme of these is Swampman. Swampman is an accidentally created, absolutely perfect, molecule-for-molecule, duplicate of some target creature who cannot be denied to be conscious (for example, *you*). It is hard to deny that Swampman is conscious, but the representational theory of consciousness seems forced to make that denial because of the argument given above. Perhaps the representational theory can bite this bullet, or perhaps it should be considered that dealing with Swampman in an intuitively satisfying way is an adequacy condition upon any theory of consciousness and the failure to deal with Swampman is a *reductio* of such a theory. Is Swampman too radically *weird* and improbable to worry about? This might, conceivably, be so if theories of consciousness had nothing to say about him, but in fact their application to Swampman is clear. Instead of being unable to say anything about Swampman, they say altogether too much in their flat denial that Swampman has any conscious experience at all. Swampman merely focusses our attention on certain consequences of making representational capabilities depend upon features external to the representing system and as such he is a legitimate thought experiment.

The problem is elementary. According to a bio-functionalist version of the representational theory, whether a brain state is a representation or not depends upon its function, which in turn depends upon its 'evolutionary history' (pretty broadly construed, but the idea is familiar from e.g. Millikan 1984, 1993 or Godfrey-Smith 1994). So any system which either lacks such a history or lacks a direct, intentional implantation of representational capacities, will have no representational states. If it lacks representational states then it simply cannot be conscious, not to the least degree. So, to take a now famous example, Donald Davidson's *Swampman* (introduced in Davidson 1987) – an atom for atom duplicate of Davidson created entirely by accident – will be utterly unconscious. Of course, Swampman will wince and moan when he twists his ankle, but he will *feel* nothing! To get personal about it, *you* face the risk that in fact you are right now utterly unconscious; whether you are conscious or not depends upon facts about the evolutionary history of your species (and ancestor species) and you cannot be sure of these facts 'from the inside' – amazingly, there is no 'inside' unless these facts obtain. This 'possibility' does not seem to be merely unlikely (actually, if it is a possibility then its probability is as incalculable as that of the possibility of deception by Descartes's evil genius); it strikes me as utterly absurd. Nor, as Dretske concedes with the above remark, can one go transcendental here with the argument that since it is evident that I am conscious I thereby know that I possess the required evolutionary history,[15] since, as Kant might say, this history is a condition for the possibility of my own consciousness. For how, from within the confines of the bio-functional theory of representation, can it be *evident* that something is a representation? Note that a champion of the bio-functional approach, Ruth Millikan, explicitly endorses the claim that this cannot be evident when she says: 'we do not have . . . certain knowledge via Cartesian reflection, even of the fact *that* we mean, let alone knowledge of what we mean or knowledge that what we mean is true' (1984, p. 93) and 'absolutely nothing is guaranteed directly from within an act of consciousness' (1984, p. 92). I think it is considerably more tempting to take the threat of this new 'sceptical possibility' as a *reductio* of Dretske's theory. Since *all* reasoning essentially presupposes a conscious engagement with some problem at hand, any theory that threatens this presupposition – or any reasoning purporting to support such a theory – must be rejected. Such theories (or reasoning) are literally unthinkable.

Since this problem will come up frequently in what follows, will form a focus of chapter 8 and constitutes a general threat to a great number of accounts of mental content when they are applied to consciousness, it deserves a name. Call it the *anti-Cartesian catastrophe* and define it as the situation that arises whenever a theory of consciousness has the consequence that it is possible that one is utterly unconscious even as one 'seems to' think and feel. Of course, this is poorly expressed since *seeming* to think and feel are states of consciousness themselves and if seemings are allowed then the catastrophe has not occurred. It is hard to come up with a more coherent description of the difficulty but it evidently must obtrude into any externalist theory of conscious mental content. Since I can't know that the requisite external relations obtain between myself and the world, I can't know that I am conscious or that I am having any experiences. That is the catastrophe.

Nonetheless, Dretske bites the bullet on Swampman. He admits that there is a strong 'internalist intuition' but goes on to say: 'aside . . . from its intuitive appeal – an appeal that we should mistrust – is there any reason to think the Internalist Intuition valid in the extraordinary circumstances described in Swampman (and similar "replacement") thought experiments?' (1995, p. 149). He goes on to claim that the internalist intuition is a brute intuition, 'one that is not justified by any defensible claim about the nature of thought or experience' (1995, p. 150). This is an odd remark. His denial of the internalist intuition – and the problems facing Dretske canvassed above – do not stem from considerations of thought and experience but rather from a certain theory of representation. On the face of it, a theory of representation has nothing to say directly about consciousness, even if one accepts a representational theory of consciousness. The logical situation is this:

(P1) Consciousness = Representation.
(P2) Biosemantics.
So, the internalist intuition is false.

Clearly, anyone who wants to defend the internalist intuition can, and I would say ought, to attack the biosemantics component of Dretske's theory. We have already seen that it is this component of Dretske's theory that leads to many problematic features. The denial of the internalist intuition is, we might say, the final straw that should lead us to overthrow the biosemantics version of the representational theory. I would say that we have as much reason to suppose that Swampman will, upon his creation, feel and think as we have to suppose that he will respond to gravity in the same way any other object of his mass will. Sure, he is an extraordinary creature, whose probability is at best only slightly greater than zero, but clearly physics will apply to him. I can see no reason, save a prior commitment, not to a theory of mind, but to the bio-functional theory of representation why psychology won't equally apply. It will sure *look* like psychology applies to him.

Swampman is a rather far fetched thought experiment though none the worse for that since, as Leibniz pointed out, 'bizarre fictions have their uses in abstract studies, as aids to a better grasp of the nature of our ideas' (1765/1981, p. 314). We can imagine somewhat more probable analogues. Soon we shall have a considerable power to manipulate the genetic machinery of our fellow organisms, and ourselves. Let us suppose that in this brave new world we decide to give a certain creature a new discriminatory ability by modifying its genetic makeup (see the PTU example discussed above). Let's say that we modify it so that it can hear – as I'm sure we would say – somewhat higher frequency sounds than its conspecifics. All we have to do to make sure that there is no consciousness or experience of these sounds, even though there *is* discrimination of them from other sounds, is to ensure that it is not the *function* of the modified sense organs to respond to the higher frequencies. Can we do this? Well, obviously evolution will not have provided this putative new function. Why, then, can we not simply and sincerely state that this experiment is not intended to provide any new functional features to this organism's perceptual repertoire? Suppose that we built a device that we knew would accurately 'track' some natural feature. That would not be sufficient to make it the function of the device to track this feature (e.g. is it the function of party banners to indicate the direction of the wind?). I suppose that one might reply that the new ability involves an *implicit* representational function (recall the distinction introduced above) since it is a simple extension of a representational 'field' already in place and will use representational machinery already in place within the organism. Maybe so, but that is an attack upon a particular feature of the example, not its principle. Let's make the response to the higher frequencies erratic and not smoothly connected to the old responses to lower frequencies. The basic question is, can we make a system that covaries with some property without making it the function of the system to represent that property? If we can then we can make Swampman analogues of sensing creatures.

Box 7.6 • Function and Intention

It seems that the designers and builders of an artifact more or less get to assign whatever functions they like to their creations. This is so even if their artifact is a copy of another artifact already in possession of a quite different function. For example, what do you think this is:

It's hard to tell from the picture, but here's a hint: this is a carefully carved mastodon tusk, created about 50,000 years ago by some Neanderthal worker. It is hypothesized that this is some kind of musical instrument (see *Discover*, April 1997, p. 19, from which this figure is adapted, where it is reported that the tusk contains '16 carefully aligned holes' – a musically significant number; this 'tuba' adds a second instrument to the Neanderthal orchestra, as what appears to be a similarly aged 'flute' was also found quite recently). Now suppose we decide to test the musical capabilities of such a device. The original is far too fragile to handle, let alone vigorously to blow into, so we build a duplicate. Letting our imaginations soar, let's suppose we build a perfect, molecule-for-molecule copy of the original. What is its function? It is *not* a musical instrument, but rather an anthropological test device. If we *wanted*, we could assemble a Neanderthal quartet, equipping it with duplicates of tuba and flute which would then be devices with a musical function. But if we have control over the functions of artifacts, what stops us from making a Swampman in the genetics laboratory (apart from formidable technical difficulties of course). If we subscribe to the representational theory of consciousness and some kind of a functional theory of representation, there could be no moral objection to such an experiment, for the resulting creature would be entirely unconscious and unfeeling, just so long as *we* decided that it had no representational functions. Is it just me, or is there something seriously wrong with the conclusion here?

In fact, if we *assembled* (from the appropriate molecular constituents) a complete Swampman with the direct intention of producing a 'human' with no genetic history, what would give that creature's sensory systems the function of representing the perceptible properties of things in the world? The fact that we copied nature? Arguably, our assembled Swampman will in fact *not* have these representational functions because the explanation of the details of his sensory systems does not essentially depend upon the functioning of his ancestors' sensory systems. He has no ancestors (of the relevant sort). Neither he nor his sensory systems are members of a 'reproductively established family'. And, I stress, we are explicitly intending to create a creature without any representational functions. Copying a system with functions does not copy the functions. To take Dretske's favourite example, I could carefully build a perfect copy of a speedometer without any intention of making something to represent speed. In fact, I could, on a whim, decide to copy a speedometer to use as a paperweight; the fact that it could be inserted into a car and used as a speedometer does not mean that it *is* a speedometer or that, as it sits faithfully pinning down my papers, it manages to represent a speed by way of its dial pointing to a certain number (0 mph). So even an assembled Swampman (I admit, an extremely unlikely creature but immeasurably more probable than the random Swampman originally envisaged) will be utterly unconscious (at least for a while). Is it just a 'brute intuition', unsupported by any reasonable theory of mind or experience, that leads us to suspect, as the creature screams and writhes as we hold its hand in the fire, that it feels pain?

Here Tye's version of the theory appears to differ significantly from Dretske's. Tye agrees with me that swampcreatures must surely be capable of having conscious experiences (1995, p. 154). So it seems paradoxical that he also agrees with Dretske that it is possible that two molecule-for-molecule identical organisms could differ in that one had sensory experiences while the other did not (1995, p. 194). The paradox is 'resolved' by Tye's disappointing admission that it is 'zombie replicas with duplicate environments and histories' that are impossible. His example of a perfect molecule-for-molecule replica that lacks the experiences of its twin involves imagining a distinct history and environment. Of course, this is no different from Dretske's theory. Bio-functional theories of representation demand that identical histories, environments and local structure will lead to identical representational content and hence identical experiences. So according to Tye, a Swampman who is utterly unconscious ought to be possible. This will ultimately depend upon whether Swampman has any representations within him at the time he is miraculously created. We should not prejudge the issue whether Swampman is the sort of *thing* that has any representational machinery within it. This harks back to the problem with Tye's definition of representation scouted above – it may be that Tye does not provide us with any theoretical way to answer the crucial question of whether Swampman has any representational states within him. Because, of course, we don't have to imagine that Swampman is created in a perfectly ordinary environment. Instead of imagining a Swampman who enters the ordinary physical world as an active participant, imagine a Swampman who comes into being in a state of reverie, remembering (as it were) certain of his (as it were) dream experiences. He or she is, say, identical to *you* on one of those occasions when you awake in a pitch dark room, overwhelmed by the memory of a dream, completely unaware of your surroundings. Let us also imagine that our swampcreature has *no* surroundings – but is created in an infinite empty space (wearing a space suit if you like). *This* swampcreature has no environment, no history and nothing for its 'representations' to covary with. According to Tye, I think, *this* swampcreature must be considered to be utterly unconscious and incapable of having any experiences. I find this no more plausible than Tye finds the conclusion that the standard Swampman is devoid of experience.

Actually, even the 'ordinary' Swampman should fail to have experiences on Tye's account. For how could one say what the optimal conditions for such a creature are? Tye says that since his behaviour is 'entirely appropriate to the states that are tracked . . . it is natural to suppose . . . that optimal conditions obtain' (1995, p. 155). This hard-ly seems 'natural' to me; the idea that there even *are* optimal (representational) conditions for such a creature seems absurd (once again, it is hard to understand this idea of 'optimal' which is supposedly utterly divorced from considerations of design, ancestral proclivities, typical environment, etc.). Anyway, couldn't our Swampman be created in a state identical to the state *I* am in one and half hours after ingesting 500 micrograms of LSD? These are, for sure, not optimal conditions for sensory representation of the world and they definitely interfere with the appropriateness of my tracking of the states of the world around me but they don't interfere with my *having* experiences. I think such a swampcreature would also have these bizarre experiences but I don't see why conditions that are optimal for me are also optimal for him. Tye's admission of Swampman into the charmed circle of consciousness is more grudging than it appears at first glance.

It's worth thinking about representation under non-optimal conditions. Basic logic applied to Tye's definition suggests that if optimal conditions do not obtain then any state, S, of subject, x, represents *anything* (by the truth of the conditional attendant upon the falsity of the antecedent). This may be taking elementary propositional logic too far, but what if optimal conditions *never* obtain for some system? The LSD Swampman is in this predicament (let's say that this Swampman dissolves after two hours). Philosophical fancy can in any case go further. Suppose that the proverbial brain-in-a-vat is a *swamp* brain-in-a-vat, created out of nothing along with its vat and attendant machinery. Now, a human brain put into a vat will retain its ability to experience on either Dretske's or Tye's account. It looks like on neither account does the swamp brain have any conscious experience.

Could Tye make his definition of representation counterfactual, so that it would become: S represents that P = if optimal conditions *were* to obtain, then S *would be* tokened iff P and this *would be* because of P? For this to help, we must suppose that optimal conditions for the brain in the vat are the same as optimal conditions for me. Why should this be so? I don't see how we could anchor to this brain any particular set of conditions as optimal without appeal to design, evolutionary history, etc. which the swamp brain utterly lacks.

The basic problem is that until you have a system whose job it is to represent, it makes no sense to speak of the optimal conditions for representing. But, from the point of view of the representational theory of consciousness, the Swampman problem starts with the question whether Swampman is the kind of thing that is in the business of representing. If you don't have an answer to this question, you can't begin to look for the optimal conditions under which Swampman's states will be representational states.

Another problem: according to Tye, representational states are not experiences unless they are poised to affect the beliefs (and other intentional states) of the system they are within (1995, pp. 137–8). So if a system is unable to get into any intentional states it cannot have any conscious experiences (1995, p. 144). So if Swampman can't have any beliefs (or other intentional mental states) then he can't be conscious. What, according to Tye, are the conditions for being able to have beliefs and desires? This is unclear; beliefs are a kind of representation, but not representations that abide by the covariational theory. What theory, then, does Tye favour for the representational content of beliefs and desires? Obviously, if he turns now to a bio-functional theory then Swampman loses consciousness for the secondary reason that his sensory representations cannot feed into the appropriate belief-desire system! Tye allows that beliefs involve *concepts*, so the answer to this worry depends, at least in part, upon the story Tye favours for the nature and acquisition of concepts. He unfortunately does not tell us this story. In Dretske's account we can allow that there is a unified account of representation, and representational capacity, from the most basic sensory representations all the way to the most complex intentional states (whether such an account, which Dretske does not elaborate, could be made to work is very unclear, but that is another issue).

Because it stems from such considerations a particular worry about Tye's theory should be mentioned here. A troubling potential difference between Dretske and Tye concerns animal consciousness. Both philosophers wish to assert that animals are conscious in the sense that there is something that it is like to be such an animal, that animals can feel pain, etc. (see Dretske 1995, p. 111 and Tye 1995, p. 5). Both Tye and Dretske subscribe to the theory of introspection outlined above in which introspection essentially requires the deployment of a field of mentalistic and mental-representational concepts. So it follows that if animals do not have such concepts (if animals don't have a 'theory of the mind') then animals are incapable of introspection. But a creature's inability to introspect would not seem to have any particular connection to the question of whether or not the creature is conscious. About this, Dretske says: '. . . are we to believe that [a dog's] itch is not conscious . . . because the dog has no conceptual resources for thinking that it is an itch . . .' (1995, p. 111). However, Tye draws very strong conclusions from their common theory of introspection. 'Without the application of concepts', says Tye, 'our sensations are concealed from us. We are like the distracted driver who sees the road ahead, and thereby manages to avoid crashing, but who is oblivious to his visual perceptions' (1995, p. 190). It appears to follow from this understanding of the relationship between consciousness and introspection that animals are perpetually and irredeemably in a state like that of the distracted driver with respect to *all* their sensations, perceptions and any other 'phenomenal' states as well, inasmuch as they lack the concepts needed for introspective knowledge. The worry is brought out clearly by applying an argument already used (see chapter 3 above) in the discussion of the HOT theory of consciousness. Tye reveals in the quoted passage that his version of the representational theory is remarkably close to the HOT theory. Suppose you have a terrible headache. You go to your doctor who recommends a new drug which while not removing the disagreeable phenomenal quality of your current states disengages it from the conceptual machinery underpinning introspection. You shall become, with respect to your headache, as the distracted driver is to the perceptions of the highway. The question is, would you be suffering, would you truly be in pain, after taking this drug? Perhaps you find yourself moaning and prone to hold your head, but you can't *feel* anything (perhaps we should add: so far as you can tell). Such a drug would be an analgesic. If this is what it is like for animals, then there seems little to be concerned about regarding their treatment or condition. They are not really *suffering*, no matter how intense their pain may appear to be to an observer of their behaviour (a philosopher who draws exactly this conclusion is Carruthers 1989).

Hopefully, the representational theory is not forced to accept this view of animal, not to mention child, consciousness. I don't think that it is. It is possible to interpret the distracted driver in a different way. It *could* be that the driver loses consciousness of the road because the information from the road simply ceases to be conscious (in Tye's terms, ceases to be *phenomenal*). On Tye's official theory one way this could happen is if this information ceases to be *poised*, that is, ceases to be ready to influence the belief and desire system. We have already seen that the theory must accommodate a distinction between representations that are conscious from those that are not and that effecting this accommodation is not a straightforward task. We can use this problem to our advantage here. The representations of the road slip from consciousness for the distracted driver because they lose what it takes to be conscious representations. So perhaps in such cases animals are unlike the distracted driver *simply* in the lack of a set of sophisticated mentalistic concepts. Maybe that is a sufficient reply, but with the reader's indulgence I would like to go a little deeper into this. We may suppose that normally the sensory information extracted from one's view of the road ahead is ported to high level cognitive systems that support *beliefs* about the road ahead and that normally we drive with, so to speak, this high level cognitive system (not entirely of course, much of the basic operation of a car really does seem to become unconscious with enough practice). But it is possible that when a driver becomes distracted, the business of keeping the car on the road becomes a much lower level activity in which rather primitive visual information sustains the link between road, eye, hand and foot. Such information is truly *sub-conscious*. Animals might, perhaps often, go into such states but we don't have to suppose that they are always like this or that they would typically be in such a state when confronted with the insistent, highly motivational representations of bodily damage that is pain.

A natural question to ask here is whether there are and, if so, what are the differences in the nature of the consciousness of a creature that has a full complement of mentalistic concepts from a creature that does not. According to both Dretske and Tye, consciousness exists only in systems that can have beliefs and desires (though, of course, these creatures need not be capable of introspective beliefs or desires). It follows that animals do possess concepts. Is this a problem? Both Dretske and Tye also agree that experiences are non-conceptual representations. So how come consciousness requires the addition of a genuinely conceptual faculty? I suspect that this view is really grounded in the fear that otherwise too many obviously lifeless and unfeeling representational systems will end up being conscious after all. This does not address the point of the question. Articulating the proper answer may require a more radical theory of representation than we have seen so far. These issues will be discussed below in chapters 8 and 9. To end this excursus, what should we now say about the hypothetical pain remedy introduced above? One should look closely at how the link between sensory representation and conceptual machinery is broken. It seems reasonable to suppose that the representations are no longer, in Tye's terminology, poised to affect the belief-desire system. If so, they are after all not phenomenal. They are truly unconscious. I think this is quite a nice result which firmly and quite properly distances the representational theory from the HOT theory of consciousness.

More, much more, will be said about Swampman below. I want to stress two points here: both the bio-functional and Tye's covariational accounts of the representational theory deal with Swampman type cases in ways that lead to many unsatisfactory conclusions (it is not simply a matter of a single clash with a dispensable intuition). And, the problems stem from the theory of representation, not from the representational theory of consciousness itself. That theory remains a plausible, intriguing and refreshingly distinctive approach to consciousness. *Any* version of it will be a hostage to the fortunes of its attendant theory of representation. And no thorough development of it can proceed without paying attention to the associated theory of representation. It was entirely proper of Dretske to present his theory in the context of the bio-functional theory of representation, for which he has in any case independently argued (see Dretske 1986, 1988). But I think we will have to evaluate the theory with some alternative theory of representation in mind. This theory will have to be fundamentally an *internalist* theory of representation. While such theories are not very fashionable at the moment, some have recognized the need for at least an internalist component in the proper theory of content (see for example McGinn 1989, Searle 1983, Devitt 1990, Loar 1988, Chalmers 1996b; for some discussion of internalism see chapter 8 below).

Unfortunately, a movement towards internalism will not eliminate all the problems which stem from Dretske's espousal of the bio-functional account of representation. A problem remains that is independent of such details. It is a problem that has been lurking in the philosophy of mind at least since Descartes but has seldom been noticed.[16] The representational theory has the virtue of making this problem disturbingly visible though whether the theory can solve it is doubtful. The problem can be stated very concisely in Cartesian language: in consciousness we are aware of the objective reality of our ideas, not their formal reality. To say this in the terms of the modern representational theory of consciousness is a little more long winded. What we are consciously aware of are the properties of objects as represented by our cognitive system[17]; but we have no awareness of the properties of the brain states which are the token representations, which properties, in part at least, account for the fact that these brain states manage to represent the properties of the objects of which we are aware in consciousness. According to the theory, there is nothing mysterious about the way that brain states represent – they get to be representations in fundamentally the same way that speedometers or bee-dances[18] do (these particular examples differ simply in the existence of a genuine background intention to *create* a representational system in the former case which is missing in the latter, but this is not supposed to make any significant difference in the representations themselves – if it did make an important difference the whole theory would be in jeopardy). However, the combination of the ideas that brain states are 'normal' representations and that we are aware of what these states represent is deeply mysterious. For it is obviously true that we come to know what a particular normal representation represents by being aware of (some of) the non-representational properties of that representation. When I come to know that some story is about a cat, this is because I was aware of the word 'cat' via its shape, its contrast with the paper on which it is printed, etc. (circumlocutions are of course possible but they don't affect the point here). When I become aware that a picture is representing a certain kind of scene this is because I am aware of the properties of the picture itself, its panoply of colours, shapes and textures.

We can also describe this problem in terms of a distinction between the *content* and the *vehicles* of representations (these are the terms in which Sedivy 1995 couches her discussion). Content is what is represented (objective reality); the vehicle of this content is the set of properties of the token representation which, in part, enables it to fulfil its representational function (an aspect of the representation's formal reality). I say 'in part' since there will, in general, also be a variety of features external to the vehicle which are required for a representation to represent. In these terms, the problem is to account for the fact that in consciousness we are aware of the content of representations *without* being aware of their vehicles.

So it now turns out that brain representations (at least some of them) are remarkably different from all the representations we are familiar with. I can become aware of what certain brain states represent (their content) in the complete absence of any awareness of the properties of the brain states which are doing the representing (their vehicles). How is this possible? And note that only *I* can have such wonderfully transparent access to my brain states' contents, for while you can perhaps find out what my brain states represent, you would have to do this by examining my brain (as well as many other things no doubt). *You*, in principle, can read my brain like a book but *I* can read my brain in an entirely different way. This is disturbingly reminiscent of Descartes's ideas of the perfect transparency of the mind to introspection. The problem is much more focussed here however. There is no need for any claim that we have infallible access to our mental states or that *all* mental states are open to conscious inspection or, indeed, that *any* mental states are introspectively accessible (though in fact of course we know that a great many are introspectible). But the representational theory must assent to the idea that we are conscious of what is represented without the necessity (or perhaps even the possibility) of being aware of the representation's 'enabling' features.

Thus the whole representational approach may be undercut with the threat of a vicious regress. *If* (1) we need to be aware of the properties of a representation in order to be aware of what that representation represents and (2) all awareness is of represented properties, *then* there will have to be an infinity of representations underlying any act of awareness. This is a vicious regress since it is required that one have an awareness of the properties of the previous representation *before* one can become aware of what the current representation represents. Since (2) just *is* the representational theory, we will have to deny (1). If the representationalist does so, we then deserve an account of some other mechanism by which one can become aware of what a representation represents. This is never tackled in Dretske's account (nor Tye's for that matter).

The problem is aggravated by the admission, which is entirely reasonable in itself, that only *some* brain representations are conscious. Only some representations have this mysterious power of 'directly' revealing their objective reality. How do they get it? It is no answer to say that it is just these representations that become conscious – that is only a thinly disguised restatement of the problem for, on this theory, consciousness is awareness of what is represented.

I confess that I can find no model – not even an implausible one – of how representations can, as it were, reveal what or how they are representing to consciousness in the absence of any consciousness of the properties of the representation which enable it to be a representation. One can, of course, assert that it is a *brute fact* that certain brain states can, as it were, deliver their content to consciousness. One can even enlist our regress to show there must be a primitive layer of representations which can enter awareness 'directly', not in virtue of an awareness of their vehicles. Well, this is an exceedingly curious property of those configurations of the physical world we call brain states. And it is doubly wonderful that it is a *brute* feature of the universe manifesting itself, despite its bruteness, *only* in extremely complex assemblies of matter (that otherwise seem to function entirely in terms of the combined contributions of their simpler physical parts). Baldly asserting that brains have such a property as a brute feature of their makeup is hardly a *solution* to the generation problem. Here is another mystery of consciousness; the deepest one of all, I fear.

But Dretske's theory does not face this difficulty alone. The representational theory remains to my mind the most plausible, most exciting and most promising approach to the problems of consciousness yet devised. Perhaps, with tinkering, everything *but* the generation problem can eventually be solved by it.

Box 7.7 • Summary

The idea that all states of consciousness are representational states faces many difficulties. What is interesting is that most of these stem from the particular theory of representation which is chosen to underlie the theory. Especially troublesome are those theories of representation which make representations depend upon a representational system standing in certain relations to things entirely external to the system itself. Rather unfortunately, it is these that are by far the most popular and most well developed theories of representation currently on offer. They are also rather plausible, until coupled to the representational theory of consciousness. This issue will lead to further insight into both representation and consciousness. The representational theory of consciousness also highlights a whole range of problems that have been given scant attention, but which are extremely interesting and, I think, help to reveal key features of consciousness. Perhaps the most striking of these is the peculiar property of consciousness that it can 'reveal' the contents of representations without any reliance upon an awareness of the nature of the representational vehicles that manage to carry those contents.

8

CONSCIOUS INTENTIONALITY
AND THE
ANTI-CARTESIAN CATASTROPHE

Box 8.1 • Preview

Whether or not one wholeheartedly adopts a representational theory of consciousness, there is at least one zone of mentality where it must be essentially correct: conscious *thought*. The core of conscious thinking is awareness of content. It is not a special sort of phenomenal or qualitative consciousness; it seems quite distinct from the consciousness of colours, sounds and other sensory qualities (on the other side of the coin, it is this difference that is supposed to give the problem of qualia its special bite). So conscious thought puts an inescapable burden on the externalist theories of representation and mental content. I argue that conscious thought in fact *shows* that externalist views of mental content cannot be correct. Perhaps this only indicates that the ambitions of these externalist views must be moderated, and there may be various ways to retreat from radical externalism. Perhaps it reveals that there is some sort of very deep misunderstanding about the nature of consciousness lurking within almost all our thinking about it. Or it may simply show that some kind of *internalist* theory of mental content or representation is needed to account for conscious thought. The details of such a theory, or even whether a non-trivial one can be coherently formulated, are unfortunately far from clear.

Our discussion of the representational theory of consciousness has focussed, somewhat by default, on perceptual consciousness. Dretske almost exclusively restricts his discussion to this domain and Tye goes only a little further in his treatment of the 'phenomenal states'. This is understandable since the really intimidating problems of qualia have always centred on the vividly phenomenal states of perception and feeling, and this is where the representational theory can make tremendous headway. It is also where one would expect the most resistance to the theory since it is far from obvious that the phenomenal is properly to be understood in representational terms.

But assuming that this last issue can be successfully addressed, a whole new level of difficulty heaves into view. Not all states of consciousness are 'purely' phenomenal, certainly not if this means that they are all either bare perceptual states or other 'feeling' states. The new problem can be raised in a very stark form if we note that both Dretske and Tye are at pains to insist that the kind of representational content assigned to the states of consciousness which they aim to discuss is *non-conceptual* content. The legitimacy of the distinction between conceptual and non-conceptual content is somewhat controversial, but even tentatively accepting it forces us to ask about the *conceptual* content of conscious states. For example, seeing a tree is a perceptual state but it is perfectly possible, normal and usual for one to be aware of the tree *as* a tree. It appears to one not only as a vague, jumbled, greenish and brownish *coloured-shape* (though this is evidently already a conceptualized version of the content)[1] but also literally as a *tree*. This is a perceptual state with conceptual content, as well as, perhaps, the non-conceptual content of some kind of a 'pure' perceptual state. It is natural to ask about the relationship between the putative non-conceptual content of the pure perceptual state and the conceptual content of 'seeing a *tree*' in the more typical, if impure, state, but this question is not addressed by Dretske or Tye. One might be tempted, philosophers have been tempted, by the answer that we somehow *infer* conceptual content from non-conceptual content. But there are great difficulties in working out how the non-conceptual can stand in inferential, or evidential, relations to the conceptual. This is the problem of the given, or the myth of the given (see Sellars 1956; for an overview of the epistemic situation see Bonjour 1985, chapter 4). One might then decide, as did Sellars, that the non-conceptual 'content' just *causes* certain beliefs to come into existence, where the general appropriateness and accuracy of these beliefs is a matter of the training we receive which actually produces in us the relevant concepts and the capacity to 'apply' them (the scare quotes are needed since despite initial linguistic appearance the *application* of a concept is certainly not an action). But this is obviously not very satisfactory since we surely want to appeal to the way the object of our vision *looks* in support of our judgement that it is in fact a tree before us. It seems that the veracity of the conceptual content of our states of consciousness can be evidentially *supported* by appearances, not just be caused by them. We have *reasons* for thinking that we are seeing a tree before us, and while these reasons are not exhausted by the appearances, they must *involve* the way the tree looks to us.

Tye says that the non-conceptual content of experiences 'stands ready and in a position to make a direct impact on the belief/desire system' (1995, p. 138). We can perhaps read this as an endorsement of the pure causal account of the relation between non-conceptual and conceptual content. But then we also have to ask, in what sense are we *aware* of this non-conceptual content? Recall Tye's statement that 'without the application of concepts our sensations are concealed from us. We are like the distracted driver who sees the road ahead, and thereby manages to avoid crashing, but who is oblivious to his visual perceptions' (1995, p. 190). Dretske almost echoes this: 'the access one has to the quality of one's experience . . . is only through the concepts one has for having thoughts about experience' (1995, p. 134). It looks rather as if we can only be aware of content through the veil of concepts but, if so, we are not ever aware of the *non-conceptual* content at all but instead are, so to speak, only aware of some conceptualization of that content. As we saw above, this cannot be the proper interpretation of this aspect of the representational theory of consciousness for it reduces the theory to the HOT theory. What Dretske says in the above ellipsis helps us to see a better interpretation; interpolate into the above quote: 'unlike the access one has to the qualities of the external objects the experience is an experience of'. So long as we strenuously remember that it is access to these qualities *as represented* we are on our way to a better understanding of the theory.

Concepts are ways of representing;[2] non-conceptual contents are also ways of representing. Thus I am intrigued by the possibility that a concept could represent the world in exactly the way that a non-conceptual content represents the world. Above (in chapter 6), I called such concepts 'substantial concepts' of how things look, or, more generally, appear in whatever sensory mode. Of course, most of our concepts do not have this very special and rather peculiar feature. The concept 'tree' for example does not represent the way that any particular tree looks to us; it could hardly serve its cognitive function if it did, which is after all to represent trees, not particular trees and still less particular tree-*appearances*. Some concepts evidently get closer to the phenomenal level. Consider for example the visual concept of 'pitch blackness'. But best of all we have ready to hand, instantly constructible (and storable in memory or forgettable), a set of indexical concepts which we – as thoroughly conceptual beings – can apply to experience whenever we like, so long as we are having the experience, recreating it in memory or imaginatively generating it: this pain, this colour, this sound, etc. It seems to me that these indexical concepts are the perfect tool with which to bring any non-conceptual contents into contact with the conceptual. Once 'indexicalized', these non-conceptual contents are ready to enter into inferential relations, they have been brought into the 'space of reasons'. This does not mean that the non-conceptual contents don't *cause* our awareness of conceptual content. No doubt they do. Indexicalization allows them to also stand in justificatory relations.[3] I take it that at bottom this means that it really doesn't matter very much whether we *call* phenomenal content *conceptual* content or not, it can be conceptualized just as it is, it represents rightly or wrongly, it meets normative conditions by which we can say that it is correctly representing or not, it is fully *intentional* content, etc.

Arguments against the given are arguments against a certain special epistemic role that primitive experiential contents were supposed to have in the creation and maintenance of knowledge. Strictly speaking, these are not arguments against the existence of primitive experiential contents as such. According to the suggestion made here, once such contents are indexicalized they are fit to enter epistemic relations (though not fit to play the crucial foundational role of the original given, but *that* was an impossible role). Un-indexicalized, they remain active in the system and remain conscious. Suppose that (non-human) animals have beliefs and desires (as both Dretske and Tye,[4] for example, allow and which, though I recognize that there is controversy here, is certainly more plausible than that they do not). This means that animals have some kind of conceptual system in which the content of *their* beliefs and desires are appropriately expressed (more than likely, their concepts are quite different from ours, especially as ours are mostly conditioned, created and maintained by linguistic mechanisms). We can say that for both animals and ourselves (perceptual) beliefs about the world around them are caused by inner events that represent the world. Some of these events are conscious experiences. For the animal there is no question of *having reasons* for the beliefs which are generated by these experiences, in the sense of knowing or appreciating the grounds for the belief.[5] Such an *epistemic* assessment of one's own cognitive position requires conceptual machinery which it is hardly likely animals possess. But we are different. The fact that we can indexicalize experiential contents permits us to see *why* – in an evidential sense – we have the beliefs (about the perceived world) that we do. Of course, it is no accident that we, and the animals, believe in accord with our experiential contents. In general, causes and reasons desynchronize on pain of death and extinction.

It is acceptable to say, then, that we are aware of a tree *as* a tree not only via a causal process but by a causal process that (at least sometimes) also constitutes an inference from something's looking *like this* to its being a tree. Nonetheless, the final product is a consciousness of a tree *as* a tree. There remains a layer of experience that is richly conceptual even if there is *also* a non-conceptual layer of experience which can be transformed into the 'barely conceptual' through the mechanism of indexical concepts. Such high level experience has to be integrated into the representational theory of consciousness if that theory is to be a complete theory of consciousness. This may seem an easy task; after all, it is *more* evident that such high level experience is representational than that the 'purely phenomenal' is representational. In fact, such experience leads to a further host of problems. Let's begin by reviewing the situation.

To say that consciousness necessarily possesses intentionality is to say that all states of consciousness necessarily have an intentional object towards which they are directed or are about or, more simply, represent. Consciousness does not essentially possess intentionality, then, if it is possible to be conscious without being conscious *of* anything. This is one of the few issues in the philosophy of mind that can rightly be settled by introspection; it is clear from conscious experience that when one is conscious one is invariably conscious of something or other. In fact, any state of consciousness involves a multitude of objects. Since we can, usually do and perhaps, in a certain sense, cannot fail to, know what we are conscious of it is reasonable to speak of our *access* to the objects of our states of consciousness. The nature of this access, as well as the philosophically appropriate way to describe it, is traditionally problematic, but its existence is not.

It does not follow simply from the fact that all states of consciousness possess intentionality that all mental states possess intentionality. The popular doctrine that certain mental states, such as pains (or sensations in general) or moods, are not intentional does not imply that one's consciousness of pain is not intentional – obviously a consciousness of pain is directed at the pain. But beware an ambiguity here. Most often, we use the expression 'aware of the pain' to mean no more than 'feel pain'. But there is an important distinction lurking here. On the face of it, the phrase 'aware of a pain' suggests an awareness of a mental state; whereas to feel pain is not to be aware of a mental state – it is to experience a state of one's body (it is grist for the representationalist's mill that pains can be 'purely intentional', that is, have as their object states of non-existent parts of one's body, as in the famous case of phantom limb pain). A toothache provides information about one's tooth, not one's mind. Of course one *can* be aware of pain, and this is to introspect and to engage in a very high level mental activity. I doubt that animals can be aware of pain in this sense though they certainly can *feel* pain. Still, a representational theory of consciousness does not have to endorse a completely representational theory of mind (though there would seem to be little to gain in such reticence – one might as well be hanged for a goat as a sheep). However, it does follow from the intentionality of consciousness that if pains are mental states that lack intentionality then they are not, in and of themselves, states of consciousness. It may well be that all pains (or all *felt* pains) must be conscious pains, but that would not by itself collapse the distinction between the pain and one's consciousness of it.

Box 8.2 • Intentionality, Content and Mode

Intentionality is the property of 'being about something'. Very many mental states possess this property: thoughts have contents which are about things (not necessarily existent things however – one can think about unicorns), desires have their objects, probably best thought of as a way the world could be rather than particular things (when I say I want some soup, I mean that I want to *eat soup* – I want the world to be truly describable as including a soup-eating by me). Perhaps all mental states have intentionality. This was Brentano's thesis, and is the core doctrine of the representational theory of consciousness, which equates 'aboutness' and representation. There are two obviously problematic mental states: sensations and 'objectless' emotions and moods. But reflection shows that sensations generally do provide information about the world or a special part of the world (our bodies). Moods and emotions that appear objectless are plausibly thought of as adding certain background representational feature to everything we are experiencing (objectless depression is a kind of representing of *everything* as more or less awful). Such general 'colourings' of states of consciousness can be called *modes* of consciousness.

However, it would be preferable to allow that pains are themselves states of consciousness. Otherwise, it seems that only those beings that can be conscious of *pain* can be said to be in pain, or to be suffering (such an extreme conclusion is drawn and accepted by Carruthers 1989 – animals do not suffer). But as just noted, feeling pain is *not* a matter of introspection, no more than seeing the cut on your finger is. On the representational theory this entails that pains themselves have intentional content. And, really, this is not difficult to appreciate: pains are located, inform us about the condition of various parts of our bodies and these are representational functions. It remains the burden of the representational theory to show that, so to speak, every element of pain is representational. What is interesting about pain is the 'motivational' force which accompanies this form of perception: we might say that pains provide relatively low resolution information with high motivational content, whereas sense perception provides high resolution information with relatively low motivational content. Sense perception is by no means devoid of motivational force however; imagine yourself as very hungry and consider the difference between perceiving a rock and a raisin. As we correctly say, the raisin *looks* good to eat. Thus I am inclined to say that the *painfulness* of the pain is a matter of representing the 'value' of the bodily state about which the pain is providing information. A more radical version of this suggestion that attempts to undercut the whole class of objections which claim that *painfulness* is a special property of pains, or the experience of pain, which is non-representational is this: the painfulness of the experience of pain is the representation of the bodily state in question *as painful* (a representational feature that is also highly motivating). Just as representing something (in vision) as red is to experience red, so too to represent a bodily state as painful is to experience pain.

It would likely be objected that unfocussed moods, objectless depressions and the like are themselves states of consciousness, and ones that lack intentional objects. One may be depressed without being conscious of one's depression, but this would hardly render one unconscious. Still (as discussed briefly above in chapter 6) it seems to me that the vast majority of such states do have their own intentional objects. We are, when depressed, mostly depressed about something or other and those cases we might like to call objectless are best thought of as *modes* of consciousness or ways of being conscious. Being depressed in this way is then a way of being conscious of things in general: everything seems worthless, or pointless, dull and profitless. That is, more or less, *everything* is represented as being worthless, or pointless, dull and profitless. It is, thankfully but also significantly, impossible for a conscious being to be in a state of consciousness which consists of nothing but unfocussed depression; there always remains a host of objects of consciousness and without these objects there would be no remaining state of consciousness. I would be the last to deny that there are many modes of consciousness and, of course, such modes are not themselves going to call for any *additional* intentional objects (any more than the distinction between *hoping* and *fearing* that p requires any surplus propositional objects to distinguish the hoping from the fearing – these are properly distinguished as ways of apprehending or thinking about p). On the other hand, one can become conscious of the way one is conscious; one can become aware that one is generally depressed, in which case the depression becomes an additional object of consciousness in the ordinary way.

A current state of consciousness should be specified jointly by the current *intentional objects* (as defined below) of consciousness and the current *mode* of consciousness, rather as one's 'propositional attitude state' has to be specified by the dual ascription of a particular proposition and a particular attitude.[6] Mostly, we can only gesture towards such a specification of a state of consciousness, for both the objects of consciousness and the ways one can be conscious of them tend to outrun the resources of language available for their description. For example, it is hard to describe with any precision the perfectly obvious phenomenological difference between having had one and two martinis, and the details of sensory experience are notoriously difficult to convey; the most detailed 'stream of consciousness' novel still leaves us with many distinct possible streams of consciousness equally in accord with the text. But since we are all conscious and can all, more or less, appreciate both the objects of our consciousness and the ways we are conscious of them, such gestures are sufficient for communication.

It may be that the distinction between objects of consciousness and modes of consciousness can help to rehabilitate Brentano's thesis that *the* characteristic of the mental is intentionality. For Brentano surely never meant to deny that there were various ways that the mind could direct itself upon intentional objects. Brentano even says something along these lines: 'every mental phenomenon includes something as object within itself, although they do not all do so in the same way. In presentation something is presented, in judgement something is affirmed or denied, in love loved, in hate hated, in desire desired and so on' (1874/1973, p. 88). Even (non-perceptual) sensations – the paradigm example of supposedly non-intentional mentality – can be regarded as modes of consciousness; that is, crudely, as the way the *body* is presented in consciousness (see Dretske 1995, pp. 102–3). Diffuse states of consciousness like moods and other non-specific emotions can be treated as indicated above, that is, as general modes of consciousness: they are ways *the world* is presented in consciousness, an extensive, background colouring of the field of consciousness. Confusion can arise when we consciously think about these modes themselves for they can then appear to be states of consciousness without objects. But in and of themselves, they simply are not states of consciousness, but require completion by a set of intentional objects. Thinking about them is a state of consciousness, but such thoughts obviously have a straightforward intentional object.

Consciousness is doubly intentional in the sense that we are always conscious of things in a certain way, or we are conscious of things *as* being such-and-such, or, as I shall prefer to speak, under a certain *aspect*. I would *define* the intentional object of a state of consciousness to be an object presented under an aspect; to consciousness there is, as it were, nothing more to the object than what is contained within the aspect (more correctly aspects) under which it appears. The classic illustrations of this feature of consciousness are the ambiguous drawings, such as the Necker cube. To be conscious of the following line drawings (fig. 8.1) at all one must be conscious of them *as* either three dimensional 'wire-frame' cubes in one of two possible spatial orientations or, as some can see them, as merely two-dimensional assemblies of lines (most people can't help but see the example on the left as a cube while many can see the right figure only as a two dimensional 'star-hexagon').[7]

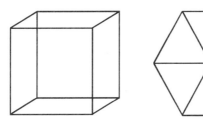

(Fig. 8.1)

This claim is not one of aspect essentialism; few if any objects of consciousness have a mandatory aspect, but all enter consciousness under some aspect or other. The precise relation between 'being conscious of . . .' and 'being conscious of . . . as -' is this:

(1) $(\forall x)\Box(\exists A)(Aw(S,x) \supset Con(S,x,A))$

where 'Aw(S,x)' stands for 'S is conscious of x' and 'Con(S,x,A)' abbreviates 'S is conscious of x as A', where A is an aspect under which x can 'appear' to consciousness. By contrast, aspect essentialism would place the necessity operator within the scope of the existential quantifier.[8] Con(S,x,A) provides the intentional object of S's state of consciousness. We are usually conscious of things under a multitude of aspects simultaneously, and among these we can make distinctions and judgements.

For obvious pragmatic reasons, the way that x is picked out in a 'conscious of . . .' construction is usually designed to reveal the relevant aspect under which the subject is conscious of x. When we ask, 'were you conscious of the stop sign on Smith Street?' we intend to ask whether you were conscious *of* the stop sign *as* a stop sign or, as we would more typically phrase it, *that* a stop sign was on Smith Street. (It is interesting that in cases where the accuracy and veracity of the ascribed aspect is important we take 'conscious of x as A' to be equivalent to 'conscious that x is A'; the latter phrase has the requisite 'witness leading' veridicality.) Certainly, it would be misleading for someone to establish that you were conscious of the stop sign by showing that you were conscious of, say, an indistinct red blob on your right which red blob, as a matter of fact, was the stop sign. Again, it is an intelligible reply to the question, 'were you conscious of the stop sign?' to say 'not as such – but I realize now that what I was conscious of was the stop sign'. So (1) allows us to make a distinction between what may be called a *de re* and *de dicto* characterization of someone's consciousness of x. From the outside, as it were, we can report that someone is conscious of x, thus specifying the object of consciousness but leaving open the way in which the person is conscious of x. This is the *de re* characterization. Sometimes, of course, the object of consciousness is a 'purely intentional' *inexistent* (to use Brentano's term) object but even in such cases the present distinction holds. We can know that someone is thinking of, dreaming of or imagining a unicorn, for example, without knowing how the person is representing a unicorn, that is, without completely knowing what I call the intentional object of this state of consciousness. Nonetheless, there must be some way or other that they are representing their unicorn. A *de dicto* characterization is one that informs us under what aspect (or aspects) someone is conscious of the object of consciousness, one that identifies the intentional object.

The exact relation between being *conscious of* and being *conscious that* involves complexities and ambiguities which ordinary talk ignores. To take an example of Dretske's (discussed in Dretske 1993), it is obvious that you can be conscious of an armadillo, on the road in front of you say, without being conscious that an *armadillo* is on the road in front of you. But, as expressed in formula (1) above, you cannot be conscious of the armadillo without being conscious of it *as* something or other (the aspect that 'presents' the armadillo as the intentional object of your state of consciousness).

Box 8.3 • Consciousness *As*

A familiar but peculiar feature of consciousness is that we are directly aware of the world *as* structured in terms of the concepts we have acquired. Thus we see the world in ways that our distant ancestors could not. Try to imagine a neolithic hunter transported to a busy intersection or an airport terminal. The hunter simply could not be aware of the world around him as full of cars (BMWs versus Chevrolets), *business*men and women, advertising placards, minor – sometimes major – transgressions of social rules, etc. (Equally, were I transported back to neolithic times, I would not be able to see the world as the hunter sees it.) But these are essential components of the way we are aware of the world. This means that both the nature and the process of concept acquisition is an important element in any theory of consciousness, as the representational theory forthrightly recognises. Serious problems arise here.

It does not follow that you are therefore conscious that a something or other is in front of you, for, it seems to me, that would require that the *aspect* be presented to consciousness as an object of consciousness. This is not what is happening – the *armadillo* is being presented to consciousness *as* a something or other; you are not necessarily conscious of any thought about that something or other, let alone the particular thought that a something or other is before you. Of course, this does not prevent you from becoming conscious of the thought, but being conscious of the armadillo does not require you to be conscious of this thought. As we have seen, the representational theory's account of conscious experience and introspection handles all this very nicely.

The aspectual nature of consciousness has often been remarked upon by philosophers and psychologists, who have respectively extended its reach to very sophisticated levels of thought and rock bottom elements of perception. An example which brings both of these tendencies together is the traditional debate about the theory-ladenness of observation in the philosophy of science. In terms of the aspects under which we can become conscious of objects, development of a richer set of conceptual resources is the acquisition of a richer set of such aspects. The entirely plausible implication is, to take a definite example, that the veteran astronomer's consciousness of the night sky is radically different from a five year old's. The fund of aspects available to the astronomer greatly enriches the state of consciousness produced by the sensory data available from the stars and planets, galaxies, satellites, etc. (see Churchland, 1985, pp. 14–15, for a nice discussion of this particular, as well as other similar examples).[9] It would be natural to say that the child and the astronomer get into distinct states of consciousness in virtue of the possession and deployment of distinct sets of available concepts which can figure as aspects under which they are conscious of the night sky. This point is reinforced when we note that the application of the richer set of 'astronomical aspects' within the astronomer is not a conscious inference from some lower level *consciousness* of mere points of light against a black background. The astronomical aspects are presented in consciousness simply as the way the sky is apprehended. Though in all likelihood there are background cognitive processes linking the 'points of light' to the 'astronomical aspects', these processes are entirely invisible to consciousness, and are emphatically not the aspect under which the night sky is consciously apprehended. Such processes are productive of the astronomer's current state of consciousness not an apprehended feature of that state. The fact that the astronomer literally *perceives* the night sky as a field of planets, stars, galaxies etc. means that this is also an example of the psychologists' tendency to assimilate perception to the (unconscious) application of concepts, which concepts are the aspects under which objects are presented in consciousness.

In terms of the discussion of indexicalized experiential content above, the astronomer example reveals that it might be very difficult, conceivably even impossible, to retreat to a 'purer' or 'more direct' apprehension of the experiential content.[10] Such content might, so to speak, be *erased* and *overwritten* with a thoroughly conceptualized version. A good example is language: I cannot, try as I might, *hear* spoken English as stream of sounds, though no doubt my cognitive machinery is at some level processing it as such a stream. At the other extreme, I can *only* hear spoken Chinese as a stream of sound; if I were to learn Chinese it would come to sound very different to me. Intermediate phenomena of this sort are common too, with 'half-learned' languages for example. To a greater or lesser extent, the entire perceived world exhibits the same phenomenon: it is 'parsed' by my conceptual apparatus and presented to my consciousness as a world of trees, cars, houses, people, etc.

These two central features of the intentionality of consciousness will engage us: the evidently conceptual character of its aspectuality and the equally evident accessibility of the aspects *to* consciousness. Together, they pose a serious challenge to a whole range of currently prominent theories about mental content and will require a transformation – but not the overturn – of the representational theory of consciousness.

For our purposes, externalism is the doctrine that the content of a mental state is, at least in part, determined by elements of the world external to the subject of that mental state. Externalism is to be contrasted with internalism (or, as it is sometimes called by detractors, individualism): the doctrine that the content of mental states is determined entirely by features of the subject. Certain other forms of externalism are quite obviously correct and can provide models with which to compare content externalism as defined here. For example, a wide class of terms marking human social relationships can be understood only along externalist lines. The properties of 'being an uncle' or 'being a widow' are clear examples.[11] Closer to our subject, many mental states are external in this benign sense. Whether a certain state of consciousness is a memory or not does not solely depend upon its 'intrinsic features'. That is, while a feeling of pain can be determined not to be a memory solely by its intrinsic features, other states of consciousness bearing all the 'internal marks' of memory will yet fail to be memories if they fail to meet appropriate external criteria such as that memories must be true – you can't remember what did not happen, and your memories must be of something *you* experienced, etc. One can consciously remember something, but there is nothing about this state of consciousness itself that guarantees that it is a genuine memory experience.[12]

So much is clear. But lately a large number of philosophers have propounded theories of the nature of mental content that have as a consequence that the *content* of mental states is itself determined, at least in part, by external features. The relevant external features vary significantly across these theories, and include such diverse mechanisms as: causal-historical connection between thinker and world (e.g. Putnam 1975, Davidson 1987), socio-linguistic community practices (Burge 1979, 1982, 1986, Baker 1987), asymmetrical counterfactual dependencies in the causal production of content bearing items (Fodor 1992), evolutionarily defined function (Millikan 1984, Dretske 1986, 1988 and, of course, 1995) and interpretation relative to the predictive desires of a specified (usually only implicitly) group of interpreters (Dennett 1987, Cummins 1989). I do not intend to review these theories here; the doctrine of externalism is well known (at least to philosophers) as is the range of arguments advanced in its favour. What all externalist theories of interest here must have in common is the claim that the very *content* of a mental state depends upon elements of the world external to the subject of that state. A useful metaphor here is to picture the content of a mental state as determined by the sum of both an internal and an external 'vector', as in fig. 8.2.

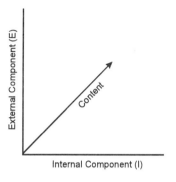

(Fig. 8.2)

In the diagram, the internal vector represents whatever intrinsic or individual features are relevant to content, the external vector abstracts from the controversial details of externalism and lets a single vector stand for whatever constellation of external factors contribute to the determination of content (even some variation in the relative importance of internal vs. external features could be represented in the metaphor by making this a 'weighted sum' (viz. *content* = $a\mathbf{I} + b\mathbf{E}$); internalism is the doctrine that $b = 0$). What the metaphor makes clear is that indistinguishable internal vectors could be involved in mental states with distinct content so long as the external vector was varied in some way.

The classic philosophical thought experiments which underpin externalism pay homage to this metaphor. The internal vector is kept constant by imagining a situation into which two intrinsically physically identical subjects can somehow be introduced (in the trade, such duplicates are called *doppelgängers*). It is then argued that these duplicates nonetheless differ in the content of (at least some of) their mental states because of a variation in external circumstances, of whatever sort is appropriate to the brand of externalism at issue.

As in the case of mental states, where the class including remembering, seeing and knowing requires an externalist account, there is a class of content carrying items for which externalism of some form or other is obviously correct. For example, words cannot be thought to carry their semantic content solely in virtue of their intrinsic features; that is, two word tokens identical in all their intrinsic non-semantical (orthographic) features need not, because of this identity, agree in their semantical features (they might after all be from different languages, as, for example, 'dos' is both a French and, by now, an English word).[13] In the case of words, the best – at least traditional – candidate for the external feature that helps fix semantic content is the content of the mental states of those who use words. It is thus a striking claim that these mental states themselves have a determinate content only because of their relation to certain features external to their subjects.

One might wonder about the legitimacy of the crucial distinction between the intrinsic and external features upon which the doctrines of externalism and internalism both depend. Almost all the participants in this debate are minimal naturalists. That is, it is accepted that the mental supervenes upon the physical in some fashion or other. If we allow that the distinction between intrinsic and external properties of an object is reasonably clear at the level of basic physical properties and thus that it is possible to mark out the intrinsic basic physical features of an object (perhaps such properties as (rest-frame) mass, charge, momentum, angular momentum, etc.) then we can draw the general distinction between intrinsic and external properties in terms of physical supervenience (as was discussed above in chapter 4). The intrinsic properties of something are those that supervene on its intrinsic basic physical properties, or, as I shall say, the intrinsic properties are *locally* supervenient upon the physical. Properties that are not locally supervenient are said to be globally supervenient upon the physical, leaving open the degree to which the supervenience base extends beyond the individual. For example, the property of 'being an uncle' surely does supervene upon the physical, but equally surely does not locally supervene upon the intrinsic physical properties of the uncle in question – it is thus an external property.[14] Notice that we need not have any good idea of exactly *how* properties supervene upon the physical to have good evidence that they *do* supervene or to have reasonable grounds for applying the distinction between local and global supervenience. Externalism, then, is the doctrine that the content of mental states globally, but not locally, supervenes upon the physical.

We have seen that both Dretske (explicitly and enthusiastically) and Tye (arguably from the 'optimal conditions' clause of his covariational account of representation) opt for an externalist theory of representation in their versions of the representational theory of consciousness. We have also seen that this option leads to severe difficulties for the theory. I want to show that such difficulties are not restricted to these particular theories, and that the consciousness of intentional states reveals the problems particularly clearly.

A very general argument against externalist theories of content can be constructed on the basis of the following inconsistent triad:

P1. States of consciousness are essentially intentional.
P2. A mental state's intentionality depends upon external features.
P3. States of consciousness are intrinsic features of their subjects.

Here, I take it that a state's being intentional involves its directedness upon an intentional object. P1 asserts that all states of consciousness have such intentional objects, as argued above. Note that P1 asserts only that intentionality is a necessary feature of consciousness; I am not making the considerably more controversial claim that in some way or other consciousness is essential to intentionality.[15] P2 is the externalist claim. P3 asserts that one's current state of consciousness supervenes locally on one's current intrinsic basic physical properties.

Once it is granted that these are indeed together inconsistent, the argument succeeds simply by showing that P1 and P3 are considerably more plausible than P2, hence leading to the rejection of P2.

Box 8.4 • Against Externalism

The argument begins by displaying an inconsistent trio of propositions. It cannot be that (1) some states of consciousness are essentially representational (or have intentionality), (2) that whether a state is representational is a matter of satisfying certain external relations *and* (3) that states of consciousness are intrinsic features of subjects. (1) seems undeniable. (2) is the target against which this argument is aimed. (3) is intuitively appealing. If (3) *is* true then externalism is wrong. In addition to its intuitive appeal, two arguments for (3) are offered. The first is that states of consciousness make a difference in the world in virtue of their content. But if states of consciousness are not intrinsic it is hard to see how this can be, for causal efficacy appears to be an intrinsic feature of states. The second argument is that consciousness is a 'real-time' feature of our being. The sense that 'something is going on' when we are conscious could not be in error. But it is metaphysically repugnant that I could know, simply in virtue of being conscious, that I stand in certain external relations (for example, that I have an evolutionary history). Crudely, I cannot know, merely from the a priori examination of my own experience, that I am *not* an accidentally, very recently created duplicate of a human being (see the 'Swampman thought experiment' in the text). Thus externalism seems to be refuted.

Let us begin with the question of inconsistency. There are various ways of understanding P1 through P3. P1 can be taken as stating merely that all states of consciousness have an intentional object or it can be taken to assert something much stronger, namely, that states of consciousness are *individuated* by their intentional objects. The latter reading is probably too strong, for it seems possible that one could be conscious of the very same object under the same aspect in various ways (e.g. regretfully, delightedly, etc.). To deny this would be to claim that all modes of consciousness are reducible to differences in the aspects under which we are conscious of objects. While such a view is not altogether indefensible, I don't think it is very plausible (but see Tye 1994 for a defence of a very limited version of this claim) nor an essential part of the representational theory. Modes of consciousness are representational but are worth distinguishing from the particular represented properties of our states of consciousness. However, denying this strong reading of P1 does not rule out the possibility that intentional objects have a crucial role in differentiating states of consciousness; that is, it may still be that distinct intentional objects imply distinct states of consciousness. Consider the states of my being conscious of you as hostile as opposed to my being conscious of you as friendly. The involvement of these distinct aspects is sufficient to guarantee that these states are distinct states of consciousness. I recognize here that the distinction between a mode of consciousness and aspect cannot be made completely precise. It seems that modes of consciousness affect the way we are conscious of many objects; aspects are tied to their particular objects.[16]

P2 also allows for stronger and weaker readings. The strongest possible reading of P2 is to regard it as claiming that a mental state possesses intentionality or content only if it satisfies the external requirements for the possession of content. That is, if a state does not enter into the appropriate relations to the proper external elements then it is not an intentional state at all and has no object whatsoever. A notable weaker reading is just that *what* the intentional object of a content carrying state is depends upon the external factors, but that these do not by themselves determine whether or not a state has such an object. A still weaker version of P2 holds that only the *referent* of a mental state depends upon external factors so that, as it were, almost everything about the state's intentional object is fixed by internal features. The strong reading of P2 allows the argument to proceed under the weak reading of P1. And somewhat remarkably, the extant versions of externalism give us very powerful grounds for asserting that P2 ought to get the strong interpretation, although some proponents of externalism are more forthright about this than others.

To make the case for the strong reading of P2, I must reintroduce the villain of our story, this time more carefully, a very peculiar and particular sort of doppelgänger known as the Swampman (or Swampwoman as the case may be). I believe it was Donald Davidson (1987) who introduced the Swampman (or we could say *his* Swampman) under his proper name with the following B-movie tale, but the notion of such a replacement goes back thousands of years in folklore and a few years in philosophy[17]:

> Suppose lightning strikes a dead tree in a swamp; I am standing nearby. My body is reduced to its elements, while entirely by coinci-dence (and out of different molecules) the tree is turned into my physical replica. My replica, the Swampman, moves exactly as I did; according to its nature it departs the swamp, encounters and seems to recognize my friends, and appears to return their greetings in English. It moves into my house and seems to write articles on radical interpre-tation. No one can tell the difference.
>
> (1987, pp. 443–4)

But, Davidson goes on, there is a difference because, he says, the Swampman cannot 'be said to mean anything by the sounds it makes, nor to have any thoughts'. Why not? Because the Swampman would lack the proper causal-historical connections to the world which underpin meaning and thought-content.

For those who look askance upon outrageous philosophical thought experiments that transcend the bounds of possibility, let me hasten to mention that at least by the August authority of Stephen Hawking (1993), the Swampman – or at any rate a randomly created duplicate of a given physical system, though maybe not one created out of a tree – is a physical possibility, of vanishing but non-zero probability.[18] According to certain quite popular theories of cosmology the Swampman is even as I write coming into being (perhaps infinitely many of them too, just for good measure). Swampman is an easy, if yet more improbable, extrapolation of these remarks of Hawking's: '. . . it is possible that the black hole could emit a television set or the works of Proust in ten leather-bound volumes, but the number of configurations of particles that correspond to these exotic possibilities is vanishingly small' (1993, pp. 112–13). On second thought, for those with no taste for it, maybe appeals to this sort of cosmology are no more palatable than Swampman himself. But let the thought experiment continue!

Another prominent externalist, Ruth Millikan, discussed her own version of Swampman somewhat prior to Davidson. Millikan says of her Swampwoman: 'that being would have no ideas, no beliefs, no intentions, no aspirations, no fears and no hopes . . . this because the evolutionary *history* of the being would be wrong' (1984, p. 93). Intriguingly, she also goes on to allow that the being would nonetheless be in the same state of *consciousness* as herself.

Although I can't go into the details here, I believe that an examination of the main externalist theories, in addition to the bio-functional and causal covariational theories considered above, will reveal that all of them share the consequence that, at least on the face of things, a swampcreature will have no content carrying mental states, that is, no intentional states. If, as Tyler Burge avers, membership in a linguistic community is required to fix the content of one's thoughts then Swampman's radically non-social and non-linguistic origin will preclude his states from carrying any content whatsoever. If we regard Hilary Putnam's efforts in 'The Meaning of "Meaning"' (1975) as providing a theory of content for mental states (it is doubtful whether this was Putnam's intention but his views have been widely adapted to the externalist platform), at least for those mental states involving concepts of natural kinds, social kinds and the large class of concepts which engage the machinery of the so-called 'linguistic division of labour', Swampman again is seen to lack the proper externalist credentials for the possession of any contentful states of mind. I believe that even the quasi-externalist theory offered by Jerry Fodor (1992) robs Swampman of content, for according to Fodor, content depends upon what he calls asymmetrical counterfactual dependence. The crucial counterfactuals depend for their evaluation upon an initial situating of the thinker into a particular milieu of causally inter-related objects. Content will vary according to the initial situation of the thinker. But Swampman has no such initial situation and thus is in no position to have any determinate content assigned to him.[19] Finally, if content depends upon external interpretation, or even interpretability, relative to the predictive and explanatory ends of some community then Swampman, who might be created in the absence of any particular community of interpreters, cannot possess any mental states with determinate content.[20,21]

Let me also mention that the strong reading seems to emerge from remarks made by Falvey and Owens (1994). This is of interest since their views do not depend upon any particular form of externalism. When considering a thought experiment which involves someone not knowing whether they are on Twin-Earth (using Twin-Earth concepts) or on Earth (using Earth concepts) Falvey and Owens claim that 'the only [mental states] that the content sceptic can confidently maintain I would be enjoying if I were on Twin-Earth are *purely qualitative* states – that is, those states that are not characterized in terms of their content' (1994, p. 122, original emphasis). This entails that, since he has absolutely no external features to provide content, Swampman possesses no content carrying states whatsoever and hence, given that consciousness essentially involves content, is entirely unconscious. I am sure that Falvey and Owens would reject the last inference here, but to do so they would have to deny P1 (as their quote may indicate). This seems to me entirely implausible.

For now then, let's interpret P2 as the strong claim that without the proper external vector Swampman will have no intentional states whatsoever (for what it is worth, the vector metaphor can easily sustain this extension if we revise the form of the content fixing vector equation to something like *content = (aE + bI) × cE*; now if **E** = **0** then content = **0**, otherwise **I** will still have a role to play in fixing content). P1 will be interpreted as the weak claim that all states of consciousness possess an intentional object. There is no inconsistency as yet. P1 and P2 are compatible, but only so long as we embrace the conclusion that not only does Swampman possess no content carrying states but also that Swampman is incapable of being in any state of consciousness. Swampman is then what philosophers sometimes call a *philosophical zombie*: a being that acts just like a conscious being but who is entirely unconscious. An *intentional zombie* is a creature that acts just like a being that possesses intentional states but who in fact lacks all content – Swampman is of course also one of these, and so we have, as a theorem, that all intentional zombies are philosophical zombies.

But I am locally physically indistinguishable from Swampman and I am a conscious being, so if consciousness were to supervene locally we would have our inconsistency. This is just what P3 asserts and thus P1, P2 and P3 together (at least under their current interpretations) are indeed an inconsistent triad.

The argument for P1 was provided above; the case for P2 has been made, and made quite strongly, by the legion of externalists. Can a case be made for P3? Considerations in its favour were presented in chapters 6 and 7 above but, at least before one begins to think about externalism, P3 is intuitively extremely plausible, given the minimal naturalism that I am presupposing throughout this paper (as we saw in chapter 7, Dretske, for one, forthrightly admits the distinct attractions of the 'internalist intuition'). There is a kind of repugnant air of metaphysical 'action at a distance' to the idea that S's consciousness could be altered via the alteration of features distant from S. This repugnance is lacking in the case of, say, widowhood, because the external nature of this property is manifest in the conditions of its properly applying to someone. But, intuitively, consciousness just does not seem to be such a property; although it reaches out to the world, as it were, my consciousness is entirely a matter of what is happening to me right now. As indicated above, at least one externalist, Millikan, actually accepts P3 on the basis of its presumed obvious truth (she must then, of course, deny P1 – such a move will be examined below). As we saw in the last chapter, Dretske attempts to defend his treatment of Swampman with the claim that the 'internalist intuition' is nothing more than a brute intuition and 'one that is not justified by any defensible claim about the nature of thought or experience' (1995, p. 150). This claim is far too strong; it is only the adoption of an externalist theory of representation that threatens the internalist intuition, *not* simply the adoption of the representational theory of consciousness. Further arguments for P3, which are not unfamiliar, can also be provided.

Argument 1. From the Presumed Causal Efficacy of Consciousness. The argument runs along these lines: states of consciousness are apparently locally causally efficacious (if you consciously will your arm to go up it is *your* arm that goes up and it goes up right away) and such causal efficacy cannot supervene upon external features of a state (here I am thinking particularly of the Davidsonian and Millikanite appeal to causal-historical or evolutionary-historical features) save inasmuch as these features determine the details of the current local state. That is, if distinct external features lead to indistinguishable current states then the difference between those features cannot retain any causal efficacy. Take one of Davidson's own examples, sunburn (which does not, of course, supervene upon local physical states). Sunburns are causally efficacious all right, but not as such. Whatever they can cause is caused by the current state of one's skin. It would be more, and worse, than physically mysterious if, for example, sunburn caused skin cancer but *physically identical* skin conditions not produced by the sun failed to cause skin cancer. The causal machinery of the world, we believe, cannot keep track of external features that leave *no* distinctive mark on current states or processes.[22]

It is natural to explain people's actions by reference to their states of consciousness. For example, suppose we show Jones a Necker cube after explaining its perceptual double aspect. Jones looks at the cube for a while and suddenly says: 'now I see what you mean'. It would be hard to explain this without appealing to the conscious experience of Jones noticing the Necker cube switch aspects. There is no reason to deny that this is a causal explanation. Is such an explanation like the sunburn example, where an implicit appeal is made to an underlying state which provides 'direct' causal force? Of course, we believe there is an underlying local physical state in such a case, but the crucial difference is that we take this underlying state to be intimately related to the state of consciousness itself (perhaps identical to it, perhaps a state which 'realizes' it, or whatever). If this underlying state was such that it might exist in the total absence of consciousness then it was not the state of consciousness as such that caused the action. When we say that sunburn explains someone's peeling skin, a philosopher's gloss would be: the sun caused a certain skin condition which in turn is causing peeling skin. What gloss could be given to 'experiencing the Necker cube aspect switch explains Jones's understanding of what we were talking about'? A gloss parallel to the one given in the sunburn case results in consciousness dropping out of the picture, for the gloss would be something like 'a certain visual scene brings about an internal state (which, in itself, might or might not be a conscious state) which then brings about an appropriate utterance'. But, of course, we meant to be claiming that it was the conscious experience *itself* that accounted for Jones's appreciation of the phenomenon. It is an extremely radical position that the causal efficacy of states of consciousness is the sort of 'by courtesy' causal efficacy of sunburns, dimes and genuine Monets.

Box 8.5 • Externalism and Money

Money provides an excellent illustration of the main points of externalist views of representation and mental content. The analogy has it that *monetary value* is to *physical embodiment* (be it coin, bill, cheque or whatever) as *mental content* is to *physical embodiment* (be it brain state or whatever else can implement mentality). Everything which has monetary value must be physically instantiated one way or another. Monetary value seems to depend upon the details of the physical world in which it is instantiated as well. But it would be a mistake to think that monetary value 'reduces' to some physical property of its instantiations. For, no matter how similar a *counterfeit* bill is to a genuine bill, it is not genuine and has no monetary value unless it has been legally minted. And whether a bill has been legally minted is not an intrinsic property of the bill – in principle it is possible to have a *perfect* counterfeit bill, but it would still be a counterfeit. Similarly, if externalist theories of representation and mental content are correct, it makes no difference if two creatures are physically identical – only the one with the proper external credentials can *really* have states that carry content.

It is of course possible to respond to this sort of argument. The natural line of reply requires a heavy reliance upon the distinction between action and behaviour on the one hand and 'mere bodily motion' on the other (see Dretske 1995, pp. 151 ff.). The basic idea is that action and behaviour are themselves externally individuated so that identical physical motions can constitute distinct actions or behaviours. There is something obviously right about this. Swampman makes motions with a pen across the paper identical to mine, but only I manage to *sell* my car by such motions.

Similarly, it is argued, only I can *speak* when my body issues forth the same sounds that Swampman produces. Moving inward, only *my*, properly historically or evolutionarily (or whatever) grounded, brain states are the genuine representations which can explain *my* genuine behaviour *as* behaviour. Once we see this distinction, it is argued, we can see how the causal efficacy of consciousness is retained with respect to its proper effects (action and/or behaviour) while Swampman's identical bodily motions are now seen to be the product of purely physical causes.

But this cannot be the whole story. *If* Swampman produces bodily motions identical to mine, and surely he does, it is because he is in a locally identical physical state. Thus, since Swampman is by hypothesis not conscious it is not in virtue of these physical states subvening (or whatever) consciousness that they have their effects. Consciousness completely drops out of the causal story here so we still have a problem of efficacy. This point can be driven home by considering Dretske's (1997) discussion of the *function* of consciousness. The value of consciousness appears to be quite obvious. Consider Dretske's example: 'let an animal – a gazelle, say – who is aware of prowling lions – where they are and what they are doing – compete with one who is not and the outcome is predictable' (1997, p. 5). Not so fast! What if the competitor is 'swamp-gazelle', very recently formed from a lightning bolt on the savannah? We've already seen how Dretske (in company with other externalists) must deny that swamp-gazelle is conscious. Yet it is obvious that swamp-gazelle will do *exactly* as well at avoiding lions as her actually evolved competitor.[23] So it is not the consciousness that is valuable to our gazelle, but the underlying physical state (which might or might not be an instance of conscious experience). As far as avoiding lions is concerned, the fact that this physical state does or does not underlie a conscious experience is causally irrelevant.

The reply now is that we need to add yet another distinction to that between action and bodily motion, namely the distinction between causation and explanation. As Dretske puts it: 'the events that reasons (here-and-now beliefs and desires) cause are not the behaviour that reasons (there-and-then content) explain' (1995, p. 155). The problem is that the relation of causation is descriptively promiscuous: it does not care how the events it relates are described (as philosophers say, causation is an extensional relation). The causal structure of events is the same in me and my Swampman. But the explanatory structure might be and, it is argued, actually is different.

A simple and clear example of how such a pair of distinctions functions to separate causal and explanatory structure is provided by *money*. Consider the difference between genuine and counterfeit money. The financial realm is an externalist's heaven for it is clear that what transforms a hunk of matter meeting certain internal specifications into a genuine dime is its history, specifically the fact that it has been properly minted. Counterfeit dimes are monetary zombies, they seem to act just like real money without any genuine fiduciary properties. A *perfect* counterfeit dime is conceivable, that is, one that is completely indistinguishable from a genuine dime by *any* test.[24] Swampdime is also conceivable and could be a perfect counterfeit just so long as its peculiar production history becomes undiscoverable. Now, what we are supposed to see is that, from a certain point of view,[25] counterfeit dimes only *appear* to act the same as real dimes. Only real dimes generate real financial effects. If you try to *buy* something with counterfeit money, it won't work, though it will look as if it worked (maybe *everyone* will be fooled). One can easily see how this comes about: *buying* and *selling* are themselves events (or descriptions of events) that require an external social underpinning to actually occur. Still, monetary transactions are locally realized in definite physical motions of matter: movements of arms, transferences of metal disks, electrical impulses through certain physical devices etc. The genuineness of money matters to these events only *as described* (as *financially* described we might say). Since causation is descriptively promiscuous, it follows that the genuineness of money has no *causal* efficacy: genuineness cannot cause anything that necessarily reveals it for what it is. Nonetheless, there is obviously an explanatory structure in which the genuineness (or counterfeitness, an equally external notion naturally) of money plays a very important role.

When I say that the genuineness of the dime has no distinctive causal effects I mean that there are no differences in the locally realizing physical events generated by the counterfeit as opposed to the genuine dime. Similarly, my Swampman and I generate indistinguishable local events, distinguishable at best only in terms of certain externalistic modes of description. So the question comes down to this: does consciousness have a causal role or exclusively an explanatory role within a structure of externalistic, description sensitive, concepts? And the problem for the externalists is that consciousness does appear to be something which plays a part in generating the locally realizing events. This can be shown simply by finding an example (one would do) in which a state of consciousness produces a 'bodily motion', something which is not an action or a behaviour (when these are *contrasted* with bodily motions). Take someone with a fear of heights. Such a phobia produces trembling, sweating, heart palpitations and other bodily manifestations which are neither actions nor even behaviour, but only when the subject is conscious (veridically or not) of being in a high place. Of course, we can distinguish between trembling induced, say, by some kind of drug, and the trembling from fear. But what we mean by the latter is a trembling *caused* by an awareness of height. Go back to the case of money. Dimes turn on photocopiers, and they do this in virtue of their intrinsic characteristics. That's why counterfeit and real dimes work equally well in photocopiers. The proper financial description of the dime does not and cannot matter to the photocopier for the turning on of the photocopier is a matter of causation which is local and description insensitive. It is not the genuineness of the dime that *explains* why the photocopier turns on when the dime is inserted, since 'turning on' is not a description which is externally sensitive to the historical properties of its causing event. Of course, we can distinguish between a photocopier turning on because a counterfeit dime was inserted and one turning on because of the insertion of a genuine dime, but that is just to distinguish the causes, not to distinguish what *makes them* cause what they do.

Similarly, it is not the external features of my state of consciousness which explain why my heart palpitates when I am in that state; this is because my state of consciousness is the *cause* of these palpitations. The point can be made another way: suppose that states of consciousness *are* explanatory creatures at home solely in a structure of externalistic, description sensitive, concepts. Then they are not the explanation of my bodily motions, since these are, like the turning on of the photocopier, not externally individuated events. With regard to my bodily motions, I am exactly like Swampman; my states of consciousness can't explain them. The *reductio* ensues when we are forced to accept that this is false: some states of consciousness do explain, causally explain, some bodily motions. Is it just a 'brute intuition' that a fear of heights causes heart palpitations or trembling, in virtue of the awareness (veridical or not) of being in a high place? I don't think so. No more than it is a 'brute intuition' that the genuineness of a dime does not matter to whether the photocopier turns on or not when the dime is inserted.

Argument 2. From Consciousness Being a 'Real Time' Feature. Consciousness is a real feature of our being which presents itself to us immediately in real time. My current consciousness is a matter of what is happening to me, now, and this, given some sort of minimal naturalism, has its source in the physical. My current consciousness should thus somehow be a matter of what is happening to me, now, at the physical level.[26] The immediacy of consciousness (which I do not claim here has any special epistemic status – this is *not* an appeal to incorrigible access) guarantees that something is going on *right now*. No certificate of representational authenticity is required to vouchsafe what is immediately presented in this sense. I can easily imagine that the referential details of my consciousness might need to be authenticated and that these details could turn out to be fraudulent in some legalistic sense. That is, I can imagine, for example, that I am in truth incapable of having thoughts about Paris by imagining that I am the victim of some complex and far reaching hoax by which my apparent connection to what I call 'Paris' is really to another city.[27] I cannot imagine that it is the external representational authenticity of my conscious states which permits them to *be* conscious. Otherwise, my consciousness would be something separate from *me*, a notion which is surely incoherent when it implies that in my own case it might be false that something is going on right now. The immediate apprehension that something is going on seems to be a part of my being – and in all probability a part of my physical being – which cannot depend upon a history I need not in any way recall and of which my very body need carry no distinctively accurate trace.

Perhaps this worry can be made more palpable if I present a Swampman tale of my own. My scenario is somewhat complicated and begins with a preamble about myself – a being which, I ask you to admit, at least for the sake of the argument, possesses ideas, aspirations, has thoughts, etc. (Although, for all you know – and, I fear, for all I know too, I might be a Swampman except of course that the fact that I am *worrying* whether I am a Swampman seems to guarantee that I am not one. Somehow this reflection does not increase my confidence in the externalist view. But I digress.) Suppose I am to have a medical operation for some complaint or other – perhaps to remove the organ responsible for outrageous philosophical imaginings (obviously in my case dangerously overactive – but I've been keeping bad company). In any event, I am told that the anaesthetic they are using, although admirable in almost every way, has the unfortunate side effect of permitting consciousness to return before sensory and motor functions. Thus I will have to spend an hour or so fully conscious on the postoperative table before I reconnect to the world. I spend this time cogitating about elementary mathematics (say I review the proof that root 2 is irrational, and such like), recalling a trip to Paris and considering the philosophical problems of consciousness. But, as you may have guessed, a strange fate intervenes: lightning strikes and, instead of a nearby tree reassembling itself as myself, the bedside table stands in. Swampman replaces me in the bed *at the beginning* of my hour of forced meditation. Now my worry is obvious. Are we to believe, with the externalists, that for the next whole hour upon that hospital bed, no thoughts occurred, no ideas were considered, no beliefs were active, no aspirations were aspired to? Are we to believe that this creature, physically identical to me in both constitution and process throughout the hour, is entirely unconscious?[28]

It is very hard to deny that my example Swampman will, as he lays upon the hospital bed, have a sense that 'something is going on now' even though he is, by his unusual creation, barred from entering into whatever external relations might be deemed necessary for content and, temporarily, cut off from the external world (both affectively and effectively) and so cannot for some time begin to enter into these relations. Of course, the primary difficulty then arises from the fact that there is no understanding of 'what is going on now' except as laden with, sometimes exhausted by, content. But, given Swampman's peculiar nature, our agreement that Swampman is conscious must stem from the fact that he is completely locally physically identical to me.

This point can be looked at from the other side, where the anti-Cartesian catastrophe (as I called it in chapter 7) can be seen. Seeing that swampcreatures are strictly speaking physically possible, it is possible that *I* am a newly created swampcreature (a picturesque way to say that I could be very mistaken about my causal/evolutionary history). This would obviously mean that I have a seriously inaccurate self-image. But if the externalists are right, it would mean much more. It would mean that it is possible that I am not conscious (right now), that right now as I type these words I am not experiencing anything. This is a truly radical possibility, far transcending anything Descartes dreamt up in the *Meditations*. Descartes thought that he could limit uncertainty. Reduced to essentials, Descartes thought that if one has a sense of existence, of something happening, of *being here now*, then indeed something is happening, there is *being here now*. On this point, if not on very many of the supposed consequences which he drew from it, Descartes was right. It is *not* possible that I am unconscious right now, that I am not experiencing anything right now, and that *nothing* is happening. So, whether or not I am a swampcreature, I am conscious. But the only point of similarity between me and this possible swampcreature is local physical qualitative identity, and so P3 is established.

I take it that P1 is more plausible than P2 and even, in a certain sense, that P2 presupposes the truth of P1: it is only the fact that we are conscious of the intentionality of consciousness that leads us to propose any theory of content at all. That is, P2 is part of a project whose goal is to explain intentionality; consciousness is the root source and paradigm case of intentionality so if the development of an externalist position involving P2 leads to the denial of intentionality to consciousness this should constitute a *reductio* of P2. So the argument comes down to the relative plausibility of P2 versus P3. It seems to me pretty clear that P3 is the winner of this controversy, and hence that externalism, at least as applied to the intentionality of consciousness, is to be rejected.

With the above work all done, we can summarize the argument in a very simple form. Externalism entails the anti-Cartesian catastrophe. Any theory which implies the anti-Cartesian catastrophe is false. Therefore, externalism is false.

How might an externalist respond to the problems stemming from the inconsistent triad? I can think of three broad strategies of reply for the externalist:

R1. Deny P1 come what may (declare a revolution in our understanding of consciousness).

R2. Claim that externalism's domain is restricted to questions of *reference*.

R3. Concede that externalism is true only for a sub-class of intentional contents.

Since R2 and R3 are defensive retreats, while R1 is a rather bold offensive, R1 should be treated first.

Millikan is the most forthright externalist on this point, explicitly wishing to divorce questions of consciousness from questions of intentionality. She says: 'we would maintain that . . . every kind of *awareness of*, is in part an external relation, the inside of the awareness – the feeling part – giving no absolute guarantee that it *is* the inside of a genuine *awareness of* relation' (1984, p. 91–2, her emphasis), and as was noted above, despite her claiming 'that [her Swampwoman] would have no ideas, no beliefs, no intentions, no aspirations, no fears and no hopes . . . this because the evolutionary *history* of the being would be wrong' (1984, p. 93) she nonetheless goes on to allow that Swampwoman would be in the same state of *consciousness* as herself (see 1984, p. 93).

Box 8.6 • Externalist Replies

Externalists ought to be moved by the arguments given above, but how should they reply? It is possible to bite the bullet and declare a metaphysical revolution. There is no consciousness without appropriate external relations and thus philosophical, or at least intentional zombies of the purest imaginable kind are possible, and so, further-more, my own consciousness guarantees the existence of the external world (at least those parts necessary for my states to carry content). This view seems to have nothing to recommend it. Much less radical replies are also possible. An extremely minimal one is to claim that externalism applies only to questions of the *reference* of representations (that is, what *object* a representation stands for). This permits Swampman to remain conscious even though he cannot think about real things in our world (such as the city of Paris, or Bill Clinton). This is not an implausible view, but it means externalism has nothing to say about consciousness. And there are some remaining problems, such as the issue of whether thoughts that don't refer to particular objects nonetheless refer to *properties* and, if so, whether there ought to be an externalist account of this sort of reference. Finally, the externalist can try to divide contents into those that are properly treated externalistically from those that are not. It is not clear that this approach can succeed; the region of the former contents might tend to shrink towards zero.

There are two ways to read these remarks. The first is the commonplace reading which has it that one cannot tell, merely by introspecting upon one's states of consciousness, whether their intentional objects are also objectively real external objects (I think Descartes said something like this). On this reading there is no doubt that one's states of consciousness have intentional objects. This is no denial of P1 then and can't save the externalist from the argument given above. It is also, of course, part and parcel of conventional philosophical wisdom. The more radical reading suggests that whether a state of consciousness even has an intentional object is a matter of the appropriate external relations being satisfied. As we've seen, Millikan does make some remarks that clearly suggest she intends the stronger reading. Consider also these further remarks: 'we do not have . . . certain knowledge via Cartesian reflection, even of the fact *that* we mean, let alone knowledge of what we mean or knowledge that what we mean is true' (1984, p. 93) and 'absolutely nothing is guaranteed directly from within an act of consciousness' (1984, p. 92).

Putting these remarks together we get the result that since Swampman has no intentional states, no states of consciousness with intentional objects, and since I am in a state of consciousness identical to Swampman's then my states of consciousness have no intentional objects just in virtue of their being states of consciousness. This, at last, is a clear denial of P1. And perhaps this position would have its attractions for those with externalist leanings, though it must be noted that it involves the complete repudiation of the representational theory of consciousness – in my view a very serious strike against it at the outset.

It might be helpful here to divide possible views about the relation of consciousness to theories of content into a range of positions reflecting how strong an externalist line is taken. The strong externalist with respect to consciousness (for short, the strong externalist) maintains that Swampman is simply and entirely unconscious (this was the externalism refuted above). The weak externalist attempts to restrict externalism's claims to issues of content alone and wishes to disavow any implications about consciousness. Various intermediate externalisms may also be possible.[29]

One could then interpret Millikan and certain other externalists, though not Dretske of course, as mere weak externalists. They would thus be seen as refusing to grant the *title* of 'belief', 'intention', etc. to the states of the swampcreatures while granting them everything else. In that case, the states of Swampman would bear a relation to genuine mental states analogous to the relationship a *perfect* counterfeit dime would bear to a genuine dime, i.e. the counterfeit is identical to the real dime in every respect *except* production history. This deflationary view of Swampman's oddity gains some currency by reconsideration of one of Davidson's own explicatory examples mentioned above: sunburn. A certain skin condition just is not a case of sunburn unless it has the proper causal history. But of course ersatz sunburn has all the forward looking causal and internal constitutive properties of sunburn – it is an identical *skin* condition. The only difference is what produced it, not what it is like. Note also how Millikan uses a functionalist analogy between intentional states and internal organs: 'That being [the swampcreature] would also have *no liver, no heart, no eyes, no brain*, etc. This, again, because the history of the being would be wrong. For the categories 'heart', 'liver', 'eye', 'brain' and also 'idea', 'belief' and 'intention' are proper function categories . . .' (1984, p. 93, original emphasis). Further support, perhaps, for the deflationary view stems from the contention, common to both Davidson and Millikan, that Swampman will *very soon* come to have intentional states, as the requisite causal historical or functional connections between Swampman and the world are rapidly established. These connections will be established without any significant change in Swampman however, for Swampman's internal states are already such that the world will smoothly connect to them. It is as if Swampman comes with a socket already perfectly shaped (though *by accident*) for the world's insertion. Like the counterfeit dime, Swampman bears the right stamp but merely fails to come *from* the right stamp.

So, on the weak externalist interpretation, when Davidson or Millikan (and by implication other externalists as well) say that Swampman has no intentional states we are to understand this as claiming that something consciously 'occurs to' Swampman which is in every respect entirely like a state which does have an intentional object except possession of the proper external credentials, and we refuse to call this occurrence a thought (perception or belief or whatever) just because of a theoretical commitment to the causal-historical or evolutionary-functional (or whatever) individuation of mental content. Thus, the issue of the intentionality of Swampman's mental states becomes a merely verbal issue and also, I think, becomes entirely trivial. Externalism about the mental ends up being of no relevance to the problem of consciousness. Like as not, externalists would welcome such a conclusion.

Unfortunately, the weak externalist position cannot be maintained. Take a randomly selected swampcreature, and let this creature be locally physically identical to me when I am consciously experiencing a Necker cube figure as a cube being looked at from above (call this orientation 1, or O1). The intentional object of my state of consciousness is, roughly, 'a wire-frame cube as O1'. Although Swampman is supposed to be in a state of consciousness identical to my own he has no such intentional object for his state of consciousness – no intentional object at all in fact (isn't your head swimming already?). Now let my state of consciousness switch, as it is wont to do while looking at a Necker cube figure, so that its intentional object becomes 'a cube as O2' (where, of course, O2 is the orientation 'a cube looked at from below'). This is a local switch in the physical state of my brain (brought about, some cognitivists would claim, by my brain trying out different *interpretations* of the incoming visual stimuli, but notice – a worrying point of digression – that such an explanation, insofar as it involves a variety of content bearing states, can't be applicable to Swampman). Let Swampman's brain follow mine in the local alteration, because, let us say, he too is facing a Necker cube figure. Now, my state of consciousness certainly has changed with the switch from O1 to O2. So Swampman's state of consciousness, being identical to mine in virtue of our local physical homology, must change as well. But what can change apart from the nature of the intentional object of my state of consciousness? The externalist, like Millikan, will say the 'feeling part' changes. But, I say, *what* feeling part? The whole difference in my state of consciousness is encompassed by the change in orientation of an intentional wire-frame cube in the (intentional) space before me. The postulation of a 'feeling part' is an *ad hoc* retreat to some vestige of the myth of the given – some pre-conceptual or non-conceptual, and also utterly *non-representational*, material which is present to consciousness somehow prior to any intentional 'values' being imposed on 'it'.

There may yet be another way to save the safely trivial position of the weak externalist. Note that according to Millikan's notion of 'proper function' a device that has the function of doing A will necessarily possess ancestors who actually *did* A but did *not* have the function of doing A (see chapter 7, note 5 above for some expansion on this). A sign has the function of delivering certain information. So, crudely speaking, there must have been ancestors of the sign that actually delivered the information even though they did not at that time have the function of providing that information. Now, if mental states have the function of carrying certain sorts of content (essentially kinds of information) and if mental states are, in the natural order, realized by brain states then this function will be grounded, at least in part, on the fact that ancestor brain states carried this content without having the function of doing so. *Voilà*: Swampman could be like that. His brain states really do carry content but merely lack the function of doing so. This could help explain how Swampman soon acquires genuine representational functions, since it could well be – it will certainly appear to be – the fact that (some of his) brain states carry information which explains why these states persist and reproduce themselves in the appropriate circumstances. Of course, now we need an account of how physical states manage to carry content *prior* to it being their function to do so, so in a sense we are back to square one here (that's where we end up anyway, I think). But at least we can say that Swampman really does possess states with genuine intentional content even though, since they lack the function of carrying this content, they cannot be *called* genuine content carrying states. I am naturally attracted to this view (now we can have an internalist theory of content with an externalist theory of functions – including even content carrying functions) but it does not cohere very well with Millikan's own remarks about the states of Swampman and her distinction between the content aspect and the 'feeling part' of states of consciousness. Nor can this approach be applied to other content externalisms.

Let us then examine the defensive retreats of R2 and R3. R2 represents the complete trivialization of externalism. It was after all Descartes who emphasized so strongly that we could not know the *reference* of our ideas from their intrinsic nature as revealed in consciousness even though this consciousness 'presented' ideas as of external objects (Descartes allowed of course that a complex rational process could take one from the totality of one's ideas to an excellent hypothesis about the reference of a good number of ideas). This shows that an externalism that accepted R2 would have no bearing whatsoever on traditional epistemological problems, contrary to the somewhat veiled hopes of many externalists (see McGinn 1989 for more deflation of the anti-sceptical hopes of externalists).

Though I have never seen it in print, there is a straightforward externalist anti-sceptical argument. Begin with the premise that I know that I am conscious. It follows from externalism that I know that I am not Swampman and therefore that I must actually stand in those external relations serving to ground (if that is the right word) consciousness. So the existence of the external world has been established. Thus it is possible to view externalist approaches to epistemology as being a strange attempt to revive Descartes's project insofar as the externalists begin with their states of consciousness and proceed from them to 'demonstrate' that our 'ideas' must have an external reference. This would, I fear, be regarded as a perverse interpretation of their project by the externalists. Nor can the argument be successful. I do know that I am not Swampman, but only for, broadly speaking, *scientific* reasons; it cannot be demonstrated a priori from a philosophical theory of content. And so at best I have scientific reasons to believe in the external world. But I had those reasons already;

externalism certainly adds nothing. In fact, the idea that externalism has any bearing on scepticism is just an epistemological aspect of the anti-Cartesian catastrophe.

In any case, R2 accepts individualism, in that it allows that the intentional nature of our states of consciousness – their intentional objects – is fixed by these states' intrinsic natures, and this would represent a galling admission of defeat for most externalists. Acceptance of R2 also means that externalism would end up having nothing of special importance to say about the nature of psychological states, since these would possess all their psychologically significant intentional properties in despite of variations in external circumstances. In short, acceptance of R2 pretty much destroys both the rationale and the supposed fruits of externalism. At the least, it restricts externalism's relevance to questions of reference, which turns out to be a rather narrow and parochial feature of the intentional content of our representational states of consciousness.

This leaves us with R3. In a sense, R3 is irrelevant to the concerns of this chapter, since it essentially concedes the truth of content internalism. But there are some interesting 'instabilities' lurking in R3 that make it worth examining. One take on R3 would have us simply divide up our concepts into those that are able, and those that are unable, to serve as aspects under which we can be conscious of things. To take a popular example, this view would hold that while we cannot be conscious of something as *water* (since this is a content that is properly given an externalist treatment) we can be conscious of that thing as a *clear, heavy, liquid* which we also think of as called *'water.'* This proposal is directly counter to the explicit pronouncements of some externalists about the extreme situation of Swampman (both Davidson and Millikan for example) and also demands some kind of a general account of the difference between those concepts that require an externalist treatment and those that do not (no such account has ever been offered so far as I know but see McGinn 1989, pp. 44 ff.). This particular case would suggest that a sharp distinction between the observable and the unobservable might do the job (and some have tried to revive the old positivist distinction; see Fodor 1984,[30] McGinn 1989, chapter 1, and, more recently, Tye 1994). But it remains completely obscure why we cannot *consciously think* of things which are unobservable and think of them as such (needless to say, common sense as well as much work in the philosophy of science suggests that we can and do have such thoughts).[31] Externalism would apparently have nothing to say about this, so again we see externalism ending up almost completely irrelevant to psychology. One might also wonder just what kind of a concept it is that cannot inform the intentional object of a conscious thought. If the concept of water (call it C[water]) does deserve an externalist treatment then Swampman cannot have any water-thoughts. I can have such thoughts, but I cannot be conscious of something *as* water (since my state of consciousness is identical to Swampman's); C[water] cannot be an aspect under which I am conscious of some liquid. In what sense then, can I be said to possess the concept of water? However we divide up concepts, we face the question of just why it is that Swampman can have the non-externalist ones given that he cannot have the externalist ones. Is it something about observability? Then why can Swampman *observe* things? Such questions cannot be answered by externalism and yet these questions will end up being the heart of a psychology of concepts and concept formation. So this interpretation of R3 seems to open a can of worms which quickly wriggle free of externalism's grasp. In the end, the failure of (at least this version of) externalism to grapple with these problems and its forced admission that some contents are, after all, *purely internal* contents suggests that externalism is nothing but an exceptionally bloated and grandiose attempt to restate the old and obvious fact that, by and large, we can't know merely from conscious introspection what external objects our intentional states involve.

Another possible way to regard R3 takes it as a call to rethink radically the *kind* of contents that can figure in states of consciousness. Although it runs counter to most externalist thinking, the notion of a distinctive kind of content which is individual or internalist in nature and which forms the aspects under which we are conscious of things might be appealing in the face of the difficulties scouted above. Lately there is even a candidate for this kind of content: narrow content. Many have said, after all, that doppelgängers share their 'narrow psychology'. But the most natural interpretation of this suggestion is that the aspects that inform conscious states are narrow aspects only in the sense that their external *reference* is not determined solely by their intrinsic nature; narrow contents are transformed into 'wide' contents simply by being given a contextually determined reference (through the usual externalist machinery). This collapses R3 into R2 – it is the thorough trivialization of externalism and the elimination of any relevance externalism might have for psychology or the understanding of psychological states (this is, pretty much, what the champions of narrow content have said all along about externalism). Roughly speaking, this would seem to be the view underlying *internalist* theories of thought such as those presented by Loar (1988) and Chalmers (1996b). However, as we shall see below, neither Loar nor Chalmers are presenting a theory of what should be strictly called *narrow* content but instead offer theories in which the posited content is already richly representational (and so much the better for their views in my opinion). A narrow content approach also inherits the difficulties, which externalists themselves have eagerly pointed out, inherent in the notion of narrow content as an element of *psychological* states and particularly as figuring in states of consciousness. Narrow content seems to be inaccessible, inexpressible, incommunicable, and thus, one could be excused for thinking, unexperienceable (surely a serious flaw in something looking for the job of *being* the aspects under which we are actually conscious of things; for more on this difficulty for narrow content see Baker 1987).

But set aside such worries, for a more peculiar and serious problem immediately arises. Suppose that narrow contents are accessible – they are in fact the only aspects that are ever accessible to consciousness. So both I and Swampman are indeed in the very same state of consciousness with the very same intentional object, at least with respect to the aspect under which we are conscious (Swampman might or might not be conscious of the very same object of which I am conscious). Of course, it seems to me that I am conscious of things under wide aspects but that's an illusion engendered by the fact that I have always and inescapably been conscious of things under narrow aspects and narrow aspects alone.

Let's say that N[c] is the narrow content associated with the wide content, c (here I'm adapting a method of referring to narrow content from Stich 1991). So N[water] is the narrow content that figures in my conscious thoughts which are, thanks to the grace of God, about water and also in Swampman's identical states of consciousness which are *not* thoughts about water (or any other wide thing). We all can understand what N[water] is supposed to be in terms of content – it's what would be linked to the stuff we call water for thinkers who were in the appropriate externally specified situations. So thinkers can, apparently, consciously consider the opposition between N[water] and C[water], where this latter is a wide content, the concept of *water*. But that presupposes that these thinkers can have both C[water] thoughts and N[water] thoughts. I am such a thinker. My Swampman cannot have such thoughts however, whether consciously or not. This is odd: I can be conscious of the difference between N[water] and C[water] but Swampman cannot. This would amount to a difference between our states of consciousness however, and, as we have seen, there is *no* difference between my and Swampman's states of consciousness. So we have a *reductio* of the suggestion that the aspects under which we are conscious of things are narrow aspects.

It might be objected that the situation has been misdescribed. Under the current hypothesis (or interpretation of R3) I am conscious of water as water only insofar as N[water] is the aspect which currently informs my state of consciousness (and appropriate external relations are satisfied). Perhaps, then, to think about N[water] is to think under the aspect N[N[water]]. But what is this monster, N[N[water]]? It must be the narrow content associated with the narrow content associated with 'water'. Is there such a thing? No. If there was it would be a content that, when appropriate external relations were satisfied, would refer to N[water] and thus allow someone to have (wide, so to speak) thoughts with N[water] contents. But no external relations are required to enable someone to have a thought with N[water] contents – narrow contents are postulated to *avoid* the need for such a distinction. For narrow content, there can be no difference between wide and narrow thoughts (we could say N[N[water]] = N[water]). So this objection fails.

This line of thought also leads to a more general problem which I shall call the paradox of the isolation strategy. The isolation strategy is something like what Fodor (1980) called 'methodological solipsism' and Stich 'the principle of psychological autonomy' (1978). It seeks to secure a place for a psychology that focusses only on the mind, leaving aside the rest of the world. It can be likened to similar strategies in physics, where certain intrinsic features of objects are selected as fundamental determinants of their behaviour. It is then attempted to isolate an object so that the only features at work are the selected ones; this can be approximately done in reality (e.g. by putting a pendulum in a vacuum chamber) or it can be done perfectly in thought experiments. This strategy has, to say the least, paid off for the physical sciences.

In psychology, the postulation of narrow contents serves an analogous end: it postulates a core feature of the mind, and the mind alone, which drives thought and behaviour in abstraction from the external situation of the thinker/behaver (although not, it would seem, from the external situation *as thought of* by the subject – but see below for a worry about this). However, this strategy only makes sense from a point of view that itself has access to both narrow and wide content. That is, the very distinction between wide and narrow content makes sense – can be understood – only from a point of view which has access to both sorts of content. Yet, according to the view we're considering, all thoughts, insofar as they are regarded as *purely psychological*, are informed solely by narrow content. According to this view, it should be impossible to *think* the difference between C[water]-thoughts and N[water]-thoughts because the closest we can get to having C[water]-thoughts is to have N[water]-thoughts (in the appropriate external circumstances, should we be lucky enough to be in such). So, if the suggestion is that all conscious thinking is thinking under narrow aspects then the theory which postulates a distinction between wide and narrow thoughts looks to be an unthinkable theory.[32]

I think the problem is, at root, that the idea of narrow thought is spurious because it assumes that one is already having wide thoughts about relatively non-particular features of the world – the features that pick out the set of possible worlds in which one's thought places one. These are very far from being simply the sensory qualities of the world as presented in consciousness for these would be duplicated in a world in which, for example, I was a brain in a vat yet such a world is not compatible with the world as I conceive it to be. It is this covert assumption of wide thoughts which persist through the various philosophical externalist thought experiments that makes us think we understand what it would be like to have only or thoroughly narrow thoughts. The externalist challenge trades on the ambiguity between the picayune fact that thought alone does not establish reference to particulars and the astonishing hypothesis that without an appropriate enabling connection to the world thought represents *nothing* and therefore must be utterly empty. But from an externalist perspective, Swampman cannot have thoughts with any wide content at all – his thoughts cannot even present a non-particular picture of the, or a, world in which they would turn out to be true (and thus wide in the picayune sense) thoughts. It is the function of the Swampman thought experiment to sever any and all of the appropriate external links to the world. Nonetheless, if Swampman is in the same state of consciousness as I am, then his thoughts do present such a 'truth-evaluable' picture of the world. So they must have some wide content after all. Non-picayune external-ism must be false.

So none of the replies, R1 through R3, is very promising. I think the conclusion to be drawn is that either there is something radically wrong with externalism or else it is a rather trivial doctrine restricted to certain points in the theory of reference and almost entirely irrelevant to psychology. This is made clear by thinking about conscious thinking. Obviously, we can think about things beyond ourselves, and we do this by engaging physical processes entirely within ourselves. We come to know this fundamental fact solely through our consciousness of the directedness of our thoughts. It is in consciousness that we have a mysterious zone of connection between ourselves and the 'outer' world. Consciousness is nothing but what is happening to us right now, but it also points beyond itself to a great world spread out in both space and time. The fundamental flaw in externalism is that it tries to reconcile these two equally basic features of consciousness by pulling them apart into, first, what is happening to me and, second, the relation between these happenings and the external situation around me as presented to me in consciousness.[33] But my current state of consciousness and the *presented* external situation cannot be separated. I don't know whether a theory of the intentionality of consciousness is possible at all, but it is clear that externalist theories of intentionality cannot provide it. This in turn makes it doubtful that externalist theories cast *any* light on the fundamental nature of intentionality.

Are some more positive remarks possible here? Evidently, what we need to crown the triumph of the representational theory of consciousness is an internalist theory of representation. Unfortunately, I don't have an internalist theory to offer. Such a theory would make (at least some of) the content of states of consciousness, and no doubt non-conscious representational mental states as well, depend solely upon the intrinsic nature of the conscious subject, in some appropriate sense of 'content' and 'intrinsic nature'. For an example of the former constraint, consider that the proper internalist theory would not attempt to fix the referents of all the elements of every content carrying state. As in the example of my thoughts about Paris discussed above, the fact that my thoughts are about the particular city we call 'Paris' cannot be internally guaranteed. What can be internally guaranteed? The simplest answer seems to be that all that is guaranteed is the 'qualitative' state of consciousness. But it is difficult to say what this encompasses. I would like to say that the qualitative state of consciousness can be expressed in terms of the *sorts* of worlds that are compatible with the way a particular state of consciousness represents, abstracting from questions of the reference of the representational elements of that state. When Swampman seems to think about Paris, although he cannot really think about Paris he is nonethe-less thinking about a world that is like thus-and-so. But the full details of the 'thus-and-so' must themselves be cashed out in the same sort of purely qualitative terms we are trying to specify. Here there are grave difficulties. For example, it seems to me that human consciousness has been (and is still being) radically transformed by the social processes of concept acquisition, especially as these are conditioned by overwhelmingly powerful linguistic processes. I can, for example, consciously think about what the world would be like without television. Such thoughts are surely highly conditioned and in fact made possible by the fact that I have a language which provides me with the vast number of concepts necessary for such thoughts. I can have these thoughts without any guarantee that there is any such thing as television in the world. I can even have these thoughts if I am in fact a recently created doppelgänger of some member of late 20th century Western civilization, and even if there is no such civilization. These last points can be taken simply to reinforce the natural internalist denial of the 'thought–reference' link. But they equally seem to indicate that reference to *properties* is preserved in the internalist theory of content we seek. How brain states, as such, can generate (or realize) content that refers to such properties as 'being a television' is the mystery before us then.

As I say, I cannot answer these questions. I suspect that the sort of qualitative content we seek to define should be mapped out in terms of the set of world transformations that maintain a relationship of *satisfaction* to the state of consciousness. My thoughts and perceptions incompletely specify a world; it is in the incompleteness of my conscious picture of the world that the qualitative content of consciousness is revealed. Qualitative consciousness cannot be reduced to the 'purely' perceptual, non-conceptual, aspects (as specified, for example, in Peacocke 1992) since the way I am experiencing now is deeply infected with complex, conceptual elements. Even to begin the delineation of such rich content would require a complete theory of the nature of concepts that would reveal how the content of concepts[34] themselves can be given an internalist explanation. No one can offer such an account at present.

Some philosophers have *posited* that internal specifications of (certain kinds of) content are possible. For example, what David Chalmers (1996a, pp. 60 ff., 1996b) calls the primary intension of a concept can be used to develop a notion of narrow content that is supposed to be fixed by the internal state of a thinker. And Brian Loar (1988) also suggests that narrow content can be seen to have some kind of intentionality. These approaches explicitly aim to meet the condition given above that internally specified content should somehow determine a set of possible worlds in which the content is 'satisfied' (Loar calls this set of worlds the *realization conditions* of a subject's beliefs; see 1988, p. 573). But it is very unclear how this satisfaction (or realization) relation can be defined – as opposed to postulated – without stepping beyond purely narrow content, solely by appeal to internal features (these conceptions are, I believe, not really of *narrow* content but rather the de-particularized wide content mentioned above). Loar says that 'the conceptual role of one's thoughts determine *how* one *conceives* things' (p. 573, original emphasis). Here, 'conceptual role' is just Loar's favoured, functionalist, notion of the internal feature of the state that supports its narrow content. The question is: *how* can conceptual role, or any purely internal feature we may select, determine how one conceives of things, since how one conceives things is a matter of wide content? Swampman has states with the required purely internal conceptual role but what set of worlds will 'satisfy' these states? Obviously we must step back from *reference* when we think about Swampman, but we shall still have to specify the satisfaction conditions in terms of the structure of the satisfying possible worlds, and won't that involve at least appeal to the properties of those worlds and their patterns of instantiation? In that case, how did Swampman's states get even *properties* as their intentional objects?

I think it is clear that we cannot give a behaviourist definition of the satisfaction relation. One could imagine, as it were, asking Swampman if he is in one of the worlds that agrees with his beliefs, and – by the nature of belief – Swampman will have to answer 'yes', but Swampman could be mistaken in his answer, just as I could be radically mistaken about the nature of the world I seem to inhabit. I might be a brain in a vat, but the 'vat-world' is not a world that satisfies my set of beliefs. Behaviourally and from my own point of view, I am equally at home in the real world or the ersatz, world of an envatted brain, but my conscious apprehension of the world is not *indeterminate* between a world with trees and television, for example, and the utterly treeless and TV-less world of laboratory and vat. What we need to know is what Swampman's (or my) inner states *represent*, and we need to be able to find this out purely on the basis of Swampman's internal state (at least we have to understand how it is that what these states represent is determined by their internal features).[35] This looks difficult; and one can certainly see what drives the externalist accounts here.

Loar makes much of the fact that we can give successful psychological explanations without any knowledge of wide contents. But, in the first place, even if Swampman was entirely devoid of every kind of meaningful psychological state we could still tell psychological stories about him that would appear to be successful (and they would succeed in predicting his behaviour exactly as well as if he really had a psychology). It would be a mistake, however, to suppose that the *truth* of our application of psychological explanations reduces to the *successfulness* of these applications in the prediction of behaviour (this is no more than logical behaviourism). More important (to me anyway, since I do agree that Swampman has a genuine psychology), the success of our psychological explanations depends upon his possessing a layer of meaningful states or representations which seems to remain wide – the representation of properties or world-structure. We need an internalist explanation of how such representation gets into place within Swampman (or any subject) that does not appeal to *any* facts about what Swampman's states already represent. Suppose a 25th century Swampman is created as a brain in a vat, being fed a program providing a virtual life in the 20th century. Swampman thinks he is an aged philosopher walking along a sea shore, on a windy day near sunset, recalling a bittersweet academic life. We are in the laboratory but have no idea what program is running. We wonder what worlds would satisfy Swampman's inner states. On the face of it, they appear to be, at least contain, worlds in which certain computer circuits send complex signal trains to various regions of Swampman's brain. But that is *not* a world that Swampman takes himself to be in. I think that internalist accounts like Chalmers's and Loar's presuppose the representational features of the mind they ought to explain.[36]

Recently, Robert Cummins (1996) has revived a kind of picture theory of meaning. In his version, the internal feature on which representation depends is *isomorphism* between the structure of the internal state and structures in the world (see Cummins 1996, especially ch. 7). At first glance, this appears to endorse a radical internalism but the second glance is disappointing. Cummins has no aim of applying his theory to consciousness – his work has an entirely different focus, but I think there are severe difficulties in applying his views to the problem of consciousness. It is far from clear how such structural content could inform states of consciousness. For example, how could one define the satisfaction conditions that delimit the set of possible worlds compatible with my conscious thoughts in terms of an isomorphism relation? It is hard to see how one could distinguish between the treed and televisioned world and the envatted brain world envisaged above in terms of isomorphism. Rather, on the face of it, the isomorphism would seem to hold equally between the subject brain and both sorts of world, if between brain and any world at all. Cummins admits that differences between isomorphs cannot be represented (p. 107) and there will never be a shortage of structures isomorphic to any given brain structure (if only ones drawn from pure mathematics). Yet in consciousness, we do *think* differences between isomorphs. Well, says Cummins, the picture theory of meaning 'does not imply that they [differences between isomorphs] cannot be conceptualized' (p. 107). This is apparently possible since Cummins regards concepts as kinds of knowledge structures rather than discrete representations (see pp. 88 ff.; on p. 107 Cummins writes: 'think of each concept as a kind of minitheory').

Of course, we cannot suppose that concepts, or knowledge structures, resolve themselves into structures of genuine representations (an obviously tempting treatment of concepts or theories) or we shall have returned to the original problem. In fact, Cummins makes a great deal of the fact that it is a mistake to suppose that because one can think about α one must therefore have a representation of α (he goes so far as to suggest that the idea that an attitude, such as belief, desire, etc., that p is to be explained as a kind of relation to a representation that p precludes any possibility of representational error, see p. 64). For example, the visual system seems to possess *edge-detectors*. Cummins takes it that an edge detector represents only *presence* but when such a detector fires 'we get a primitive attitude with the content that a visual edge is present' (p. 63, note 12). But, crudely speaking, we are conscious of these attitudes – we can see edges. How we become consciously aware of such attitudes is quite mysterious. Features of the world that we *cannot* represent are the features that inform our states of consciousness! But what is most worrying from my point of view is that when Cummins moves from representation to attitude, which essentially involves what he calls the *target* of a token representation Cummins leaves internalism behind and embraces a teleological account that depends upon the mechanism which produces representations having representational *functions* (see ch. 8, especially p. 118). Cummins does not offer any sort of internalist theory of function (and indeed hints at some kind of evolutionary account). Thus, since Swampman lacks representational functions, even though his states do represent (they are isomorphic to *something*), they cannot have any targets. But since, in Cummins's terminology, states of consciousness are of targets rather than of what is represented, Swampman again ends up with no states of consciousness.

In any event, an account of qualitative content and its relation to internally explicated contents would still leave open the central question. How does the brain (or any other possible substratum of consciousness) generate the content carrying states which inform states of consciousness? This is the ultimate generation problem, created by the dual need for a theory of representation and the fact (discussed at the end of chapter 7 above) that in consciousness we are aware of *what* a state represents but not its intrinsic properties in virtue of which it represents. But I don't think that anyone knows how to begin addressing this problem. It is important here to distinguish carefully how we *know* that some system possesses representational states from the fact that there *are* such states within the system. For example, it seems to me likely that the only way to discover and unravel a representational system is to find a set of states within the system whose interrelationships are sufficiently and appropriately homomorphic to (a part of) the world under an interpretation, and which direct behaviour appropriate to the content assigned by that interpretation. That would not be the same as *identifying* representation with 'homomorphism under an interpretation'. Presumably, the homomorphism exists because the representing states are representations, not *vice versa*.

It would be nice to take refuge in a resolutely naturalistic picture of the world and the place of the mind within the world. Why not echo Charles Darwin that since the 'exuding' of gravity by matter is not thought to call for any appeal to the supernatural and can simply be accepted as an intrinsic feature of matter, we should also willingly accept thought as a 'secretion of the brain' (as reported in Desmond and Moore 1994, p. 251).[37] This would be to take the representational capacities of the brain (within a very difficult to specify class of 'intrinsically intentional' devices) as a brute metaphysical fact of the world. As remarked at the end of chapter 7, taking up the position that intentionality is a brute fact is less than comfortable. Darwin's example of gravity reveals one discomforting aspect. It may be that there is no explanation of matter's propensity to gravitate but we can reduce gravitation to the action of the elementary constituents of the world. Brute facts *ought* to reside at that level, not suddenly appear in full flower upon the fortuitous assembly of a vastly complicated material structure. Reflection on this worry, along with a respect for the generation problem, suggests a strange return to one of the truly ancient doctrines of the mind–body relation. The final chapter will indulge in this speculation.

Box 8.7 • Summary

When faced with the problem of conscious thought, externalist treatments of representation and mental content face severe difficulties. There are reasons for holding that states of consciousness are intrinsic features of the conscious subject and so, for those states of consciousness which essentially involve awareness of content – i.e. conscious thoughts – this content cannot be given a thoroughly externalistic treatment. Externalists can attempt various lines of reply to this argument, but none that plausibly leave conscious thought dependent upon an externalist view of content. Thus, an internalist theory of representation or mental content would seem to be needed. Unfortunately, it is far from clear how to construct such a theory. Functionalist attempts seem to fail, either because they circularly presuppose the very content carrying states they are supposed to explain or because they dissolve into an unacceptable behaviourism. Perhaps some kind of view of representation as 'structural isomorphism' between an object and its representation holds promise, but isomorphisms are too easy to come by and attempts to restrict the field might lead back to externalism.

9

CONSCIOUSNESS,
INFORMATION AND PANPSYCHISM

Box 9.1 • Preview

The problems of providing physicalist explanations of the nature and generation of states of consciousness seem so perplexing that some radical speculation might be in order. The views of David Chalmers provide a springboard into deep and dark speculative currents. Chalmers espouses a kind of dualism, in which consciousness figures as an absolutely fundamental feature of the world, essentially linked to *information* as well as to the functional architecture of the brain (or other possible physical realizations of consciousness). All of these ideas lead to riddles. How can a brute or fundamental feature of the world appear *only when* associated with exceptionally complex physical structures, such as the brain? No other fundamental feature of the world (mass, energy, charge, etc.) has such a peculiar property. Also, how can a fundamental feature link to physical structure as *functionally* described? To speak in metaphysical metaphor, surely the world doesn't know anything about functional architecture or 'levels' of functional descriptions. Perhaps it would be better to accept that a fundamental feature of the world should appear at the simplest structural levels. This leads one to consider the old view that *everything* has a mental aspect – panpsychism. Many objections can be raised against this strange and implausible view. Responses to these objections seem possible, if we increase the speculative content of the view by drawing on certain ideas from quantum physics, especially ideas about the nature of *information* and ideas about how quantum systems can form distinctive 'wholes', irreducible to the parts which appear to constitute them. Strangely, there are a variety of possible links between the quantum and the mind, and a kind of panpsychism that connects to them in interesting ways. But if such speculative exercises are ultimately unsatisfactory, we must again consider the generation problem, and what it is trying to tell us about the place of consciousness in the natural world.

What I've been calling the generation problem is evidently very close to a problem recently returned to prominence by David Chalmers at the first of the now famous Tucson conferences on consciousness. What Chalmers calls the *hard problem of consciousness* is explaining precisely why and exactly how experience is generated by certain particular configurations of physical stuff. We should be a little wary about this characterization since we must bear in mind that the term 'generates' might be misleadingly causal: the explanatory relation we seek might be identity, instantiation, realization or something else altogether. The generation problem has been around for a long time; a clear formulation is given by John Tyndall (as quoted by William James): 'The passage from the physics of the brain to the corresponding facts of consciousness is unthinkable. Granted that a definite thought and a definite molecular action in the brain occur simultaneously; we do not possess the intellectual organ, nor apparently any rudiment of the organ, which would enable us to pass, by a process of reasoning, from one to the other' (as quoted in James 1890/1950, p. 147; from Tyndall 1879). As Thomas Huxley put it, less directly but more poetically: 'given the molecular forces in a mutton chop, deduce Hamlet or Faust therefrom' (as quoted in Desmond and Moore 1994, p. 560). Now, we've seen that there are at least two problems that enter into the *hard problem*: what makes some state an 'intrinsic representation' as well as the more traditional generation problem of what makes one of these representational states conscious. Perhaps these two questions are not as distinct as they appear.

Chalmers's approach to consciousness is distinguished in the way it places the 'hard problem' at the very centre of the issue. But while the generation problem has the outward appearance of a genuine scientific problem, one might dispute whether it is useful, mandatory or, even, intelligible. As discussed in chapter 1, we always have the option of trying to dissolve rather than solve an intractable problem. Though I discounted the chances of dissolving the generation problem, let's look again now that we have seen a variety of theories of consciousness. To begin with a familiar and tendentious example, suppose one tried to divide the problems of statistical thermodynamics into the easy and the hard. The easy problems would be ones like 'how and why do gases expand when heated', 'why and how does pressure increase with increasing temperature', etc. By contrast, the supposedly hard problem would be to account for the generation of thermodynamic properties by the 'thermodynamically blank' particles which form the subject of statistical mechanics. What a mystery! Not only does a collection of independent particles *act like* a gas with thermodynamic properties, the collection somehow *generates* these very properties.

It is easy to see through this sham mystery[1] and there are philosophers who would suggest that the case of consciousness is no different. Once you have explained the appropriate and, no doubt, exceedingly complex internal structures which, ultimately, generate behaviour there is simply nothing more to be explained. Don't mistake a task impossible because it is utterly senseless for one that embodies a deep metaphysical mystery. Chalmers insists that because consciousness is not a functional property, someone asking for an explanation of how a 'behaviourally sufficient' functional organization generates experience is 'not making a conceptual mistake' (Chalmers 1995a, p. 8; Chalmers 1996a, pp. 104 ff.). Certainly, this is not as obvious a mistake as that which would demand an independent, additional explanation of how *heat* arises apart from the account of the functional isomorphism between statistical and phenomenological thermodynamics provided by statistical mechanics. But how can one show that the case of consciousness is not fundamentally similar to that of thermodynamics?

A straightforward reply is simply to point out the intelligibility of the classical problem of other minds. There is no a priori argumentation that can eliminate this problem; everyone who thinks about it can see that each of us is, in a fundamental sense, *alone*. Perhaps against this, Wittgenstein once said: 'if I see someone writhing in pain with evident cause I do not think: all the same, his feelings are hidden from me' (1953/1968, p. 223). A naive but not necessarily incorrect reply is: of course not, for we operate on the very deeply held assumption that other people do indeed have experience and this is no time to question basic assumptions. But what if it is a beetle writhing about as it is impaled on the specimen seeker's pin or a lobster squirming as it's dropped into the boiling water? There is no easy answer, let alone a philosophically innocent a priori answer, to the question of where in the chain of biological development experience emerges, although even at the levels of the beetle and lobster one certainly sees behaviour similar (at least) to that caused by pain.

As became clear in the discussion of his theory in chapters 4 and 5, Daniel Dennett's view of consciousness (1991b, 1993) can be seen as fixated on debunking the generation problem. His discussion of philosophical zombies, those hypothetical creatures that act just like us but who are entirely without experience, is reminiscent of Wittgenstein's remark, and is similarly perplexing.[2] At one point Dennett says (1991b, pp. 405–6) that if zombies were possible, you wouldn't be able to really tell whether something was a zombie or not (every coin has two sides) so it would be immoral to treat a putative zombie as an entirely unconscious being. This is no argument against the possibility of zombies and so even less an argument undermining the intelligibility of the generation problem.

Elsewhere, Dennett allows that animals do have experiences even though they do not have the fully developed consciousness of human beings (1991b, pp. 442 ff.). He intimates that many distinct functional architectures could underwrite the ascription of (I avoid saying 'generate'[3]) experience and with regard to bats in particular remarks that we can know something of the range of bat experience by finding out what the bat nervous system can represent and which representations actually function in the modulation of behaviour (1991b, p. 444). Although nicely in the spirit of a representational theory of consciousness, this only tells us what the bat *could be* conscious of, it does not tell us whether the bat *is* conscious of these things, for there can be no question – certainly not for Dennett – of eliminating the distinction between conscious and unconscious representations which 'modulate behaviour'. So here we find a very stark form of the generation problem located in a theory that was supposed to banish it: given the viability of the conscious/unconscious representation distinction (endorsed by Dennett even as he asserts that this distinction is not absolutely clear cut) and given the undeniable fact that some unconscious representations modulate behaviour, what makes the difference between conscious and unconscious behaviour modulating representations in non-verbal animals? Why is it that the states that represent bodily injury in bats are conscious experiences, if they are, whereas those representing the details of wing positioning during the hunt are not, if they aren't? (Here I am just imagining that bats are like me: I feel the pain in my ankle but am not usually aware of the complex foot work involved in running over an uneven surface, yet both involve behaviour modulating representations.) We have no recourse to the usual behavioural test of consciousness here – verbal behaviour – since, of course, bats can't *tell us* what they are aware of, but Dennett generously, if puzzlingly, admits that animals have experiences despite this.

Or again, in his discussion of split-brain cases Dennett denies that 'commissurotomy leaves in its wake organizations both distinct and robust enough to support . . . a separate self' (1991b, p. 426). But the issue should be, does the right hemisphere have *experiences*? Whether or not it is a full-fledged self, is it like a non-verbal animal and is it distinct from the human self that unquestionably remains after commissurotomy? As the mass of split-brain research amply reveals, the right hemisphere deploys various *representations* and many of these modulate behaviour (for a review of research on the rich distinctions in functions across the cerebral hemispheres see Springer and Deutsch 1985). So what makes them, or some of them, into experiences? If it is not simply the behaviour modulating powers of a representation, is it a representation's having behaviour modulating power above degree n (on some scale of efficacy)? Obviously, this is the generation problem all over again: what makes n (or a vaguely defined region around n) the right sort of thing to enable consciousness?[4]

A theory of consciousness ought to tell us what consciousness is, what things in the world possess it, how to tell whether something possesses it and how it arises in the physical world (both synchronically from physical conditions and diachronically as an evolutionary development). The hard problem of consciousness is evidenced by the very real 'zombie problem' we have with animals. The honey bee, for one more example, acts like a creature that has experiences – visual, olfactory, as well as painful and pleasurable – as well as enjoying an apparently cognitive relation to its environment (see Griffin 1992 or Gould 1988, 1990 for more on the 'mental life' of the honey bee). Its behaviour, we have reason to suppose, is modulated by a complex system of internal representations generated, maintained and updated by a sophisticated neural parallel processor, rather like our own, if much less complex (though the nervous system of the bee contains around one million neurons as compared to our own perhaps 100 billion, it is nonetheless an extremely complex network). These representations may be coordinated, for all I know, by the famous 40 Hz oscillations (the 'sign' of consciousness in the visual system according to Francis Crick and Christof Koch; see Crick 1994). Now, on which side of the fuzzy line between sentience and non-sentience does the bee reside, or in the fuzzy zone itself? More important, for whatever answer, *why*? Suppose we made a robot bee that fitted well into bee life (beginnings are being made, see Kirchner and Towne 1994). Suppose also we were sure the robot could not have experiences (it was truly an 'apian zombie'). Would that show that *bees* do not have experiences? *Why*? On the other hand, suppose we think that bees most certainly do experience things. Would that show that the robot also experiences (it certainly passes a *bee-level* Turing Test)? Again we have to ask *why*?[5]

We've seen that Chalmers is right to claim that no extant theory of consciousness really addresses this range of questions in a satisfactory way, even as these theories admit that questions about, for example, bees' experiences are perfectly intelligible. Forgive me for harping on this, but the existence of the generation problem is absolutely crucial. Without it, there is *no* hard problem of consciousness. With it, the problem looks very hard indeed.

So hard, in fact, that Chalmers looks to a radical solution to bridge the so-called explanatory gap between physical system and conscious system. He suggests that consciousness is an absolutely fundamental feature of the universe, which must be simply accepted as the First Datum in the study of the mind (see Chalmers 1996a, ch. 4, especially pp. 126 ff.). Of course, this is the idea that consciousness is somehow one of the brute facts of the universe, an idea which we have seen force its way into our theories quite regularly. It is a neat way to finesse the generation question since there can be, by definition, no explanation of why fundamental features of the world arise whenever they do arise. For example, there is no explanation of why fundamental particles come in their observed mass ratios and if this is indeed one of the brute facts of our universe then this lack of explanation simply has to be accepted. Perhaps, once we accept the reality of the generation problem, there is no other way to proceed. And since I am strongly inclined to see the generation problem as a real problem, I can feel the attraction of some kind of brute fact solution of it. On the other hand, Chalmers's 'solution' involves the denial of physicalism – Chalmers labels it *naturalistic dualism*, and this is a radical leap in the dark which I am loath to endorse. Furthermore, I confess to find some disturbing elements in Chalmers's account, which I will argue suggest that a yet *more radical* view of the problem of consciousness is dictated by the assumption that consciousness is a fundamental feature of the universe. I want to spend some time developing this radical view; perhaps it *is* the way to go. Or it may be another indication that the appeal of the idea that consciousness is somehow a fundamental feature of the world is bogus.

Begin with Chalmers's idea of the conditions under which consciousness arises, what he calls the principle of organizational invariance (see 1996a, ch. 7). Strictly speaking, this principle asserts only that 'any two systems with the same fine-grained functional organization will have qualitatively identical experiences' (1995a, p. 19).[6] But it follows from this that whether or not a system, S, is conscious depends upon its fulfilling some *functional* description. For suppose not: then there is some other, non-functional feature of S, call it Q, on which consciousness depends. We could then build a system functionally isomorphic to S that lacks Q which will, by hypothesis, not be conscious, which is impossible by the organizational principle.[7] This argument seems to leave open the possibility of additional, non-functionally defined, generators of consciousness, but they will fall victim to Chalmers's 'fading qualia' argument considered below. It is very disturbing that consciousness can be an absolutely fundamental feature of nature while being dependent upon particular systems satisfying purely functional descriptions, with the relevant similarity among these descriptions being *behavioural* capacities. No other fundamental feature of the world has this character, or a character even remotely like it. It is rather as if one declared that 'being a telephone' was a fundamental feature of the world, generated by a variety of physical systems agreeing only in fulfilling the relevant, highly abstract, behaviourally defined functional descriptions.

Also, since Chalmers is adamant that consciousness presents a hard problem because it is *not* itself a functional feature it is very odd that consciousness should depend solely upon whether a system meets a certain abstract functional description. Of course, if consciousness is truly a fundamental feature we are barred from asking *how it is* that all and only systems meeting certain functional descriptions are conscious, yet this idea does seem only to deepen rather than to dispel the mystery of the generation problem.

Box 9.2 • Silicon Isomorphs and Fading Qualia

Imagine that some high-tech lab produces microchips that are perfect *functional* duplicates of individual neurons. Further supposing that these silicon functional isomorphs can be integrated into a biological brain, imagine that *your* neurons are gradually replaced by such isomorphs. Would you notice any difference? Would there be any difference in your states of consciousness? If the isomorphs are incapable of supporting states of consciousness we might expect that your qualia would gradually 'fade out' as more and more of your genuine neurons were replaced. But there would be no behavioural difference from the outside (since the isomorphs would direct your movements and speech utterances just as before). You will *insist* that nothing has changed. But on the inside are you desperately and hopelessly trying to get your voice to utter your real thoughts? Chalmers thinks this is highly implausible and argues for the principle of organizational invariance on the basis of it.

We also face here a variant of the generation problem which grows out of the inherent vagueness in the phrase 'fine-grained functional organization'. Chalmers provides the example of a brain suffering a gradual substitution of its neurons, one by one, by 'silicon isomorphs' (electronic devices with neural signalling input–output functions identical to the biological neurons they replace) as an instance of his principle of organizational invariance (see 1996a, pp. 253 ff., 1995a, p. 19). Chalmers's 'fading qualia' argument in support of the principle of organizational invariance is that *if* the silicon isomorphs do not support consciousness then there should be a fading out of consciousness as the number of replacements climbs (or, possibly, consciousness will simply 'cut out' after some number of replacements; this alternative possibility does not significantly affect Chalmers's line of argument). But the subject of the experiment will, since the input–output chains of neurological signalling must remain unchanged within the brain, show no signs of fading qualia. Indeed, the subject will give every sign that no change in qualitative experience has occurred and will – if asked – *insist* that he is just as conscious and in the same ways conscious as he was before the start of the replacement procedure.[8]

But how do we know that neural input–output function is the appropriate level of specificity of functional description to satisfy the principle of organizational invariance?[9] The silicon isomorphs, we may suppose, are not *internally* functionally identical to the neurons they replace, yet the internal workings of a neuron certainly satisfy some quite complex functional description. Or, from the other direction, why couldn't we replace large groups of neurons with a single silicon device that mimics the input–output relations of the whole neural group it replaces? This experiment would seem to affect the subject's behaviour no more than Chalmers's original neural replacement experiment.

It is possible to develop an alternative version of Chalmers's qualia argument, one that does *not* preserve the 'fine-grained functional structure' of the subject, yet which is just as good at supporting the intuitions against fading qualia. Suppose that the proper level of functional fine-grainedness is located at the level of the neuron. That is, replacement of real neurons with functionally identical artificial neurons maintains support of states of consciousness qualitatively identical to those induced by the genuine neurons. Internally, the replacement neurons are functionally very different from real neurons but they duplicate the input–output capacities of the neurons they replace and *that*, we are supposing, is what matters. Now, none of the neurons in the brain is connected to every other neuron. In fact, a typical neuron might connect to about 10,000 other neurons. If the brain has around 100 billion neurons we have a connectivity ratio of about 0.00001 per cent. Obviously, the brain is organized into myriads of sub-networks and there is abundant evidence that the brain is in fact arranged into robust, functionally distinct and localized sub-networks. At a pretty fine-grained level it is possible that the neural columns found throughout the cortex could be modelled as distinct sub-networks and, at the other end of the scale, each cerebral hemisphere is a gigantic sub-network capable of independent operation and even, more or less, able to take over the functions of its twin. In any case, such sub-networks certainly exist and our thought experiment consists in replacing entire sub-networks instead of individual neurons. So, for each sub-network defined at some level well above that of the individual neuron, let's build a silicon chip which is the functional duplicate of the whole sub-network. Now, let's gradually, one by one, put these sub-network isomorphs into *your* head properly connected (both to each other and the appropriate sensory inputs and motor outputs). What will happen? Presumably, your behaviour will not change in any way whatsoever (how could it?). Will your state of consciousness change or disappear altogether, will you suffer from fading qualia? *If* the relevant level of fine-grained functional organization was indeed the level of individual neural interconnection then we might expect that the network replacement version of your brain no longer supports consciousness or supports a different sort of consciousness. Yet the new system supports all the conditions which Chalmers gives for believing that conscious experience remains in place – that qualia do not fade. The new system – perhaps it is still *you* – will *say* that it is as vividly conscious as it was before the replacement operation, it will discriminate stimuli exactly as well as before; as Chalmers says 'on a functional construal of belief, Joe [i.e. the victim of the isomorph replacement operation] will even *believe* that he has all these complex experiences . . .' (1996a, pp. 256–7).

The obvious reply is that our thought experiment shows only that we had misidentified the appropriate level of fine-grainedness required to support consciousness. We have 'proven' that this level is the level of the neural sub-networks rather than the level of individual neuron. But of course there are alternative functional architectures that will preserve both the behaviour and the associated functional analysis of belief which are not isomorphic to the particular level of neural sub-network we chose for our thought experiment. For example, there are many, many distinct levels of sub-networks ready to be discovered in the brain. A more exotic possibility is the replacement of the entire neural system with a pure Turing machine simulation of it. If the input–output function of each neuron is well defined then it is guaranteed that such a Turing machine simulation exists.[10] It is hard to avoid the suspicion that *any* internal structure that preserves all behavioural dispositions will meet the conditions of the fading qualia argument, and have to be granted consciousness.[11] Essentially, this is an unacceptable behaviourism.

Box 9.3 • Levels of Organization

Even if we accepted the principle of organization invariance, there would remain a question about what *level of organization* was appropriate for the generation of consciousness. The silicon isomorphs are functionally equivalent to the neurons they replace at the level of neural inputs and outputs. They must be functionally very different from these neurons on the inside (there is no reason for the isomorphs to have little silicon *faux* mitochondria within them for example). But how could we know what was the proper level for the generation of real consciousness? Maybe the inner workings of the neurons do matter. Who knows? Or maybe the *individual* neurons don't matter but only larger networks of neurons. Perhaps all that matters is that the whole individual simply remain behaviourally indistinguishable after the switch to the silicon surrogates (of whatever functional architecture). Of course, this puzzle is a version of the generation problem.

An adaptation of a thought experiment invented by Leibniz and discussed above in chapter 1 will drive the point home.[12] Recall that Leibniz imagined an artificial duplicate of a human being run by internal devices that were 'keyed' or pre-programmed so as to produce, at precisely the right time, behaviour exactly appropriate to the events that the duplicate would face throughout its (artificial) life. Though utterly mindless this artificial human would give every sign of intelligence and consciousness. Leibniz assumed Newtonian determinism so that, as he puts it, 'it is certain that a finite spirit could be so enlightened as to understand and to foresee demonstratively everything which would occur in a determinate time' (1702/1976, p. 575). Perhaps such determinism is not true of the actual world, but the point of the thought experiment to come is independent of such 'mere facts' (anyway, it is quite possible that the level of the neuron is deterministic, though like as not it is a chaotic, complex determinism). Now, imagine that we replace each neuron in your head, one by one – slowly if you like, with an artificial device that does not *respond* to input signals from other neurons but simply fires according to a predetermined pattern that corresponds exactly to the firing pattern of the real neuron it replaces (call these things *shneurons*). Each shneuron fires exactly in the way its corresponding neuron *would have* fired throughout its life in response to all the neurological conditions that *that* neuron *would have* faced throughout its existence. Shneurons are like alarm clocks, set to go off at exactly the times their neural counterparts would have gone off in the course of their natural commerce with connected neurons. After a while your whole head is full of shneurons.[13] Do you notice any change? Well, it appears that we can use all of Chalmers's arguments about fading qualia to argue that you will notice no change and that you therefore remain conscious throughout the replacement process, and indeed through the rest of your life even though your actions are all coordinated by the entirely predetermined, canned responses of the programmed replacement shneurons. But this seems preposterous. Such a 'brain' would surely not be conscious. You have become a completely inflexible robot incapable of responding to any but one predetermined set of events (although, it must be admitted, it is, by hypothesis, physically impossible for you to meet with any event for which you have not been properly pre-programmed). Why, at the end of the replacement process, all the shneurons except those governing motor responses could be thrown away – you would still behave as before and appear to respond intelligently and appropriately to the world. I think this thought experiment shows that Chalmers's fading qualia argument cannot be correct.

The shneuron thought experiment can also be developed further. We could for example preserve a more robust causal connection between the shneurons if we wanted; they can be linked together so that if, *per impossibile*, the shneurons that seem to provide the input signal to a given shneuron do not fire appropriately then the given shneuron will not fire. Of course, this causal link will never really interfere with the action of the given shneuron since its input shneurons will always fire just as they should. Should we believe that the existence of this never-to-be-used 'cutoff' switch restores you to true consciousness? We could even rig the shneurons so that, although they are all firing completely independently (just like alarm clocks) they *would* alter their internal program in an appropriately neuron-like way *if* the shneurons they have as apparent inputs should happen to alter their firing pattern (which, of course, they won't – the very laws of physics forbid it). Since the shneuron thought experiment involves what I called decounterfactualization in chapter 1 above, we could call this last notion the *re-counterfactualization* of the shneurons. It's hard to see how this operation could all by itself make consciousness spring back into existence!

The upshot of all this is a new generation problem: why does just a *particular* level of functional description generate consciousness, exactly which level performs the feat and how could we ever find out which was the correct level? The problem is that functional duplicates of a system isomorphic to the original system on various *distinct* functional levels could, in principle, duplicate the whole system's behaviour. Would any system that acts like a conscious system be judged conscious by the principle? If not, suppose we have two systems which are functionally isomorphic at level n but are not functionally isomorphic at level $n-1$ (as in Chalmers's own example as I take it). Whether they share the same states of consciousness apparently depends upon which level is the appropriate level of description, but who decides? What does the *universe* know about levels of functional description?

Lately, this problem has emerged in a somewhat more serious form with the hypothesis of Hameroff and Penrose (see Hameroff 1994, Penrose 1994)[14] that the fundamental underlying elements subserving consciousness are a special sort of structure deep *within* the neurons: the microtubules. Only within these peculiar structures can the essentially quantum mechanical processes which – according to Hameroff and Penrose – underpin conscious experience be maintained. So, it is possible to imagine building microtubule-less neuronal surrogates that preserve the input–output relations of their originals but which cannot generate any conscious experience.[15] The question at issue is how Chalmers's replacement argument could show, a priori, how to solve this 'practical' version of the functional levels problem.

Furthermore, a pernicious problem of explanatory exclusion – to borrow a term from Kim 1993 – arises from the aligning of consciousness with functional description. Any functionally described system must be actually instantiated by some assemblage of physical parts, if it is to take any part in the workings of the world. The causal efficacy of the system depends entirely upon the causal efficacy of its physical instantiation. Thus when we say such things as 'the thermostat turned on the furnace' the efficacy of the thermostat is entirely explained by the particular physical instantiation of *this* thermostat (say by the physical details of its thermocouple, or whatever else lets it serve its function). Perhaps a better example would the power of water to dissolve salt: this is entirely explained by the interactions of individual H_2O molecules with the NaCl molecules that constitute salt, and these interactions are in turn entirely explained by the ultimately quantum mechanical properties of Hydrogen, Oxygen,

Sodium and Chlorine. There is no room for water to have any causal powers save those grounded in its constituents. The *principle of causal grounding* states that the causal efficacy of any complex, whether functionally or mereologically described, is entirely dependent upon the causal efficacy of the basic constituents of its physical instantiation. The problem is now worrisomely clear. Does consciousness have *any* causal power in the world? If the causal powers of conscious systems obey the principle of causal grounding so that the causal powers of any conscious system are entirely dependent upon the powers of its instantiation then, since consciousness is a fundamental feature of the universe which cannot be *reduced* to its instantiations, consciousness has no efficacy in the world – consciousness turns out to be completely epiphenomenal. (This is a problem of efficacy independent of the rather similar one that arises in the debate about the internal vs. external nature of consciousness which was discussed in chapter 8.) On the other hand, if this conclusion is resisted and some independent causal power is granted to consciousness, then some assemblages of physical parts have causal powers that don't depend entirely upon the causal powers of those parts. This is what philosophers call *radical emergentism* (a doctrine interesting in its own right and especially popular earlier in this century; see Kim 1993, ch. 8 for more on emergentism and its connection with the problem of explanatory exclusion). Only here we have an ultra radical form for it is not the mere assembling of physical parts into particular molar combinations that yields the emergent properties, but rather it's the assemblage managing to fulfil a certain abstract *functional* description that produces the miracle (we might call this the doctrine of radical functional emergentism). Neither horn of this dilemma is very attractive.

This problem of explanatory exclusion can also be seen to arise from another of Chalmers's principles: that equating the phenomenal character of conscious experience with 'information states' (see 1996a, ch. 8). Now, every physical state is an information state relative to some possible information receiver, and the causal differences which correspond to differences in the information encoded into any physical state are normally thought to obey the principle of causal grounding (this fact, of course, is what underlies our ability to exploit physical processes to transmit information). So again we have our dilemma: if conscious experience is isomorphic to information load then the causal powers of conscious experience are either (1) entirely dependent upon the physical properties of the information bearer or (2) some information bearers violate the principle of causal grounding. If (1) we have explanatory exclusion and conscious experience is epiphenomenal. If (2) we have another form of radical emergentism, now somehow dependent upon the information carried by the physical state in question. Again, neither horn is attractive. In fact, it appears that Chalmers opts for the first horn (see 1996a, chs. 4 and 5).[16] His theory of 'naturalistic dualism' entails that phenomenal experience has no causal explanatory relevance, even with respect to our judgements about consciousness itself – yes, even our judgements about our own self-consciousness. Despite Chalmers's attempts to ease our worries about this it is deeply implausible.

Box 9.4 • Emergence and Efficacy

An emergent property is one whose appearance cannot be predicted on the basis of underlying, fundamental theory. Emergentism is the view that there are emergent properties (of which consciousness is a prominent and venerable candidate). Unsurprisingly, there are different kinds of emergentism. *Benign* emergence essentially claims that emergent properties are simply new ways to *describe* complex situations. Such new descriptions cannot be predicted from underlying theory – nothing in atmospheric dynamics, for example, predicts the concept 'thunderstorm'. But if one was given a new descriptive concept ('thunderstorm' say) and a simulation of the world based solely on fundamental laws (a simulation of the atmosphere on a hot, dry afternoon in Alberta say), one would see that complexes in the simulation deserved to be described by the new concept (things acting just like thunderstorms would appear spontaneously in the simulation). *Radical* emergence goes further, asserting that the emergent properties make a real difference to the workings of the world. Radical emergentism claims that the simulation based only on fundamental physical law would simply *fail* to simulate the world accurately (if thunderstorms were radically emergent, the atmospheric simulation, no matter how perfect, would go on and on, but never generate anything like a thunderstorm). Chalmers's view seems to be somewhat different from both these positions and, as it were, in between them. On the one hand, consciousness is emergent, and not merely as a high-level description of the underlying phenomena. But on the other hand, consciousness is epiphenomenal.

What is more, I think there is a serious problem with supposing both that consciousness is a fundamental feature of the world, a brute upwelling from the functionally described physical world, and that it is causally impotent. It seems to me that a fundamental feature of the world must do something in the world, an intuition I'll elevate to the *principle of fundamental causation*. This principle asserts that no brute feature of the world is causally impotent. A brute feature is any property which has no explanation in terms of simpler features of the world but which must be simply accepted as part of the way the world is structured. Roughly speaking, a *brute fact* reports a brute feature (for example, if the mass of the electron is a brute feature of the world then the fact that the mass of the electron is 9×10^{-31} kg is a brute fact). It is safe to say that none of the brute facts currently posited in physics are causally impotent. If the mass of the electron is a brute feature of the world it is certainly one that makes a huge causal difference in a great many physical processes. Similarly for the gravitational constant or any other candidate physical brute feature I can think of. If this principle is correct then an epiphenomenal consciousness cannot be a fundamental feature of the world, or, equivalently, a fundamental consciousness cannot be causally impotent. I will conjecture below that a more radical view of the connection between consciousness and information might relieve some of the epiphenomenalist stress here.

It is also worth mentioning a familiar ambiguity in the notion of information, which can mean nothing more than the 'bit capacity' of a physical process or it can mean some *semantically* significant content carried by the transmitted bits. It is not clear which sort of information Chalmers means to assign to the phenomenal qualities of conscious experience, though what he says inclines me to the former interpretation. The bit capacity of the brain is no doubt gigantic, but it is obviously doubled by considering *two* brains as a single system, yet it is doubtful that there is a kind of *third* consciousness associated with the interaction of two human beings, even though these two brains then form a causally interacting system. So we have yet another generation problem: which information states actually yield consciousness, and why/how just those?

Chalmers conjectures that perhaps information is itself a fundamental feature of the world, which makes it a 'natural associate' of consciousness. But consciousness and information connect at the level of semantic significance, not at the level of bit capacity. Insofar as the classical theory of information is situated at the level of bit capacity it would seem unable to provide the proper (or *any*, for that matter) connection to consciousness. Furthermore, the classical theory treats information as a feature, albeit a very abstractly conceived feature, of certain causal processes, which is to say that information is a functional notion: information is embodied in causal processes that can be variously instantiated, and obeys the principle of causal grounding (so leading to the problems of explanatory exclusion discussed above). Since information so conceived obeys the principle of causal grounding it is not itself a fundamental feature of the world, for if it was it would be epiphenomenal in exactly the way consciousness seems to be according to Chalmers and similarly violate my principle of fundamental causation. Of course, on the usual understanding of 'information', it is most certainly not a fundamental feature of the world and thus is not an obvious partner of consciousness conceived as an absolutely fundamental feature of the world.

All of these considerations suggest to me that if we want to pursue the idea that consciousness is a *fundamental* feature of the world, we need a theory which is even more removed from orthodoxy than Chalmers's. We can begin to move towards a more radical view of the fundamental nature of consciousness with a move towards a more radical view of information. This view of information sees causal processes as one species of information transfer but does not expect that all information 'connections' will be restricted to such processes. The natural place to seek a notion of information like this is in quantum mechanics (henceforth simply QM).

It was in 1935 that Albert Einstein, with his collaborators Boris Podolsky and Nathan Rosen, noted that QM demands that systems maintain a variety of 'correlational properties' amongst their parts no matter how far the parts might be separated from each other (see Einstein, Podolsky and Rosen 1935, the source of the famous EPR paradox). In itself there appears to be nothing strange in this; such correlational properties are common in classical physics no less than in ordinary experience. Consider two qualitatively identical billiard balls approaching each other with equal but opposite velocities. The total momentum is zero. After they collide and rebound, measurement of the velocity of one ball will naturally reveal the velocity of the other.

Box 9.5 • Quantum Essentials I

In quantum mechanics, systems are represented by a 'wave function' which describes a kind of undulation over time in a purely abstract space, whose axes can be associated with measurable properties. What undulates is *probability*. For example, if you measure the position of a particle, your *chances* of finding the particle in a certain region are given, roughly, by how 'high' the wave is over the region of the space axis which represents that position. Wave functions can be added together to give new wave functions (superpositions). In the famous two-slit experiment (see text below) the two wave functions corresponding to a particle going through either the one or the other of the slits are added together and, characteristically for waves, this addition generates interference effects. This works even if we set up the experiment so that only a single particle passes through the apparatus for each measurement. If we perform a measurement on a particle, revealing its position as x for example, we force its wave function into one corresponding to a very high probability (ideally, a probability of 1) for finding the particle at position x. In the two-slit experiment, finding out through which slit the particle travelled amounts to such a position measurement and thus must alter the wave function as described. This alteration in the wave function destroys the interference effect.

But EPR coupled this observation with the orthodox Copenhagen interpretation of QM, which states that until a measurement of a particular property is made on a system, that system cannot be said to possess any definite value of that property. It is easy to see that if distant correlations are preserved through measurement processes that 'bring into being' the measured values there is a *prima facie* conflict between the Copenhagen interpretation and the relativistic stricture that no information can be transmitted faster than the speed of light. For if we measure one part of a system, and find that the correlated property of that part is say, +1, then we know that if we were to measure the distant part of the system it would reveal that property to have value −1 (to preserve the correlation). It is rather as if, in our billiard ball example, we knew that the total momentum was zero but that we believed that neither ball had a particular velocity *until* we measured it. Then there is an evident problem of how the other ball 'knows' what value we got for its partner's velocity. If the system's components are separated to a sufficient distance there can be no possibility of any ordinary sort of 'communication' between the parts (i.e. any communication process which operates at light speed or below). The obvious answer, championed by EPR (as well as the classical picture of the world), was that there are some hidden elements of reality that both parts of the system carry with them as they are separated; these hidden elements are initially correlated and maintain that correlation until they are measured, at which point they merely reveal a value that they had possessed all along. This natural solution was spectacularly criticized by the work of John Bell (1964, 1987) who showed that if QM was correct in its predictions then any version of the EPR model of 'carried correlations' must be incorrect.[17] Bell showed that the measurement statistics of all hidden variable theories must obey some form of a relatively simple algebraic relation now called the 'Bell inequality'. In recent years, QM has been vindicated in a series of experiments directly aimed at testing the Bell inequality, some of which explicitly eliminate the (remote) possibility that there is any kind of secret, sub-light speed, signalling between the separated parts (for a discussion of these experiments see Shimony 1989 or Ruhla 1992, ch. 8).

QM demands that the distant parts of systems remain 'aware' of what is happening to the other parts. This is an information link but a most peculiar one: no information, in the sense of bit capacity, can be transmitted over the link. The resolution of this 'paradox' requires us to distinguish causal chains from information links. Ordinary information theory *reduces* information transmission to causal connection, but it seems there is a more fundamental sort of information laden *connection* in the world. It is possible to view information as the basic element at work here, so that causal processes come to be seen as just one, albeit particularly visible and salient, form of information link. The paradox of correlated systems is resolved if we note that if it were possible to transmit information by manipulation of the distant parts of some QM correlational system one could set up a *causal* process from one to the other. This is ruled out by relativity theory. But if other sorts of information links are envisaged, then of course *an* information link can remain in despite of the absence of any causal link.

It is also interesting that since the source and, in some sense, maintenance, of the correlations between the distant parts of some system are dependent on fundamental physical conservation laws, such as the conservation of momentum, the constraints imposed on the world by these laws are not always enforced by causal processes. It has always seemed remarkable to me that laws can constrain the world in 'abstract' ways so that the mechanisms of their observance vary from system to system (each candidate perpetual motion machine can be seen to fail, but the failure in each case depends upon the details of the machine at issue). It is surely significant that the 'mechanisms of law observance' transcend the realm of causal process and seem to enter a more general sphere of pure informational commerce.

But the notion of 'pure information' I want to develop can be better illustrated in a less exotic setting, through a simple discussion of the famous two-slit experiment. A beam of photons, electrons, atoms or whatever is directed towards an appropriately separated pair of slits in an otherwise opaque surface. A detector screen is set up behind the slits. QM predicts, and less ideal but more practical experiments amply verify, that the 'hits' on the screen will form an interference pattern, which results in some way from the interaction of the two possible paths an element of the test beam can take to the screen.

Box 9.6 • Quantum Essentials II

If we ask what is the nature of the 'wave' described by the wave function, a possible answer is that it essentially contains *information*, but not in the form of any energy or other source of physical influence. In the two-slit experiment the particles seem to travel through either one or the other of the slits, but the wave of probability is everywhere and in a way carries information about the configuration of the slits. Exactly how to interpret this is an open question, but the phenomena are not unhappily described in terms of there being information exchange between all the 'components' of the experimental setup. But this information exchange is not via any transfer of energy, so it is entirely unlike familiar information transmission such as TV or radio. Nor is this sort of information connection fully manipulable – there is no way to rig up a QM experiment so as to send a message instantaneously from one component to another.

More particularly, the QM formalism demands that the atoms, say, in the beam be represented as a *superposition* of the states associated with each spatial path, for example:

(1) $\Psi = \sqrt{\tfrac{1}{2}}(\Psi_1 + \Psi_2)$

(where the coefficient, $\sqrt{\tfrac{1}{2}}$, is merely a normalization factor required to insure that the output probabilities upon measurement remain between 0 and 1). Here, Ψ represents the 'total state' of the particle which passes through the apparatus, Ψ_1 represents the particle taking the left slit – call this path 1, and Ψ_2 represents the particle taking the right slit – call this path 2. The probability that the screen will be hit in a certain region, r, is given by a variety of formal mechanisms. In general, probabilities are given by the following *inner product*:

(2) $\langle \Psi | P_r \Psi \rangle$,

where P_r is an operator which projects on to the subspace representing those states in which the atom is found in r (how this works doesn't matter – to us P_r and the computations involved in taking inner products are just 'machines' for producing the number we are interested in).[18] Writing out the inner product in full we get:

(4) $\langle \sqrt{\tfrac{1}{2}}(\Psi_1 + \Psi_2) | P_r \sqrt{\tfrac{1}{2}}(\Psi_1 + \Psi_2) \rangle$.

The expansion of this, using the fact that operators like P_r and the inner product algorithm are both linear, ends up as:

(5) $\frac{1}{2}[\langle\Psi_1|P_r\Psi_1\rangle + \langle\Psi_2|P_r\Psi_2\rangle + \langle\Psi_1|P_r\Psi_2\rangle + \langle\Psi_2|P_r\Psi_1\rangle]$.

The first two terms respectively represent the probability of the particle being in region r if it takes path 1 or if it takes path 2. The final two terms are the unavoidable 'cross terms' which, at least mathematically, account for the interference between the two paths. Schematically, the situation can be pictured as in the following sketch.

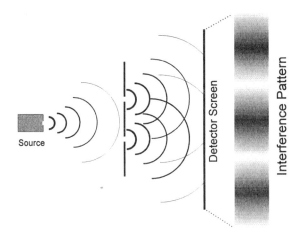

(Fig. 9.1)

Here, the darker regions of the interference pattern correspond to a greater number of detected particles. Right behind the slits we find a very low number of particles, contrary to classical expectations for particles (though perfectly in line with the expectations for wave phenomena).

As everyone knows but which is still amazing, the interference pattern disappears if we have some way of determining through which slit a given atom has passed on its way to the screen. This is sometimes explained in terms of the *causal disturbance* of the atom's state which such a measurement will involve, and sometimes it is said that such a disturbance is unavoidable and is the proper account of this aspect of the two-slit phenomena (and, in general, of the uncertainty relations in QM). But there is no need to posit disturbance in order to explain the loss of the interference pattern; mere *information* about which path the atoms take will suffice. For suppose that there was a *perfect detector* that could determine which path an atom has taken without altering the atom's state. Such a detector would be capable of only two detection states, let's say L, R (for left slit and right slit respectively), and the output of the detector would be perfectly correlated with the components of the atomic state, Ψ_1 and Ψ_2. The atom plus detector state, after detection – which I'll label Ψ_d, would be written as a superposition of *tensor products* (again, the details of the tensor product machine don't matter to us, though I provide some of the manipulation rules – not very complicated ones – as needed below) as follows:

(6) $\Psi_d = \sqrt{\tfrac{1}{2}}[(\Psi_1 \otimes L) + (\Psi_2 \otimes R)]$.

Now if we wish to compute the probability of finding an atom in region r, we require an operator that works on the so-called tensor product space of the particle *plus* detector. Since we are only interested in measuring the position of the particle and have no wish to do anything at all to the detector, this operator is $P_r \otimes I$, where I is the identity operator (i.e. for any Ψ, $I(\Psi) = \Psi$).[19] The basic form of our probability equation is just as above, but taking into account the existence of the detector; the probability of finding the particle in region r is now:

(7) $\langle \Psi_d|(P_r \otimes I)\Psi_d\rangle$.

Written out in full this gets rather messy:

(8) $\langle\sqrt{\tfrac{1}{2}}[(\Psi_1 \otimes L) + (\Psi_2 \otimes R)]|(P_r \otimes I)\sqrt{\tfrac{1}{2}}[(\Psi_1 \otimes L) + (\Psi_2 \otimes R)]\rangle$,

but if we abbreviate $(\Psi_1 \otimes L)$ to X, $(\Psi_2 \otimes R)$ to Y and the operator $(P_r \otimes I)$ to O, the fundamental form will become apparent:

(9) $\langle\sqrt{\tfrac{1}{2}}(X + Y)|O \sqrt{\tfrac{1}{2}}(X + Y)\rangle$

which is analogous to (4) above. However, when (9) is expanded the cross terms take on a distinct form; the first step gives us:

(10) $\tfrac{1}{2}[\langle X|OX\rangle + \langle Y|OY\rangle + \langle X|OY\rangle + \langle Y|OX\rangle]$.

The expansion of just the first and last term (which is a cross term) of (10) should be enough to reveal what will happen to the probabilities in this case.

(11) $\langle X|OX\rangle$ $= \langle(\Psi_1 \otimes L)|(P_r \otimes I)(\Psi_1 \otimes L)\rangle$
  $= \langle(\Psi_1 \otimes L)|(P_r\Psi_1 \otimes L)\rangle$
  $= \langle \Psi_1|P_r\Psi_1\rangle \times \langle L|L\rangle$.[20]

Since all our state vectors are normalised, $\langle L|L\rangle = 1$ and (11) is simply the probability of the particle being in region r if it took the first path. As we would expect, the detector state has no effect on this probability.

Consider now a cross term of (10), say $\langle Y|OX\rangle$:

(12) $\langle Y|OX\rangle$ $= \langle (\Psi_2 \otimes R)|(P_r \otimes I)(\Psi_1 \otimes L)\rangle$
$= \langle (\Psi_2 \otimes R)|(P_r\Psi_1 \otimes L)\rangle$
$= \langle \Psi_2|P_r\Psi_1\rangle \times \langle R|L\rangle.$

Note that this cross term is accompanied by the factor $\langle R|L\rangle$ (the other cross term of (10) will be accompanied by $\langle L|R\rangle$). But in a perfect detector, distinct indicator states are orthogonal, which is to say that these inner products have the value 0 and the interference terms thus disappear. The probability that the particle will be found in region r is now just the sum of the probability of its being in r if it takes the first path and the probability of its being in r if it takes the second path. Fig. 9.2 is a schematic representation of the situation where we have 'which path' detectors at work destroying the interference phenomena.

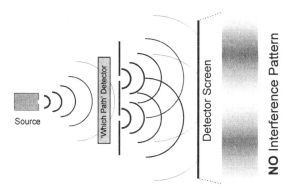

(Fig. 9.2)

This is of some interest to those who need to be reminded that complementarity is not the result of the clumsiness of measurement, but is rather an intrinsic and ineradicable feature of QM. The mere fact that our detectors carry the relevant *information* is sufficient to destroy the interference effects, whether or not the detector in some way 'disturbs' the system under measurement. The kind of information at issue here is not bit capacity but the semantically significant correlation of 'distinct' physical systems, where there is no requirement that the correlation be maintained by some causal process connecting the two systems (which is not to say that there is no *influence* of one part of the system on another but there is no transfer of energy characteristic of causal processes). The properties of the QM system are of course fully explicated by the structure of the wave function describing the whole system, but what we seek to understand is the connection between the purely mathematical, abstract space in which the wave function evolves and the solidly real, 'spread-out' physical space in which the properties of the system are actually discovered by us.

This remarkable feature of QM is made more apparent by my final excursion into the formalism, only slightly more complex. The notion of a perfect detector suggests the possibility of retrieving the original interference patterns simply by *erasing* the information within the detector. Since the atomic states have not been altered by the initial operation of the detectors, this would appear to be at least theoretically feasible. To speak figuratively: the atoms, now far along on their way towards the screen upon which their position will eventually be recorded, have no idea whether their paths have been registered or not. Such an interference retrieval device is called a *quantum eraser* (see Scully and Drühl 1982 and Scully *et al.* 1991; see also Englert *et al.* 1994; for an interesting discussion of the nature and significance of quantum erasers see Davies 1996, ch. 7).

Box 9.7 • Quantum Erasers

The idea that *information* plays a crucial role in the interpretation of QM is strongly supported by a strange device known as a quantum eraser, for what is erased is information. Return again to the two-slit experiment. As we know, if one places a device to detect which slit the particle takes on its way to the detector screen, this device will always register the particle in but one of the slits (never two at once) and if we choose to use the detector then the characteristic interference pattern upon the detector screen disappears (or is not formed). It doesn't matter whether our 'path detector' actually disturbs the particle or not, just acquiring the path information will destroy the interference pattern. This suggests a question: supposing that we have the information about which path has been taken sitting in the memory of our detector, what would happen if we erased the information before anyone looked at it? Yes, the answer is that the interference pattern returns. What matters is the presence or absence of the *information* itself.

The simplest imaginable or *naive* quantum eraser would be modelled by some operator that transformed either of the detector states, R or L, to the same neutral third state, say a ground state, G. Call this hypothetical operator, $\Re$, the *reset* operator. Then we could represent the eraser as $\Re$ acting on the detector states thus: $\Re(L) = \Re(R) = G$. Since $\Re$ acts only on the detector it would be represented in the tensor product space as $(I \otimes \Re)$. We could choose to turn on the eraser or not. If we did, its action on Ψ_d would be this:

$$(13) \quad (I \otimes \Re)\Psi_d = \sqrt{\tfrac{1}{2}}[(\Psi_1 \otimes \Re(L)) + (\Psi_2 \otimes \Re(R))]$$
$$= \sqrt{\tfrac{1}{2}}[(\Psi_1 \otimes G) + (\Psi_2 \otimes G)].$$

Now, upon expansion, the terms $\langle L|R \rangle$ and $\langle R|L \rangle$, which previously eliminated the interference, become $\langle G|G \rangle$, which we may suppose has unit norm and so the interference terms are back!

The quantum eraser just outlined might be called a perfect eraser, and I hope it does illustrate the idea behind the eraser, but unfortunately it is entirely impossible as it is presented here. No such operator as $\mathfrak{R}$ is allowable in QM since it violates the laws governing the time-evolution of quantum mechanical states. The temporal evolution of a quantum system is governed by the system's time-dependent Schrödinger equation, but this evolution can also be given by a set of operators, U_t, such that Ψ_t (i.e. the state at time t) is $U_t \Psi_0$ (where Ψ_0 is the initial state of the system whose time is taken to be zero). These operators are *unitary*, and this entails (among other things) that they preserve orthogonality (in fact, $\langle X|Y \rangle = \langle UX|UY \rangle$). Thus, there is no way that our two orthogonal detector states, R and L, could both be reset to the *same* state, G.[21]

We should have had our doubts about the quantum eraser anyway. If there was a perfect quantum eraser it would be a truly *magical* machine. For consider. We can choose to activate (or not) the eraser at any time before the relevant atom reaches the screen (probably even after it reaches the screen) and, in principle, the screen could be a goodly distance away. But so long as we do activate the eraser the atom will be 'directed' to a region of the screen compatible with interference; if we do not activate the eraser the atom goes to a non-interference part of the screen. Of course, such regions overlap so those limited to observing the screen might only receive statistical evidence about whether the eraser is on or off but after a time it would become clear, and sometimes the atom would hit the screen in a place that would make it very unlikely that the eraser had been turned on. Now suppose that whether or not the eraser is activated will be determined by a randomizing device which renders its decision just prior to eraser activation or non-activation. To make things vivid, if rather impractical, let's say the randomizer is a certain roulette wheel in Monte Carlo ('red' means turn the eraser on, 'non-red' means leave it off).

Let us also suppose that the distance between screen and slits/detector/eraser apparatus and the delay between the atom's passing the slits and activation (or not) of the eraser are considerable enough to ensure that the two events of eraser activation and atom detection on the distant screen are space-like separated. In that case, there is a moving observer for whom the atom will hit the screen *before* the quantum eraser is activated. Such an observer will then know (at least to a degree better than chance) the outcome of the spin of the roulette wheel before the wheel has been spun. More particularly, there are certain regions of the screen such that if an atom is registered in them then it is very likely that the roulette wheel will come up non-red. But I take it as given that no one, especially someone with no particular knowledge about the roulette wheel in question, can have this sort of knowledge.

Worse still, the perfect quantum eraser would permit superluminal signalling. For suppose that instead of randomly engaging the eraser we try to use it as a kind of Morse code transmitter. Again, because of the overlap between interference and non-interference regions, we might have to send the same signal repeatedly to ensure a reasonable likelihood of proper reception, but that is no difficulty of principle. By waiting until the last second, as it were, to activate (or not) the eraser, we can direct a distant atom to various regions of the screen with some level of control. It is this possibility, perhaps, which appals the physicist E. T. Jaynes. He writes about a related quantum device but I adjust the quote here to accord with the eraser example: 'by applying [the eraser] or not . . . we can, at will, force [the atoms] into either (1) a state with . . . no possibility of interference effects . . . (2) a state [in which] interference effects are then not only observable, but predictable. And we can decide which to *do* after the [atoms have passed the slit/detector] so there can be no thought of any physical influence on the [atoms]' (Jaynes 1980, p. 41; this quote appears, and is discussed, in Scully *et al.* 1991). Jaynes goes on to insult QM as having 'more the character of medieval necromancy than of science' (1980, p. 42).[22]

Such remarks would seem to presuppose that a perfect quantum eraser is possible, but as we have seen this is in fact not the case. That is to say, we have discovered that what I called the *perfect eraser* is impossible. However, despite the considerations given above, quantum erasers *are* possible. Their construction is just a little more complicated than appeared at first sight.

Consider again the state of our atoms as they proceed through the quantum eraser apparatus. After passage the state of the system is that given in (6) above. We cannot reset the detector in the way required for the perfect eraser, but it will suffice if we can discover appropriate, possible states that the detector can achieve which will still allow the eraser to function. Such states are possible. What is needed is a mathematical trick, which is the heart of the Scully *et al.* scheme for eraser construction. Define four new states as follows:

$$\Psi_+ \equiv \sqrt{\tfrac{1}{2}}(\Psi_1 + \Psi_2)$$
$$\Psi_- \equiv \sqrt{\tfrac{1}{2}}(\Psi_1 - \Psi_2)$$
$$G_+ \equiv \sqrt{\tfrac{1}{2}}(R + L)$$
$$G_- \equiv \sqrt{\tfrac{1}{2}}(R - L)$$

Since any linear combination of quantum states is a quantum state, these are all perfectly legitimate states of our hypothetical system. They are all observable states (i.e. there are (Hermitian) operators of which they are eigenstates). The states G_+ and G_- are to be thought of as states the detector can enter through the operation of the eraser. Furthermore, the original state, Ψ_d, can be written in terms of our new states, as follows:

(14) $\Psi_d = \sqrt{\tfrac{1}{2}}[(\Psi_+ \otimes G_+) + (\Psi_- \otimes G_-)]$.

This can be verified quite easily, from the properties of the tensor product.[23] So, as it must, this state exhibits no interference since the cross terms contain the vanishing $\langle G_+|G_-\rangle$ and $\langle G_-|G_+\rangle$.

But suppose we ask, what is the probability of the particle being in region r *given* that the detector is in the state G_+? On the assumption that the detector is in G_+ the second term of (14)'s left side must vanish and the probability will be calculated from the state $\Psi_+ \otimes G_+$.[24] This calculation proceeds normally; so the probability of the particle being in region r given that the detector is in state G_+ is:

(15) $\langle \Psi_+ \otimes G_+|(P_r \otimes I)(\Psi_+ \otimes G_+)\rangle$.

This quickly reduces to

(16) $\langle \Psi_+|P_r\Psi_+\rangle \times \langle G_+|G_+\rangle$.

It is easy to see that $\langle G_+|G_+\rangle$ equals 1 so the probability we seek is simply $\langle \Psi_+|P_r\Psi_+\rangle$. The expansion of this inner product is however very interesting. Given the definition of Ψ_+, this probability expression is just (4) above. That is, we have recovered the original two-slit configuration with its interference effects despite the operation of the detector and we have done so via the operation of the eraser!

What happens to the probability on the assumption that after the operation of the eraser the detector goes into state G_-? This probability will be equal to $\langle \Psi_-|P_r\Psi_-\rangle$, which is:

(17) $\langle \sqrt{\tfrac{1}{2}}(\Psi_1 - \Psi_2)|P_r\sqrt{\tfrac{1}{2}}(\Psi_1 - \Psi_2)\rangle$

which expands by the following steps:

$$= \tfrac{1}{2}\langle (\Psi_1 - \Psi_2)|P_r(\Psi_1 - \Psi_2)\rangle$$
$$= \tfrac{1}{2}[\langle \Psi_1|P_r\Psi_1\rangle - \langle \Psi_1|P_r\Psi_2\rangle - \langle \Psi_2|P_r\Psi_1\rangle + \langle \Psi_2|P_r\Psi_2\rangle].$$

Here too we have interference effects, but they are the opposite of those attendant upon (16). The *sum* of these two interference effects produces a pattern at the screen identical to the no-interference pattern produced by the operation of the detector without the eraser.

So have we produced a quantum eraser with the magical properties discussed above? The best answer seems to be 'yes and no'. We have a quantum eraser all right, but it cannot be *used* in any of the ways imagined above. This is because the peculiar effects of the eraser are evident only if we *know* which state the detector is in after the passage of each atom and there is no way to get *this* information to someone in the vicinity of the screen except by ordinary means, which precludes such things as superluminal signalling or 'predicting' the outcomes of roulette wheels. In order to use the eraser to achieve such ends, the eraser would have to send the detector into a determinate state, and this, we have seen, it simply cannot do. On the other hand, from the point of view of the universe, as it were, something quite mysterious is going on. For the atoms are 'responding' to the operation of the eraser and they are doing so instantaneously across (in principle) any distance.

The story is not quite over. It might be objected that the idea of the eraser can't even get off the ground since it presupposes the existence of 'perfect detectors' which are in reality entirely impossible. However, perhaps surprisingly, it is *not* the impossibility of perfect detectors which do not disturb the state of their target atom which destroys the idea of the quantum eraser. As outlined in Scully *et al.* (1991), it is possible to construct a 'micromaser cavity' that will guarantee that an excited atom will de-excite (via emission of a photon of characteristic wavelength) while passing through the cavity. The emission of the photon will have no significant effect on the 'centre-of-mass' wave function of the atom, but the photon left behind in the cavity is a marker indicating that the atom passed through it. Scully *et al.*'s version of the quantum eraser involves two such micromaser cavities which serve as the detectors yielding information about which slit an atom has traversed. By activating a photo-detector placed between the cavities, it is possible to erase this information, via the absorption of the information carrying photon. Significantly however, detailed analysis reveals that such a device can detect the photon only half the time, at random, and it is only if the eraser actually detects the photon that the normal interference effects are to be expected. In fact, the situation is such that when the eraser works one gets the normal interference pattern, when it fails one gets an anti-interference pattern. These two patterns sum to the normal no-interference pattern. Thus only if one already knows the state of the eraser can one detect the interference pattern, as a *distinct* pattern, on the distant screen. Perhaps one could say that such a device permits superluminal signalling in some very attenuated sense, but the receivers would not know what message had been sent until they got detailed records of the action of the eraser. *Then* they could correlate atom hits with eraser records and see which hits were parts of dots and which of dashes, but, of course, in such a case no useable information has been sent faster than light. In fact, it is this record of eraser operation which *is* the message.

The 'microwave cavity eraser' follows the abstract analysis given above (which is no surprise, as that analysis just *is* an abstract presentation of the Scully *et al.* technique). But just why a *particular* quantum eraser will necessarily follow this analysis is a matter of detailed examination of that eraser scheme.

We can see that the eraser will not establish a bit channel between the eraser and the detector screen, so preventing use of the eraser to send instantaneous signals across the universe. But the operation of the eraser irresistibly suggests that each particle is responsive to the state of the eraser. And there can be no question of any causal process between the particle and the eraser operation if we arrange our experiment properly (we could, for example, make the distance between detector screen and the eraser so great and delay the operation of the eraser so long that a light signal could not reach the particle from the eraser before it got to the screen).

The reasonable, if not required, interpretation of both the quantum eraser and the simpler, basic two-slit experiment is that there is a non-causal, but *information laden* connection amongst the elements of a quantum system. And this connection is *not* a bit channel or any sort of causal process. It is a kind of 'influence' with which we were totally unfamiliar before the advent of QM. Here, perhaps, we find a new, non-trivial and highly significant sense in which information is truly a fundamental feature of the world (maybe *the* fundamental feature).[25]

It seems to me possible to use this more robust sense of the fundamental nature of information to mold a theory which takes consciousness to be itself a fundamental feature of the world, where I mean by fundamental something elemental, not dependent upon the satisfaction of any functional description by any physical system, and not subservient to the principle of causal grounding. Chalmers himself makes a friendly gesture towards such a theory in his remarks on information and notes that such a theory is 'not as implausible as it is often thought to be' (1995a, p. 21) and that 'it deserves a close examination' (1996a, p. 293). We might as well be blunt about it: the theory at issue is *panpsychism*, which is the doctrine that 'all matter, or all nature, is itself psychical, or has a psychical aspect' (this from the OED), and it is indeed thought to be implausible and little deserving close examination. I offer a defence of it only with great diffidence. The generation problem seems real to me and sufficiently difficult to warrant fairly untrammelled speculation, especially at such an early stage in the investigation of the natural basis of consciousness. Strange to say, several strands of thought, some in defence of and some attacking panpsychism also come together in a curiously satisfying way once we unite the ideas that consciousness is a foundational feature of the world with our new notion of information and its significance.

I said above that on Chalmers's account, consciousness appears to be a radically emergent phenomenon and hence is fundamental only in the sense that it cannot be explained in terms of the properties of the relevant complex systems that exhibit it. Chalmers is also adamant that consciousness cannot be reduced to these subordinate properties. It was noted some time ago, by Thomas Nagel (1979), that the *denial* of radical emergentism coupled with non-reductionism seems to entail panpsychism. The argument is straightforward: if consciousness is not reducible then we cannot explain its appearance at a certain level of physical complexity merely in terms of that complexity and so, if it does not *emerge* at these levels of complexity, it must have been already present at the lower levels.[26] Thus, if we are to *reject* a radical emergentism and yet respect the generation problem we will be driven naturally towards panpsychism.

Panpsychism has seen better times. Perhaps it was the favoured doctrine of our forebears, echoed in the animism of many pre-scientific cultures. The polymathic philosopher Leibniz endorsed a form of panpsychism, essentially for the reasons given by Nagel. But panpsychism was always at the fringe of scientific and philosophical respectability and tended to decrease in respectability as the scientific understanding of the world expanded. So it is somewhat ironic that the revolution in biology wrought by Darwin occasioned a rekindling of interest in panpsychism. In a paper which still retains interest W. K. Clifford (1874)[27] presented an argument that was evidently in the air: the theory of evolution's application to the mind requires that some element of consciousness be present in all matter. Apparently in recognition of a form of the generation problem, Clifford says of consciousness (in words highly reminiscent of Tyndall's quoted above) that:

> ... we cannot suppose that so enormous a jump from one creature to another should have occurred at any point in the process of evolution as the introduction of a fact entirely different and absolutely separate from the physical fact. It is impossible for anybody to point out the particular place in the line of descent where that event can be supposed to have taken place. The only thing that we can come to, if we accept the doctrine of evolution at all, is that even in the very lowest organism, even in the Amoeba which swims about in our own blood, there is something or other, inconceivably simple to us, which is of the same nature with our own consciousness . . . .
>
> (1874, p. 266)

Is this not Nagel's argument in a nutshell? Emergence is impossible, reduction is absurd – so elements of consciousness must be found in the basic construction materials of the universe (in Clifford's restriction of his argument to organisms we see a vitalistic error, for the generation problem will arise no less for the gap between organism and non-organism than for any gap in the intra-organism hierarchy). The addition of the theory of evolution which gives (though in Clifford's time it was entirely hypothetical) a palpable mechanism by which the simple is differentially compounded into the complex adds impetus to the slide towards a true panpsychism.

On the other hand, one can raise potent objections against panpsychism. Perhaps the single most concentrated and insightful attack on panpsychism is found in William James's *Principles of Psychology* (1890/1950)[28]. James vigorously scourges the view he derisively terms the 'mind-dust' theory and presents what I think is the gravest difficulty facing any panpsychist theory of consciousness. I will label this (1) *the combination problem*, which is the problem of explaining how the myriad elements of 'atomic consciousness' can be combined into a single, new, complex and rich consciousness such as we enjoy. At bottom, isn't this just the generation problem all over again? James is characteristically engaging on this:

> Take a sentence of a dozen words, and take twelve men and tell to each one word. Then stand the men in a row or jam them in a bunch, and let each think of his word as intently as he will; nowhere will there be a consciousness of the whole sentence. We talk of the 'spirit of the age' . . . but we know this to be symbolic speech and never dream that the spirit . . . constitute[s] a consciousness other than, and additional to, that of the several individuals whom the word 'age' . . . denote[s].
>
> (1890/1950, p. 160)

Or again,

> Where the elemental units are supposed to be feelings, the case is in no wise altered. Take a hundred of them, shuffle them and pack them as close together as you can (whatever that might mean); still each remains the same feeling it always was, shut in its own skin, window-less, ignorant of what the other feelings are and mean. There would be a hundred-and-first feeling there, if, when a group or series of such feeling were set up, a consciousness *belonging to the group as such* should emerge. And this 101st feeling would be a totally new fact; the 100 original feelings might, by a curious physical law, be a signal for its *creation*, when they came together; but they would have no substantial identity with it, nor it with them, and one could never deduce the one from the others, or (in any intelligible sense) say that they *evolved* it.
>
> (1890/1950, p. 160, original emphasis)

In sum, James thinks that the *second* fundamental posit of panpsychism – that units of experience can *merge* into higher forms of experience – is 'logically unintelligible' (1890/1950, p. 158), but without it panpsychism offers no escape to those enthralled by the generation problem.

If James is right then the combination problem points to a distinctive generation problem in panpsychism which is formally analogous to the problem of generating consciousness out of matter. Panpsychism will have no advantage over physicalism if essentially the same problem lurks at its heart, and of course, it faces the intrinsic implausibility of asserting that atoms are conscious (in whatever degree you like – it remains undeniably implausible). If James is right then nothing whatever is gained by the *first* postulate of panpsychism, and hence the utility of making it in the first place is entirely undercut.

Another objection flows from this one[29] which might be called (2) *the unconscious mentality problem*. One might be inclined to avoid the implausibility of the first posit by accepting the *mentality* of the elemental units of mind while denying that they are actually *conscious* experiences. But this would of course leave the generation problem unsolved and might even be thought to exacerbate it; for how are we to account for the generation of conscious experience from the combination of non-conscious entities, even if they are in some sense mental entities? In this case, panpsychism faces a problem which is *strictly* analogous to the generation problem facing physicalists.

Box 9.8 • Some Objections to Panpsychism

The Combination Problem. Even if we grant that all elements of reality have some kind
   of mental, conscious aspect to them, how is it that some groups of such elements
   form higher level and unified states of consciousness? Isn't this just the generation
   problem all over again?
The Unconscious Mentality Problem. It would be easier to believe in an all pervasive
   mentality if we didn't have to swallow the extra implausibility of this being
   conscious mentality. But then the generation problem is back with full force. What
   is the secret ingredient that turns certain *combinations* (see the first problem) of
   utterly unconscious mental elements into complex states of consciousness? There
   seems to be no escape from the requirement that panpsychism posit some kind of
   'micro-consciousness'.
The Completeness Problem. The physical world view as presented by and in fundamental physics seems to be causally complete. But a truly irreducible, basic feature of
   the world *ought* to make a causal difference to the world. Thus panpsychism would
   seem to threaten a plausible doctrine of physical causal closure.
The No Sign Problem. There appears to be no direct evidence whatsoever that every
   element of reality has an associated mentalistic and in fact conscious aspect.
The Not-Mental Problem. Even supposing there was some evidence for a fundamental,
   non-physical property that pervaded the world and had some kind of causal
   influence upon events, why would we call it a *mental* property? (In particular, why
   not call it a new kind of *physical* property?)

Yet another serious problem arises upon considering the role of mentality in the workings of the world. One might expect that a fundamental feature as significant as consciousness should take some part in the world's causal commerce. But if it does play such a role, then we should expect it to turn up in our investigation of the physical world; we should expect, that is, to see *physically* indistinguishable systems at least occasionally diverge in their behaviour because of the lurking causal powers of their mental dimension. In that case, our physical picture of the world is radically incomplete and many would find this extremely implausible. I often have to worry about whether my car will start, but I thankfully don't have the additional worry about its failing to start even when there is absolutely nothing mechanically wrong with it but just because it 'feels like' staying in the garage today! Let's call this (3) *the completeness problem*. I will reserve my replies to these objections until later, but one unsatisfying reply to (3) should be discussed here. A panpsychist could urge that physically identical systems will have, in virtue of their physical identity, identical mental features and so physically identical systems will always behave in exactly similar ways even if the mental aspect is providing some of the driving force. This is unsatisfying because it immediately raises the explanatory exclusion problem: what ground for positing any mental influence at all if the physical properties of the system *can* account for all its behaviour (where – bear in mind – we continue to assume that the mental cannot be *identified* with the physical)? The mental then becomes, at the very least, *explanatorily* epiphenomenal and threatens to be an entirely superfluous appendage. So the problem is that either panpsychism asserts that our physical picture of the world is incomplete or that mentality is explanatorily epiphenomenal. The first horn is implausible and the second undercuts much of the point of the panpsychist enterprise.

Finally, there are the two simplest objections. We have (4) *the no sign problem*: there is no evidence whatsoever of a non-physical dimension to the elemental units of nature and, (5) *the not-mental problem*: even if there was some feature of these units which was in some sense non-physical and even if we chose to *label* this feature as 'mental', what possible ground could one provide to justify this label. Surely we would like to see some 'sign' of mentality, as such, in the basic features of the world before we could think there was any real content to the doctrine of panpsychism.

There is a coherent view of panpsychism that can go some way towards answering *all* of these objections. I want to examine them back to front since it seems to me that by and large they were presented in order of decreasing difficulty. As to (5): if one takes consciousness to be a truly fundamental feature of the world then it should not seem odd that it might manifest itself in regions remote from our normal encounters with it and in ways difficult to recognize. There is no apparent sign of any gravitation between sub-atomic particles but since we take gravitation to be fundamental we are willing to accept that the gravitation force between two electrons really does exist.[30] But we must always remember that those philosophers who deny that there is any generation problem for consciousness will be likely to regard the ascription of consciousness to anything that gives no behavioural sign of consciousness as more than implausible but utterly unintelligible. I have tried to argue above, and throughout the book, that the generation problem is a real problem and this means that one can postulate with at least bare intelligibility that consciousness is a fundamental feature of the universe.

And this provides something of a reply to (4) as well. For if the analogy with gravitation is acceptable, then we would expect that the effects of the 'degree' of consciousness associated with the elemental units of physical nature would be entirely undetectable. There is no requirement that fundamental features provide operationally observable effects at every possible scale. This reply may be sufficient, but it also may not be necessary for, significantly, it is not entirely clear that the elemental units present absolutely *no* evidence of their postulated non-physical (and indeed mental) aspect.

To explain what I mean is to address (3). I think it is reasonable to expect that a truly fundamental feature of the world should take a distinctive causal role in the world (I codified this intuition above in the principle of fundamental causation). And so we would expect that a picture of the world that is expressed in purely physical terms, without making any reference to this fundamental feature, would be incomplete. Occasionally, that is, the world should act in ways that are inexplicable from the purely physical viewpoint. No one really knows whether human thoughts and actions are entirely determined by physical features, so no one really knows whether human behaviour is purely physically determined either. But leaving that aside, let us observe the elemental units of physical nature and see if *they* ever act in a way that is inexplicable from a purely physical standpoint. Of course they do – the quantum theory insists upon this. As a physical theory, QM asserts that there is no explanation of certain processes since these involve an entirely random 'choice' amongst alternative possibilities. In a curious way, the world's behaviour does at least leave room for an additional fundamental feature with its own distinctive role.

There are various proofs the QM cannot be extended into a fully deterministic physical theory (see Jammer 1974 or Hughes 1989). As I understand it, these proofs all depend on disputable assumptions. But we might nonetheless take them as a sign of the ineradicable incompleteness of a purely physical picture of the world.

It will be urged, along the lines of (5), that the incompleteness appealed to here has absolutely no relation to consciousness, but this is not entirely clear. If we ask what features of the world our elemental units seem to respond to, one major influence is *information*. In the two-slit experiment, we might say that the particles are *informed about* the results of the perfect detector; in the quantum eraser the particles are *informed whether* information has been erased or not, in the demonstrable absence of any causal connection between them and the detector or eraser. It is the content of the information 'received' that affects the particles' trajectories. Responsiveness to information is hardly foreign to the realm of mentality although here it applies in an admittedly very circumscribed and impoverished sense, but perhaps this is to be expected of a fundamental feature manifesting itself at an elemental level. It may be worth repeating here that the kind of information at issue is not just the bit capacity of classical information theory but something more like semantically significant information, and this *is* a notion of information more akin to mentality. I don't say that such considerations are very plausible (or even very clear), but they seem to be in line with a view that takes consciousness as a truly fundamental feature of the world, and, so far as they go, they seem to be in line with the world as it is observed.

On this view, the elemental units of physical nature possess a mental aspect which plays a distinctive causal role in the behaviour of those units. Thus it grasps the first horn of the dilemma: the physical viewpoint *is* incomplete. But, I urge, at the level of the elemental units, the physical picture of the world does indeed, from a certain point of view, *look* incomplete. And it may be that this incompleteness extends upward through the complex hierarchy of physical composition.

Reflecting upon the composition of more complex physical entities brings us naturally to the most difficult problem facing panpsychism: the combination problem. For while it is manifest that the basic physical elements combine in a multitude of ways to produce molecules, proteins and people, it is far from clear that it even makes sense to speak of the combination of basic mental elements, even granting they are in some sense conscious,[31] into distinct and more complex conscious experiences.

I doubt that the difficulty of the combination problem can be completely overcome, but I think that a fairly natural response to it springs from a little deeper look at the metaphysical presuppositions underlying James's position. According to James, the combination problem stems from a very general consideration:

> no possible number of entities (call them as you like, whether forces, material particles, or mental elements) can sum *themselves* together. Each remains, in the sum, what it always was; and the sum itself exists only *for a bystander* who happens to overlook the units and to apprehend the sum as such; or else it exists in the shape of some other *effect* on an entity external to the sum itself. Let it not be objected that H_2 and O combine of themselves into 'water', and thenceforward exhibit new properties. They do not. The 'water' is just the old atoms in the new position H-O-H; the 'new properties' are just their combined *effects* . . . .
>
> (1890/1950, pp. 158–9)

Or again:

> Just so, in the parallelogram of forces, the 'forces' themselves do not combine into the diagonal resultant; a *body* is needed on which they may impinge, to exhibit their resultant effect. No more do musical sounds combine *per se* into concords or discords. Concord and discord are names for their combined effects on that external medium, the *ear*.
>
> (1890/1950, p. 159)

I won't dispute that such a view has a certain attractiveness; it seems no more than a reasonable generalization of the mereological reductionism for which the world provides so much evidence. But we know it to be false. The most startling revelations of its error spring, as the reader knows or guesses, from QM. Consider again the two-slit experiment. It is the most natural assumption in the world to regard the particles as they pass through the two slits as forming a *mixture* which contains one-half the particles in state Ψ_1 (a state representing, recall, the particle as having passed through the left slit) and one-half the particles in state Ψ_2 (particle having passed through right slit). But they do not. They instead are in the *superposition* of the two possible states, $\Psi_1 + \Psi_2$, and the superposition is a 'combination' of states which itself forms a genuinely new state with properties observably different from the properties of the mixture. A *quantum* whole is not simply the sum of its parts, the effects of the whole are not just the combined effects of the parts.

Yet the ability to enter into superpositions like $\Psi_1 + \Psi_2$ is a reflection of the properties of the elements that enter into it. So the notion of mereological reductionism is not to be expunged from our philosophy altogether, which is surely a good thing for this sort of reductionism lies at the heart of our notion of scientific explanation itself. However, we cannot accept the principle of mereological composition espoused by James, and thus there is no argument from general principles against the panpsychist's combinations of elemental mental units into distinctive mental wholes.

Thus can the philosophical objections against panpsychism be answered. The kind of panpsychism I have envisaged states that the physical world view is incomplete, as evidenced by the fact that physically identical systems can nonetheless act in different ways. The 'hidden variable' is not physical but a form of elementary consciousness (although, as Clifford remarks, the kind of consciousness 'which goes along with the motion of every particle of matter is of such inconceivable simplicity, as compared with our own mental fact, with our consciousness, as the motion of a molecule of matter is of inconceivable simplicity when compared with the motion of the brain' (1874, p. 267)) – this is the 'psychist' part of the picture. The 'pan' part of the picture comes to the assertion that consciousness is an utterly fundamental feature of the world: not one element of physical reality is lacking its associated mental aspect. These mental elements combine according to some principle by which the summing together of parts yields more than just the assemblage of parts in causal interaction, just as do the physical elements.

We might speculate that there is a connection between the summation principles, so that in cases of superposition of states of physical elements we have mental combination as well. If we extend this idea to the case of multi-particle systems immersed in a non-ideal environment, which in truth we must, we arrive at the notion that *quantum coherence* might underlie more complex states of consciousness, for only coherent multi-particle systems will preserve the peculiar quantum mechanical properties that underlie the appropriate 'summation rules'. However, just *how* large systems could maintain coherence in the face of a highly energetic environment is quite unclear. Still, this idea has been espoused by a surprisingly large number of authors (see Michael Lockwood's 1991 discussion of this issue; more recently Roger

Penrose 1994 has adopted a version of it) but they fail to see the rather natural connection between panpsychism and their views. I mean that quantum coherence *cannot* solve the generation problem satisfactorily, but it might solve the combination problem.

In any event, a series of yet more speculative ideas suggest themselves if we entertain this approach, which I would like just to sketch here. The first idea is that only systems that can maintain quantum coherence will permit 'psychic combination' so that complex states of consciousness will be associated only with such systems. Given that the brain supports animal and human consciousness, the brain (or some significant part of it) is such a quantum system (this is *almost* the hypothesis of Penrose in *Shadows of the Mind* 1994; it differs from Penrose in that it denies that there is any new physics behind the phenomena). On the other hand, we may suppose that envisageable computers will not sustain quantum coherence; let's say that they are devices that *de-amplify* quantum effects, and so they will not support complex, unified states of consciousness.[32] Here we have a modern reincarnation of an old idea, which goes back at least to Leibniz, distinguishing unified entities, or what Leibniz called *organisms*, from mere aggregates.

It might be objected that most quantum coherent systems could hardly be thought to sustain any kind of complex conscious mental life, as for example a pot of liquid helium. This seems a cogent objection fostering further speculation: could we not imagine that the nature of the combinatory consciousness is connected to the informational structures of the physical system at issue? The essential simplicity of the structure of liquid helium is informationally grossly impoverished as compared to the complex structures of the brain (even though, we are assuming, both somehow maintain coherence). Thus while our speculative panpsychist ought to (in fact, has to) admit that the liquid helium does indeed have an associated unified state of consciousness, it would remain an extremely primitive state of consciousness, perhaps not so different from the state of consciousness, whatever it may be, associated with the single lowly helium atom.

Looking at this point from another direction, modern computers have an informationally rich internal structure, which is what permits the complex range of behaviours they can exhibit. Yet since they are quantum de-amplifiers, panpsychism (at least of the stripe we are discussing here) denies that they have any conscious mental life. Thus the panpsychist might support Searle's contention (drawn from his famous 'Chinese Room' thought experiment, Searle 1980) that computers have no understanding, and at the same time *explain* it, in terms a little clearer than Searle's brute insistence that the brain simply 'secretes intentionality'.

I must reiterate my diffidence in presenting such speculations. To borrow a phrase from Nagel, they reek all too obviously of the 'faintly sickening odour of something put together in the metaphysical laboratory'. The panpsychism offered here is a purely philosophical theory; as it stands, it has no distinctive empirical consequences. Still,

I find it remarkable that a number of issues involved in the question of consciousness get a surprisingly unified treatment under panpsychism. It does seem to me that the acceptance of the reality of the generation problem and the subsequent perception of its extreme difficulty leads quite naturally, as Chalmers notes, to the idea that consciousness is a *fundamental* feature of the world. I would like to urge that panpsychism is the most natural way to incorporate consciousness as *truly* fundamental. Given the natural antipathy almost everyone feels towards panpsychism, I would actually expect the argument to lead many back towards the difficult task of denying the reality of the generation problem.

But we have seen that the generation problem – like all serious philosophical problems – resists dissolution. The coherence of the idea that matter can somehow yield – at the very least, bear a specifiable relation to – consciousness is not to be gainsaid. Neuroscience will tell us more and more about the conditions under which brains are conscious, but that knowledge is only a step-up to the generation problem. If you don't like the idea that consciousness could be a fundamental feature of the universe but the generation problem seems utterly intractable to you, then mysterianism is your last option (the classic expositions of mysterianism are to be found in Nagel 1974 (only hints of it here though), 1986 and McGinn 1989, 1991).

Mysterianism grows out of a persistent failure to naturalize consciousness and a suspicion that the generation problem is philosophically and scientifically unique. Normally we discover some new or strange phenomenon by stumbling upon its relations to other things, and these relations provide the key to connecting the new phenomenon to what we already know. The strange mysteries of the quantum world of which we are now the masters grew out of intransigent difficulties in the theory of electromagnetic radiation and weird problems in the early attempts to model the newly discovered atom in classical terms. But consciousness doesn't enter the arena of scientific explanation in this way. It is not something we stumbled on during our deepening scientific investigation of the world and must now integrate with our scientific understanding. It is not for consciousness to be integrated with science; the emphasis must be the other way around. Science has to be integrated with consciousness, but it is not clear that there is any way to *naturalize* consciousness.

What is it to naturalize some phenomenon? It is to be able to see the phenomenon as just another part of what we already accept as natural. The rules of naturalism are straightforward and remain at heart reductionist in spirit: they require us to provide an explanation of a phenomenon, X, in terms of Something Else which does not itself appeal to or depend upon X itself for its understanding. We can codify the rules of naturalization as follows:

> X has been *naturalized* iff
>> (1) X has been explained in terms of Something Else.
>> (2) The Something Else does not logically involve X.
>> (3) The Something Else is *properly* natural.

The present case sets X = consciousness, Something Else = features of the brain (or body, or, I suppose, possibly still other elements of the physical world). The brain is certainly properly natural and, of course, our notions of the brain (or the body or behaviour) do not logically involve the notion of consciousness. If they did, there would be no problem, or we could say that it had been dissolved by noting the relevant logical (or analytic, or 'grammatical') linkages.

The kind of explanation which clause (1) demands is one that makes it intelligible exactly how X arises from the workings of the Something Else alone. Thus it is that such domains as chemistry or thermodynamics have been more or less successfully naturalized (though it is worth pointing out again that the traditional case of the reduction of thermodynamics to statistical mechanics can still generate rather more controversy than many might think, see Sklar 1993). Such examples reveal that naturalization is relative: both chemical and thermodynamic properties are, at least when compared to mental properties of consciousness, unproblematically natural. But relative to the more austere view of the world provided by physics they cry out for integration into the physical picture. To naturalize consciousness it will suffice to relate it properly to neurological properties, trusting that this will enable a cascade of naturalization right down to the basic physical components which compose the brain. (Of course this is not necessary for naturalization – it could be after all that consciousness is not a brute feature of the world but is, rather, *explicable* directly in terms of lower level physical elements.)

It is important to distinguish naturalization from outright reduction. The two notions are intimately connected but I think we should mark the distinction by allowing that the requirements for naturalization are much less stringent than for reduction. That is, the kinds of explanations suitable for naturalization are looser or vaguer than those suitable for reduction. For example, Davidson's (1970) *anomalous monism* could be part of a project to naturalize at least intentional mental states. For it explains why such mental states 'must' be physical and gestures towards an explanation of how brain states could, one by one, token by token, fill the causal roles of the intentional states. Completion of such a project would be enough to naturalize this aspect of the mental.[33] Roughly speaking, naturalization only requires that we be able to see how the world as described in natural (especially basic physical) terms could 'act' so as to sustain a characterization in the target non-natural terms.

But this won't work in the case of consciousness. We can already agree that human behaviour is well on the way towards being naturalized in the sense that we have something of an idea how brain systems can generate behaviour. Let's suppose that we come to see how the brain produces the kind of behaviour that generally underwrites the ascription of consciousness. This might tell us *that* brains, perhaps even certain features or parts of brains, are the source of consciousness, it might tell us how to disentangle and even understand the representations in the brain and it might even tell us which of these representations are conscious representations. None of this will tell us why and how these brain features *are* or *generate* conscious experience.

McGinn (1989) has provided particular arguments based on possible limitations of human cognitive capacity that a naturalizing explanation of the how and why of consciousness is impossible, or, at least, unattainable by us. I won't discuss the merits of these arguments here because I think a more general roadblock stands in the way of the naturalizing project. This is the disturbing fact that there is nothing we could know about the brain that can explain how or why consciousness arises from it. That's because we are asking the brain to provide an extra layer of effects for which it could have no *discoverable* resources. Once the brain lays down its representational machinery, categorizes the world so as to coordinate behaviour and perception, produces or realizes states which *are* conscious and does all this because of its neurological structure, it has done all it can. After figuring out all this, raising the question of how it is that some of what is going on in the skull is *also* subvening states of *consciousness* is a knife in the back. Everything we can learn about the brain must be taken up with the former concerns. How could it be otherwise?

Consciousness happens. Without it there is no science, no questions, no projects of naturalization. Only through consciousness is the world revealed to itself. So we *must* ask how this thing arises. How, for instance, does the neural source of behavioural aversion turn into pain? It happened a long time ago, in a comparatively simple brain. But presumably nothing dramatic happened to these brains, as brains. Nor does it matter if there was a dramatic change. For any such change is, again, a change in the brain's ability to lay down representational machinery, a change in its ability to categorize the world, to coordinate behaviour and perception. No change in the brain could do more than simply *signpost* the arrival of consciousness, and that only in retrospect.

Maybe the generation of consciousness is not *hard* to explain but simply unsuitable for a naturalizing explanation. Since every explanation is necessarily advanced from, as well as aimed at, the perspective of a conscious explainer, there is always an element of consciousness standing apart from the explanation – the part that takes up, that *understands* the explanation. Normally this doesn't matter since this background element has nothing to do with the offered explanation. And sometimes the implicit presence of consciousness can be positively employed in the limiting of science's ambitions to what is currently seen as feasible, as in the 17th century separation of primary and secondary qualities: troublesome entities are consigned to the realm of consciousness and the scope of scientific explanation is usefully, if only temporarily, contracted. But in trying to explain consciousness itself, this independent element, the standpoint from which the explanation is offered and in terms of which it is understood, contains the very thing we want to explain. Nor can we remove it since the standpoint of consciousness is an essential part of any offered explanation. Naturalizing consciousness is akin to a camera trying to take a picture of itself; the best it can capture are reflections. But quietism is not an option. It is indecent to have a ragged and unpatchable hole in our picture of the world. Cold comfort to end with the tautology that an unpatchable hole is . . . unpatchable.

Box 9.9 • Summary

This chapter indulged in the speculative idea that the seriousness of the generation problem requires a radical approach. The view that consciousness is a fundamental feature of the world is attractive, but the most coherent, as well as the version most likely to come to grips with the generation problem is the venerable but rather implausible doctrine of panpsychism. Yet there are features of the world, hinted at by certain interpretations of modern quantum physics, that have a strange affinity with consciousness as well as a panpsychist approach to mentality. But still, such speculations are hard to swallow. Wishing to remain within the world as we know it and to remain as much a part of the grand project of scientific naturalization of all phenomena as possible, *mysterianism* is a final option. Perhaps there are reasons why the generation problem is unsolvable. Perhaps, to speak metaphorically, to expect to see consciousness take an ordinary place in the scientific world picture is like expecting to be able to see one's own eyes, directly and without the aid of any imaging equipment.

NOTES

1 THEMES FROM DESCARTES

1 The situation is analogous to one in biology. It is possible to discover much about the world around an organism by studying the organism itself. But the possibility of decoupling organisms from evolutionary history is there, and is now being exploited in, e.g., recombinant DNA research. I imagine that the 'evolutionary history' of the new tomato plants which incorporate certain fish genes (to help them withstand cold weather by producing a kind of antifreeze fluid) or the bacteria which have been modified to produce human insulin would appear deeply mysterious to the unknowing. Sometimes, though, I have an unworthy suspicion that evolutionists could come up with a story of how the ability to produce insulin was crucial to the survival of these strange organisms' ancestors (and it *is* crucial to them now of course if their gerrymandered genetic line is to persist).

2 In fact this is vital to intellectual accomplishment, for, Descartes says, learning depends upon memory and memory is aided by the passion of wonder: 'when something previously unknown to us comes before our intellect or our senses for the first time, this does not make us retain it in our memory unless our idea of it is strengthened in our brain by some passion'. Thus it is that 'people who are not naturally inclined to wonder are usually very ignorant' (1649/1985, p. 354).

3 In this respect Descartes's views turn out to be not so very far from those of his accuser, Damasio. Emotions are necessary for the survival of the body through their influence upon the mind, according to Descartes. Of course, Damasio is right to point out that 'survival' extends, especially for humans, into the social and cultural domains, and even into intellectual ones. Descartes did not see this very clearly, or at least failed to emphasize it.

4 There are niceties of Descartes's views that I'm skating over here. For example, Descartes allows that there is a class of ideas that are what he calls 'materially false'. For example, if *cold* is a mere privation of heat rather than something in itself, then the idea of cold represents *nothing*. Perhaps it has no objective reality. On the other hand, Descartes explicates the notion of material falsity as follows, in a passage from the *Meditations* that is thoroughly representationalist: 'there is another kind of falsity, material falsity, which occurs in ideas, when they represent non-things as things. For example, the ideas which I have of heat and cold contain so little clarity and distinctness that they do not enable me to tell whether cold is merely the absence of heat or vice versa, or whether both of them are real qualities, or neither is. And since there can be no ideas which are not as it were of things, if it is true that cold is nothing but the absence of heat, the idea which represents it to me as something real and positive deserves to be called false . . .' (1641a/1985, p. 29).

5 I note here that Churchland (1985) states that after we begin observing our brain states under the new neurophysiological conceptual scheme they will 'feel' just the same! Coming from Churchland this is an extremely cryptic remark; it will be discussed more in later chapters.

6 Unwise as it might be to give in, the temptation is strengthened by other remarks of Descartes: '. . . these [memory] traces consist simply in the fact that the pores of the brain through which the spirits previously made their way owing to the presence of this object have thereby become more apt than the others to be opened in the same way when the spirits again flow towards them. And so the spirits enter into these pores more easily when they come upon them . . .' (1649/1985, p. 343).

7 Though Descartes is much less clear on this, and seemingly much less committed to any kind of computationalism than, for example, Hobbes who famously stated that: 'by ratiocination, I mean computation' (1656, chapter 1, p. 3, as quoted by Haugeland 1985, p. 23) or Leibniz who, if not reducing thought to computation, seemed to think the reduction could be effected, as when he says '. . . to calculate and to reason will, in the future, be the same . . .' (1679/1989, p. 10). For a nice discussion of the birth of computationalism see chapter 1 of Haugeland (1985).

8 The brain really can do this kind of thing at a Cartesian level too, as recent studies of victims of post-traumatic stress syndrome as well as animal and human research on the function of the amygdala reveals; see Caldwell 1995 or LeDoux 1996, especially chapter 8. For example an American Vietnam veteran, many years after returning home, may upon hearing a car backfire find himself uncontrollably running across the street seeking cover.

9 We might find in Descartes a hybrid theory in which memory experience depends upon *scenes* – reactivated sensory memories – and the ever present *judgements* which are crucial for consciousness of the scene as representing this or that past experience. Such a hybrid theory is very briefly sketched in Hacking 1995, pp. 251 ff., and seems quite congenial to Descartes. The hybrid theory would also make memory experience strictly analogous to conscious perception where we also find *input + judgement* yielding particular consciousness. Perhaps it is worth stressing that for Descartes there could be no consciousness of the bare scene save through the intercession of the function of judgement.

10 My thanks to Lorne Falkenstein for pointing out the significance of Locke's theory of memory here.

11 Descartes says: 'In our early childhood the mind was so closely tied to the body that it had no leisure for any thoughts except those by means of which it had sensory awareness of what was happening to the body. It did not refer these thoughts to anything outside itself, but merely felt pain when something harmful was happening to the body and felt pleasure when something beneficial occurred. And when nothing very beneficial or harmful was happening to the body, the mind had various sensations corresponding to the different areas where, and ways in which, the body was being stimulated, namely what we call the sensations of tastes, smells, sounds, heat, cold, light, colours and so on – sensations which do not represent anything located outside our thought' (1644, p. 218). These last words

are somewhat problematic on the reading of Descartes I am urging here. I take them to mean that while these sensations do in fact represent the body, they do not do so *for* the infant at such an early stage of development.

12 More grist for this mill: why did Descartes allow that talk of images and other cognitive mechanisms was appropriate in the description of the *brain*? One might interpret this as groundwork for a more thorough mechanism which puts *all* cognitive and mental function into the brain.

13 It seems that Descartes considered the chances of this happening to be negligible, but that joint effects that were more or less contrary to each other were common and psychologically significant. Thus what are often mistakenly called 'conflicts of the will' are really to be explained by such contrary effects, only one of which is due to the will: '. . . there is no conflict here except in so far as the little gland in the middle of the brain can be pushed to one side by the soul and to the other side by the animal spirits (which, as I said above, are nothing but bodies), and these two impulses often happen to be opposed, the stronger cancelling the effect of the weaker' (1649/1985, p. 345). This seems to me an interesting anticipation of a modern line on the problem of the weakness of the will, particularly the view of Donald Davidson (1969). For Descartes can say that cases of weakness of will are explained by sub-doxastic states of a subject: the causal forces impinging on the pineal gland which are *not* from the mind itself. At the same time though, Descartes does not have to deny that weakness of will has a cognitive explanation, for the non-mental forces on the pineal gland might nonetheless be the products of a variety of cognitively significant brain states (e.g. images, states which are in some way the product of inference, and the like).

14 Although the more I think about Descartes's views, the less I can understand *how* such pure, disembodied thought would be possible, except in the VR situation of experience as it were of and from a body. Hence my absurd conjecture that Descartes was no dualist.

15 Such is the radical line of Dennett, as we shall see below. I suspect that Dennett's view is that *any* solution to the binding problem that puts forth some particular brain function as the 'binding agent' is a version of Cartesian Materialism, which means that an awful lot of people interested in the brain–consciousness connection are closet Cartesian Materialists (as Dennett hints he believes in a few places). For example, it seems that Dennett ought to consider Paul Churchland a Cartesian Materialist, given Churchland's views on qualitative consciousness, as we shall see in chapter 2.

16 Dennett's views will be discussed below, but it is hard to see how any implementation of his slogan that 'consciousness is cerebral celebrity' (see Dennett 1993), where 'celebrity' appears to be, roughly, the amount of control of the system as a whole which a current representation commands, would not appeal to a multitude of forces (of some kind or other) whose joint actions account for the degree of 'celebrity' of any set of cerebral representations. This is not quite to say that Dennett is, after all, a closet Cartesian Materialist himself but simply indicates the generality of Descartes's proposal which in fact stands as almost a constituent part of the very notion of scientific explanation.

17 The sense I have in mind is brought out very well by this pro-functionalist remark from

Richard Boyd: 'there are certain configurations such that whenever they are realized by a physical system, whatever substances compose it, the qualitative feeling of pain is manifested' (1980, p. 96).

18 This problem goes by various names. Joseph Levine calls it the problem of the 'explanatory gap' (see Levine 1983, 1993). David Chalmers labels it the 'hard problem' of consciousness (see Chalmers 1993, 1995a, 1995b, 1996a). See also Nagel (1974, 1986); McGinn (1989, 1991). There are differences between these. For example, Levine leans towards the view that the explanatory gap is essentially an epistemic problem whereas Chalmers draws strong metaphysical conclusions from the Hard Problem (see below for discussion of the distinction between the epistemic and metaphysical aspects of the generation problem). Furthermore, Block and Stalnaker (1997) argue that both Chalmers and Levine assume that, in general, explanatory gaps are filled by 'conceptual analysis', an assumption that they go on vigorously to criticize. But my notion of the generation problem rests on no such assumption about the nature of explanation, as will become clear.

19 I mean my hyperbolic assumption to include the possibility that some systems are put in a grey area between conscious and non-conscious but that this inclusion is not based on ignorance but a *knowledge* that, in some relevant and sufficiently well defined sense, consciousness comes in degrees.

20 Aldous Huxley's grandfather, Thomas, is philosophically famous for his espousal of epiphenomenalism. I believe that he considered epiphenomenalism the only intellectually honest position he could endorse, largely because of the force he saw in the generation problem, which he put thus: 'how it is that anything so remarkable as a state of consciousness comes about as a result of irritating nervous tissue, is just as unaccountable as the appearance of Djin when Aladdin rubbed his lamp' (1866, 8, p. 210). Other early expressions of the generation problem are given at the beginning of chapter 9 below.

21 The nature of brute facts is actually complex and interesting. For instance, the set of 'brute facts' changes with the advance of science. The velocity of light appeared to be a brute fact until Maxwell deduced it from independently measurable magnetic and electric parameters; since 1983 the velocity of light has been a matter of *definition*. But there seems to be little prospect of science altogether eliminating brute facts.

22 One radical option is to make consciousness itself a fundamental feature of the world, for then there could be no requirement to provide an explanation of consciousness in physical terms. A philosopher who embraces this position is David Chalmers (see, especially, his 1995a, 1996a). There are options within this option. Chalmers's idea is that consciousness is ontologically fundamental but only manifests itself as the result of certain functional configurations coming into being. This view has difficulties of its own. Another, perhaps yet more radical, version is *panpsychism*: the view that consciousness is fundamental and, in some sense, is everywhere and always present. See chapter 9 below for discussion of these options.

23 It is not *absolutely* clear that even Leibniz's example suffers from this defect. It depends upon how you read the counterfactual. If we imagine the world being different around the

robot then we might suppose that the creators of the robot would have taken this change into account and re-programmed the robot.

24 For one limiting case: imagine a 'mirror-world' made of antimatter (perhaps a better version of Twin-Earth than Putnam's original, in Putnam 1975). This world would be internally detectably different from ours in subtle ways but, I believe, complex organisms just like us, except for their being formed from antimatter, could exist in it (for some early but I think not yet entirely discounted speculations about the possibility of antimatter zones within our own universe see Alfvén 1966; recently, clouds of antimatter have been discovered in our own galaxy). If we suppose that such creatures would be conscious, and it is rather difficult to suppose otherwise, then we know that consciousness does not depend upon whether one, or one's brain, is made from matter or antimatter. This is somewhat interesting for a really strict reading of 'brain state X' would seem to entail that X was the kind of brain-state that *we* get into and these states one and all involve matter, not antimatter. So, could we replace the particles which make up our brains with just any old things which could, in the end, duplicate the causal role of these particles (as in the various thought experiments of Block 1978, Searle 1992, chapter 3, Chalmers 1995a, 1995b, 1996a, ch. 7)?

25 By the way, I don't think that this analogy is correct. For my worries see Seager 1991a, chapter 6, or 1991b.

26 Do Zeno's paradoxes provide an example of a dissolved philosophical problem? I don't think so, but they do illustrate a common fate for philosophical problems, which is to be solved by scientific (or, in this case, mathematical) appropriation. Is it possible that the birth of cognitive science is the harbinger of a new round of problem appropriation and that the philosophy of mind will disappear into this new science just as 'natural philosophy' disappeared into the physical sciences as they matured? We shall just have to wait and see.

27 For an optimistic acceptance of this sort of 'scientistic' view see the Churchlands (e.g. Paul Churchland 1981 or Patricia Churchland 1986), though they have also in the past offered identity theories of at least certain aspects of consciousness and seem to be moving more towards that view, becoming less eliminativist (see Churchland and Churchland 1982, Paul Churchland 1986, 1995 – for discussion of which see chapter 2). Champions of the first, more radical sort of dissolution strategy will likely see the intrusion of science as a worsening of the situation. The hope for a *scientific* solution to the problem will strike them as dependent upon the very conceptual confusions that generated the pseudo-problem in the first place. More on this below.

28 Another toy problem: consider theories of perception which posit a device which must do some *perceiving* in order for the system in which it is embedded to perceive the world. This is not an incoherent view of perception, I guess, but it is not one that is very explanatorily satisfactory. By the way, this 'problem of the homunculus' (i.e. the 'little man' within us whose seeing will 'explain' our seeing) was clearly stated by Descartes. With regard to the images which are passed from the retina into the deeper recesses of the brain, he said: 'we must not think that it is by means of this resemblance [of the image to

the object of perception] that the picture causes our sensory perception of these objects – as if there were yet other eyes within our brain with which we could perceive it' (1637b/ 1985, p. 167). The essentials of Descartes's superpositional theory of the generation of consciousness – whatever its other faults – does not seem to me to reintroduce the homunculus but is, rather, an attempt to explain the conditions under which a selection of the range of information loose in the brain is made, and prepared, for presentation in consciousness (but see Hacker 1993, p. 70, for the opposite view).

29 We could coin the term 'grammatical behaviourism' for Wittgenstein's view, but insofar as a truth of philosophical grammar is an analytic truth, grammatical behaviourism would not seem to differ significantly from logical behaviourism.

30 Unfortunately, theoretical linguistics seems to feel no qualms about the brain's possessing 'internal representations' which it uses by following hidden 'rules'. Of course, as Hacker points out, Wittgenstein would have seen through Chomsky: 'Chomsky's argument in favour of an innate knowledge of universal grammar . . . would . . . have struck him as yet another house of cards' (Hacker, 1993, p. 114 n.) . For a detailed Wittgensteinian attack on Chomsky see Hunter 1973 and for a trenchant reply Chomsky, 1980, pp. 73 ff.

31 Although of course not a Wittgensteinian option, the identity theory's attractions beckon here for surely there is no special problem about how brain stimulations cause (other) brain states which, by the identity theory, are all there is to states of consciousness. But as I argued above, although its attractions are manifest, the core of the generation problem remains even if we yield to them. See the next chapter for a more detailed look at identity approaches.

32 There are differences between Loar and Lycan of course. Lycan emphasizes an analogy between knowledge of one's own states of consciousness and indexical knowledge in general, but the account of the appearance of the generation problem is nonetheless similar to Loar's. Lycan says: 'my mental reference to a first-order psychological state of my own is a tokening of a semantically primitive Mentalese lexeme. My mental word is function- ally nothing like any of the complex expressions of English that in fact refer to the same (neural) state of affairs . . .' (1996, p. 64). Lycan's approach is very similar to that of Georges Rey (1991, 1993).

33 However, I believe that actual *physics* rules out the existence of any phenomenological doppelgänger of water (at a minimum, surely any candidate would be heavier than water and thus have to be less dense in which case it would be easily detectable as different from water). Thus, strictly speaking, Putnam's infamous XYZ is physically impossible.

2 IDENTITY THEORIES AND THE GENERATION PROBLEM

1 In what follows I will give a severely compressed outline of the theory of neural networks; for more see the works referred to above, or Rumelhart and McClelland 1986. A more biologically oriented discussion can be found in Churchland and Sejnowski 1992. For

philosophical perspectives on this work see Bechtel and Abrahamsen 1991 or Clark 1989, 1993.

2 The rules for the transformation are to take the inner product of the input vector and each column of the matrix to form the two components of the output vector. The inner product of $\langle x,y \rangle$ and [m,n] – using [m,n] to represent a column of the matrix – is defined as (x × m) + (y × n).

3 The exclusive-or network and its logical relatives are useful for tasks beyond the domain of logic. Negated exclusive-or networks can be used to match inputs across a model retina in order to discover displaced input patterns, a task fundamental to stereo vision (see for example Paul Churchland's very clever if not, perhaps, biologically plausible Fusion-Net as described in Churchland 1995).

4 The simple term 'feedback' is perhaps misleading here if it implies that the 'back connections' must wait for an input before feeding back signals into the network. In the brain, the back connections have an independent ability to actively transform the network even as it feeds signals forward. This is one reason why Edelman (1987, 1992) is so adamant in distinguishing what he calls 're-entrant' connections from mere feedback relationships.

5 It is interesting to note that Armstrong is following Locke, almost word for word, in his definition of consciousness. Locke wrote '[c]onsciousness is the perception of what passes in a man's own mind' (1690/1975, Bk 2, chapter 1, p. 115).

6 It is strange, then, that Flanagan displays such a deep antipathy to McGinn's version of mysterianism. McGinn asserts that though there is an explanation of how the physical processes in the brain generate consciousness, it lies beyond the limits of our cognitive abilities (see 1989; reprinted in McGinn 1991 but with additional relevant material in chapters 2, 3 and 4). Flanagan seems to be asserting rather that there is no such explanation at all, and surely such appeal to brute fact is simply another form of mysterianism.

3 HOT THEORY: THE MENTALISTIC REDUCTION OF CONSCIOUSNESS

1 Impressions are introduced by Hume thus: 'those perceptions which enter with most force and violence, we may name impressions; and, under this name, I comprehend all our sensations, passions, and emotions, as they make their first appearance in the soul' (1739/1973, Bk 1, Pt 1, § 1, p. 1). Of course, Hume agreed with Descartes about the perfect transparency of the mind, even as he divided Descartes's class of ideas into impressions and (Humean) ideas: '. . . since all actions and sensations of the mind are known to us by consciousness, they must necessarily appear in every particular what they are, and be what they appear' (1739/1973, Bk 1, Pt 4, § 2, p. 190).

2 Dennett's account of consciousness is closely related to that of the HOT theories, but differs from it sufficiently to require a detailed independent treatment, for which see below, chapters 4 and 5.

3 Although the distinction is decidedly reminiscent of Hume's division between impressions and ideas, there is, of course, no commitment on Rosenthal's part to any sort of 'copy theory' of the nature of the intentional states or, for that matter, any particular relation between the phenomenal and intentional states.

4 We can follow Dretske in a very liberal understanding of 'object' as including things, events, processes, conditions, states of affairs, etc. Unlike these sorts of objects, facts, as Dretske sees them, are referred to by that-clauses, have truth values and are often said to be 'made' true or false by certain objects and, in turn, to 'make' sentences true or false. Facts are conceptual, objects are not. To be conscious *that* such-and-such requires that one possess concepts requisite for specifying such-and-such whereas to be conscious *of*, to take Dretske's example, an armadillo does not require that one possess the concept of an armadillo.

5 As we shall see below, there is a dangerous ambiguity in this expression. It allows for at least two *sorts* of fact consciousness of pain. The first is the normal case of conscious pain providing the underpinning of the fact awareness; the second is the anomalous case of somehow merely knowing that one is in pain. It is perhaps a strength of HOT theory that it brings out this distinction, but the possibility of 'mere knowledge' of unexperienced phenomenal states is highly problematic and will lead to severe difficulties for the theory. Such difficulties will be examined below – they are not problems which Dretske addresses.

6 For Rosenthal's response to this line of objection, see 1986, pp. 350 ff. The objection that animals lack the appropriate conceptual resources to be conscious can also be deployed with seemingly still more damaging force in the case of children. It is an empirical question whether animals and sufficiently young children have the appropriate concepts (or any at all), but it is an unhappy conclusion that they may be unconscious beings. Since I think there are more basic problems with the theory I won't try to develop this objection here, though Dretske takes it to be 'decisive'; see 1995, chapter 4, §2.

7 Actually, this statement is somewhat oversimplified. As discussed above, if α is a mental state with an intentional object then α's being a conscious state of S is to be identified with S's being conscious of that intentional object. So a more accurate version of Dretske's question would be: can there be conscious states in a person who is not thing aware of them or their intentional objects. The argument to follow is not affected by this nicety.

8 The compatibility here is just like that between saying, of the lottery, both that there is necessarily someone who holds the winning ticket and that nevertheless everyone is a possible loser.

9 By contrast, the theory of consciousness espoused in Dennett's (1991b and 1993), though bearing traces of Dennett's earlier views, is of a radically different sort. It is also worth mentioning that in *Consciousness Explained* Dennett draws on but ultimately rejects Rosenthal's theory on the grounds that the theory is too closely wedded to the traditional, and in Dennett's opinion inadequate, categories of folk psychology (see Dennett 1991b, pp. 307 ff.). Dennett's views will be discussed in the following two chapters.

10 I use the scare quotes since HOT theory certainly does not require that intentional mental states require some sort of phenomenal characteristic in order for them to become

conscious. The consciousness of intentional states is rather different than the consciousness of sensations, but of course it does not follow that we cannot *be* conscious of our intentional states. An apparent advantage of HOT theory is that it gives a unified account of consciousness for both intentional and phenomenal mental states without resorting (as, notoriously, did Hume) to the ascription of phenomenal properties to intentional states.

11 Within the context of this debate, the existence of phenomenal properties of mental states is taken for granted. This being given, the argument above cannot be taken as merely demanding an eliminativist reply.

12 The proper response to this sort of problem is not, I think, to adopt an eliminativist stance about the phenomenal but rather to rethink the nature of the phenomenal. The central 'revision' in the idea of the phenomenal is to regard it as the *content* of experience, conceived of as thoroughly representational. This option is extensively considered below, in chapters 6, 7 and 8. The eliminativist option – at least Dennett's version of it – will be considered immediately below in chapters 4 and 5.

13 I am appealing here to a model of the grounds of consciousness that is advanced and explored in great detail in Dennett 1991b. This part of Dennett's model has an independent plausibility that, I think, makes my appeal to it far more than an appeal to a mere abstract possibility.

14 The term 'experience' might seem to carry the force of 'being conscious', but I mean to use the term neutrally, to mean whatever Rosenthal means by an unconscious mental state that possesses phenomenal properties, such as pains with their painfulness, or 'sights' with their visual phenomenal properties. There are certainly contentious issues involved in such a conception of phenomenal properties, as I have tried to argue above. I will not rehearse these here, but will rather provisionally accept this conception to advance my current objection.

4 DENNETT I: EVERYTHING YOU THOUGHT YOU KNEW ABOUT EXPERIENCE IS *WRONG*

1 The specific difficulties which consciousness creates for a variety of theories of intentionality will be addressed below, in chapters 6, 7 and, especially, 8.

2 In chapter 9 below I provide a concise description of these quantum phenomena, and even try to relate them to the problem of consciousness.

3 There is no doubt that experiences can be evoked by direct neural stimulation, as the classic work of Wilder Penfield demonstrated (see Penfield 1958 or for a more recent report on Penfield style procedures see Calvin and Ojemann 1994). There is doubt whether such stimulation activates memories or can produce genuinely new experiences.

4 The Churchlands' acceptance of the kind of ineffability at issue here is revealed in their attempt to argue that the infamous Mary (well known as the poor neurophysiologist –

introduced in Jackson 1982 – who has complete neurological knowledge but has never seen any colours for herself) must, and can, imagine what it is like to see red on the basis of her neural knowledge. There are many problematic features to such a response to Jackson (see my discussion in Seager 1991a, chapter 5) but the important point here is that if Mary must imagine *seeing red* to know what it is like to see red then the experience is ineffable in the sense defined above.

5 Page references for Dennett 1988 are to the reprint in Lycan 1990.

6 This notion of intrinsicness is a version of Lewis's (1983b) 'second way': taking the notion as primitive. The assumption of physical determination allows us to limit the range of the pure postulation of intrinsicness to a relatively small set of physical properties which, I think, have a pretty clear claim to the title of being intrinsic. Once that is granted everything else follows along nicely. For example, the two properties that Lewis uses to refute Kim's (1982) attempted definition of 'intrinsic property' are easily seen to be extrinsic by our criterion. These are the properties of 'being accompanied' (i.e. being in a world with other contingent things) and 'being lonely' (i.e. being alone in a world). Obviously, by either adding things to a world or removing them one can alter these properties of something without having to make a physical alteration in it (though of course a physical alteration in the subject will *later* follow upon such a change in its world via the operation of natural law).

7 Pure representationalists, like Dretske 1995 or Tye 1995, will try to move the qualia information completely out into the world but, as we shall see in chapters 6 and 7, this attempt cannot be entirely successful.

8 Physical determination posits a nomic link between qualia and brain states but does not demand identification of qualia with physical states of the brain. But information is carried by nomic links so brain states will carry information about qualitative aspects of consciousness under the assumption of physical determination. The doctrine of phenomenal information claims that there are possible worlds completely alike physically that differ in the phenomenal properties exemplified in them. Such worlds break the nomic link between physical state and qualia, but the defender of phenomenal information need not deny that *in fact* there is a nomic link between physical state and phenomenal state.

9 For a fascinating account of awareness in the face of temporary but almost complete loss of linguistic knowledge and ability, see Lecours and Joanette 1980.

10 Steven Rose (1993, p. 17) gives away the secret which destroys the relevance of Armstrong's example; Rose claims that one day old female chicks have a double row of wing feathers, males but a single row. The point of the example remains.

11 A good verificationist might wonder how we could have independent grounds for assigning any neural process a role in the generation of consciousness. Pondering the pair of unverifiable hypotheses that underlie this verificationist 'insight' is put off until the next chapter.

12 Such peripheral qualia inversion may actually occur in a small subset of the population. Nida-Rümelin 1996 reports that a rare genetic condition of 'double' colour blindness

could result in the mutual replacement of the 'green' and 'red' cones in the retina in a tiny fraction of the male population. Such males *might* suffer a sort of colour inversion heretofore only seen in philosophical science fiction.

13 It would be rather like denying the existence of Napoleon on the grounds that there are certain aspects of him that are unverifiable, e.g. exactly how many hairs did he have on his head at 9 a.m. (local time) on the day of the battle of Waterloo. We might say that the problem with Dennett's verificationist approach to qualia examined here is that it is too weak or circumscribed to succeed; whereas, as we shall see in the next chapter, the full application of verificationism to consciousness is too *strong* to succeed. This is somewhat reminiscent of Wittgenstein's remark that 'it would strike me as ridiculous to want to doubt the existence of Napoleon; but if someone doubted the existence of the Earth 150 years ago, perhaps I should be more willing to listen, for now he is doubting our whole system of evidence' (1969, § 185).

14 It is not immediately relevant here, but externalism has a perplexing and fascinating relationship to consciousness which will be examined in chapters 7 and 8 below.

15 Even on Dennett's own views this is implausible. Since the nearest thing to qualia are the bases of discriminative reactions (including verbal behaviour) and since any two physical duplicates will exactly duplicate these reactions in the face of any discrimination task, physical duplicates ought to be assigned identical qualia, or 'ersatz-qualia'. That is, qualia or 'ersatz-qualia' are intrinsic.

16 As noted, qualia will fail to be intrinsic if we can apply externalism to a representationalist account of qualitative consciousness. Although such a possibility is irrelevant to the arguments of Dennett's now under discussion, it is highly relevant to Dennett's overarching strategy of replacing qualitative experience with some class of content carrying states amenable to his analysis of intentionality. This strategy will be discussed in the next chapter, and the general problem of intentionality and consciousness in chapters 6, 7 and 8 below.

5 DENNETT II: CONSCIOUSNESS FICTIONALIZED

1 Most important of the other sources for our intentionalizing proclivities – and this in fact utterly eclipses the desire for predictive/explanatory success – is the simple fact that we cannot see our fellows as *persons* except by the attribution of intentional states. Needless to say, it is rather a deep part of our being to see ourselves as living amongst other *people*. It is a gross scientist distortion to imagine that predictive and explanatory purposes are the foundation of our viewing other people as people.

2 No doubt many would feel threatened if the new theory was good enough and practical enough to replace our intentional idioms. That wouldn't show that the intentional stance fails to pick out real patterns, just that another set of patterns and pattern-catching talk had taken our fancy (I think Dennett draws this lesson near the end of 'Real Patterns'

1991a). It is interesting that on this view the kind of scientific threat to folk psychology sometimes invoked by eliminativists is entirely without force. Even the overthrow of folk psychology would not impugn the reality of intentional states, since intentional state ascription would still work if anyone bothered to use it. This can seem to be a very disturbing conclusion, as it appears to imply that *phlogiston* still has some claim to reality, seeing as phlogiston talk captured and presumably still would capture some real patterns in the world. One reply is that phlogiston talk was not a very 'good' way to capture the real patterns evinced in oxidation and combustion (see Dennett 1991a, pp. 28–29). This is Pandora's Box. But with respect to folk psychology, I think the correct reply is to distinguish those ways of talking that *aim* to be modelled in the world from those that do not. Phlogiston was part of a scientific hypothesis about the fundamental forces and entities of the world. Folk psychology is not. We will see below that this misunderstanding about the nature of our intentional idioms is one of the forces which leads people toward what Dennett calls 'Cartesian materialism'.

3 And, of course, even our fundamental conception of the brain as made up of a myriad of distinct (though richly interconnected), utterly microscopic nerve cells is the product of a lengthy and intense scientific controversy, one which is not entirely settled yet (see Shepard 1991 for a history of the 'neuron doctrine').

4 We don't have to appeal to quantum indeterminacy here though for all we know it may well have a role to play in the brain. The kind of extreme sensitivity to initial conditions we are familiar with from studies of chaotic systems would do.

5 However, no less a philosopher than Hume asserts that imagination and belief *are* distinguished by a feeling. Hume says 'the difference between fiction and belief lies in some sentiment or feeling, which is annexed to the latter, not to the former, and which depends not on the will, nor can be commanded at pleasure. It must be excited by nature . . . ' (1748/1962, §5, Pt 2, p. 48). Hume is driven to this position by a variety of dubious propositions about the mind and its powers. On the other hand, Hume is quite clear that beliefs are individuated by their contents, that is, by differences of ideas.

6 As remarked above, I myself have grave doubts about the legitimacy of the particular analogy Johnson employs, the liquidity of water. For whereas we have at least a good idea of how the interactions of the water molecules yield a liquid, we have nothing remotely comparable to offer as a tale relating neural activity to conscious experience (as opposed to *behaviour* generation, for which we may be allowed to have some dim glimmerings). For expansion of these doubts see, again, Seager 1991a, chapter 6, or 1991b.

7 For the original work on the colour phi phenomenon see Kolers and von Grünau 1976. I've tried it on myself and could not observe the effect, perhaps because I was too suspicious a subject or perhaps because the various temporal and chromatic parameters were not adjusted properly (I just tried it on a PC).

8 This is a perfectly good reason to decide between apparently or, we might say, *locally* unverifiable options. Consider the proposition that there are entire universes, spatially and temporally similar to The Universe but absolutely causally isolated from it. Obviously there is no way to contact such universes to verify their existence. But if their existence

is a consequence of a theory which is acceptable for other reasons (as in, it may end up, inflationary cosmological theories – see Guth and Steinhardt 1989), then we may have good grounds for allowing their existence.

9 I'm kind of sidestepping a fascinating issue here: does the speed of those processes which 'implement' consciousness make any difference to whether or not consciousness will actually be generated? Dennett has flirted with the idea that a 'slow consciousness' is not a notion entirely innocent of conceptual difficulties (see 1987, ch. 9). But it seems to me that, on the face of it, consciousness generating operations can run at a very slow rate and still produce consciousness. This appears actually to *follow* from the special theory of relativity, which demands that all processes will slow down if they are in motion. Someone speeding by us in a rocket ship travelling at 99.99% the speed of light will appear to us to be thinking quite slowly. An astronaut falling into a black hole will take a thousand of our years to have a single conscious thought (though everything will appear normal to the unfortunate astronaut). Given this, I don't see any reason to deny that in general very 'slow' processes could implement an equally slow consciousness.

10 Dennett's position is reminiscent of, and a development of the extreme logical behaviourist position of Norman Malcolm 1959. Recent work on what is called 'lucid dreaming' would seem to present strong evidence that dreams are indeed experiences (see LaBerge 1985; see also Baars 1997, pp. 109–111).

6 REPRESENTATIONAL THEORIES OF CONSCIOUSNESS, PART I

1 Even more recently William Lycan 1996 has also defended a representational theory. Some interesting anticipations of the core notions of the representational view can be found in Harman 1989, 1990.

2 A somewhat more detailed defence will be provided below in chapter 8; see also Tye 1995, especially chapter 4 and Dretske 1995, especially chapter 3 and for a characteristically vigorous treatment of a set of specific anti-representationalist arguments see Lycan 1996, chapters 6 and 7.

3 Although I suspect that Dennett would resist the bald claim that he is an eliminativist about qualitative conscious experience, he spends so much time and effort undermining the very notion of qualitative experience and his own judgement based approach is so radical (see chapters 4 and 5 above) that I think the label is fair enough.

4 Thus I take it that my criticisms of Dennett in chapter 4 above are compatible with a representational theory of consciousness.

5 It is perhaps possible to read the traditional empiricists as advancing just such a view. According to them, maybe, the concept of a horse just *is* some peculiar assemblage of phenomenal features. But the empiricist theory of concepts has not stood up too well, succumbing to numerous objections. And, in fact, the purely phenomenal reading of the empiricists is probably a misreading, unless we also suppose that their notions of

reflection, expectancy, etc. are all to be reduced to the phenomenal as well. Perhaps Hume's infamous 'discovery' that there is a special 'feeling' associated with believing as opposed to merely entertaining a proposition can be construed as evidence in favour of such a reductive hypothesis. Against this, it seems pretty clear that Hume's rules of association allow for 'second order' associations between ideas stemming from the associations of what these ideas *stand for* as well as simply associations between the corresponding impressions (as Hume says: '. . . there is no relation, which produces a stronger connexion in the fancy, and makes one idea more readily recall another, than the relation of cause and effect betwixt their objects', 1739/1973, Bk 1, Pt 1, §4).

6 Incidentally, while Block's official definition of phenomenal consciousness includes the notion of awareness of B-qualia, the role of phenomenal consciousness versus what Block calls access consciousness can easily be duplicated within the representational theory (see Block 1995). Access consciousness involves inferential readiness and behaviour control (including speech control in linguistic animals). The representational theory has no problem in positing the existence of representation tokens that are not access-conscious, or are more or less access-conscious. Of course, if Block really intends that phenomenal consciousness be restricted to consciousness of B-qualia, then the representational theory denies its existence.

7 For example, what is the status of the principles which connect the adverbial properties of experience with the perceptible properties of objects? Some such principle would have to be added to the sub-argument by the adverbialist. Perhaps it would read so: sometimes when I experience *red-object-in-front-of-mely* there is a red object in front of me. If so, we require an infinitude of principles connecting these predicates to their correlates in the perceived world. And, the second premise of the sub-argument is now true only in a Pickwickian sense; in fact, objects are never really red in the sense that they have the property of which I become aware in experience, for I am only ever aware of properties *of* experiences (this is the other, unfortunate, side of the coin which is the very point of the adverbial theory).

8 This traditional requirement raises a question for the self-interpretation view. In order to ascribe intentional states to myself I must, according to the view, first observe my own behaviour or 'overhear' my own 'silent colloquies' (as Ryle put it). But surely to go from this data to a mentalistic ascription I must *know* what action I performed, or actually, but worse for the theory, what action I *intended* to perform, and *know* what words I uttered to myself (silently). Isn't this introspective knowledge of a kind unaccounted for by the self-interpretation theory?

9 Although Tye 1995 does not deal with introspection at the same length as Dretske, he makes frequent remarks that show an affinity for this view of introspection. For example: '. . . when we introspect such states and form a conception of what it is like for us, we bring to bear phenomenal concepts' (1995, p. 191).

10 It is also possible, of course, that the development of our 'theory of mind' required a dual use of the new concepts, both as other *and* self ascriptive. For such a view see Barresi and Moore 1996.

11 For lots of information about bats' lives and senses, and gorgeous illustrations, see Fenton 1992.

12 Thus Dretske is led to endorse the rather implausible 'ability' analysis of knowing what it is like to experience something advanced by Nemirow 1980, 1990 and Lewis 1988. It seems to me preferable to have a unified theory of introspective knowledge. Tye, who takes a line very much like the one offered here, calls the ability analysis 'very counterintuitive' (1995, p. 175). In fact, the representational approach to 'knowing what it is like' offers substantial objections to the ability analysis, as given below. For more criticism of the ability analysis see, Loar 1990, Lycan 1996, chapter 5 or Seager 1991a, chapter 5.

13 Is it possible to imagine an experience so novel that it fits under no determinable concept? No, because any experience can at the very least be indexically specified as *that experience* (as opposed to the more determinate *that colour*, *that sound*, etc.).

14 In fact, Loar identifies such concepts with 'recognitional dispositions' of the appropriate sort (see 1990, pp. 88–89). It seems to me that this won't do since it is possible to be having some sort of experience, to thereby 'know what it is like' to have that experience, but not have any recognitional disposition by which one could, in the future or even counterfactually at that time, recognise the experience again as being of *that* sort. I think that knowing what it is like primarily involves directing one's introspective attention towards what one is experiencing (which is *not* a matter of attending to the experience itself, for one is not experiencing the experience); there is no a priori requirement that this act of attention create any dispositions (though obviously it often does and it may even by one of the functions of attention to create such dispositions).

15 I suppose the most obvious possible examples are *sensations*. But sensations as normally conceived are representations of the state of the body. They are tingles, itches, twinges that happen in various parts of our body and inform us of the state of those parts. Philosophers have extended the language with talk of such mongrels as 'visual sensations', but these, if anything, are the visual representations of the world that constitute *seeing*. If you favour a perceptual model of introspection then you will think that there are lots of these explicitly mentalistic substantial concepts. But you will face a strange problem. Why is it that the *experience* of tasting strawberries, when introspected, retains (or still 'delivers') the taste of the *strawberries*? When I – and I trust it is the same for you – taste strawberries all the phenomenology I can find is the taste of the berries. Introspection does not add any phenomenology. But on a perceptual model of introspection one could be forgiven for supposing that there ought to be a distinctive phenomenology of introspection, as different from tasting as is seeing. Perhaps one could say that the only qualitative features we are aware of when we have experiences are features of our mental states, rather than of the objects of our experiences, but I see nothing to recommend such a position. For more on this point see Dretske (1995, ch. 2).

16 I draw my information on Gymnarchus from a wonderful article by H. W. Lissmann (1963/1974). The drawings presented below are adapted from Lissmann's article. Page references are to the 1974 reprint.

17 There is evidence that electrically sensing fish will alter the frequency of their pulse discharges in the presence of other such fish, perhaps to enable them to distinguish *their* signals from those of the others.

7 REPRESENTATIONAL THEORIES OF CONSCIOUSNESS, PART II

1 Tye, on the other hand, employs a causal covariation theory of representation. Differences will be discussed below.

2 Just *what* makes a representation into an experience is a lurking question here; it is not simply a matter of the representational function of the systems at issue. Of course, this is nonetheless a crucial problem which we'll examine below.

3 It is not just through sustained, specialized use that a system's meta-function of altering its function may be invoked. A possible alternative is suggested by an hypothesis of Margie Profet (1995) that food aversions developed by pregnant women are adaptations to protect the foetus from various toxins in common foods. Women's olfactory systems, on this hypothesis, become hypersensitive during pregnancy – a beautiful illustration of a transition from a K-type to a J-type device. It is a virtue of the bio-functional version of the representational theory that such hypotheses fit so naturally into its framework. However, the idea that *no* taste qualia are shared by a woman and her pre-pregnant self seems rather extreme.

4 The vector coding identity theory we considered above (chapter 2) provides a nice way to express the radical distinctness between the new and old qualia spaces. We can suppose that more discriminating systems deploy more dimensions in their sensory encodings. So, as it might be, before training the wine taster coded tastes in, perhaps, a 10-dimensional quality space but, after training, this enlarges to, say, a 50-dimension space. *All* the old tastes were 10 element vectors; *all* new tastes are 50 element vectors. One can also sense more or less faint echoes of the old incommensurability debate in the philosophy of science, especially with regard to so-called observation terms, as well as a resonance with issues in the conflict between holist and atomist semantics.

5 The answer is to be found in the explanation of the discrimination device's current capabilities. For example, on Millikan's account (roughly) the function of a device D is to perform A iff ancestors of D actually did A and the explanation of why D does A is *because* these ancestors did A. So a device, D, would have the function of altering its functional precision in way ϕ iff its ancestors did alter their discriminatory precision in way ϕ and this explains D's precisional alteration. It seems entirely reasonable to imagine that it would be more efficient to build a device that could alter its functional precision rather than build in all possible levels of precision, especially if the device is one whose detailed sensory requirements cannot easily be specified in advance. That is, devices like *us*.

6 As Dretske explains it (1995, p. 68), for something, x, to phenomenally look ϕ to S

requires that (1) x looks the way ϕs normally look to S and (2) x looks different from non-ϕs to S (i.e. S can discriminate ϕs from non-ϕs). Dretske notes that this definition is not circular so long as we take 'looks the same' and 'looks different' as primitive (see 1995, p. 176, note 1). The legitimacy of this move is doubtful since there is clearly a similar distinction at work within these terms. X and y *doxastically look the same* to S just in case there is a ϕ such that S takes x and y both to be ϕ (S might say 'they both look like dogs to me'). Dretske must have in mind as the primitive notion 'phenomenally looks the same (different)'. To me, this looks suspiciously like 'indiscriminable on the basis of the way the objects look', where the 'look' here must, unfortunately, be 'phenomenally look' (mere indiscriminability will obviously not ground the notion of *looking* the same or different since two objects can look exactly alike while one is beeping, the other silent).

7 I was drawn to this example by a reference to it in Dennett 1991a, but note that Dennett gets the taster/non-taster proportions backwards (though the figures are correct in Dennett 1988 where he first uses the example). Dennett's original source, Bennett 1965, gets it right though Bennett makes the taster/non-taster proportion appear to be more precise and less variable than it actually is.

8 There is a difficulty right here, which I will not go into beyond this note. The notion of implicit representation presupposes that the represented properties fall into a 'family' of coherently related elements. The appropriate notion of a family of properties is not very clear. The examples used suppose that the represented property comes from a set that possesses a clear mathematical ordering but it is far from clear that *all* 'qualia properties' meet this condition.

9 A representationalist might reply that the PTU tasters are actually *misrepresenting* the taste of PTU. They are misrepresenting it as having the property which more paradigmatically bitter substances possess and which both tasters and non-tasters of PTU can taste. PTU tasting would then be likened to widespread visual illusions such as the Müller-Lyer. This response depends upon PTU (and the family of substances tasters can taste) being indiscriminable from other bitter substances. I don't know if this is the case. In any event, the response is not very plausible; we do not, I think, want to say that it is an illusion that saccharin or aspartame are sweet.

10 Of course, the possibility discussed above of developmental functional alteration also permits a class of acquired phenomenal states, but these do not pose the same sort of threat to Dretske's scheme, and Dretske is not altogether unsympathetic to such possibilities (see the discussion in 1995, note 4, pp. 169–70).

11 Tye explicitly concedes this and makes some brief remarks in support of objectivism – it is especially required for the account of representation he favours as we shall see immediately below. But whether the proper theory of colour is objectivist, subjectivist or something else altogether remains highly controversial (see Hardin 1988 or Thompson 1995).

12 At higher cognitive levels this is dubious. It is possible to imagine that evolution selects or would select for 'an optimistic outlook' or for believing that 'life is worth living' even if there is or were little objective support for this outlook or belief.

13 Other problems are obvious. For example, one can (some did) believe in phlogiston without the term 'phlogiston' covarying with phlogiston or being brought about by the presence of phlogiston. Tye concedes that the covariational theory can work, if at all, only for sensory representation, indeed only for what he calls 'simple perceptual sensations' (1995, p. 102). There are, perhaps, some exotic difficulties even at the level of simple perceptual sensations. I take it that the perception of the three-dimensionality of space is such a sensation; that is, our visual system represents the space we find ourselves within as three dimensional. Yet some *recherché* physical theories – so-called supersymmetric string theories – posit the existence of ten (or more) spatial dimensions. Only three dimensions are evident to our senses since the others are 'compactified' or curled up around the familiar dimensions at a scale of around 10^{-33} metres! These theories evidently possess very wonderful properties promising a mathematically satisfying unification of all the fundamental forces (as Abdus Salam notes: 'one can only hope that nature is aware of our work on all this', Salam 1989, p. 490). It is entirely possible that such theories are *true*, in which case one of the most fundamental aspects of our visual representation of the world is, in fact, as false as phlogiston. I do not see how this universally false visual representation can be given a covariational account, since there is nothing for the representation to covary with, save the *appearance* of three-dimensionality, but of course one cannot appeal to such appearances without introducing a vicious circularity into the theory, for all appearances are – according to the theory – themselves representations. This point is quite analogous to the problem with *redness* discussed above, save that the bio-functional theory would seem to be able to deal with it. If we suppose that the visual representation of 3-space in the presence of an actual 10-space (with compactification) will serve to enhance fitness, then I think we can account for the prevalence *and* falsity of our spatial visual representation. This sort of account will not be available for the *redness* problem (given the assumption that objectivism about colour is false) since our cognitive systems *are* able to represent the complex truth about reflectances, and it is this representational ability which accounts for the success of our colour vision. Thus I think that Cummins (1996, p. 48) is wrong to suppose, as I think he does, that a bio-functional account of representation could not account for the Euclidean content of visual perception, as well as our thoughts about space. The covariational account is in trouble here, but there is hope that the *explanation* of the success of our visual senses and thoughts involves their being about Euclidean space rather than – even though they would thus be more accurate – the non-Euclidean space we actually inhabit. Appeal to what *explains* reproductive success can be sensitive to content that is false though obviously it is impossible for a representation to causally covary with something that does not exist!

14 Tye has his own version of this process, worked out in rather greater detail than Dretske, which he labels the 'PANIC theory', which stands for *p*oised, *a*bstract, *n*on-conceptual, *i*ntentional *c*ontent. 'Poised' just means ready to influence the beliefs and desires (or, in general, the conceptual representational states) of the system. The essential similarity with Dretske's view is clear.

15 There is also the possibility that I am an artifact, in which case the fact that I have functioning representations within me will, I suppose, depend upon the intentions of my

creators. I leave, as an exercise for the reader, the development of this line of thought into an argument for theism.

16 McGinn notes it in 1991 but does not give it the prominence it deserves. A detailed look at the problem can be found in Sedivy 1995, but she does not focus on the aspect of the problem which involves consciousness. The *title* of Dennett 1993 is a good statement of the problem but it is never addressed in that paper.

17 As Tye puts it (but you could find almost identical expressions in Dretske): 'introspection of your perceptual experiences seems to reveal only aspects of *what* you experience, further aspects of the scene, as represented' (1995, p. 136, original emphasis).

18 The nature of the dance of the bees is endlessly fascinating but notice that on Dretske's theory bees would seem to meet the conditions required for them to be conscious. There is lots of evidence that they possess acquired representations and that their sensory systems function to alter these to improve the efficiency of bee behaviour. Bees remember landmarks, recognize particular kinds of flowers and, of course, communicate information in an abstract form to their sisters (see Gould 1975, 1988, 1990; see also Griffin 1992). The nature of the representational capacity is highly controversial; it might be, for example, that bees represent the location of nectar sources via the use of 'cognitive maps' or, perhaps less exciting, 'path integration' (see in opposition to Gould's cognitive map theory, Kirchner and Braun 1994). In any case, it seems their systemic representations interact with a system of acquired representations in exactly the way that Dretske takes to underlie conscious experience. While I remain uncertain about the acceptability of this result, it is a very good thing that a theory of consciousness produce a definite answer about the issue of animal consciousness, and it is evident that the representational theory is in a better position to produce such answers than other theories of consciousness.

8 CONSCIOUS INTENTIONALITY AND THE ANTI-CARTESIAN CATASTROPHE

1 The exact nature of this putatively non-conceptual content of experience is difficult to spell out for obvious and, perhaps, significant reasons. For an attempt see Peacocke 1992. As Peacocke notes, the fact that we cannot specify the content without the use of concepts does not *imply* that the content itself is conceptually infected. But this purely logical point cannot contribute to a positive belief in the existence of non-conceptual content.

2 It does not follow from this remark that concepts are simple *representations*. I have no theory of concepts to offer here, but it is evident that most concepts are in some way or other complex structures of constituent sub-concepts. Perhaps, in general, it is better to view concepts as abstract knowledge (or belief) structures more like theories than words (a view defended in Cummins 1996). Be that as it may, it remains a striking fact and, on the concepts as mini-theories view, maybe an astonishing fact that we experience the world in terms of our conceptual capacities (e.g. it is entirely possible for something literally *to look like* a scanning tunnelling electron microscope to someone with a grasp

of the appropriate conceptual machinery). So according to the representational theory of consciousness, concepts are ways of representing (at least, applications of concepts are ways of representing but I think this nicety is of no moment).

3 Such a view has obvious affinities with McDowell's in 1994 but I am unsure how close my remarks are to McDowell's position since McDowell appears flatly to deny the existence of non-conceptual experiential content.

4 Both Dretske and Tye make it a condition of a content's being conscious that it 'stand ready' to impact upon a system of beliefs and desires (in Dretske's case, at the very least a system of 'acquired representations' but he seems pretty much to equate acquired representations with beliefs, desires and judgements, see 1995, pp. 18–20). So it appears that if animals cannot have beliefs and desires (perhaps because of conceptual impoverishment) then they cannot be conscious. This is a serious issue with a deep bearing on the generation problem which I cannot go into here (but a few further comments on this issue are made in chapter 9 below).

5 But note that *we* can take up an epistemic stance towards the relation between the experiential contents and the animal's beliefs and thus provide a second-hand assessment of the rationality of these beliefs, according to the evidence that (we take) the animal to have from its experience.

6 While it is natural to speak of there being many objects of consciousness at any time, we could equally regard all of these objects as elements of a single, unified object of consciousness, for it is a particularly striking feature of consciousness that it forms a single 'field' by which we are aware of many things at once as somehow unified and complete. It is within this field that one's *attention* can move, selecting elements of consciousness and thereby also altering one's state of consciousness. The exact relation between consciousness and attention is very complex; I will not try to say any more about it here.

7 Perhaps other ways of being conscious of such drawings are possible. It may be that certain sorts of visual agnosia would leave their victims unable to be conscious of these figures as unitary objects at all except as mere assemblages of line segments. These fractured awarenesses are no less awarenesses under an aspect than are the ways we are normally conscious.

8 The distinction between (1) and aspect essentialism has, I think, troubled at least one discussion of consciousness, namely that in Dretske 1993. For details see Seager 1994 or chapter 3 above.

9 This is contrary to what Dretske says in one place: 'how things seem$_p$ . . . is independent of what one believes (or is disposed to believe) about the k one experiences' (1995, p. 132; here 'seem$_p$' is short for 'phenomenally seem'). In fact, this is highly contentious. There seems to be nothing to prevent the cognitive changes involved in acquiring new concepts also causing changes in one's 'systemic' representational capacities. It seems quite evident that things do *look* different to the trained observer than to the novice and this difference is to be, at least in part, accounted for by the conceptual differences between them.

10 I do not mean to suggest here that the astronomer would be absolutely or necessarily

unable either to appreciate the sort of consciousness enjoyed by the five year old or to be unable to re-enter this pre-theoretic state of consciousness. It is an interesting and difficult question to what extent perceptual consciousness becomes irretrievably bound up with one's conceptual apparatus; my sketchy remarks here do not even begin to do justice to this issue.

11 It is worth remembering that some philosophers have denied even these apparently benign forms of externalism. Leibniz says: 'there are no extrinsic denominations, and no one becomes a widower in India by the death of his wife in Europe unless a real change occurs in him' (unknown/1976, p. 365). Such an aversion to externalism is driven by Leibniz's extreme individualistic metaphysics; I suspect that contemporary externalists about mental content are similarly driven by metaphysics, but of a rather different sort.

12 That there is real difference between the experience of memory and that of mere recalled knowledge marks an important distinction in psychological theories of memory dividing *semantic* from *episodic* memory. My knowledge that cows are animals must depend upon a kind of memory, but I do not have any sense of *remembering* this fact; I just know it. My recall of events in my life is quite different, carrying with it a conscious sense of remembrance (see Tulving 1985). We know very well that this consciousness can be delusory, hence the point of our expression 'I seem to remember such-and-such'.

13 Note that syntactic form no less than semantic content requires an externalist treatment (see Seager 1992b). There is no test by which one could in general determine the syntactic class of a word merely from its form. Some formal languages at least attempt to make, and perhaps any 'logically perfect' language would make, syntax apparent in word- or symbol-form (although in fact these always presuppose some *understood* conventions of sign use). Is it significant that there is no way that semantics can similarly be encoded into individual word- or symbol-form?

14 For more on the notion of supervenience – perhaps rather more than the reader cares to find out, see Kim 1993 or Seager 1991a, chapter 4.

15 As does Searle (see 1992, chapter 7). What seems to me to be essential to intentionality is aspectuality. This is also the source of *intensionality*. The aspectuality of some mental states explains the intensionality of the linguistic contexts that involve reference to these states (as in 'believes that . . .', 'looks like . . .', etc.). It is another – presumably non-mental (?) – sort of aspectuality that explains the intensionality of contexts like 'the probability of . . . is n' which are true only relative to a description. For example, the probability of the next roll of the die coming up 5 is 1/6; the probability of the next roll which comes up 5 coming up 5 is 1. But the next roll of the die and the next roll of the die that comes up 5 may be exactly the *same* event. So probability works on descriptions as such. If we regard probability as a matter of subjective likelihood based upon current *knowledge* then the intensionality of probability can be reduced to the intentionality of mental states. But if probability is considered to be an objective feature of the world, then I think there is a serious problem about explaining how the *world* is sensitive to the content of descriptions. I don't think this problem has ever been successfully addressed. Given the essential role of probability in quantum mechanics, one might suspect that the metaphysical foundation

of the world is somehow based upon 'information' rather than the more familiar features of physical states. In the final chapter below, I offer some speculations about this.

16 The 'as' construction helps to mark out the distinction between mode and aspect. For example, I can be conscious of something *as* a depressing object but I can also be conscious of it in a 'depressed sort of way'. These are distinct; I can be conscious of x as a depressing object without being at all depressed, but being conscious (of x or anything else) in a depressed sort of way *is* to be depressed. It also seems very odd to suppose that I could be conscious of x, and x alone, in a depressed sort of way – another sign of a mode of consciousness.

17 Stephen Stich's 'replacement argument' for methodological solipsism is presented in his 1978. The really radical conclusions drawn by externalists, however, seem to begin with Millikan and Davidson. Deborah Brown informs me that a version of the Swampman thought experiment can be traced back to Avicenna!

18 I have recently seen a reported estimation of the probability of a person materializing out of nothing (see Crandall 1997). The probability is, however, of a particular person (a *duplicate* of the person, that is) materializing on Mars after having been de-materialized upon Earth. The probability is given as odds: 10 raised to the power of 10^{51} to 1. Since the conditions upon the Swampman needed for our thought experiments are so much less stringent, the probability of Swampman is presumably much greater than this!

19 Fodor would resist this conclusion since he takes the Swampman case to be a virtual *reductio* of (other) externalist theories of content (see Fodor and Lepore 1992, p. 237). Nonetheless, I doubt he can escape allowing a sizeable externalist component to his theory of content. Fodor's attempt to give Swampman determinate content as presented in Fodor 1995a obviously fails. Fodor claims that 'Swampman means *water* by 'water' for all that [i.e. despite the fact that none of Swampman's tokens of 'water' (if any) have been caused by *water*]. The reason he does is that it's water that *would* cause his 'water' tokens in the worlds that are closest to the one that Swampman actually lives in' (1995a, p. 118, original emphasis). To see that this won't do, simply suppose that Swampman is created suspended half-way between Earth and Twin-Earth.

20 It is interesting that Dennett, the foremost interpretationist (at least when he is not advocating an evolutionary function theory of content), has sometimes, and quite forcefully, denied the possibility of 'zombies', i.e. beings who act just like they have a mental life but who in fact have none (see his 1991b, especially chapters 10, 12 and appendix A). His denial is made possible, I think, by always placing the putative zombie within an interpretative community, even if only for the purposes of exposition. A radically disengaged creature like the Swampman, utterly cut off from such communities, no more has determinate content than Dennett's two-bitser (see Dennett 1987, chapter 8) would be already set to recognize any particular sort of coin if it were randomly ejected from some distant blackhole. Dennett's position is, I think, fundamentally confused on this point. If you deny that zombies are possible then you cannot be an externalist (unless you can show that Swampman is flat out impossible). The question is which do you like the least: zombies or externalism about content?

21 Nor should we forget Wittgenstein, the prototypical externalist. An obvious interpretation of the private language argument coupled with the arguably Wittgensteinian thesis that without language there is no thought gets us to the conclusion that Swampman has no intentional states (at least, no thoughts or other intentional mental states).

22 Of course, there might be subtle differences between genuine sunburn and other similar skin conditions, say ones caused by UV lamps. The point is that if sunburn is to be causally efficacious *as such* then there must be such differences. And if there are such differences then we have returned to the view that it is *local* conditions that govern causal efficacy. One can however speculate that the world actually does keep track of the history of a system in some way independent of the local state of that system (it is perhaps possible to view certain features of some special quantum mechanical states in this way; see the discussion of the 'quantum eraser' in chapter 9 below). One could further speculate that this 'non-local' tracking governs the causal powers of the system in question. This would be a metaphysically exciting externalism but none of the externalisms on offer have any desire to be metaphysically exciting in this way. Quite the contrary, they positively aim to fit into the traditional, physicalist picture of the world. They most certainly do *not* think that philosophical reflection upon the mind–body problem should lead to a radical change in our view of how the physical world operates. Nonetheless, there are some deep metaphysical issues lurking around this issue.

23 Dretske's slip here was brought to my attention by Mary Leng.

24 Unless there are non-local tests. Tests that somehow reveal causal history, for example, without relying upon a correlation between current physical state and that history. Of course, the proper metaphysics forbids there being any such tests. History can only be revealed by the current state, though the current state of other objects besides the target are often relevant. There is nowhere else for the information about history to reside except in the current state of the world. Furthermore, information degrades over time; the further we are from an event, the less information remains about it (I imagine that this is at bottom a matter of thermodynamics). So I say anyway – this issue raises some of the deep metaphysical questions hinted at above.

25 I don't know if the point of view I have in mind is the *legal* point of view. I am told that, for the sort of practical reasons that often move the law, unsuspecting users of counterfeit money get to keep what they 'buy' with it. If so, I wonder if the size of the bank accounts of unsuspecting depositors of counterfeit money remains the same after the mistake is discovered?

26 It is possible, I suppose, to counter this argument by speculating that individuals, like me and you, are really, as physical beings, somehow 'spread out' in space and time. This is a bizarre metaphysical notion one should prefer to avoid. It is however somewhat reminiscent of the view of physical objects in orthodox quantum theory, but heaven forbid that externalism should get together with quantum mechanical mysticism. I'll warn the reader though that a kind of quantum mysticism and *internalism* will begin to get together in the next chapter.

27 Perhaps this hoax could work as follows: all occurrences of the word 'London' in my

upbringing are to be replaced with the word 'Paris' along with an appropriate alteration in the attendant information, coupled with the complete elimination of any reference to the real Paris. In such a case, it is arguable that my conscious thought that, say, *Paris is large* is really a thought about London. Of course, in such a case it is nonetheless perfectly clear that I am really thinking about what *I* think of as Paris, that my thoughts have a determinate content and that I am indubitably conscious.

28 Many other scenarios of roughly the same sort can be envisaged. Here is another nice one. Suppose I am undergoing 'open-brain' surgery (say to cure intractable epilepsy). During the preliminary investigation, the surgeon stimulates various parts of my brain and some of these stimulations generate vivid experiences (these effects are very well known; see Penfield 1958, Calvin and Ojemann 1994) which I can report and describe while they are occurring. But Swampman on the operating table is merely a machine within which certain cortical stimulations lead to 'reports' and 'descriptions' of experience without there being any experience at all. This conclusion is not only implausible but even distasteful.

29 Perhaps it is worth noting that my distinction is *not* the distinction that Colin McGinn labels with the same words in *Mental Content* (1989).

30 For a vigorous criticism of Fodor's argument which maintains that perception is inextricably laced with conceptual elements, see Churchland 1988a.

31 The idea that all concepts are somehow combinations (logical, associational, etc.) of observation-level concepts would mean that people on Earth and Twin-Earth actually have identical sets of concepts and thus this idea would simply destroy externalism. In any case, few nowadays would look fondly on such a blatantly empiricist view of concept formation.

32 Argumentation here can become very intricate however. For example, it is possible to claim that N[water] has two 'aspects' or 'modes of presentation'. The basic aspect is what we are familiar with in ordinary thinking about water; a secondary aspect arises when we think of N[water] *as* N[water]. So, when we think we are thinking of the difference between C[water] and N[water] we are really only noticing the difference between these two aspects of N[water].

33 Perhaps externalists are misled by the correct perception that reference (at least to some ranges of things) cannot be determined strictly internally. But this is an insight as old as Descartes and it should not blind us to the fact that the intentionality of consciousness which presents an 'outer' world is a phenomenon that exists quite independently from questions of the referential relations between these states of consciousness and the world beyond it.

34 I say the 'content of concepts' since it is the content that matters. It might be that *concepts* themselves deserve an externalistic, social treatment. But the content they embody must transcend that account since the contents are shared by all doppelgängers, even if some of these are not to be granted the possession of genuine concepts. Perhaps this disturbingly fine distinction could be grounded in a way similar to the distinction between something *carrying* content and it having the *function of carrying* content which we briefly explored above.

35 See also Devitt 1990. Devitt does not discuss our problem but it seems to me that Devitt's narrow representational theory of the mind lacks the resources to explain how internally specified states can represent anything in the way needed to set up the satisfaction or realization relation. Essentially, this is because Devitt's narrow psychology focusses on the relation between *stimuli* and inner mental states. It is hard to see how Swampman, for example, can have inner states that distinguish (with respect to the satisfaction relation) between worlds that agree on the set of stimuli, such as the actual versus the vat world. Also, at one point Devitt appears to allow that at least some aspects of narrow meaning are 'dependent upon these [causal-external] links' (p. 380). If so, Swampman lacks these aspects altogether with the obvious unpleasant consequences.

36 In Chalmers's case, the primary intensions of thoughts are, in essence, dependent upon what the thinker decides his thoughts apply to 'upon reflection' about certain kinds of counterfactual cases. But such reflection already presupposes that there is content at work in the system, the system's access to which or representation of which must be explained. Some of the critical remarks of Block and Stalnaker (1997) bear on this aspect of Chalmers's view.

37 Desmond and Moore report that Darwin was taken with the views of the so-called strongest materialist of the day, John Elliotson, who wrote 'thought . . . seems as much function of organ, as bile of liver' (as quoted in Desmond and Moore 1994, p. 251). The phrase is curiously similar to some, more guarded, remarks of John Searle (see for example Searle 1987, p. 217). If one pauses to think, it is difficult to know how to understand the secretion metaphor. As William James noted: '. . . "the brain secretes thought, as the kidneys secrete urine, or as the liver secretes bile," are phrases which one sometimes hears. The lame analogy need hardly be pointed out . . . we know of nothing connected with liver and kidney activity which can be in the remotest degree compared with the stream of thought that accompanies the brain's material secretions' (1890/1950, pp. 102–3). Still true today.

9 CONSCIOUSNESS, INFORMATION AND PANPSYCHISM

1 Well, not altogether easy. The passage from micro-physics to thermodynamics is still fraught with difficulties, both scientific and conceptual. For example, the passage from the deterministic micro-physics to the probabilistic macro-physics is not completely understood, depending upon many non-obvious substantive assumptions. Another and related mysterious area involves the notions of entropy and information. Macroscopic thermodynamic intuitions suggest that information can be lost (this is the information theoretic counterpart to entropy), but the micro-physics (either classical *or* quantum) insists that no information ever disappears from the world. There are unresolved tensions here that may go to the heart of the scientific picture of the world. For an appreciation of the complexities of the micro/macro relation in thermodynamics see Sklar 1993.

2 Another perplexing point to note: Dennett is pretty clearly an externalist about content; in many writings he approvingly supports a Millikan style bio-functional approach (although in other writings he champions an 'interpretationist' view of content and content ascription, interpretationism is no less a kind of externalism than is bio-functionalism). But on such views, as we saw in the last two chapters, there is no way to avoid the possibility of what I called intentional zombies. Swampman is one. But Dennett's theory of consciousness provides the assumptions needed to generate the theorem: all intentional zombies are philosophical zombies. The argument is dead simple: externalism implies that Swampman has no content carrying states, Dennett's theory of consciousness implies that without such states there is no consciousness, so Swampman has no consciousness and is hence a zombie (see chapter 8, note 20).

3 But I recall to our attention that the reviewer for the *New York Times*, George Johnson (1991), took Dennett to be providing a generation theory of consciousness: '. . . from the collective behaviour of all these neurological devices consciousness emerges – a qualitative leap no more magical than the one that occurs when wetness arises from the jostling of hydrogen and oxygen atoms'. We saw above why Dennett dare not accept this interpretation of his theory.

4 See chapter 5's discussion of Dennett's notion of 'cerebral celebrity' for a little more on this sort of unsuccessful attempt to dissolve the generation problem.

5 Imagine we try to answer by, to take a current example, noting that the bee brain deploys the 40 Hz oscillation binding system whereas the robot's processor does not. Then: why does only the 40 Hz BS generate consciousness? Aren't other binding systems possible, and if not, *why* not? Of course, this worry holds for any putative purely physical correlate of consciousness.

6 Chalmers means by this *local* functional organization. Roughly speaking, this is just the input–output relations of the (somehow specified) functional units of the brain. This highly non-biological, non-teleological notion of function should be kept in mind in what follows and carefully distinguished from the notion of function we have considered in earlier chapters.

7 Thus Chalmers's position is a generalization of the view, quoted in chapter 1 above, of Richard Boyd (1980, p. 96): 'there are certain configurations such that whenever they are realized by a physical system, whatever substances compose it, the qualitative feeling of pain is manifested'. Boyd's restriction of the realizing systems to 'physical systems' is somewhat puzzling. A hard-core functionalist shouldn't care anything about the realizing systems. It may be that Boyd thinks that non-physical realizing systems are *impossible*, but this would need a strong argument (see the discussion of this feature of functionalism in chapter 1 above).

8 For an example of some fading qualia thought experiments identical to Chalmers's but that are in direct opposition to Chalmers's intuitions see Searle 1992, ch. 3. Chalmers discusses Searle's thought experiment, claiming that only dualist presuppositions could support Searle's interpretation (see Chalmers 1996a, pp. 258 ff.).

9 The danger of ignoring the problem that there are a great many possible levels of

functional organization, and thinking solely in terms of a functional versus a non-functional description, has been much emphasized by William Lycan, who labels it *two-levelism* (see Lycan 1987, 1996).

10 It remains, perhaps, a slightly open question whether this is so. Roger Penrose has defended the view that the brain is not describable solely in terms of 'computable' functions (see 1989, 1994) and so would not have a Turing machine simulation. It seems to me that such an idea is about as speculative as the quantum mechanical tale to be told below.

11 Chalmers comes close to admitting this in his discussion of Searle's famous Chinese room thought experiment (see Chalmers 1996a, pp. 322 ff.; see also Chalmers's discussion at pp. 262–3). However, Chalmers claims that if we observe the internal workings of the Chinese room (the paper shuffling) 'we will see a whir of causal interaction that corresponds precisely to the whir among the neurons' (p. 325). However, watching the actions of a Turing machine simulation of the set of high-level neural sub-networks of a brain will not reveal a correspondence with the actions of the individual neurons, but it will of course duplicate the behavioural capacities of the simulated brain.

12 The following thought experiment has some similarity to the Arnold Zuboff's delightful fantasy 'The Story of a Brain' (see Zuboff 1981).

13 Each shneuron is somewhat like the monads Leibniz posited as the ultimate existents and, in good Leibnizian fashion, the shneurons are operating in *pre-established harmony*. From the outside, they all seem to know what the shneurons they are connected to are doing but, as Leibniz said about the monads, they have no windows.

14 For a stinging rebuff of the Hameroff–Penrose mechanism of quantum generation of consciousness see Grush and Churchland 1995. For an equally stinging reply see Penrose and Hameroff 1995.

15 Actually, the situation would be a little more complicated from Penrose's point of view since he thinks that the quantum machinery within the microtubule gives human intelligence an insurmountable edge over machine 'intelligence' which would show up in certain sorts of behavioural tests. This is the ultimate import of Penrose's version of Lucas's 1961 argument that Gödel's theorem reveals limitations to machine abilities which are surpassed by those of humans; see Part One of Penrose 1994; of course, Penrose's – and Lucas's for that matter – interpretation of Gödel's theorem remains highly contentious. But we could, I suppose, in principle, build microtubule-less surrogates that exploited the relevant quantum processes in another way which preserved functional distinctness.

16 This element of Chalmers's theory of consciousness particularly irks Searle, as he makes clear in his review (Searle 1997).

17 More accurately, Bell showed that no *local* carried correlation theory can be correct. If we allow that the parts of the system can 'communicate' (more or less instantaneously across any distance) then we can maintain a hidden variable theory (since the separated parts can through their intercommunication manipulate the measurement statistics to bring them in line with those of ordinary QM). And there is such a hidden variable theory,

developed by David Bohm (see Bohm and Hiley 1993, Bohm 1980). In Bohm's theory all the positions and trajectories of the particles in a system are always determinate but there is non-local 'communication' via the so-called quantum potential (a new kind of field that, in essence, carries information rather than energy). The nature of this communication is mysterious however and I believe it remains unclear whether Bohm's theory can be properly integrated with quantum field theory. Bohm's theory certainly does not vindicate the EPR intuition and in fact champions the 'spooky action at a distance' that Einstein deplored.

18 In the special case of position, the famous Born-rule can be used according to which the probability of finding the particle in a certain region is simply a function of $|\Psi|^2$ over that region. Basically, if the region r ranges from n to m then the probability of finding a particle in state Ψ within r is equal to (3) $\int |\Psi(x)|^2 dx$ evaluated from n to m. We are not trying to do any calculating here though, so I'll stick to the abstract projection operator form in what follows.

19 And, in general, if O and P are operators we have $(O \otimes P)(\Psi \otimes \Phi) = O\Psi \otimes P\Phi$.

20 This follows from the definition of the inner product in the tensor product space, which is: $\langle \Psi_1 \otimes \Phi_1 | \Psi_2 \otimes \Phi_2 \rangle = \langle \Psi_1 | \Psi_2 \rangle \times \langle \Phi_1 | \Phi_2 \rangle$.

21 One might, perhaps, entertain some doubts about this argument since, notoriously, the normal time evolution of a quantum state seems to fail in the case of measurement where the so-called collapse of the wave function occurs. There is no question that two orthogonal states can both 'collapse' to the same state. E.g. the result of a measurement of spin in the z-direction of an electron already prepared to be spin-up in the x-direction could be spin-down in the z-direction; the very same result could, of course, be obtained from a measurement of a spin-down in the x-direction electron. But in the case above, we *maintain* the superposition of states which is characteristic of the normal time-evolution of quantum states; we did not invoke any collapse of the wave function in the operation of the eraser and, it seems, any such collapse would necessarily eliminate one of the terms of the superposition and thus would also eliminate any possibility of interference.

22 There are several distinct proofs that superluminal signalling is quite impossible within quantum mechanics. For an interesting and somewhat sceptical review of these proofs see Peacock 1991.

23 The crucial properties are that $c\Psi \otimes d\Phi = cd(\Psi \otimes \Phi)$ and that $(\Psi_1 \otimes \Phi_1) + (\Psi_2 \otimes \Phi_2) = (\Psi_1 + \Psi_2) \otimes (\Phi_1 + \Phi_2)$. The proof of (14) follows by the expansion of the left term thus. The left term is equal to:

$$\sqrt{\tfrac{1}{2}}[[\sqrt{\tfrac{1}{2}}(\Psi_1 + \Psi_2) \otimes \sqrt{\tfrac{1}{2}}(R + L)] + [\sqrt{\tfrac{1}{2}}(\Psi_1 - \Psi_2) \otimes \sqrt{\tfrac{1}{2}}(R - L)]]$$

$$= \sqrt{\tfrac{1}{2}}[\tfrac{1}{2}[(\Psi_1 \otimes R) + (\Psi_1 \otimes L) + (\Psi_2 \otimes R) + (\Psi_2 \otimes L)] + \tfrac{1}{2}[(\Psi_1 \otimes R) - (\Psi_1 \otimes L) - (\Psi_2 \otimes R) + (\Psi_2 \otimes L)]]$$

$$= \sqrt{\tfrac{1}{2}}[\tfrac{1}{2}[(\Psi_1 \otimes R) + (\Psi_2 \otimes L) + (\Psi_1 \otimes R) + (\Psi_2 \otimes L)]]$$

$$= \sqrt{\tfrac{1}{2}}[\tfrac{1}{2}[2(\Psi_1 \otimes R) + 2(\Psi_2 \otimes L)]]$$

$$= \sqrt{\tfrac{1}{2}}[(\Psi_1 \otimes R) + (\Psi_2 \otimes L)]$$

$$= \Psi_d.$$

24 Scully *et al.* are somewhat sloppy when they report that the probability of interest is that of 'finding both the detector excited [i.e. finding the detector in our state G₊] and the atom at R on the screen' (1991, p. 115). One can easily see that this is not the probability of interest here by imagining that r is the 'region' $-\infty$ to $+\infty$. The probability that the particle will be found in this region is 1, but the probability of finding the particle in this region *and* the detector in state G₊ is just ½. Of course, the probability of the particle being in this region *given* that the detector is in G₊ is still equal to 1.

25 I am not here trying to develop a wholesale interpretation of QM but only to point out that it is not unnatural to think that information plays a fundamental role in the quantum world. Since interpretations of QM range from the ultra anti-realist or instrumentalist to the fully realist and even deterministic, not all may agree that information is a fundamental feature of QM's world view. But it is interesting to note that Bohm's realist interpretation does give information a very special role. For example, Bohm and Hiley claim that 'the quantum field does not act mechanically, but rather . . . it acts as *information* that guides the particle in its self-movement . . .' (Bohm and Hiley 1993, pp. 79–9, my emphasis). The role of what Bohm and Hiley call *active information* is stressed throughout their interpretation of QM.

26 I think that Nagel's argument is invalid, as it stands, because of an equivocation on the notion of 'reduction', which can be taken in either an epistemic or an ontological sense. Chalmers is pretty clear that his notion of reduction is an ontological one (but see his remarks at 1995a, p. 16) and this clarity rescues Nagel's argument (at the cost of making the 'no reduction' premise less secure, a problem exploited in James van Cleve's 1990 criticism of Nagel's argument). An alternative to panpsychism is, then, the view that while there is no *explanatory* relation between matter and consciousness – no solution to the generation problem that is – consciousness is, at the bottom of its being so to speak, a physical phenomenon. Such a view has been derisively labelled by Owen Flanagan (1992) as the New Mysterianism. However, as discussed in chapter 1 above, Flanagan's attachment to neural *correlates* of consciousness does not, I fear, even begin to address the generation problem. In fact mysterianism is quite attractive if one accepts the seriousness of the generation problem while retaining an attachment to physicalism. Note that the mysterianism just advanced may differ from McGinn's (as expounded originally in McGinn 1989 and further developed in the initial chapters of his 1991). McGinn allows that there is an explanation of the matter consciousness connection but that human cognitive capacities are insufficient to discover and/or grasp it. It does not seem to me that it obviously follows from there being an ontological link between matter and consciousness that therefore there is an explanatory link as well. The inference seems to depend upon certain obscure but interesting theses about both language, such as that every relation in the world can be described 'appropriately' in some language, and cognition, such as that there are no intrinsic limits to possible cognitive powers, as well as questions about the nature of explanation (for some discussion of this last feature, see Seager 1991a, chapter 1).

27 This is the same Clifford whose early speculations about the curvature of space prefigured General Relativity and John Wheeler's more radical program of geometrodynamics that attempted to reduce matter to 'knots' of tightly curved spacetime.

28 This despite the fact that James can be seen as a kind of panpsychist himself. However, James's overall theory is very difficult to untangle from his coil of writings about the mind; for the complexities involved see Cooper 1990.

29 In these objections, I am indebted both to Colin McGinn's critical remarks on David Griffin's manuscript (1994, now forthcoming) as well as this manuscript itself which defends a Whiteheadian style panpsychism. These were presented to a conference on *Consciousness in Humans and Animals* held at Claremont School of Theology in 1994. I would like to express my gratitude to Professor Griffin for organizing this conference and inviting me, and to the other participants for their vigorous debate. I cannot hope to deal with the intricacies of Process Philosophy panpsychism here but I thank Professor Griffin for stimulating my interest in the doctrine.

30 This unutterably tiny level of force can nonetheless play a role in the world which is 'visible' under special circumstances. If we imagine a perfect, frictionless billiard table possessed of perfectly elastic billiard balls, then a computation of their interactions which neglected only the *gravitational* force exerted by a single electron on the other side of the Galaxy would be hopelessly inaccurate in just a few minutes (such an example is discussed in Ekeland 1988, pp. 67–69).

31 This is the only answer to problem (2). The panpsychist must proclaim that it is consciousness itself that divides down to the elemental units. Otherwise the generation problem returns with its full force. But given the considerations adduced above which ameliorate its implausibility, there is no reason why the panpsychist cannot make this basic postulate. Here's a case where the correct response – which I've heard Paul Grice once gave in reply to a question – is: that's not a counterexample to my theory, that *is* my theory.

32 Of course, an intentionally designed quantum computer, if such can be constructed, would not necessarily suffer from this weakness. See Deutsch 1985 and Lockwood 1991, pp. 246–52, for discussions of this remarkable device; there are now some signs – Gershenfeld and Chuang 1997 – that quantum computers can be built.

33 This is not to say that the project is likely to succeed. There are severe difficulties in marrying the demands of Davidson's causal-historical account of representation, and hence his account of the nature of belief, desire and the other intentional mental states, with his token physicalism, for which see Seager 1992a.

BIBLIOGRAPHY

Alfvén, Hannes (1966). *Worlds – Antiworlds*, San Francisco: Freeman.

Armstrong, David (1968). *A Materialist Theory of the Mind*, London: Routledge and Kegan Paul.

Armstrong, David (1980). *The Nature of the Mind and Other Essays*, Ithaca, NY: Cornell University Press.

Armstrong, David (1996). 'Qualia Ain't in the Head: Review of *Ten Problems of Consciousness: a Representational Theory of the Phenomenal Mind* by Michael Tye', in *PSYCHE: an interdisciplinary journal of research on consciousness*, Internet journal at URL http://psyche.cs.monash.edu.au.

Arnauld, Antoine (1641/1985). 'Objections', in Cottingham *et al.* (1985, v. 2).

Baars, Bernard (1997). *In the Theater of Consciousness: The Workspace of the Mind*, Oxford: Oxford University Press.

Baker, Lynne (1987). *Saving Belief: A Critique of Physicalism*, Princeton: Princeton University Press.

Barresi, John and Chris Moore (1996). 'Intentional Relations and Social Understanding', *Behavioral and Brain Sciences*, 19, 1, pp. 107–22.

Bechtel, William and A. Abrahamsen (1991). *Connectionism and the Mind: An Introduction to Parallel Processing in Networks*, Oxford: Blackwell.

Bell, John (1964). 'On the Einstein–Podolsky–Rosen Paradox', *Physics*, 1, p. 195.

Bell, John (1987). *Speakable and Unspeakable in Quantum Mechanics*, Cambridge: Cambridge University Press.

Bennett, Jonathan (1965). 'Substance, Reality and Primary Qualities', *American Philosophical Quarterly*, 2, pp. 1–17.

Bilgrami, Akeel (1992). *Belief and Meaning*, Oxford: Blackwell.

Block, Ned (1978). 'Troubles With Functionalism', in Wade Savage (ed.) *Perception and Cognition: Minnesota Studies in the Philosophy of Science*, v. 9, Minneapolis: University of Minnesota Press.

Block, Ned (1990). 'Inverted Earth', in J. Tomberlin (ed.) *Philosophical Perspectives*, v. 4, pp. 53–79.

Block, Ned (1993). 'Consciousness Explained' [review of Dennett 1991b], *Journal of Philosophy*, 90, pp. 181–93.

Block, Ned (1995). 'On a Confusion about a Function of Consciousness', *The Behavioral and Brain Sciences* 18, 2, pp. 227–247.

Block, Ned and R. Stalnaker (1997). 'Conceptual Analysis and the Explanatory Gap', ms. (http://www.nyu.edu/gsas/dept/philo/faculty/block/papers).

Bohm, David (1980). *Wholeness and the Implicate Order*, London: Routledge and Kegan Paul.

Bohm, David and Basil Hiley (1993). *The Undivided Universe: An Ontological Interpretation of Quantum Theory*, London: Routledge.

BonJour, Laurence (1985). *The Structure of Empirical Knowledge*, Cambridge, MA: Harvard University Press.

Boyd, Richard (1980). 'Materialism without Reductionism: What Physicalism Does Not Entail', in Ned Block (ed.) *Readings in the Philosophy of Psychology*, v. 1, Cambridge, MA: Harvard University Press.

Brentano, Franz (1874/1973). *Psychology From the Empirical Standpoint*, O. Kraus (ed.), A. Rancurello, D. Terrell, L. McAllister (trans.), London: Routledge and Kegan Paul.

Broughton, R. (1994). 'Homicidal Somnambulism: A Case Report', *Sleep*, 17, 3, pp. 253–264.

Brown, Deborah (1993). 'Swampman of La Mancha', *Canadian Journal of Philosophy*, 23, 3, pp. 327–48.

Burge, Tyler (1979). 'Individualism and the Mental' in P. French, T. Uehling and H. Wettstein (eds), *Midwest Studies in Philosophy, v. 4: Studies in Metaphysics*, Minneapolis: University of Minnesota Press.

Burge, Tyler (1982). 'Other Bodies', in A. Woodfield (ed.) *Thought and Object: Essays on Intentionality*, Oxford: Oxford University Press.

Burge, Tyler (1986). 'Individualism and Psychology', *Philosophical Review*, 95, pp. 3–45.

Caldwell, Mark (1995). 'Kernel of Fear', *Discover*, 16 (June), pp. 96–103.

Callwood, June (1990). *The Sleepwalker*, Toronto: Lester and Orpen Dennys.

Calvin, William and G. Ojemann (1994). *Conversations with Neil's Brain: the Neural Nature of Thought and Language*, Reading, MA: Addison-Wesley.

Carruthers, Peter (1989). 'Brute Experience', in *Journal of Philosophy*, 89, pp. 258–69.

Chalmers, David (1993). *Towards a Theory of Consciousness*, Indiana University doctoral dissertation, Bloomington, IN.

Chalmers, David (1995a). 'Facing Up to the Problem of Consciousness', in the *Journal of Consciousness Studies*, 2, 3, pp. 200–19.

Chalmers, David (1995b). 'The Puzzle of Conscious Experience', *Scientific American*, 273, pp. 80–87.

Chalmers, David (1996a). *The Conscious Mind: In Search of a Fundamental Theory*, Oxford: Oxford University Press.

Chalmers, David (1996b). 'The Components of Content', ms.

Chomsky, Noam (1980). *Rules and Representations*, New York: Columbia University Press.

Churchland, Patricia (1986). *Neurophilosophy: Toward a Unified Science of the Mind–Brain*, Cambridge, MA: MIT Press.

Churchland, Patricia and Terrence Sejnowski (1992). *The Computational Brain: Models and Methods on the Frontier of Computational Neuroscience*, Cambridge, MA: MIT Press.

Churchland, Paul (1979). *Scientific Realism and the Plasticity of Mind*, Cambridge: Cambridge University Press.

Churchland, Paul (1981). 'Eliminative Materialism and Propositional Attitudes', *Journal of Philosophy*, 78, pp. 67–90.

Churchland, Paul (1985). 'Reduction, Qualia, and the Direct Introspection of Brain States', *Journal of Philosophy*, 82, pp. 8–28.

Churchland, Paul (1986). 'Some Reductive Strategies in Cognitive Neurobiology', *Mind*, 95, pp. 279–309.

Churchland, Paul (1988a). 'Perceptual Plasticity and Theoretical Neutrality: A Reply to Jerry Fodor', *Philosophy of Science*, 55, pp. 167–87.

Churchland, Paul (1988b). *Matter and Consciousness: A Contemporary Introduction to the Philosophy of Mind*, Cambridge, MA: MIT Press.

Churchland, Paul (1995). *The Engine of Reason, The Seat of the Soul*, Cambridge, MA: MIT Press.

Churchland, Paul and Patricia Churchland (1982). 'Functionalism, Qualia and Intentionality', in J. Biro and R. Shahan (eds) *Mind, Brain and Function: Essays in the Philosophy of Mind*, Norman: University of Oklahoma Press.

Clark, Andy (1989). *Microcognition: Philosophy, Cognitive Science and Parallel Distributed Processing*, Cambridge, MA: MIT Press.

Clark, Andy (1993). *Associative Engines: Connectionism, Concepts and Representational Change*, Cambridge, MA: MIT Press.

Clifford, William K. (1874). 'Body and Mind', reprinted in *Lectures and Essays*, Leslie Stephen and Frederick Pollock (eds), London: Macmillan, 1886.

Cooper, W. E. (1990). 'William James's Theory of Mind', *Journal of the History of Philosophy*, 28, 4, pp. 571–93.

Cottingham, John, Robert Stoothoff and Dugald Murdoch (eds) (1985). *The Philosophical Writings of Descartes*, Cambridge: Cambridge University Press.

Crandall, Richard (1997). 'The Challenge of Large Numbers', in *Scientific American*, 276, 2 (February), pp. 74–8.

Crick, Francis (1994). *The Astonishing Hypothesis: The Scientific Search for the Soul*, London: Simon and Schuster.

Cummins, Robert (1982). 'What Can be Learned From *Brainstorms*', in J. Biro and R. Shahan (eds) *Mind, Brain and Function: Essays in the Philosophy of Mind*, Norman: University of Oklahoma Press.

Cummins, Robert (1989). *Meaning and Mental Representation*, Cambridge, MA: MIT Press.

Cummins, Robert (1996). *Representations, Targets and Attitudes*, Cambridge, MA: MIT Press.

Damasio, Antonio (1994). *Descartes' Error: Emotion, Reason, and the Human Brain*, New York: G. P. Putnam.

Davidson, Donald (1969). 'How is Weakness of Will Possible?', in Joel Feinberg (ed.) *Moral Concepts*, Oxford: Oxford University Press.

Davidson, Donald (1970). 'Mental Events', in L. Foster and J. Swanson (eds) *Experience and Theory*, University of Massachusetts Press. Reprinted in Davidson's *Essays on Actions and Events*, Oxford: Oxford University Press, 1980.

Davidson, Donald (1984). 'First Person Authority', *Dialectica*, 38, pp. 101–11.

Davidson, Donald (1987). 'Knowing One's Own Mind', *Proceedings and Addresses of the American Philosophical Association*, 60, pp. 441–58.

Davies, Martin and Glyn Humphreys (eds) (1993). *Consciousness*, Oxford: Blackwell.

Davies, Paul (1996). *About Time: Einstein's Unfinished Revolution*, New York: Simon and Schuster (Touchstone).

Dennett, Daniel (1969). *Content and Consciousness*, London: Routledge and Kegan Paul.

Dennett, Daniel (1971). 'Intentional Systems', *Journal of Philosophy*, 68, pp. 87–106. Reprinted in Dennett's *Brainstorms*, Montgomery, VT: Bradford Books, 1978.

Dennett, Daniel (1976). 'Are Dreams Experiences?', *Philosophical Review*, 85, pp. 151–71. Reprinted in Dennett's *Brainstorms*, Montgomery, VT: Bradford Books, 1978.

Dennett, Daniel (1978). 'Why You Can't Make a Computer Feel Pain', *Synthese*, 38, pp. 415–49. Reprinted in Dennett's *Brainstorms*, Montgomery, VT: Bradford Books, 1978.

Dennett, Daniel (1987). 'Evolution, Error and Intentionality', in Dennett's *The Intentional Stance*, Cambridge, MA: MIT Press.

Dennett, Daniel (1987). *The Intentional Stance*, Cambridge, MA: MIT Press.

Dennett, Daniel (1988). 'Quining Qualia', in A. Marcel and E. Bisiach (eds), *Consciousness in Contemporary Science*, Oxford: Oxford University Press. Reprinted in William Lycan (ed.) *Mind and Cognition: A Reader*, Cambridge, MA: MIT Press, 1990.

Dennett, Daniel (1991a). 'Real Patterns', *The Journal of Philosophy*, 89, pp. 27–51.

Dennett, Daniel (1991b). *Consciousness Explained*, Boston: Little, Brown and Co.

Dennett, Daniel (1993). 'The Message is: There is no Medium', *Philosophy and Phenomenological Research*, 53, 4, pp. 919–31.

Dennett, Daniel (1995). *Darwin's Dangerous Idea: Evolution and the Meanings of Life*, New York: Simon and Schuster.

Descartes, René (1637a/1985). *Discourse on Method*, in Cottingham *et al.* (1985, v. 1).

Descartes, René (1637b/1985). *Optics*, in Cottingham *et al.* (1985, v. 1).

Descartes, René (1641a/1985). *Meditations*, in Cottingham *et al.* (1985, v. 2).

Descartes, René (1641b/1985). 'Objections and Replies', in Cottingham *et al.* (1985, v. 2).

Descartes, René (1644/1985). *Principles of Philosophy*, in Cottingham *et al.* (1985, v. 1).

Descartes, René (1649/1985). *The Passions of the Soul*, in Cottingham *et al.* (1985, v. 1).

Descartes, René (1664/1985). *Treatise on Man*, in Cottingham *et al.* (1985, v. 1).

Descartes, René (1684/1985). *Rules for the Direction of the Mind*, in Cottingham *et al.* (1985, v. 1).

Desmond, Adrian and James Moore (1994). *Darwin: The Life of a Tormented Evolutionist*, New York: Norton.

Deutsch, David (1985). 'Quantum Theory, the Church–Turing Principle and the Universal Quantum Computer', *Proceedings of the Royal Society of London*, A400.

Devitt, Michael (1990). 'A Narrow Representational Theory of the Mind' in William Lycan (ed.) *Mind and Cognition: A Reader*, Cambridge, MA: MIT Press, pp. 371–98.

Dretske, Fred (1986). 'Misrepresentation', in R. Bogdan (ed.) *Belief: Form, Content and Function*, Oxford: Oxford University Press.

Dretske, Fred (1988). *Explaining Behavior: Reasons in a World of Causes*, Cambridge, MA: MIT Press.

Dretske, Fred (1993). 'Conscious Experience', *Mind*, 102, pp. 263–83.

Dretske, Fred (1995). *Naturalizing the Mind*, Cambridge, MA: MIT Press.

Dretske, Fred (1997). 'What Good is Consciousness?', *Canadian Journal of Philosophy*, 27, 1, pp. 1–16.

Edelman, Gerald (1987). *Neural Darwinism*, New York: Basic Books.

Edelman, Gerald (1992). *Bright Air, Brilliant Fire*, New York: Basic Books.

Einstein, Albert, B. Podolsky and N. Rosen (1935). 'Can Quantum Mechanical Description of Physical Reality Be Considered Complete?', *Physical Review*, 47, pp. 777–80. Reprinted in John Wheeler and W. Zurek (eds) *Quantum Theory and Measurement*, Princeton, NJ: Princeton University Press, 1983.

Ekeland, Ivars (1988). *Mathematics and the Unexpected*, Chicago: Univ. of Chicago Press.

Englert, B., M. Scully and H. Walther (1994). 'The Duality in Matter and Light', *Scientific American*, 271, 6, pp. 86–92.

Falvey, Kevin and J. Owens (1994). 'Externalism, Self-knowledge, and Skepticism', *Philosophical Review*, 103, pp. 107–37.

Fantz, Robert (1958). 'Pattern Vision in Young Infants', *The Psychological Record*, 8, pp. 43–7.

Fantz, Robert (1961). 'The Origin of Form Perception', *Scientific American*, May, pp. 61 ff. Reprinted in W. Greenough *The Nature and Nurture of Behavior: Developmental Psychobiology*, San Francisco: Freeman, 1973, pp. 66–72.

Fenton, Brock (1992). *Bats*, New York: Facts on File.

Flanagan, Owen (1992). *Consciousness Reconsidered*, Cambridge, MA: MIT Press.

Fodor, Jerry (1980). 'Methodological Solipsism Considered as a Research Strategy in Cognitive Science', *Behavioral and Brain Sciences*, 3, pp. 63–109.

Fodor, Jerry (1984). 'Observation Reconsidered', *Philosophy of Science*, 51, pp. 23–43.

Fodor, Jerry (1987). *Psychosemantics*, Cambridge, MA: MIT Press.

Fodor, Jerry (1992). *A Theory of Content and Other Essays*, Cambridge, MA: MIT Press.

Fodor, Jerry (1995a). *The Elm and the Expert: Mentalese and its Semantics*, Cambridge, MA: MIT Press.

Fodor, Jerry (1995b). 'West Coast Fuzzy: Why We Don't Know How Minds Work', *Times Literary Supplement*, August 25, pp. 5–6.

Fodor, Jerry and Ernest Lepore (1992). *Holism: A Shopper's Guide*, Oxford: Blackwell.

Gazzaniga, Michael (ed.) (1994). *The Cognitive Neurosciences*, Cambridge, MA: MIT Press.

Gershenfeld, Neil and Isaac Chuang (1997). 'Bulk Spin-Resonance Quantum Computation', in *Science*, 275, 17th January, pp. 350–55.

Godfrey-Smith, Peter (1994). 'A Modern History Theory of Functions', *Noûs*, 28, 3, pp. 344–62.

Goldman, Alvin (1989). 'Interpretation Psychologized', *Mind and Language*, 4, pp. 161–85.

Gopnik, Alison (1993). 'How do We Know Our Minds: The Illusion of First Person Knowledge of Intentionality', *Behavioral and Brain Sciences*, 16, pp. 1–14. Reprinted in Alvin

Goldman (ed.) *Readings in Philosophy and Cognitive Science*, pp. 315–46, Cambridge, MA: MIT Press, 1993.

Gould, J. L. (1975). 'Honey-Bee Communication: The Dance Language Controversy', *Science*, 189, pp. 685–93.

Gould, J. L. (1988). *The Honey Bee*, New York: Scientific American Library, Freeman.

Gould, J. L. (1990). 'Honey Bee Cognition', *Cognition*, 37, pp. 83–103.

Gould, Stephen J. (1989). *Wonderful Life: The Burgess Shale and the Nature of History*, New York: Norton.

Gregory, Richard (1990). *Eye and Brain: The Psychology of Seeing*, Princeton, NJ: Princeton University Press.

Griffin, David (1994). *Unsnarling the World Knot: Consciousness, Freedom and the Mind–body Problem*, ms. Now forthcoming from University of California Press.

Griffin, Donald (1992). *Animal Minds*, University of Chicago Press.

Grush, R. and Patricia Churchland (1995). 'Gaps in Penrose's Toilings', *Journal of Consciousness Studies*, 2, pp. 10–29.

Guth, Alan and Paul Steinhardt (1989). 'The Inflationary Universe', in Paul Davies (ed.) *The New Physics*, Cambridge: Cambridge University Press.

Hacker, Peter (1993). *Wittgenstein: Meaning and Mind, Part I: Essays*, Oxford: Blackwell.

Hacking, Ian (1995). *Rewriting the Soul: Multiple Personality and the Sciences of Memory*, Princeton, NJ: Princeton University Press.

Hameroff, Stuart (1994). 'Quantum Coherence in Microtubules: A Neural Basis for Emergent Consciousness', *Journal of Consciousness Studies*, 1, pp. 91–118.

Hardin, C. L. (1988). *Color For Philosophers: Unweaving the Rainbow*, Indianapolis: Hackett.

Harman, Gilbert (1989). 'Some Philosophical Issues in Cognitive Science: Qualia, Intentionality and the Mind–body Problem', in M. Posner (ed.) *Foundations of Cognitive Science*, Cambridge, MA: MIT Press, pp. 831–48.

Harman, Gilbert (1990). 'The Intrinsic Quality of Experience' in J. Tomberlin (ed.) *Philosophical Perspectives*, v. 4, pp. 31–52.

Haugeland, John (1985). *Artificial Intelligence: The Very Idea*, Cambridge, MA: MIT Press.

Hawking, Stephen (1993). *Black Holes and Baby Universes and Other Essays*, London: Bantam Books.

Heal, Jane (1986). 'Replication and Functionalism', in J. Butterfield (ed.) *Language, Mind and Logic*, Cambridge, Cambridge University Press, pp. 135–50.

Hobbes, Thomas (1656). *The Elements of Philosophy*, London: R. and W. Leybourn.

Hughes, R. I. G. (1989). *The Interpretation of Quantum Mechanics*, Cambridge, MA: Harvard University Press.

Hume, David (1739/1973). *A Treatise of Human Nature*, London: John Noon. Page references to the edition of L. Selby-Bigge, Oxford: Oxford University Press.

Hume, David (1748/1962). *An Enquiry Concerning Human Understanding*, London: Millar, Kincaid and Donaldson. Page references to the (2nd) edition of L. Selby-Bigge, Oxford: Oxford University Press.

Humphrey, Nicholas (1984). *Consciousness Regained: Chapters in the Development of Mind*, Oxford: Oxford University Press.

Humphrey, Nicholas (1992). *A History of the Mind: Evolution and the Birth of Consciousness*, New York: Simon and Schuster.

Hunter, John (1973). 'On How We Talk', in Hunter's collection *Essays After Wittgenstein*, Toronto: University of Toronto Press.

Huxley, Aldous (1963). *Point Counter Point*, London: Chatto and Windus.

Huxley, Thomas (1866). *Lessons in Elementary Physiology*, London: Macmillan.

Jackson, Frank (1982). 'Epiphenomenal Qualia', *Philosophical Quarterly*, 32, pp. 127–36.

Jackson, Frank (1986). 'What Mary Didn't Know', *Journal of Philosophy*, 83, pp. 291–5.

James, William (1890/1950). *The Principles of Psychology*, v. 1, New York: Henry Holt and Co. Reprinted in 1950, New York: Dover. (Page references to the Dover edition.)

Jammer, Max (1974). *The Philosophy of Quantum Mechanics*, New York: Wiley.

Jaynes, E. (1980). 'Quantum Beats', in A. Barut (ed.) *Foundations of Radiation Theory and Quantum Electrodynamics*, New York: Plenum Press, pp. 37–43.

Johnson, George (1991). 'What Really Goes On In There', *New York Times*, November 10.

Johnson, Mark (1987). *The Body in the Mind: The Bodily Basis of Meaning, Imagination and Reason*, Chicago: University of Chicago Press.

Jones, P. and G. McLachlan (1991). 'Fitting Mixture Distributions to *Phenylthiocarbimide* (PTC) Sensitivity', *American Journal of Human Genetics*, 48, 1, pp. 117–20.

Kalmus, H. and S. Hubbard (1960). *The Chemical Senses in Health and Disease*, Springfield, IL: Charles Thomas.

Kim, Jaegwon (1982). 'Psychophysical Supervenience', *Philosophical Studies*, 41, pp. 51–70.

Kim, Jaegwon (1989). 'The Myth of Non-Reductive Materialism' in *Proceedings of the American Philosophical Association*, 63, pp. 31–47.

Kim, Jaegwon (1993). *Supervenience and Mind*, Cambridge: Cambridge University Press.

Kirchner, W. and U. Braun (1994). 'Dancing Honey Bees Indicate the Location of Food Sources using Path Integration rather than Cognitive Maps', *Animal Behaviour*, 48, pp. 1437–41.

Kirchner, W. and W. Towne (1994). 'The Sensory Basis of the Honeybee's Dance Language', *Scientific American*, 270, pp. 74–81.

Kolers, Paul and M. von Grünau (1976). 'Shape and Color in Apparent Motion', *Vision Research*, 16, pp. 329–35.

Kripke, Saul (1980). *Naming and Necessity*, Cambridge, MA: Harvard University Press.

LaBerge, Stephen (1985). *Lucid Dreaming*, New York: St. Martin's Press.

Lakoff, George (1987). *Women, Fire and Dangerous Things: What Categories Reveal about the Mind*, Chicago: University of Chicago Press.

Lecours, André and Yves Joanette (1980). 'Linguistic and Other Psychological Aspects of Paroxysmal Aphasia', *Brain and Language*, 10, pp. 1–23.

LeDoux, Joseph (1996). *The Emotional Brain: The Mysterious Underpinnings of Emotional Life*, New York: Simon and Schuster.

Leibniz, G. W. (1679/1989). 'Samples of the Numerical Characteristic', in R. Ariew and D. Garber (eds) *G. W. Leibniz: Philosophical Essays*, Indianapolis: Hackett.

Leibniz, G. W. (1702/1976). 'Reply to the Thoughts on the System of Preestablished Harmony Contained in the 2nd Edition of Mr. Bayle's *Critical Dictionary*, Article Rorarius', in L. Loemker (ed. trans.) *Gottfried Wilhelm Leibniz: Philosophical Papers and Letters*, 2nd Edition, Dordrecht: D. Reidel.

Leibniz, G. W. (unknown/1976). 'On the Method of Distinguishing Real from Imaginary Phenomena', in L. Loemker (ed. trans.) *Gottfried Wilhelm Leibniz: Philosophical Papers and Letters*, 2nd Edition, Dordrecht: D. Reidel.

Leibniz, G. W. (1765/1981). *New Essays on Human Understanding*, P. Remnant and J. Bennett (ed. and trans.), Cambridge: Cambridge University Press.

Levine, Joseph (1983). 'Materialism and Qualia: The Explanatory Gap', *Pacific Philosophical Quarterly*, 64, pp. 354–61.

Levine, Joseph (1993). 'On Leaving Out What It is Like', in Davies and Humphreys 1993.

Lewis, David (1983a). 'Postscript' to 'Mad Pain and Martian Pain', in *Philosophical Papers*, v. 1, Oxford: Oxford University Press.

Lewis, David (1983b). 'Extrinsic Properties', *Philosophical Studies*, 44, pp. 197–200.

Lewis, David (1988). 'What Experience Teaches', in J. Copley-Coltheart (ed.) *Proceedings of the Russellian Society*, Sydney: University of Sydney Press. Reprinted in William Lycan (ed.) *Mind and Cognition: A Reader*, Cambridge, MA: MIT Press, 1990.

Lissmann, H. (1963/1974). 'Electric Location by Fishes', *Scientific American*, March. Reprinted in D. Griffin (ed.) *Animal Engineering*, San Francisco: Freeman, pp. 56–65.

Loar, Brian (1988). 'Social Content and Psychological Content', in R. Grimm and D. Merrill (eds) *Contents of Thought*, Tucson: University of Arizona Press, pp. 99–110. Reprinted in D. Rosenthal (ed.) *The Nature of Mind*, Oxford: Oxford University Press, 1991. (Page references are to the reprint.)

Loar, Brian (1990). 'Phenomenal States', in J. Tomberlin (ed.) *Philosophical Perspectives*, v. 4, pp. 81–108.

Locke, John (1690/1975). *An Essay Concerning Human Understanding*, London: Basset. Page references are to the Nidditch edition (Oxford: Oxford University Press).

Lockwood, Michael (1991). *Mind, Brain and the Quantum*, Oxford: Blackwell.

Lucas, John (1961) 'Minds, Machines and Gödel', in A. Anderson (ed.) *Minds and Machines*, Englewood Cliffs, NJ: Prentice-Hall.

Lycan, William (1987). *Consciousness*, Cambridge, MA: MIT Press.

Lycan, William (ed.) (1990). *Mind and Cognition*, Oxford: Blackwell.

Lycan, William (1996). *Consciousness and Experience*, Cambridge, MA: MIT Press.

Lyons, William (1986). *The Disappearance of Introspection*, Cambridge, MA: MIT Press.

Malcolm, Norman (1959). *Dreaming*, London: Routledge and Kegan Paul.

Marr, David (1982). *Vision*, San Francisco: Freeman.

Mattes, R. and J. Labov (1989). 'Bitter Taste Responses to Phenylthiocarbamide are not

Related to Dietary Goitrogen Intake in Human Beings', *Journal of the American Dietary Association*, 89, 5, pp. 692–3.

Maudlin, Tim (1989). 'Computation and Consciousness', *Journal of Philosophy*, 86, pp. 407–32.

Mayr, E. and C. Sagan (1996). 'The Search for Extraterrestrial Intelligence: Scientific Quest or Hopeful Folly?', *The Planetary Report*, 16, 3, pp. 4–13.

McDowell, John (1994). *Mind and World*, Cambridge, MA: Harvard University Press.

McGinn, Colin (1989). 'Can We Solve the Mind–Body Problem?', *Mind*, 98, pp. 349–66. Reprinted in McGinn (1991).

McGinn, Colin (1989). *Mental Content*, Oxford: Blackwell.

McGinn, Colin (1991). *The Problem of Consciousness*, Oxford: Blackwell.

Menzel, R. (1979). 'Spectral Sensitivity and Colour Vision in Invertebrates', in H. Autrum (ed.) *Comparative Physiology and Evolution of Vision in Invertebrates: Handbook of Sensory Physiology*, v. 7/6A, Berlin: Springer-Verlag.

Millikan, Ruth (1984). *Language, Thought and Other Biological Categories*, Cambridge, MA: MIT Press.

Millikan, Ruth (1989). 'Biosemantics', *Journal of Philosophy*, 86, 6, pp. 281–97. Reprinted in Millikan (1993).

Millikan, Ruth (1993). *White Queen Psychology and Other Essays for Alice*, Cambridge, MA: MIT Press.

Nagel, Thomas (1974). 'What is it Like to be a Bat?', *Philosophical Review*, 83, pp. 435–50. Reprinted in Nagel's *Mortal Questions*, Cambridge: Cambridge University Press, 1979.

Nagel, Thomas (1979). 'Panpsychism', in Nagel's *Mortal Questions*, Cambridge: Cambridge University Press, 1979.

Nagel, Thomas (1986). *The View From Nowhere*, Oxford: Oxford University Press.

Nelkin, Norton (1989). 'Propositional Attitudes and Consciousness', *Philosophy and Phenomenological Research*, 49, pp. 413–30.

Nemirow, Laurence (1980). 'Review of Thomas Nagel's *Mortal Questions*', *Philosophical Review*, 89, pp. 473–7.

Nemirow, Laurence (1990). 'Physicalism and the Cognitive Role of Acquaintance', in William Lycan (ed.) *Mind and Cognition: A Reader*, Cambridge, MA: MIT Press, 1990.

Nida-Rümelin, Martine (1996). 'Pseudo-Normal Vision: An Actual Case of Qualia Inversion?', *Philosophical Studies*, 82, pp. 145–57.

Oakley, David (ed.) (1985). *Brain and Mind*, London, New York: Methuen.

Papineau, David (1987). *Reality and Representation*, Oxford, New York: Blackwell.

Peacock, Kent (1991). *Peaceful Coexistence or Armed Truce: Quantum Nonlocality and the Spacetime View of the World*, University of Toronto Ph.D. dissertation.

Peacocke, Christopher (1983). *Sense and Content*, Oxford: Oxford University Press.

Peacocke, Christopher (1992). 'Scenarios, Concepts and Perception', in T. Crane (ed.) *The Contents of Experience: Essays on Perception*, Cambridge: Cambridge University Press.

Penfield, Wilder (1958). *The Excitable Cortex in Conscious Man*, Liverpool: Liverpool University Press.

Penrose, Roger (1989). *The Emperor's New Mind*, Oxford: Oxford University Press.

Penrose, Roger (1994). *Shadows of the Mind*, Oxford: Oxford University Press.

Penrose, Roger and Stuart Hameroff (1995). 'What "Gaps" – Reply to Grush and Churchland', *Journal of Consciousness Studies*, 2, pp. 98–111.

Perner, Josef (1993). *Understanding the Representational Mind*. Cambridge, MA: MIT Press.

Petit, T. and G. Ivy (eds) (1988). *Neural Plasticity: A Lifespan Approach*, Proceedings of a symposium held at the University of Toronto in 1987, New York: Liss Inc.

Profet, Margie (1995). *Protecting Your Baby-to-be: Preventing Birth Defects in the First Trimester*, Reading, MA: Addison-Wesley.

Puccetti, Roland (1978). 'The Refutation of Materialism', *Canadian Journal of Philosophy*, 8, pp. 157–62.

Putnam, Hilary (1975). 'The Meaning of "Meaning"', in Keith Gunderson (ed.), *Language, Mind and Knowledge: Minnesota Studies in the Philosophy of Science*, v. 7, Minneapolis: University of Minnesota Press. Reprinted in Putnam's *Mind, Langu..ge and Reality: Philosophical Papers*, v. 2, Cambridge: Cambridge University Press, 1975.

Putnam, Hilary (1981). *Reason, Truth and History*, Cambridge: Cambridge University Press.

Quine, Willard (1953). 'Two Dogmas of Empiricism', in Quine's *From a Logical Point of View*, Cambridge, MA: Harvard University Press.

Rey, Georges (1991). 'Sensations in a Language of Thought', in E. Villanueva (ed.) *Philosophical Issues 1: Consciousness*, Atascadero, CA: Ridgeview.

Rey, Georges (1993). 'Sensational Sentences', in Davies and Humphreys (1993).

Rock, Irvin (1985). *The Logic of Perception*, Cambridge, MA: MIT Press.

Rose, Steven (1993). *The Making of Memory: From Molecules to Mind*, New York: Anchor Books.

Rosenthal, David (1986). 'Two Concepts of Consciousness', *Philosophical Studies*, 49, pp. 329–59.

Rosenthal, David (1993a). 'State Consciousness and Transitive Consciousness', *Consciousness and Cognition*, 2, pp. 355–63.

Rosenthal, David (1993b). 'Thinking That One Thinks', in Davies and Humphreys (1993).

Rosenthal, David (1995). 'State Consciousness and What It is Like', ms.

Ruhla, Charles (1992). *The Physics of Chance*, G. Barton (trans.), Oxford: Oxford University Press.

Rumelhart, David and James McClelland *et al.* (1986). *Parallel Distributed Processing: Explorations in the Microstructure of Cognition*, Cambridge, MA: MIT Press.

Ryle, Gilbert (1949). *The Concept of Mind*, London: Hutchinson & Co.

Salam, Abdus (1989). 'Overview of Particle Physics', in Paul Davies (ed.) *The New Physics*, Cambridge: Cambridge University Press.

Santayana, George (1923). *Skepticism and Animal Faith*, New York: Scribner.

Scully, M., B. Engleret, and H. Walther (1991). 'Quantum Optical Tests of Complementarity', *Nature*, 351, pp. 111–116.

Scully, M. and K. Drühl (1982). 'Quantum Eraser: A Proposed Photon Correlation Experiment Concerning Observation and "Delayed Choice" in Quantum Mechanics', *Physical Review A*, 25, pp. 2208–2213.

Seager, William (1991a). *Metaphysics of Consciousness*, London: Routledge.

Seager, William (1991b). 'The Worm in the Cheese: Leibniz, Consciousness and Matter', *Studia Leibnitiana*, 23, 1, pp. 79–91.

Seager, William (1992a). 'Externalism and Token Identity', *Philosophical Quarterly*, 42, pp. 439–48.

Seager, William (1992b). 'Thought and Syntax', *PSA 1992* (proceedings of the 1992 Philosophy of Science Association meetings), v. 1, pp. 481–91.

Seager, William (1993a). 'The Elimination of Experience', *Philosophy and Phenomenological Research*, 53, 2, pp. 345–65.

Seager, William (1993b). 'Verificationism, Scepticism and Consciousness', *Inquiry*, 36, pp. 113–33.

Seager, William (1994). 'Dretske on HOT Theories of Consciousness', *Analysis*, 54, 4, pp. 270–6.

Seager, William (1995). 'Consciousness, Information and Panpsychism', *Journal of Consciousness Studies*, 2, pp. 272–88.

Seager, William (1996). 'A Note on the Quantum Eraser', *Philosophy of Science*, 63, 1, pp. 81–90.

Seager, William (1997). 'Critical Notice of Dretske's *Naturalizing the Mind*', *Canadian Journal of Philosophy*, 27, 1, pp. 83–110.

Searle, John (1980). 'Minds, Brains and Programs', *Behavioral and Brain Sciences*, 3, pp. 417–24.

Searle, John (1983). *Intentionality*, Cambridge: Cambridge University Press.

Searle, John (1987). 'Minds and Brains Without Programs', in C. Blakemore and S. Greenfield (eds) *Mindwaves: Thoughts on Intelligence, Identity and Consciousness*, Oxford: Blackwell.

Searle, John (1992). *The Rediscovery of the Mind*, Cambridge, MA: MIT Press.

Searle, John (1997). 'Consciousness and the Philosophers', in *The New York Review of Books*, 44, 4 (March 6), pp. 43–50.

Sedivy, Sonia (1995). 'The Vehicle-less Nature of Experiential Content', ms.

Segall, M., T. Campbell and M. Herskovitz (1966). *The Influence of Culture on Visual Perception*, Indianapolis: Bobbs-Merrill.

Selfridge, O. (1970). 'Pandemonium: A Paradigm for Learning', in P. Dodwell (ed.) *Perceptual Learning and Adaptation* (Penguin Modern Psychology Readings), Harmondsworth: Penguin Books.

Sellars, Wilfred (1956). 'Empiricism and the Philosophy of Mind', in H. Feigl and M. Scriven (eds) *Minnesota Studies in the Philosophy of Science*, v. 1, Minneapolis: University of Minnesota Press. Reprinted in Sellars's *Science, Perception and Reality*, London: Routledge and Kegan Paul, 1963.

Shepard, Gordon (1991). *Foundations of the Neuron Doctrine*, Oxford: Oxford University Press.

Shimony, Abner (1989). 'Conceptual Foundations of Quantum Mechanics', in Paul Davies (ed.) *The New Physics*, Cambridge: Cambridge University Press.

Shreeve, James (1995). *The Neandertal Enigma: Solving the Mystery of Modern Human Origins*, New York: Morrow.

Sklar, Lawrence (1993). *Physics and Chance: Philosophical Issues in the Foundations of Statistical Mechanics*, Cambridge: Cambridge University Press.

Smith, K. and W. Smith (1962). *Perception and Motion: An Analysis of Space-structured Behaviour*, Philadelphia: Saunders.

Sperling, George (1960). 'The Information Available in Brief Visual Presentations', *Psychological Monographs*, 74, no. 11.

Springer, Sally and Georg Deutsch (1985). *Left Brain, Right Brain*, revised edition, New York: Freeman.

Stich, Stephen (1978). 'Autonomous Psychology and the Belief–Desire Thesis', *The Monist*, 61, 4, pp. 573–91.

Stich, Stephen (1991). 'Narrow Content meets Fat Syntax', in B. Loewer and G. Rey (eds) *Meaning in Mind: Fodor and His Critics*, Oxford: Blackwell.

Stoerig, P. and A. Cowey (1989). 'Wavelength Sensitivity in Blindsight', *Nature*, 342, pp. 916–18.

Thompson, Evan (1995). *Colour Vision: A Study in Cognitive Science and the Philosophy of Perception*, London: Routledge.

Tulving, Endel (1985). 'Memory and Consciousness', *Canadian Psychology*, 26, pp. 1–12.

Twain, Mark (1883/1961). *Life on the Mississippi*. My page reference is to a *Signet Classics* edition of 1961, New York: New American Library of World Literature.

Tye, Michael (1994). 'Qualia, Content and the Inverted Spectrum', *Noûs*, 28, 2, pp. 159–183.

Tye, Michael (1995). *Ten Problems of Consciousness: A Representational Theory of the Phenomenal Mind*, Cambridge, MA: MIT Press.

Tyndall, John (1879). *Fragments of Science: A Series of Detached Essays, Addresses, and Reviews*, London: Longmans, Green and Co.

van Cleve, James (1990). 'Mind-Dust or Magic?', in J. Tomberlin (ed.) *Philosophical Perspectives*, v. 4, pp. 215–26.

van Fraassen, Bas (1980). *The Scientific Image*, Oxford: Oxford University Press.

van Gelder, Tim (1995). 'What Might Cognition Be, If Not Computation?', *Journal of Philosophy*, 91, 7, pp. 345–81.

Varela, Francisco, Evan Thompson and Eleanor Rosch (1991). *The Embodied Mind: Cognitive Science and Human Experience*, Cambridge, MA: MIT Press.

Weiskrantz, L. (1986). *Blindsight: A Case Study and Implications*, Oxford: Oxford University Press.

Weiskrantz, L., E. Warrington, M. Saunders, and J. Marshall (1974). 'Visual Capacity in the Hemianopic Field Following a Restricted Occipital Ablation', *Brain*, 97, pp. 709–28.

Wilkes, K. (1988). '_____, Yishi, Duh, Um, and Consciousness' in A. Marcel and E. Bisiach (eds) *Consciousness in Contemporary Science*, Oxford: Oxford University Press.

Wittgenstein, Ludwig (1953/1968). *Philosophical Investigations* (3rd English edition), Oxford: Blackwell.

Wittgenstein, Ludwig (1980). *Wittgenstein's Lectures, Cambridge 1930–32, from the Notes of John King and Desmond Lee*, Oxford: Blackwell.

Wittgenstein, Ludwig (1969). *On Certainty*, G. Anscombe and H. von Wright (eds), Oxford: Blackwell.

Young, Andrew and Edward De Haan (1993). 'Impairments of Visual Awareness', in Davies and Humphreys (1993), pp. 58–73.

Zuboff, Arnold (1981). 'The Story of a Brain', in D. Hofstadter and D. Dennett (eds) *The Mind's I: Fantasies and Reflections on Self and Soul*, New York: Basic Books.

INDEX OF NAMES

296

SUBJECT INDEX